Liberty and American Experience in the Eighteenth Century

Liberty and American Experience in the Eighteenth Century

Edited and with an Introduction
by David Womersley

amagi®

an imprint of Liberty Fund, Inc.

Liberty Fund

Indianapolis

Amagi books are published by Liberty Fund, Inc.,
a foundation established to encourage study of the
ideal of a society of free and responsible individuals.

The cuneiform inscription that appears in the logo and serves
as a design element in all Liberty Fund books is the earliest-known
written appearance of the word "freedom" (*amagi*), or "liberty."
It is taken from a clay document written about 2300 B.C.
in the Sumerian city-state of Lagash.

"Federalism, Constitutionalism, and Republican Liberty: The First
Constructions of the Constitution" reprinted from Lance Banning,
Conceived in Liberty (Lanham, Md.: Rowman and Littlefield, 2004),
35–70. © 2004 by Rowman and Littlefield.
"The Dialectic of Liberty" reprinted by permission of the publisher
from Robert Ferguson, *Reading the Early Republic* (Cambridge, Mass.:
Harvard University Press, 2004), 51–83. © 2004 by the President
and Fellows of Harvard College.

Printed in the United States of America

10   09   08   07   06   P   5   4   3   2   1

Library of Congress Cataloging-in-Publication Data

Liberty and American experience in the eighteenth
century/edited and with an Introduction by David Womersley.
    p.   cm.
  Includes bibliographical references and index.
  ISBN-13: 978-0-86597-629-0 (pbk.: alk. paper)
  ISBN-10: 0-86597-629-5 (pbk.: alk. paper)
1. Liberty.   2. Civil rights—United States—History—18th century.
I. Womersley, David.   II. Liberty Fund.   III. Title.
JC585 .L424   2006
323.440973'09033—dc22   2005034720

LIBERTY FUND, INC.
8335 Allison Pointe Trail, Suite 300
Indianapolis, Indiana 46250-1684

Contents

Contributors

LANCE BANNING was Professor of History at the University of Kentucky, where he taught since 1973. A native of Kansas City, he received his B.A. from the University of Missouri at Kansas City in 1964 and his M.A. and Ph.D. degrees from Washington University (St. Louis) in 1968 and 1971. He held fellowships from the National Endowment for the Humanities, the John Simon Guggenheim Foundation, the National Humanities Center, and the Center for the History of Freedom.

Banning was coeditor of the University Press of Kansas series "American Political Thought," editor of *After the Constitution: Party Conflict in the New Republic,* and author of many articles and essays on the American Founding and the first party struggle. His first book, *The Jeffersonian Persuasion: Evolution of a Party Ideology,* received the international book award of Phi Alpha Theta and was nominated by the press for Pulitzer, Bancroft, and other prizes. *Jefferson and Madison: Three Conversations from the Founding,* a revision of his 1992 Merrill Jensen Lectures at the University of Wisconsin, and *The Sacred Fire of Liberty: James Madison and the Founding of the Federal Republic* were published in 1995. The latter received the Merle Curti Award in Intellectual History from the Organization of American Historians and was a finalist for the Pulitzer Prize.

During the spring of 1997, Banning held the John Adams Chair in American History, a senior Fulbright appointment, at the University of Groningen in the Netherlands. During the fall of 2001, he was Leverhulme Visiting Professor at the University of Edinburgh.

His last publications were *Liberty and Order: The First American Party Struggle,* an anthology of primary sources from Liberty Fund, and *Conceived in Liberty: The Struggle to Define the New Republic, 1789–1793.* He died in 2006.

JOHN W. DANFORD was educated at Dartmouth College, Berkeley, and Yale University, from which he has a doctoral degree in political science. He is the author of three books: *Wittgenstein and Political Phi-*

losophy, David Hume and the Problem of Reason, and *Roots of Freedom: A Primer on Modern Liberty.* He has published articles on Thomas Hobbes, Adam Smith, and David Hume, among others, in journals such as *Western Political Quarterly, American Journal of Political Science,* and *Journal of Politics.* He has taught at the University of Chicago, University of Houston, and Loyola University Chicago and served as the Charles Evans Hughes Professor of Jurisprudence at Colgate University.

After working on issues in the philosophy of science (or social science) during the first part of his career, his work on David Hume led to a keen interest in the Scottish Enlightenment, and in the foundations of the kind of free societies (large modern commercial republics) studied and recommended by the Scots. More recently his attention has returned to the thought of the ancient Greeks, and in particular to Herodotus and his understanding of freedom and its importance for human flourishing.

ROBERT A. FERGUSON is the George Edward Woodberry Professor of Law, Literature, and Criticism at Columbia University. His books include *Law and Letters in American Culture; The American Enlightenment, 1750–1820;* and most recently, *Reading the Early Republic*—all from Harvard University Press. He has also published numerous articles on American literature, legal history, the literature of public documents, and the relationship of law and legal institutions to American writing.

He teaches jurisprudence, law and literature, and early American constitutionalism at Columbia Law School and English and American literature for the English Department of Columbia University.

R. G. FREY is Professor of Philosophy at Bowling Green State University, where he is also Senior Research Fellow in the Social Philosophy and Policy Center. His Doctor of Philosophy degree is from Oxford University, and he taught in the United Kingdom and Canada before coming to Bowling Green. He has published numerous books and articles on normative ethics, applied or practical ethics, and the history of eighteenth-century British moral philosophy. In addition to an edition of Bishop Butler's ethical writings, he is at work on a book entitled *Virtue and Interest: The Moral Psychologies of Shaftesbury, Butler, and Hume.*

JACK P. GREENE is a student of colonial British America. He has published widely on this subject, including such works as *The Quest for Power: The Lower Houses of Assembly in the Southern Royal Colonies, 1689–1763; Peripheries and Center: Constitutional Development in the Extended Polities of the British Empire and the United States, 1607–1789; Pursuits of Happiness: Social Development of the Early Modern British Colonies and the Formation of American Culture; Imperatives, Behaviors, and Identities: Essays in Early American Cultural History; The Intellectual Construction of America: Exceptionalism and Identity from 1492 to 1800; Negotiated Authorities: Essays in Colonial Political and Constitutional History; Explaining the American Revolution: Issues, Interpretations, and Actors;* and *Interpreting Early America: Historiographic Essays.*

Having earlier taught at Michigan State University, Western Reserve University, and the University of Michigan, he became in 1966 a member of the Department of History at Johns Hopkins University, where since 1976 he has been Andrew W. Mellon Professor in the Humanities. From 1990 to 1992, he was Distinguished Professor at the University of California, Irvine. He has been a visiting professor at several institutions, including Oxford University, Hebrew University of Jerusalem, and the École des Hautes Études en Science Sociale. He has held fellowships from the Guggenheim Foundation, the Institute for Advanced Study, the Woodrow Wilson International Center for Scholars, the Center for Advanced Study in the Behavioral Sciences, the National Humanities Center, and the John Carter Brown Library.

RONALD HAMOWY is Professor Emeritus of Intellectual History at the University of Alberta. He is a graduate of the Committee on Social Thought of the University of Chicago and has taught at Stanford University and Simon Fraser University in Vancouver before moving to Alberta.

Mr. Hamowy is the author of *The Scottish Enlightenment and Spontaneous Order* and numerous articles on the Scottish Enlightenment and F. A. Hayek. He is the editor of the 1995 Liberty Fund two-volume edition of Trenchard and Gordon's *Cato's Letters.*

BARRY SHAIN is Associate Professor of Political Science at Colgate University. His publications include *The Myth of American Individualism: The Protestant Origins of American Political Thought* and *Man,*

God and Society: An Interpretive History of Individualism and numerous book chapters and reviews. His teaching specialties are American political thought (especially that of the Founding period), modern political philosophy, political theology, early-modern natural and international law, and American political culture. After earning two B.A.'s, one from San Jose State University and one from San Francisco State University, he received his M.A. and his Ph.D. from Yale University. He was the John M. Olin Foundation Faculty Fellow in History in 1993, and a National Endowment for the Humanities Fellow in 1992 and 2005, and has been invited to speak at many lectures and conferences around the world. His research interests include the history and meanings of the most significant Western political concepts in the early-modern period, such as liberty, individual rights, slavery, and the self; and contending conceptions of the good as they developed in this period.

DAVID WOMERSLEY is the Thomas Warton Professor of English Literature at the University of Oxford and a Fellow of St. Catherine's College. His publications include *The Transformation of the Decline and Fall of the Roman Empire*, a three-volume edition of *The History of the Decline and Fall of the Roman Empire*, a collection of *Contemporary Responses to Gibbon*, the proceedings of the Gibbon Bicentenary Colloquium entitled *Edward Gibbon: Bicentenary Essays, Gibbon and the Watchmen of the Holy City: the Historian and his Reputation, 1776–1815*, and *"Cultures of Whiggism": New Essays on English Literature and Culture in the Long Eighteenth Century*. He has also edited Edmund Burke's *Pre-Revolutionary Writings*, a collection of *Augustan Critical Writing, English Literature: Milton to Blake*, an abridged edition of *Gibbon's Decline and Fall*, *Restoration Drama: An Anthology*, and Samuel Johnson's *Selected Essays*.

His current projects include a biography of Gibbon; two monographs provisionally entitled *Literary Whiggism 1680–1730* and *Religion, History and Drama 1530–1603*; and an edition of James Boswell's *Life of Johnson*. He is a General Editor of *The Complete Writings of Jonathan Swift*, for which he is editing the volume devoted to *Gulliver's Travels*.

GORDON S. WOOD is Alva O. Way University Professor and Professor of History at Brown University. He received his B.A. degree from Tufts University and his Ph.D. from Harvard University. He taught at Harvard and the University of Michigan before joining the faculty at Brown in 1969.

He is the author of many works, including *The Creation of the American Republic, 1776–1787,* which won the Bancroft Prize and the John H. Dunning Prize in 1970, and *The Radicalism of the American Revolution,* which won the Pulitzer Prize for History and the Ralph Waldo Emerson Prize in 1993. He is currently working on a volume in the *Oxford History of the United States* dealing with the period of the early Republic from 1789 to 1815. His book entitled *The Americanization of Benjamin Franklin* was published in 2004.

Professor Wood is a fellow of the American Academy of Arts and Sciences and the American Philosophical Society.

DAVID WOOTTON is Anniversary Professor of History at the University of York, England. He has published widely on intellectual and cultural history between the Renaissance and the Enlightenment in France, Italy, and the English-speaking countries. His most recent book is *Bad Medicine: Doctors Doing Harm since Hippocrates.*

Liberty and American Experience in the Eighteenth Century

Introduction:
A Conservative Revolution

All students of the political thought of the eighteenth century are familiar with the broad outlines of the mature political philosophy of Edmund Burke, as it was expressed in his most famous work, *Reflections on the Revolution in France* (1790; hereafter cited as *Reflections*). Dismayed by the achievements of Jacobinism across the Channel and appalled at the enthusiasm for the principles of the Revolution evinced by many amongst both the lower orders and the propertied in England, Burke was impelled to articulate his own contrasting vision of healthy politics. In place of the Jacobinical abolition of the past, Burke proposed a careful cherishing of a nation's political tradition as a kind of accumulated property or inheritance of practical political wisdom. In place of abstract, "natural," rights, Burke preferred those different rights which had arisen as a result of concrete, legal decisions. In place of lofty but in his eyes vacuous protestations of an attachment to the whole of humanity, Burke preferred instead to rely on a politics which was aligned with the natural affections which arose in the more restricted setting of the family. In place of the Jacobins's anti-clericalism, Burke respected the rights of national churches in a spirit of wise toleration. And above all Burke came ever more to respect the rights of property as the expropriations of the revolutionaries reached new heights and the economic policy of revolutionary France became ever more disastrous. As he would write to the Duke of Portland on September 29, 1793:

> It is truly alarming to see so large a part of the Aristocratick Interest engaged in the Cause of the new Species of democracy, which is openly attacking or secretly undermining the System of property, by which mankind has hitherto been governed: But we are not to delude ourselves. No man, who is connected with a party, which professes publickly to admire, or be justly suspected of secretly abet-

ting, this French revolution, who must not be drawn into its vortex, and become the instrument of its designs.[1]

But how did Burke's political thought assume this character? The speed of his response to events in France, written and published as they were at a period when much moderate opinion in England saw nothing to be alarmed about in the course and nature of the Revolution, surely inhibits us from imagining that they were created by the events on which they comment. Indeed, the speed and apparent prescience of Burke's analysis of the Revolution requires us to believe that the political philosophy he deployed against the Jacobins was already fully formed before 1790 and that thereafter it acquired additional intensity but did not noticeably change its shape. So the question remains: how did Burke's political thought acquire its final, memorable character?

The question becomes both more curious and also more capable of being answered when we recall that there was much in Burke's earlier writings which, while not in flat contradiction with the *Reflections,* nevertheless was certainly in tension with that later work. *Thoughts on the Cause of the Present Discontents* (hereafter cited as *Thoughts*) was published by Burke in 1770 in protest at what he called the system of "Double Cabinet" introduced by the Earl of Bute on the accession of George III in 1760—a system, as Burke represented it, which aimed at the enlarging of the powers of the Crown by means of a methodical undermining of the independence of the House of Commons. In the process, Burke also composed what was tantamount to the political creed of the Rockingham Whigs, the party to which he was then attached. It is in these more expansive passages, when Burke raises his eyes from the minutiae of British high politics in the 1760s and allows his prose to take wing at the thought of the Whiggish principles he was serving, that we meet emphases which jar when we recall the rather different elations of the *Reflections.* For instance, in the *Reflections* Burke would define man's proper and healthy political disposition in terms of consecration, piety, and awe:

1. Edmund Burke, *Correspondence,* ed. T. Copeland et al., 10 vols. (Cambridge: Cambridge University Press, 1958–78), 7:437 (hereafter cited as *Correspondence*).

We have consecrated the state, that no man should approach to look into its defects or corruptions but with due caution; that he should never dream of beginning its reformation by its subversion; that he should approach to the faults of the state as to the wounds of a father, with pious awe and trembling sollicitude. By this wise prejudice we are taught to look with horror on those children of their country who are prompt rashly to hack that aged parent in pieces, and put him into the kettle of magicians, in hopes that by their poisonous weeds, and wild incantations, they may regenerate the paternal constitution, and renovate their father's life.[2]

Twenty years earlier, however, in the course of writing *Thoughts,* Burke had painted the character of an ideal Member of Parliament in hues drawn from a less reverential palette:

A strenuous resistance to every appearance of lawless power; a spirit of independence carried to some degree of enthusiasm; an inquisitive character to discover, and a bold one to display, every corruption and every error of Government; these are the qualities which recommend a man to a seat in the House of Commons.[3]

Or, to take another example, we might cite from *Thoughts* Burke's pungently Whiggish understanding of the fundamental importance of the people in the British constitution:

The King is the representative of the people; so are the Lords; so are the Judges. They are all trustees for the people, as well as the Commons; because no power is given for the sole sake of the holder; and although Government certainly is an institution of Divine authority, yet its forms, and the persons who administer it, all originate from the people (292).

But the *Reflections* would, twenty years later, be written in a spirit of angry denunciation against Richard Price's *A Discourse on the Love of Our Country,* which also articulated the principle of popular sovereignty:

---

2. Burke, *Reflections on the Revolution in France* in *Writings and Speeches of Edmund Burke,* ed. Leslie Mitchell (Oxford: Oxford University Press, 1989), 8:146.
3. Burke, *Thoughts on the Cause of the Present Discontents,* ibid., 2:296.

Civil governors are properly the servants of the public and a King is no more than the first servant of the public, created by it, maintained by it, and responsible to it; and all the homage paid him is due to him on no other account than his relation to the public. His sacredness is the sacredness of the community. His authority is the authority of the community, and the term *Majesty,* which it is usual to apply to him, is by no means his own majesty, but the majesty of the people.[4]

From this, Price had concluded that the people enjoyed a "right to chuse our own governors, to cashier them for misconduct, and to frame a government for ourselves" (190). Burke was at great pains in the *Reflections* to refute the interpretation of 1688 which undergirded Price's portrait of the British constitution, and in particular he wished to repudiate this notion of popular sovereignty. Furthermore, it was when Fox echoed Price's sermon in the House of Commons (saying, for instance, that "the Sovereignty was absolutely in the people, that the Monarchy was elective, otherwise the Dynasty of Brunswick had no right, and that the majority of the people, whenever they thought proper to change the form of Government, had a right to cashier the King") that Burke realized that he must separate himself from his former allies.[5] Yet, were Price and Fox so very far away, at least in point of language, from the Burke of 1770?

At this point let me be very clear about what I am saying when I bring the Burke of 1790 up against the Burke of 1770 and touch on the discrepancies which seem to divide them. I am decidedly not contending that there is an utter contradiction between *Thoughts on the Cause of the Present Discontents* and *Reflections on the Revolution in France.* To do so would be at the very least to subscribe to a laughably one-sided interpretation of the *Thoughts,* which as well as the passages I have quoted

4. Richard Price, *A Discourse on the Love of Our Country* in *Richard Price: Political Writings,* ed. D. D. Thomas (Cambridge: Cambridge University Press, 1991), 185–86.

5. Report of Fox's speech in the House of Commons on February 1, 1793, in a letter from Lord Sheffield to Edward Gibbon of February 5, 1793, in *The Private Letters of Edward Gibbon,* ed. R. E. Prothero (London: John Murray, 1896), 2:368.

above contains also sentiments such as the following concerning the congruence of domestic and political affections which would be entirely at home in the *Reflections:*

> Commonwealths are made of families, free commonwealths of parties also; and we may as well affirm, that our natural regards and ties of blood tend inevitably to make men bad citizens, as that the bonds of our party weaken those by which we are held to our country.[6]

It was presumably because of passages such as this that *Thoughts* attracted the criticism of nascent metropolitan radical circles when it was first published.[7] Yet what Catherine Macaulay and others objected to is precisely what now makes the *Thoughts* so fascinating, namely the simultaneous presence within it of both an element which can be easily aligned with the political doctrines Burke was to espouse in the 1790s and another element which points in a different direction and down an unchosen path. Between 1770 and 1790 something occurred to impel Burke away from becoming that alternative, Commonwealth Whig which, on the showing of *Thoughts,* was at that point equally available to him. What was it that moved Burke toward the path he eventually followed?

I suggest that it was the experience of colonial conflict and colonial war which decisively drove Burke down the path of political reflection which terminated in his great works of the 1790s: that is to say, in *Reflections on the Revolution in France* (1790), *An Appeal from the Old to the New Whigs* (1791), *A Letter to a Noble Lord* (1796), and *Letters on a Regicide Peace* (1795–97). The conflict between Great Britain and her American colonies was the first of the three overlapping crises which occupied Burke from the mid-1770s onwards. Before peace had been concluded with the United States in 1783, he was deep in Indian affairs and preparation for the prosecution of Warren Hastings, and before that prosecution had drawn to a close, revolution had broken out in France. So the American crisis inaugurated the final phase of Burke's public career in which he was unremittingly preoccupied with international and imperial issues at the highest level until his death in 1797.

6. *Writings and Speeches of Edmund Burke,* 2:315.
7. On which response, see the endnote by Paul Langford, ibid., 322.

In the final twenty years of his life, Burke cleaved to the political insights generated by the American crisis.

Burke's central thought about the colonial war between Britain and America was simple. He unflinchingly saw it as an entirely avoidable conflict between a high-handed administration and a colonial population whose breeding and *mores* had disposed them to vigorous resistance when menaced by oppressive innovation from the mother country. As he said in *Conciliation with the Colonies* (1775), one of the two major speeches Burke made in the House of Commons at the outset of the conflict, the American colonists "snuff the approach of tyranny in every tainted breeze."[8] This strong polarity between, on the one hand, innovating and oppressive politicians at home and, on the other, hardy, resilient and suspicious colonists abroad organizes everything Burke writes on America. For instance, we might cite many passages on the character of the colonists from *Conciliation with the Colonies.* In the first place, Burke emphasized the strength of the colonists' commitment to liberty:

> The people of the Colonies are descendents of Englishmen. England, Sir, is a nation, which still I hope respects, and formerly adored, her freedom. The Colonists emigrated from you, when this part of your character was most predominant; and they took this biass and direction the moment they parted from your hands (120).

But he then went on immediately to stress the particular and focussed quality of their attachment to liberty:

> They are therefore not only devoted to Liberty, but to Liberty according to English ideas, and on English principles. Abstract Liberty, like other mere abstractions, is not to be found. Liberty inheres in some sensible object; and every nation has formed to itself some favourite point, which by way of eminence becomes the criterion of their happiness (120).

In America as in England, this "favourite point" is taxation:

8. A phrase as remarkable for its characterizing of the policy of Lord North's administration as tyrannous, as for its ascription of suspicious vigilance to the colonists, *Speech on Conciliation with America,* ibid., 3:124.

They [the House of Commons] took infinite pains to inculcate, as a fundamental principle, that, in all monarchies, the people must in effect themselves mediately or immediately possess the power of granting their own money, or no shadow of liberty could subsist. The Colonies draw from you as with their life-blood, these ideas and principles. Their love of liberty, as with you, fixed and attached on this specific point of taxing. Liberty might be safe, or might be endangered in twenty other particulars, without their being much pleased or alarmed. Here they felt its pulse; and as they found that beat, they thought themselves sick or sound (120–21).

It was a political outlook irresistibly reinforced by two auxiliary influences—one religious, the other legal. In the matter of religion, the disposition of the colonists was such that the commitment to liberty which governed their actions during the working week was also recommended to them on the Sabbath, with an unquestionable sanction:

Religion, always a principle of energy in this new people, is no way worn out or impaired; and their mode of professing it is also one main cause of this free spirit. The people are protestants; and of that kind, which is the most adverse to all implicit submission of mind and opinion. This is a persuasion not only favourable to liberty, but built upon it . . . The dissenting interests have sprung up in direct opposition to all the ordinary powers of the world; and could justify that opposition only on a strong claim to natural liberty. Their very existence depended on the powerful and unremitted assertion of that claim. All protestantism, even the most cold and passive, is a sort of dissent. But the religion most prevalent in our Northern Colonies is a refinement on the principle of resistance; it is the dissidence of dissent; and the protestantism of the protestant religion (121–22).

In the matter of law, the prevalence of legal expertise amongst the colonists[9] endowed with technical accomplishment an attachment to

---

9. "In no country perhaps in the world is the law so general a study. The profession itself is numerous and powerful; and in most provinces it takes the lead" (ibid., 123).

liberty which might otherwise have been easily circumvented by the politicians of Westminster, for

> when great honours and great emoluments do not win over this knowledge to the service of the state, it is a formidable adversary to government. If the spirit be not tamed and broken by these happy methods, it is stubborn and litigious. *Abeunt studia in mores.* This study renders men acute, inquisitive, dextrous, prompt in attack, ready in defence, full of resources (124).

What is striking however in this analysis of the character of the colonists is the absence of any suggestion that their love of liberty disqualifies them to be the subjects of a monarchy. Indeed, Burke is at pains to underline the temperamental and political consanguinity of the colonists with their English cousins. According to Burke, the colonists were not looking to become the citizens of a republic. They were driven to that undesired expedient as a consequence of the short-sightedness and arbitrary conduct of ministers.

On the pernicious innovativeness of those ministers, we can do no better than to recall the peroration of *American Taxation* (1774) in which Burke summarized with great power his acute understanding of where government was going wrong in its dealings with the colonists:

> Again, and again, revert to your old principles—seek peace and ensue it—leave America, if she has taxable matter in her, to tax herself. I am not here going into the distinctions of rights, nor attempting to mark their boundaries. I do not enter into these metaphysical distinctions; I hate the very sound of them. Leave the Americans as they antiently stood, and these distinctions, born of our unhappy contest, will die along with it. They, and we, and their and our ancestors, have been happy under that system. Let the memory of all actions, in contradiction to that good old mode, on both sides, be extinguished for ever. Be content to bind America by laws of trade; you have always done it. Let this be your reason for binding their trade. Do not burthen them by taxes; you were not used to do so from the beginning. Let this be your reason for not taxing. These are the arguments of states and kingdoms. Leave the rest to the schools; for there only they may be discussed with

safety. But if, intemperately, unwisely, fatally, you sophisticate and poison the very source of government, by urging subtle deductions, and consequences odious to those you govern, from the unlimited and illimitable nature of supreme sovereignty, you will teach them by these means to call that sovereignty itself in question. When you drive him hard, the boar will surely turn upon the hunters. If that sovereignty and their freedom cannot be reconciled, which will they take? They will cast your sovereignty in your face. No body will be argued into slavery. Sir, let the gentlemen on the other side call forth all their ability; let the best of them get up, and tell me, what one character of liberty the Americans have, and what one brand of slavery they are free from, if they are bound in their property and industry, by all the restraints you can imagine on commerce, and at the same time are made pack-horses of every tax you choose to impose, without the least share in granting them?[10]

So much here invites and deserves comment: the bold dismissal from the arena of mature political deliberation of abstract questions of right, the untroubled equation of settled habits with political rectitude, the allocation of blame for the crisis squarely on the shoulders of the British administration, and finally the implication that the rejection of British sovereignty was not the primary aim of the colonists but rather a collateral consequence of their entirely laudable refusal to enter into conditions of slavery. For Burke, then, the colonial war was a struggle between insensitive, innovative government and an independent and self-reliant colonial population. It was the crime of that government to drive that colonial population down the path of armed insurrection and ultimately political separation by a misguided insistence on an abstract right to tax. And it was this crisis within empire which sensitized Burke to the political values which in the 1790s would become so closely associated with his name.

So one can easily understand why Burke so vehemently denied the allegation of the radicals, that when he attacked the French Revolution he was an apostate from his support of revolution in the 1770s. For Burke, although these two events were both labelled "Revolutions," they were utterly unlike, and the difference between them can be easily

10. Ibid., *American Taxation*, 2:458.

seen if we reflect on the source of innovation (to which Burke professed himself a perpetual foe) in each case.[11] In France it is the revolutionaries themselves who are the peddlers of political, financial, legal, and moral innovation. In America, political and legal innovation had come from Great Britain and had been resisted by the colonists. So in Burke's opposed responses to the American and French Revolutions, we can see an implicit understanding of the American Revolution as, at least in its origins, that paradoxical thing, a conservative revolution.

Burke's insight into the originally conservative nature of the American Revolution is a useful landmark to bear in mind as one begins to read the essays collected in this volume. For they, too, bear witness to the conservative character of the colonists' resistance to Great Britain. Two essays explore—picking up a theme from Burke's *Conciliation with the Colonies*—the religious commitments of the American colonists. Robert Ferguson's exploration of the relation between religious and legal understandings of the concept of liberty maps the tensions between them and seeks to explain how it happened that the religious conception of liberty was superseded by a legal conception: "For while ministers gave Revolutionary Americans much of their moral and intellectual courage to fight, lawyers defined the event and capped its directions." Ferguson poses four searching questions: "If the religious sources of liberty are powerful and significant, *why* did they disappear from civil discourse so rapidly in the early republic? *Where,* in the continuing dialectic, are the religious contributions to civil and political liberty in American life? *How* did religious and legal sources of liberty interact to produce a distinct American understanding? *What,* if anything, does a closer look at religious explanation restore to a balanced understanding of American liberty?" The questions become all the more urgent when Ferguson establishes the strength and inevitability of religious frames of reference for the early Americans: "Early Americans had no choice but to think through a religious frame of reference; it was the mental equipment that people brought to daily life, and it was the ordering device for larger conceptions of history

11. See Burke's letter to the Duke of Richmond of May 8, 1780, in which (with litotes) he confesses to "a timidity that I have, partly from nature and partly from principle, in making very quick, strong and bold alterations in the fundamental parts of the Constitution under which I was born," *Correspondence,* 4:236.

and communal well-being. Furthermore, the root of this conception required the thinker to accept a premise that Samuel Adams, the organizer of Boston mobs, gave most succinctly. In words that came from many lips throughout the crisis, Adams claimed 'The Religion and public Liberty of a People are intimately connected; their interests are interwoven, they cannot subsist separately; and therefore they rise and fall together.'" Yet this was not a durable ascendency: "After the Revolution, ministers maintained the spiritual keeping of their congregations, but they lost the capacity to represent the gathered community in political thought." The result was in at least one respect a diminution: "Religion remained a concern and for many a central concern, but it was no longer the pillar, no longer the explanatory tool, no longer the primal articulator of liberty. Ministers had ceased to be the guardians of social well-being. The keeping of liberty, once a joint responsibility, had passed rather suddenly to the legal mind in America. Something, however, had been lost in the process, and at crucial moments, communal sense of that loss would lead to resurgence in the religious side of the dialectic. Religion spoke to the people in a way that law never can. For while the law possesses many virtues, it smells of the lamp, of calculation and reason, of an elitest response; none of these elements ever tells the wistfully searching subject much about happiness." And the key text in which this relegation of religious conceptions of liberty was effected was *The Federalist:* "In sum, *The Federalist* did more than cap the Revolution by calling for the ratification of the Federal Constitution; it confirmed, once and for all, the dominance of legal over religious explanation in civic discourse. Learned contrivance, practical artifice, and hard-headed institutional planning were the keys to a new mental adventure where those engaged knew they were neither angels nor under the control of angels." Ferguson notes the dangers for liberty in the comparative extinguishing of religious conceptions of liberty and the apparently unchallenged ascendancy of legal positivism, with its eschewal of all recourse to underpropping notions of natural law: "the power and authority of the state to make and enforce law have increased a hundredfold while acceptance of liberty as a rhetorical guide to action has dwindled." As he does so, he reveals a conservative tendency in the American Revolution: "Somewhere in the dialectic of liberty, a republic defined by the right of revolution has been replaced by a modern nation-state where the test of membership has become loyalty."

Barry Shain's essay stands shoulder to shoulder with Robert Ferguson's in its insistence on the centrality of religion to the outlook of the colonists. Shain's essential contention is that "at its revolutionary Founding, America was a nation of mostly British Protestants and Protestant communities whose culture was controlled by varying and contending Protestant categories of thought," and in defending this view he moves forward on two related fronts:

> Accordingly, I explore two key, if tension-ridden, facets of the Protestant inheritance that shaped America's cultural landscape for well over a century before the Founding and thereafter continued to powerfully influence it. First is the American elevation of the freedom of religious conscience to a hallowed and inalienable individual right. Its persistent influence on the American political and religious culture resulted from the transformation of one of eighteenth century's most traditional and dominant meanings of liberty, spiritual or Christian liberty, into the form of a right. And second is the formative role played by Americans' acceptance of the Reformed Protestant understanding of original sin and its ubiquitous deformation of each and every human being. Only through a proper recognition of original sin's centrality do key features of American political thought, such as America's localism and hostility towards long chains of hierarchy, become readily understandable.

Shain argues passionately for the dominant religious conception of liberty among the colonists: "Americans, then, were predominantly Protestants, though certainly not all of one piece. And for all Protestants, the most important form of liberty was not the instrumentally critical liberty of communal self-government or that of liberal natural rights but instead the liberty through which Christ could make them free, that is, spiritual liberty." And he carefully explains the communitarian rather than individualistic nature of this liberty: "In America this traditional Protestant sense of liberty was understood to eschew all claims of worldly liberation at the individual level while consistently and enthusiastically promoting and conflating a mixture of spiritual and political liberty at the corporate level. The result was that, among most Americans, spiritual liberty was used to defend the freedom of the community while simultaneously limiting that of the individual." Furthermore and in support of Robert Ferguson, he notes how the Protestant freedom of conscience became overwhelmed in the welter of other "natural" rights which the successful outcome of colonial rebellion produced: "The Protestant freedom of religious conscience was thus clearly separate from the panoply of personal rights that its defenders, in the main, unintentionally helped create via their war efforts. Intentional or not, the most revolutionary fallout of the war was indeed the universalization, secularization, and extension of unalienable individual rights. Here, Zuckert and others, even if wrong in their historical reconstruction of the reasons and influences which produced this particular outcome, are right in closely associating the rise of the language of natural rights and the American Revolution." Yet it seems that it was this particular right which acted as Trojan horse to introduce other "natural" rights into the mainstream of American political life in the aftermath of successful rebellion. For it happened that "the unalienable individual right of religious conscience, expansively extended to broader rights claims by Americans in their support of the prosecution of the War for Independence, had created the foundation upon which a new class of rights would be constructed."

Shain then goes on to trace the complicated process whereby the language of rights in America shifted and developed, before moving on to examine the second main legacy of this Protestant matrix—as well as freedom of conscience, there is also the pervasive awareness of original sin: "But the enduring influence of the hallowed status attached to the individual right of conscience is not the only lasting Protestant presence that continues to shape American culture and politics. For in any attempt to understand late-eighteenth-century American thought and its continuing influence, one must take note not only of the freedom of religious conscience and those natural rights which followed in its train but of the American conception of the controlling power over society and men of the Christian understanding of original sin." Shain brings out with great clarity the democratic character of the entailments of this penetrating conviction of original sin—its power to drive from the field any kind of hierarchy or intrinsic authority vested in merely human instruments. Shain describes the consequence of this Protestant character of colonial society as follows: "Thus, late-eighteenth-century Americans learned from almost every public source, Christian humanist, secular rationalist, Calvinist, and pietistic separatist (theologically Calvinist) that a life of liberty rather than license demanded that passions, lusts, and selfishness be tightly controlled through communal living." In his account the Revolution thus emerges as a calamitous event whose ultimate tendency was to cut colonial society loose from its historical moorings. For as Shain observes, "It would only be with the birth of the new world of the late 1780s, which was to witness a rapid decline in confidence among elites in their willingness to accept scriptural claims, that there would be in America a willingness of the elite to embrace the dictates of liberalism and correspondingly to abandon the effort to bend recalcitrant sinful human nature to accord with the dictates of the guiding force of Reformed Protestantism." So the former colonies began their tentative and faltering journey into the future. Shain's conclusion is provocative but inescapable: "the heart of America's Revolutionary-era's political culture and aspirations was Reformed Protestantism and, thus, America was born neither secular nor liberal." And the result of this is modern America's indelibly ambiguous heritage from its colonial past: "Today, Protestant design and conceptions continue to shape many of our inherited political and cultural institutions; if you will, they are active cultural artifacts. Americans, clearly the most religious of any modern industrial people, continue to live within a world subtly formed by the shadows of our Protestant foundations. Most importantly, we continue to live in the shadow of the hallowed freedom of religious conscience and the delimiting consequences of belief in the Christian dogma of original sin. The former, knowing no natural limits, has proven to be a superb solvent of all societal boundaries, while the latter has often served societal aims that stand in opposition to such individualistic and antinomian propensities. Albeit tension-ridden, our political and cultural inheritances are eminently Protestant rather than secular in origin."

The strongly religious character of colonial society set out in Ferguson's and Shain's essays is corroborated indirectly by the essays of Danford and Frey, which question the extent to which it makes sense to think of the American Revolution under the rubric of Enlightenment. Raymond Frey focuses on a particular tension in the intellectual matrix of the Founding: "I want to suggest that there is a tension between some of these ideas, specifically, between moral sense theory and the claim that there are natural rights, a tension that has in the end to do with different kinds of reflections upon the foundation of morality." What Frey demonstrates is "how the attempt to ground morality in human nature puts pressure upon the attempt to hang on to natural rights." Thus there was a moral confusion in the background of the Founding for "natural rights do not bind our moral sense, and it is the latter, not the former, that is the ground of virtue." Furthermore, "moral-sense theory gives us no real way of privileging certain of our concerns, of marking them off as fundamental in a way that bars another person's moral sense in principle from objecting," and this is why it is in tension with natural-rights theory which demands that some of our concerns are elevated in this way.

That the engagement of the Founders with the thought of the European Enlightenment was merely shallow and opportunistic is the conclusion also of John Danford, whose essay reflects on the shortcomings of the economic understanding of the Founders. Danford argues that in one important area—political economy—the Founders were more nostalgic than progressive and were too bewitched by ancient republics to appreciate the different effects which might flow from commercial activity in a modern republic. So this essay sensitizes us to the regressive elements in the American Revolution and reminds us that its proximate cause was a resentment against innovation.

At first sight, however, David Wootton's subtle and deep essay seems to stand out against the findings of Frey and Danford. Wootton's central contention is that the Founders had a new way of thinking about politics and in particular about constitutional design: "the Founders had a new way of thinking of a constitution as a system, one which could be analyzed in the terms provided by a new 'science of politics.'" This makes the Founders seem not confused and lagging behind developments in Europe but rather dazzlingly up-to-date: "Madison, Hamilton, and Hume were all the beneficiaries of a conceptual shift which had taken place around 1700, one which expressed itself through the adoption of a new mechanistic language. It is, I maintain, the mechanical metaphor which lies at the origins of modern constitutionalism. This metaphor was used to argue that constitutions are interacting systems in which, as Hume put it, 'Effects will always correspond to causes,' and that consequently what matters is not the moral quality of the rulers but the structure of the institutions within which the rulers operate." Wootton's ground-breaking essay excavates the surprisingly complicated meanings digested into the familiar phrase "checks and balances." Buried within this phrase, argues Wootton, was an insight about the cardinal principle of constitutional design, deliberately placed there by the Commonwealth Whigs who coined and publicized the metaphor: "their claim was that good men would eventually be replaced by bad men (it was only a short step, but one they hesitated to take, to claim that power tends to corrupt and turns good men into bad), and that in the long run what counts is not the quality of the men or the rectitude of their intentions but the nature of the political system within which they operate." However, although in technical terms this extension of the conceptual tool kit of political thought was innovative, its tendency—the additional potency with which it armed would-be political theorists—was the very reverse of progressive. As Wootton understands, its effect was to enshrine within the founding political language of the American republic a massive bias in favor of resistance to substantive innovation since the encouragement it could give to novelty is at one remove beyond the immediate comfort it gives to those who favor a certain immobility in the arrangements of government.

Ronald Hamowy's essay moves us towards the afterlife of the colonial conflict, a territory entered also by Lance Banning and Gordon Wood. Hamowy's theme, addressed by way of the disagreement between Richard Price and Adam Ferguson, is the stimulus which events in the colonies imparted to inquiries into the nature of liberty and of the imperial system proper to Great Britain. His essay pays tribute, then, to the intellectual potency of American affairs. Yet it was an ambiguous potency: "A reading of Price's *Observations* and Ferguson's response naturally raises the question: in which ways did these two writers, who shared so much of the Whig tradition and who were both highly regarded for their political insights by so many colonists, differ from each other in their assessment of the events in America?" The two men shared common ground in their understanding of social liberty:

"both Price and Ferguson, by completely divergent routes and despite differing epistemological underpinnings, arrive at similar conclusions respecting the nature of liberty. Independent of exactly how rights are defined, both Price and Ferguson agree that a free society is one, in Ferguson's words, 'which secures to us the possession of our rights, while it restrains us from invading the rights of others.'" But Price and Ferguson differed sharply in their understanding of rights. For Price, these were natural and irrefragable. For Ferguson, they were historically produced and thus artificial and changeable. Hamowy's conclusion is perhaps too blandly eirenic:

> It is a reflection on the scope of the eighteenth-century Whig tradition that it could encompass two writers whose views were as dissimilar in certain particulars as were those of Price and Ferguson. Yet both were legatees of the Revolutionary Settlement of 1688 and both accepted its ideological premises. Both agreed that a free society was one that recognized the primacy of private property and the critical importance of the rule of law and both identified individual liberty with the rights of citizens to act as they chose, limited only by a modestly intrusive government. Finally, both had original insights into the nature of freedom and despotism that enlightened and informed. In light of this, it is not difficult to see why, despite their differences, the American colonists were receptive to both these thinkers.

Well, yes: but that receptivity also says something about the diversity of conviction amongst the colonists themselves—diversities which we can see also in the numbers of emigrants to Canada and in the profound divisions which opened up even amongst the successful rebels in the aftermath of 1783.

Those divisions are the subject of the essays by Lance Banning and Gordon Wood. Banning muses over the ambiguity of the significance of the successful struggle with Britain and reflects on how it did not point in any completely clear way towards the kind of form which the new American government should take beyond that it should be republican in spirit. As Banning describes them, the scope and extent of the debates in the early republic indicate how ambiguous, various, and fluid were the understandings of different Americans of goodwill concerning the nature of the liberty they had grasped and how that liberty was to be preserved. The dispute between Madison and Hamilton over the founding of a national bank illustrates well how colleagues might harbor strongly opposed conceptions of the kind of liberty proper to be enshrined in the American Constitution and of the institutions which might support or undermine it. The effect of Banning's essay is to pose with renewed force Hamilton's searching question, which challenges so many of the central elements of American self-identity: "And is it really possible in any large and populous nation for a single government to be republican in character and spirit—'republican,' that is, in something like the sense in which the great Virginians and many others of the Founding generation defined that term?"

Gordon Wood's essay on Madison seeks to reconcile the early and late phases of his political thought. First there is the Madison of the 1780s: the fervent nationalist who feared the states and their vicious tyrannical majorities and wanted to subject them to the control of the central government. Then there is the Madison of the 1790s: the strict constructionist, states' rights cofounder of the Democratic-Republican party who feared the national government and its monarchical tendencies and trusted the popular majorities in the states. How can these two figures be made to cohabit? As Wood epigrammatically puts it: "For the early Madison, popular majorities within states were the source of the problem; for the later Madison, these popular majorities in the states became a remedy for the problem. It is hard to see how these two seemingly different Madisons can be reconciled." Wood's solution is to posit a Madison whose deepest political instincts were regressive, and he underlines the backwards-looking, even perhaps nostalgic character of Madison's political thought: "With this conception of the new national government as a neutral disinterested umpire, Madison becomes something other than the practical pluralist that many scholars have believed him to be. He was not offering some early version of modern interest-group politics. He was not a forerunner of twentieth-century political scientists like Arthur Bentley or David Truman. He did not envision public policy or the common good emerging naturally from the give-and-take of hosts of competing interests. Instead, he turns out to be much more old-fashioned and classical in his expectations. He expected that the clashing interests and passions in the enlarged national republic would neutralize themselves in the society and allow liberally educated, rational men—men, he said, 'whose enlightened views and virtuous sentiments render them superior to local prejudices, and to schemes of injustice'—to decide questions of the public good in a disinterested adjudicatory manner."

According to Wood the really modern man amongst the Founders was Hamilton, and thus it was entirely in keeping with the nostalgic coloring of Madison's political thought that he should resist Hamilton's efforts to turn the United States into a modern fiscal-military entity along the lines of eighteenth-century France and Great Britain: "Madison may have wanted a strong national government to act as an umpire over contending expressions of democracy in the states, as his Virginia Plan suggests. But he had no intention of creating the kind of modern war-making state that Hamilton had in mind. Which is why he had no sense of inconsistency in turning against the state that Hamilton was building in the 1790s." The key which unlocks Madison's consistency, then, turns out to be nostalgia and the resolve to resist the advent of political modernity: "republican idealism—this fear of the modern fiscal-military state and this desire to find peaceful alternatives to war—is the best context for understanding the thinking of Madison and other republicans."

The only essay in this collection which seems to challenge a conservative reading of the American Revolution is Jack Greene's excavation of colonial attitudes in mid-eighteenth-century Jamaica (notwithstanding the palinode of its two final paragraphs but one, composed and added after Professor Greene had been given the opportunity to read this introduction in proof). Greene wants to "unpack the meaning of liberty among settler populations in the latent republics that had emerged out of the first century and a half of British imperial activity in the Americas" by looking at the tensions which arose between the colonists of Jamaica ("Britain's most economically important and politically precocious colony") and government in London. Greene explains and narrates in some detail "the overwhelming influence of the local political establishment and the lack of gubernatorial independence in Jamaica's internal affairs, giving the provincial Jamaican polity a quasi-republican character." But is that really the story that his archival labor puts before us? There is much virtue certainly in that "quasi"—the weakness of this essay is surely that it makes it too easy for the colonists to be republicans. But sturdy independence did not, at this time or any other, have as its inescapable companion republican politics. Greene is implausibly sharp-sighted in seeing the seeds of what was to come in these dealings of the Jamaican colonists with the administrators of Whitehall. For it is a striking fact that at no point in his narrative does Greene produce an utterance or a written comment by a Jamaican colonist which is couched in republican language or which makes a republican claim. Instead, what the colonists' words plainly show is that they intended to maintain and support their rights as subjects of the British Crown. To be a subject is not (*pace* Professor Greene) to be a slave. That is why the Assembly insisted on retaining "the rights of the people, their own liberties, and the happy constitution which they have enjoyed under his present most gracious majesty, and his royal predecessors, for above seventy years." There is not much that smacks of republicanism here. Nor is it easy to make *The Respondents Case,* the pamphlet at the center of Greene's essay, wear a republican aspect, extolling as it does "those brave *Britons* who made the Conquest of Jamaica" and who in so doing would automatically have taken their inheritance ("all the old and valuable Laws of *England*") with them. By which presumably they did not mean only those laws passed during the fleeting months of republican government which England had enjoyed in the mid-seventeenth century. So Greene deduces an elaborate narrative of events, but does he understand its real significance? One can only reject his labelling of Jamaica as a "de facto settler republic." It was no such thing, as the material he himself brings forward vividly demonstrates. Rather, the story Greene has elicited from the archives corroborates Burke's insight into the conservative dynamic at the heart of the American Revolution—an insight which admonishes that, however much some of us may wish the cherishing of liberty to be found in company with the advocacy of progressive causes, they are much more likely to be antagonists than allies.

David Womersley
St. Catherine's College
Oxford

"Of Liberty and of the Colonies": A Case Study of Constitutional Conflict in the Mid-Eighteenth-Century British American Empire

I

The early modern English/British Empire in America was a negotiated empire. From the beginning, the weakness of coercive resources in the colonies forced London officials to build metropolitan authority upon settler-created structures of power. To an important extent, therefore, metropolitan colonial authority had always coexisted with extensive local autonomy on the part of provincial governments dominated by colonial settlers.[1] Increasingly aware of the growing economic and strategic importance of the American colonies, some officials at Whitehall began in the late 1740s and early 1750s to take a deeper and more sustained interest in their affairs and governance. More than at any time since the 1670s and 1680s, metropolitan officials exhibited a growing preoccupation with the political and constitutional organization of the overseas empire, stimulating the first serious metropolitan theorizing about the nature of the empire since its inception at the end of the sixteenth century.[2] The same metropolitan concern manifested itself more concretely in a variety of measures designed to bring the highly autonomous and implicitly republican regimes in the American colonies under closer London supervision.

With little influence among the settler regimes that had long con-

1. Jack P. Greene, "Negotiated Authorities: The Problem of Governance in the Extended Polities of the Early Modern Atlantic World" in Greene, *Negotiated Authorities: Essays in Colonial Political and Constitutional History* (Charlottesville, Va.: University Press of Virginia, 1994), 1–24.

2. Peter N. Miller, *Defining the Common Good: Empire, Religion and Philosophy in Eighteenth-Century Britain* (Cambridge: Cambridge University Press, 1994), 195–213.

trolled most colonial polities, metropolitan officials more and more in the early 1750s bullied Crown governors into trying to enforce London directives. Threatened with reprimands and dismissal and desperately trying to stay in favor with their London superiors, governors in many colonies in turn endeavored to enforce metropolitan directives by any means they could contrive. Where polities were deeply divided or contained latent fissures, governors sometimes managed to enlist considerable local support in these efforts, but they everywhere encountered spirited opposition from settler leaders who interpreted their actions as subversive of long-standing settler rights and liberties, both inherited and customary. Throughout the 1750s and early 1760s, Britain's American empire was riven with conflicts of varying intensity over such issues.[3]

Providing occasions for the activation of ancient settler demands to spell out the precise nature of settler rights and liberties and to obtain metropolitan recognition of them, these conflicts raised again old constitutional questions of the most fundamental nature, centered on the problem of how or whether Britons overseas were to enjoy the same liberties and identities as Britons at home, questions that would lie at the heart of the great settler revolt of thirteen of Britain's continental colonies twenty years later. So intense did these conflicts become that in many colonies neither side could sustain them, with the consequence that during the late 1750s the empire reverted, at least for the short run, to its traditional negotiated state, with the balance of political power lying in the hands of settler leaders. Seeking to illuminate this important episode in metropolitan-colonial relations, this essay focuses on the experience of Jamaica, Britain's most economically important and politically precocious colony. It will also use this experience to unpack the meaning of liberty among settler populations in the latent republics that had emerged out of the first century and a half of British imperial activity in the Americas.

In the eighteenth century, contemporary metropolitans widely regarded Jamaica as Britain's most significant overseas colony. Economi-

3. Jack P. Greene, "'A Posture of Hostility': A Reconsideration of Some Aspects of the Origins of the American Revolution," *American Antiquarian Society Proceedings* 87 (1977): 27–68.

cally, it was by far the highest-volume producer of sugar products among Britain's Caribbean colonies, it took vast quantities of British manufactured goods in return for those products, and it offered the most extensive market for Britain's profitable slave trade. Strategically, its situation in the heart of the Caribbean provided Britain both with an important forward position in the contest for empire and offered British traders, usually clandestine but sometimes legal, a base for tapping the wealth and markets of Spain's American colonies.

Like every other British colony, Jamaica had its own special character and situation. What principally distinguished it from British continental colonies was the large proportion of black slaves, who outnumbered whites by nearly ten to one. This figure was lower than that for the Leeward Island colonies of Antigua, Montserrat, Nevis, and St. Kitts but considerably higher than that for Barbados or South Carolina. What made Jamaica different from other British West Indian colonies were its size (as one of the four Greater Antilles, it was many times larger than the small island colonies in the eastern Caribbean) and its proximity to the heart of Spanish America. As Jamaican free settlers were acutely aware, these two conditions made this valuable colony especially vulnerable to attack—from its own unruly slaves and from potential foreign enemies. As a result, they solicited and received far more metropolitan naval and military aid from London than did any other British colony, at least before the late 1740s.

Because it enjoyed such extensive metropolitan bounty and because that bounty operated as a vivid illustration of the insecurity, even impotence, of its settler population, one might expect that Jamaican settler leaders would, out of gratitude and fear of losing that bounty, have been the meek adherents of metropolitan commands and the exponents of an ideology of moderation and accommodation. That this was emphatically not the case is powerfully revealed by the history of Jamaican-metropolitan interactions from 1748 through the early 1760s. That history suggests that Jamaica may well have been Britain's politically most precocious and most militantly assertive colony in defense of what it regarded as its constitution and liberties. Repeatedly during this era, Jamaican political leaders, operating through their elected Assembly (or Parliament), openly and unequivocally defied metropolitan directives, invoking what they referred to as "the principles of our happy constitution, *and* the liberties and privileges of Englishmen" in defense of local rights and liberties against metropolitan measures they regarded as efforts to subvert them. No other colony matched Jamaica in terms of its consistent and vigorous defiance of these measures.[4]

II

When London authorities began to intensify their supervision of the colonies in the late 1740s, they paid particular regard to Jamaica, principally because of its economic and strategic importance. They soon identified a number of problems, most of them long-standing. These included the small proportion of free people in the population, the engrossment of thousands of acres of uncultivated land by some of the principal planters, the disorganized state of the militia, the incendiary character of the island's politics, and the strong Jamaican lobby in the city of London. They showed a special interest in its lack of white population and, reviving an older metropolitan concern, toyed with the project of forcing Jamaica's largest landholders to relinquish title to vast tracts of lands they could not or did not cultivate. This scheme never got very far but it remained an underlying issue throughout the third quarter of the eighteenth century.

Much more important were several contested issues of governance. The Crown had long exerted authority over royal colonies to disallow colonial laws that seemed inimical to metropolitan interests or subversive of metropolitan control, and when, expressive of the new and more intense engagement with colonial administration, the British Board of Trade, the government body chiefly concerned with colonial oversight, began in the late 1740s to review Jamaica legislation more closely, it found a number of problems arising out of the weakness of royal restraints on the Assembly. One problem involved the duration of colonial laws. Because the process of legislative review in Britain was cumbersome, lengthy, and sporadic, legislatures throughout the colonies had long since learned to pass controversial laws for only short

4. George Metcalf, *Royal Government and Political Conflict in Jamaica 1729–1783* (London: Longman, 1965), provides an excellent general narrative of mid-eighteenth-century Jamaican politics.

durations of one to three years so that they would expire before the review process could have any effect, and the Jamaica legislature was no exception. As early as 1747, the Board of Trade complained to Governor Edward Trelawny that many Jamaica acts had been "passed for so short a time that there" was "no room left for the Royal Assent or Disapprobation."[5]

A second problem involved the colonial legislatures' extensive control over provincial finance. In Jamaica's case the Board discovered that the Assembly was routinely using its financial powers to establish its jurisdiction over a wide range of activities that in Britain were the exclusive province of the Crown. These extended to the auditing of public accounts, the regulation of the militia, and even the making of orders and regulations concerning the King's troops stationed in Jamaica.[6] In his letters to the Board of Trade, Trelawny, who had been governor of Jamaica since 1738, explained how the Assembly operated. Whenever it sought his approval of a bill "of a new and extraordinary nature," he reported, he could do little more than protest because the members of the House invariably "made use of their old prevailing method," keeping "back one of their Money Bills, so" that he "was forc'd to yield."[7] By such measures, the Assembly had effectively nullified the royal veto power in Jamaica and turned the colony into a self-governing polity in terms of its local affairs, a virtual settler republic.

Because they had no direct control over colonial legislatures, which in every province derived their authority from an entirely independent power base, metropolitan officials had no effective devices for getting around such evasions of royal control. Indeed their only option was to put pressure on governors to veto any laws that expanded local legislative authority. Accordingly they began in the late 1740s increasingly to issue special and formal instructions to governors forbidding them to assent to measures through which legislatures encroached upon royal

5. Board of Trade to Edward Trelawny, June 16, 1747, Colonial Office Papers (hereafter cited as CO) 137/19, p. 70, Public Record Office, London.

6. See Board of Trade to Trelawny, January 31, 1749, CO 138/19, pp. 103–4; royal instruction, #28, *Journals of the House of Assembly of Jamaica* (hereafter cited as *Assembly Journals*), 7 vols. (Kingston, 1798), April 27, 1748, 4:118.

7. Trelawny to Board of Trade, May 10, 1748, CO 137/26, f. 28.

prerogative powers, chastising and threatening with dismissal any governors who violated these instructions.

Trelawny was one American governor who was not so easily intimidated. Not only had he compiled a strong record as governor over the decade from 1738 to 1748, his most notable achievement being the pacification of the Maroon rebels early in his administration, but he was also extremely well connected in London. Born in 1699 to a prominent Cornish family who controlled at least three seats in Parliament, he had himself entered Parliament for the borough of West Looe in 1724 and had sat for the borough of East Looe for the next decade. He seems to have traded his family's political patronage for office, becoming a commissioner of customs in 1733 and the governor of Jamaica four years later.[8] A client of Henry Pelham, who became the head of the British ministry in 1748, Trelawny was unusually well protected against complaints from either his London superiors or political adversaries in Jamaica and England.[9]

Yet, not even Trelawny managed to escape the Board's censure for failure to adhere to his instructions. In response to an early admonishment, he told the Board in June 1749 that he always obeyed his instructions when he could do so "without danger or inconvenience to the Publick Tranquility." However, he explained in justification of his repeated capitulation to the measures of the Assembly that because the Assembly paid no heed to those instructions and raised money only with the conditions that pleased it, the "infallible consequence" was "that it will often happen, that either the soldiers must be without their Country Subsistence or His Majesty's Instructions deviated from." Requesting the Board "to consider this matter, & then let me have positive Orders not to recede from my Instructions," he declared that he would not thereafter "recede one tittle from them on any account." But he warned that the need to provide for the soldiers gave the Assembly a powerful lever with which to disrupt the colony's public life. Until a standing revenue was established to secure the soldiers' payment, he predicted, the royal instructions could never be

8. On Trelawny's governorship, see Metcalf, *Royal Government*, 58–108.

9. Trelawny's political clout in England may be followed in Francis Gashry to Trelawny, February 3, 1750, Vernon-Wager Manuscripts, Box 15, Peter Force Papers, 8D, Library of Congress, Washington, D.C.

enforced against the wishes of the Jamaica Assembly.[10] Constitutional reality in Jamaica dictated that Crown directives could not be implemented without legislative consent.

Trelawny had elaborated upon this situation two months earlier in two letters to Henry Pelham. These letters constituted an elaborate critique of existing constitutional arrangements within the Empire and proposed changes designed to bring the colonies under much tighter metropolitan supervision. The principal defects in British imperial governance, Trelawny wrote, were structural. The "grand error in the first decoction of Colony Government," he declared, in echoing the complaints of virtually every governor who held office in the early modern British Empire, was in the balance of power within colonial governments. While "too great power" had been "lodged in the Assemblies," the governors, endowed with "pompous enough" titles, effectively had very "little power." In the specific example of Jamaica, this situation made it possible for any assembly that was resentful of having been badly "us'd by their mother" government in London or was stirred up by "a popular Assembly-man" who was "disoblig'd by the Governor" to make sure that the government would be "without mon[e]y, however necessary it may be for the Soldiers, & forts." With no resources to use to "perswade or terrify an assembly," a governor, Trelawny complained, was impotent against "the great power that comes to the Assembly from the sole right they assume of framing mon[e]y-bills." Moreover, in every colony the assembly represented the predominant property interest. For that reason, to place power in the assemblies was to lodge it, in Trelawny's words, "in the Planters themselves," a mistake that, he was convinced, was "the Pandora's box from whence our evils have issu'd;" hence, in Jamaica's case, "the engrossing of lands, the paucity of white inhabitants, the bad state of the Militia &c &c &c."[11]

10. Trelawny to Board of Trade, June 8, 1749, CO 137/25, ff. 89–92.

11. Trelawny to Pelham, April 13 and 29, 1749, in Jack P. Greene, ed., "Edward Trelawny's 'Grand Elixir': Metropolitan Weakness and Constitutional Reform in the Mid-Eighteenth-Century British Empire," in Roderick A. McDonald, ed., *West Indies Accounts: Essays on the History of the British Caribbean and the Atlantic Economy in Honour of Richard Sheridan* (Barbados, Jamaica, and Trinidad & Tobago: University of the West Indies Press, 1996), 93, 95–97.

To remedy these problems, Trelawny, picking up on the central assumption animating the new drift in colonial administration in London, called for metropolitan officials to "consider our Colonies" not as would "a Merchant or Planter," but "in a more general & political sense." Although he proposed a number of measures to shore up executive authority in the colonies, he regarded such measures as "palliatives only." To get at the root of the problem of imperial governance, he proposed that "a State of the Colonies . . . be laid before the Parliament." Declaring that it was "high time" that the ministry take such a step, he argued "that unless there is an hearty & steddy intent to go to the bottom of things, unless there is resolution to consider fully the state of the Colonies & make a thorough reformation to be settled by Act of Parliament, all other things will be ineffectual, productive of no lasting good, but [be] a meer transitory amusement" (92, 95–96).

The most important element in that reformation, Trelawny made clear in setting forth his boldest proposal, was to take most of the authority to raise revenue out of the hands of the assemblies. "Whereas now a Colony Government is supported from year to year, as it were from hand to mouth, by annual bills rais'd by the Assembly, the standing revenue of the Island being very inconsiderable," he observed, "an Estimate should be made, (by a medium of former actual expenses for any numbers of years the Board of Trade should think proper) of what the future services of Government may be suppos'd to amount to, & then, that those very funds, (as the duty on negroes, rum, &c) which now are rais'd annually should be settled perpetually by Act of Parliament to answer those services." Once "a proper & ample Revenue [had been thus] settled by Parliament for the current & ordinary services of the Country," Trelawny noted, governors would have "no need to trouble the Assembly for a supply but upon extraordinary occasions" (92, 96).

In Trelawny's view, such a measure, which he referred to as his "grand Elixir," could not fail to produce "unaccountable . . . good": "all squabbles between Governors & Assemblies would cease at once as it were by some charm. There will be an authority in a Colony Government, which will be rescued from the dependence on the humour of an Assembly, Who will then 'tis to be hoped turn their thoughts from Politicks to Planting, & to the real good of the Colony. It will not then be in the power of a popular man to blow the assemblies up into a blaze, & all Westminster to the very Palace under the Greatest alarms." "Let this once be set right," he predicted, "& all other things will go right; Trade & Planting will of course necessarily prosper" (95, 96).

In expressing his conviction that such an action by Parliament was "agre[e]able to the *ancient* [emphasis added] constitution of England," a constitution whereby Parliament itself had met only to grant "aids upon extraordinary occasions," Trelawny implicitly acknowledged that it was contrary to the tradition of active and regular Parliamentary government that took shape in England—and the colonies—during the seventeenth century and had been institutionalized during the Glorious Revolution. Whether colonial political leaders might have opposed such a drastic revision of existing governing arrangements seems not to have occurred to him, albeit he was certainly aware that it would be necessary to have their approval or acquiescence (92, 96).

But Trelawny's proposals seem never to have made it beyond Pelham's chambers. No doubt, at least some men in power, including the Earl of Halifax, Pelham's new president of the Board of Trade, would have been sympathetic to Trelawny's call for sweeping reforms. Weak politically, Pelham's ministry, like most of those which succeeded it over the next quarter century, seems not to have been agreed on when or under what circumstances reforms in imperial governance should be undertaken or how far they should go. As a result, the Board of Trade had little choice but to fall back on its old stratagem of insisting upon strict gubernatorial adherence to the royal instructions. Thus did the Board in November 1749 again admonish Trelawny for "passing Bills for imposing Duties upon Rum & other strong Liquors for a shorter Term than one Year." Denouncing his behavior as "an Innovation of a very dangerous Tendency & expressly contrary to his Majesty's Instructions," it expressed its great concern "that any Exigence should have obliged you even once to acquiesce in a Method of raising Supplys so extreamly improper in every light & on every good Reason of State." Reason of State, not considerations of local rights and liberties or local convenience, the Board thus suggested in an important departure from traditional modes of metropolitan-colonial relations, should determine the nature of imperial governance. The Board did not deny "that Circumstances may fall out and Exigencys do sometimes occur in the Administration of Government to make a Deviation from His Majesty's general Instructions expedient & indeed necessary," but it added "that to justify such Deviations the Necessity must be very apparent and such Deviations cannot be too seldom Practiced."[12]

The difficulty with such an approach was that governors rarely had means at their disposal to persuade assemblies to comply with their instructions. Thus, when, in response to an earlier chastisement from the Board, Trelawny in October 1749 exhorted the Jamaica Assembly "to make your bills agreeable to his majesty's instructions, and to consider what a cruel dilemma you will otherwise put me to, either to risk the security of the country for want of supplies for the pay of the soldiers, the forts, and other necessary services, or else to go contrary to his majesty's instructions, which are and must be the rules of my conduct," the Assembly expressed its "extreme regret . . . to put your excellency under any dilemma" but quickly moved on to take other measures that brought Trelawny still further censure from London authorities.[13]

Indeed, the Assembly at this session took one of its boldest steps yet. Annoyed by the actions of the Crown's receiver general, it insisted upon passing a revenue bill that placed the monies raised by the bill into the hands of a commissioner of its own choosing, and Trelawny again had no choice but to accept it. Such a measure, while common enough in other colonies, represented a substantial innovation in Jamaica, where the receiver general had customarily handled all public monies. Moreover, to add to Trelawny's difficulties, the Assembly the following April signaled that it intended thenceforth to keep all public monies in the hands of officers of its own appointment by again including a clause to appoint a receiving commissioner in the annual supply bill. Though he "rejected the first Bill that came up with that Clause, & prorogu'd the Assembly," members of that body "continued fixt [in their determination] to insert this Clause in all their Bills," whereupon Trelawny explained to his London superiors he "was forced to yield; but not till I had the unanimous opinion of the Council," the governor's advisory board, and the Upper House of the legislature "that it was for His Majesty's Service as the case was, that I should do so."

12. Board of Trade to Trelawny, November 10, 1749, CO 138/19, p. 119.
13. *Assembly Journals,* October 24 and 26, 1749, 4:190, 194.

Trelawny acknowledged that this action was directly "contrary to my 17th Instruction" and professed "that this deviation from my Instructions gave me the utmost concern, & that nothing but the necessity I was really under, of otherwise losing all the Mon[e]y Bills, could have oblig'd me to submit to it."[14]

The Assembly's actions did not escape the notice of London authorities. Already in January 1750, Trelawny's London agent Francis Gashry informed him that the Assembly's measures had immediately "occasioned much speculation & a variety of opinions in the Ministry &c," with some being "for having the Instruction [forbidding such a measure] strictly insisted on" and others thinking it "better to take your advice and temporize a little and at a proper opportunity to Endeavour to bring this affair into its old Channels."[15] As Gashry put it in reference to another contemporary dispute involving Trelawny, the debate seems to have been over whether "this matter should be consider'd Legally" or "in a Political Light."[16] In the end, the exponents of a tough line won out, the Board of Trade denouncing the Assembly's efforts to appoint revenue officers as "an extraordinary Insult upon his Majesty's Government" and "a dangerous Precedent." "Unless a firm stand be made against the Encroachments of the Assembly," the Board told Trelawny in September 1750, "they will continually avail themselves of the same Plea of Necessity whenever they think proper to attempt further Infringements upon his Majesty's Authority, already too much weakened in many of his Colonies by Proceedings of a like Nature."[17]

Over the next year, the Board kept up the pressure on Trelawny. Indeed, the more deeply it dug into the recent laws of Jamaica the more convinced it became that Trelawny had repeatedly breached his instructions. He had, the Board discovered, passed many tax acts in which the Assembly had appointed commissioners to receive money

14. Gashry to Trelawny, January 25, 1750, Vernon-Wager Manuscripts, Box 15, Peter Force Papers, 8D, Library of Congress; Trelawny to Board of Trade, April 10, 1750, CO 137/26, f. 126.

15. Gashry to Trelawny, January 25, 1750, Vernon-Wager Manuscripts, Box 15, Peter Force Papers, 8D, Library of Congress.

16. Gashry to Trelawny, February 3, 1750, ibid.

17. Board of Trade to Trelawny, September 1, 1750, CO 138/19, pp. 132–33.

that the Board felt should have been "lodged in the hands of the Crown's receiver general," and in August 1751 it wrote Trelawny "highly condemn[ing] your Conduct in giving your Assent to these Laws in open violation & contradiction to an express Instruction. We every day experience the fatal Effects of the Encroachments of American Assemblys upon the Prerogative of the Crown more especially in Money Bills," it added in expanding upon a point made in its letter of the previous September, "and therefore it more earnestly behooves every Person Whom His Majesty has entrusted with the Powers of Government in his Plantations to guard against every Attempt to lessen the Power & Authority of the Crown." Further, it instructed him to persuade the Assembly to pass acts for the same ends without including the objectionable clauses.[18]

Trelawny remained unrepentant, essentially replying that he expected to be relieved by a new governor the following year and would wait on the Board to explain himself orally when he got to London.[19] In the meantime however, he made little effort to check the Assembly. On instruction from London, he did manage to persuade the Assembly to consider a measure to oblige all people with uncultivated land either to dispose of it or plant it, attributing his success in this matter to the threat in the instruction that failure to handle this problem in Jamaica would lead to the Board's bringing the matter before the British Parliament. This threat, Trelawny wrote, had "a great weight with many & will be a principal cause of our succeeding if we do succeed." In the end however, the Assembly failed to produce such a law, hinting that it was inconsistent "with our constitution and present circumstances" and in fact persuaded Trelawny to consent to several other measures regarding the administration of the judicial system and the regulation of officer's fees that the governor knew the Board would find equally objectionable.[20]

Writing to the Board several months after he had passed these laws, Trelawny admitted that they should have included suspending clauses.

18. Board of Trade to Trelawny, August 6, 1751, CO 138/19, pp. 163–65.
19. Trelawny to Board of Trade, June 13, 1751, CO 137/25, f. 208.
20. Trelawny to Board of Trade, September 16, 1751, CO 137/25, f. 215; *Assembly Journals*, September 10, October 3, December 14, 1751, 4:277, 282, 322.

More and more during the late 1740s and early 1750s, the Board had insisted upon the inclusion of a suspending clause in many types of legislation, including especially laws that modified statutes already confirmed by the Crown and laws affecting the Crown's prerogative claims. Such a clause suspended the operation of a law until it had been formally approved by the British Privy Council. An old device, such clauses were much disliked by colonial assemblies because they sharply reduced their capacity to handle problems expeditiously and represented a check upon their legislative independence. This dislike meant that they had been relatively little used during the first century of British imperial governance. The Jamaica Assembly was no exception. As Trelawny informed the Board in March 1752, this was "a point they could never be brought into."[21]

But Trelawny never again had to carry the battle over the enforcement of royal instructions to the Assembly. Despite opposition from people in the administration in London, his considerable political capital with Pelham enabled him to resign and to designate his successor, Admiral Charles Knowles, a person often stationed in Jamaica. With great applause from the Jamaican settler establishment for his political accomplishments during fourteen years in office, Trelawny left Jamaica in November 1752, a few months after Knowles's arrival. Before he could ever appear before the Board of Trade, he died in January 1754 as a result of a malady contracted on shipboard during his passage to England. As Knowles would later charge, Trelawny's enormous popularity in Jamaica was a function of his thorough capitulation to the Jamaican political establishment. When he arrived as governor, Knowles later wrote the Duke of Newcastle, secretary of state in charge of colonial matters, he discovered that his

> Predecessor had so far Yielded up his Power that he had not Authority left, without the Consent of the Ruling Demagogues [in the Assembly], for to make a Common Majestrate or even an Ensign in the Militia; Three fourths of the Money rais'd for the Current Services of the Year was likewise solely in their Disposition, and they appropriated it as they Pleased, without ever Accounting to His Maj-

21. Trelawny to Board of Trade, March 25, 1752, CO 137/25, ff. 236–37.

esty[']s Auditor General here for one Penny; The Method of Levying and Paying in of the Taxes, was likewise solely in these Great Men, and was to be paid by their Commissioner to such Favorites & to such purposes as they thought proper; by these and such like means, They invested themselves with all the Power both Civil & Military, and the Arbitrary manner in which They exercized it, has been the Occasion for near this Century past of the continual disputes, between them and their Governors & kept up a Spirit of Animosity & dissention amongst the People.

The Assembly's preponderance of authority was not, as metropolitan officials assumed, a relatively new phenomenon, a function of gubernatorial capitulations to recent innovations, but, as Knowles thus suggested with far more accuracy, one that stretched back to the colony's earliest days.[22]

III

With no powerful patrons in London, Knowles never had the option of following Trelawny's example, albeit Trelawny did his best to try to make it possible. In a masterful political stroke, Trelawny had paved the way for a similar accommodation between Knowles and the Jamaican political establishment. In the fall of 1751, he assembled twelve of the colony's most prominent public figures, many of whom had long been bitter political rivals, and persuaded them to bury the hatchet for the sake of political peace. Trelawny drew up a written "Association," which they all signed, pledging themselves to put aside the "great heats & animosities" and the pursuit of the "private resentments" that had frequently characterized Jamaican politics during Trelawny's administration and to support Knowles "as long as he appears to us to have at Heart the public Service." In letters to Knowles and his London agent, Francis Gashry, Trelawny congratulated himself upon his success. The association, he reported, produced "a happy reconciliation between the Parties of this Island" that brought immediate "Peace, harmony & joy" and laid "a sure foundation . . . for those blessings to continue during the whole time of Mr. Knowles's Administra-

22. Charles Knowles to the Duke of Newcastle, May 21, 1755, Newcastle Papers, Additional Manuscripts 32855, ff. 80–82, British Library, London.

tion." The implicit assumption underlying the association, of course, was that Knowles, like Trelawny, would allow himself to be guided by its members' advice. As Trelawny told Knowles, no one knew "the interest of the country better" than "all the principal Gentlemen of the Island on the spot."[23] The formation of the association was a de facto acknowledgment of the overwhelming influence of the local political establishment and the lack of gubernatorial independence in Jamaica's internal affairs, giving the provincial Jamaican polity a quasirepublican character.

Knowles was at first quite happy with this arrangement. Trelawny, he wrote Gashry, had "installed me to my heart[']s wishes, & I hope by reconciling Men, has so temper'd their Minds that I shall have a quiet Administration."[24] Indeed, Knowles seems to have operated under the naive belief that he could use Jamaica's new-found political harmony to enhance royal authority in the colony. In November 1752, shortly after his arrival, he wrote the Board of Trade a long letter in which he manifested his own desire to be a constitutional reformer. Speaking directly to the Board's long-standing concern with "the difficulties most of the Governors of this Island have laboured under to execute his Majesty's Instructions, by the Balance of power being constantly in the House of Representatives," he pointed out what the Board already knew as a result of its recent dealings with Trelawny: that the Jamaica Assembly had "long (tho' contrary to His Majesty's Instructions) assumed to themselves the Sole power of raising and appropriating Money exclusive of the Council" and that the Assembly's use of this power meant that it was "indeed the Government." Moreover, he added, the fact that the Assembly "was never so filled before with so many Gentlemen of Figure and Substance" meant that its "weight" was "even heavier and the Consequences more to be dreaded." With "no Mol[l]ifications or Gratifications left here in the disposal of the Administration," he observed, a remedy through which the Crown could

23. Trelawny to Knowles, October 23, 25, 26, November 2, December 9, 1751, and Trelawny to Gashry, November 2, 1751, Vernon-Wager Manuscripts, Box 15, Peter Force Papers, 8D, Library of Congress; Jamaicanus, *The Jamaica Association Develop'd* (London, 1757), 5–7.

24. Knowles to Gashry, Vernon-Wager Manuscripts, Box 5, Peter Force Papers, 9, Library of Congress.

acquire its "just weight" in island governance had proven to be "next to impossible."[25]

Knowles traced the source of this imbalance to the "first Concoction" of the Jamaica constitution, specifically to the weakness of the Royal Council, which was too small and dependent on the governor to act as an effective counterweight to the Assembly. In consultation with "Mr. Trelawny and several of the ablest Gentlemen of this Community," probably some of the twelve members of the association, Knowles devised a scheme to redress this situation. This scheme proposed to increase the size of the Council "so far as to take in every Gentleman of weight in the Country," thereby at once making the number of its members roughly equivalent to that of the Assembly and depriving the Assembly of all its "Gentlemen of Figure and Substance." To render the Council's members more independent, he proposed to raise property requirements for membership, thus presumably excluding dependent placemen from the metropolis. Although he suggested that the governor be permitted to designate from this larger number of councillors a smaller group to act as his advisers on executive matters, the members of which he could change at will, Knowles proposed to free all councillors from dependence on the governor by making it impossible for him to remove them from office without the consent of the majority of the Council or a hearing before the Crown. With its new independence, Knowles thought, the Council would be able to act more "freely in" its "Legislative Capacity." At no point in the letter did Knowles reveal any awareness of the extent to which such an arrangement, by giving local leaders control of both Houses, would have vested virtually all of the remaining vestiges of metropolitan authority in the hands of the local establishment.[26]

If such an arrangement would have been satisfactory to Jamaican political leaders, it "greatly alarm[ed]" the Board of Trade and other colonial officials. As Gashry reported from London in July 1753, it was "so little Relished here that People talk[']d of it with great warmth," and he predicted that it would "never go downe."[27] For its part, the

25. Knowles to Board of Trade, November 18, 1752, CO 137/25, ff. 279–80.
26. Ibid; Knowles to Board of Trade, September 13, 1753, CO 137/26, ff. 5–11.
27. Gashry to Knowles, July 26, 1753, Miscellaneous Papers, 1619–1783, Additional Manuscripts 19038, ff. 50–51, British Library.

Board of Trade dismissed Knowles's ideas out of hand. Although it acknowledged that the colonial assemblies had shifted the balance of power in colonial governments to themselves, it insisted that this development derived "from an improper Administration of Government," not "from any original Defect in the Constitution." "By a prudent & steady Exercise of the Powers given him by his Commission and Instructions," the Board told Knowles, the governor had all the authority he needed "to check and divert the Attempts of any one Branch of the Legislature to encroach upon any other, and whenever such a Disposition appears, the Conjuncture calls upon him to exert his Resolution as well as his Sagacity."[28]

How far the Board was willing to go in insisting upon strict gubernatorial adherence to the royal instructions was revealed in its relations with Knowles during his first two years in office. Reinforced by formal opinions from its own legal counsel and the Crown's attorney and solicitor generals,[29] the Board had already in February 1753 laid out its legislative standards following an extensive review of Jamaica legislation passed during the last two years of Trelawny's governorship. Many of these laws were in violation of the instructions in that they expired in a year, they appointed commissioners to collect and hold public revenues, or they altered or repealed laws already confirmed by the Crown without including a suspending clause. The Board denounced such practices as "lessen[ing] His Majesty's just and necessary Authority over his Colonies, by which their Connection with and Dependence upon their Mother Country can only be preserved." It directed Knowles to assent to no laws "which may contain any Provisions contrary to any of His Majesty's Instructions," assuring him that all such acts would be disallowed. By forcing Knowles into a strict adherence to his instructions, the Board signaled its intention to rein in the authority of the Jamaica Assembly by restricting its capacity to pass temporary legislation, to appoint provincial revenue officers, and to frame legislation free of suspending clauses.[30]

Knowles's response plaintively underlined the difficulties this ap-

28. Board of Trade to Knowles, May 16, 1753, CO 138/19, pp. 473–74.
29. Matthew Lamb to Board of Trade, November 20, 1752; Dudley Ryder and William Murray to Board of Trade, January 22, 1753, CO 137/25, ff. 261–62, 267.
30. Board of Trade to Knowles, February 13, 1753, CO 138/19, pp. 378–82.

proach presented for him. He immediately agreed that the Assembly's refusal to include suspending clauses in any of its laws carried "such an Air of Independence and trenches so much on the Just Authority of the Crown" that he would in future veto any bills that altered those that had already been confirmed by the Crown or contained "matters of a new and extraordinary nature." But he warned that this approach might produce a political impasse. Men of the "best abilities and greatest weight in the Community," he told the Board in expanding upon Trelawny's earlier assessment, had assured him that suspending clauses were "what the People are in general averse to, and that if His Majesty will not permit them to make Laws where the nature and evident necessity of the Case calls upon them, they must dutifully submit, and must be contented to live under the Common Laws of England, and such Statute Laws as are now in force." He asked "for His Majesty's orders how I am to act in Case matters should come to such an extremity that" the Assembly would "chuse to be deprived of having the benefit of such new Laws as the Exigencies of Affair may require, rather than give up the point of a suspending clause."[31]

This threat was the first in a series. Over the next decade, the Jamaica Assembly would several times express its adamant opposition to metropolitan restrictions upon its legislative capacity and repeatedly reveal its conception of the Jamaica constitution as an arrangement that, while providing room for metropolitan review of provincial statutes, placed control over all internal contingent affairs in the hands of the Jamaica legislature. These threats would cumulatively expose how far the Jamaican political establishment was willing to go to preserve the local autonomy it had so long enjoyed as a quasi-republican polity within a nominally monarchical empire.

Nor did Knowles expect any more cooperation in the Board's program to force the Assembly to pass supply bills for more than one year or to give up the appointment of revenue officers. Of such "long usage" was this method of raising supplies that he predicted that it "would throw the Government into the utmost Confusion and disorder if I should keep back these Supply's upon either of these Accounts." He then asked for the Board's orders as to "how far you would

31. Knowles to Board of Trade, June 27, 1753, CO 137/25, ff. 376–77.

recommend it to me to go, in Case the Assembly," as he anticipated, refused to give in. "When I have Your Lordship[']s definitive orders," he promised, "I shall inviolably adhere to them without adverting to any Consequences," vowing, like the obedient admiral that he was, always to make "His Majesty's Commands the sole Rule of my Conduct" and to adhere to them "steadily and with the utmost precision."[32]

Long before the Board of Trade could have received this plea for direction, however, that body had sent Knowles still another expression of its wrath. In drawing up Knowles's formal instructions in 1752, the Board at the request of the House of Commons had included a special clause directing him to prepare "an exact and full account" of the "present State of the island of Jamaica," giving particular attention to the problem of uncultivated lands and the paucity of white settlers. Not knowing enough to prepare this report himself, Knowles, to the great dismay of the Board, which regarded this instruction as a private communication to the governor, had sent this instruction to the Assembly. Even more objectionable to the Board, Knowles had proceeded to pass an act to disable placemen, including all Crown officers from sitting in either the Council or the Assembly. For several years the Board had been receiving complaints about Jamaica legislation to regulate the fees of those officers, contrary, as one of them said, to "a long series of practice or Custom supposed," within the British constitutional tradition, "to be of equal Authority with the Law." With this exclusion act which the Board complained was "probably the first of it's [*sic*] kind which has ever been transmitted from any of His Majesty's Colonies," the Assembly had boldly sought to diminish the status and influence of Crown bureaucrats in Jamaica, thereby once again enhancing its own authority at the expense of that of the Crown. For Knowles to have passed such an extraordinary measure without a suspending clause, the Board informed him, was "so manifest a Violation of your Instructions[,] so unbecoming a Sacrifice of the prerogative of the Crown[,] & such an Injustice to it's [*sic*] Officers as deserves the severest Censure."[33]

32. Ibid.

33. Leonard W. Labaree, ed., *Royal Instructions to British Colonial Governors 1670–1776*, 2 vols. (New York: D. Appleton-Century, 1935), 2:744; Board of

Such severe censures provided the impetus for a constitutional confrontation in Jamaica. Stung by the Board of Trade's critique, Knowles thenceforth rigidly insisted upon adhering to his instructions. At his next meeting of the Assembly in September 1753, he opened the proceedings with a recommendation that the Assembly comply with an instruction that it digest all Jamaica's "laws into one code or system." The Virginia legislature's general revision of the laws of that colony in 1749 had enabled the Board to undertake a systematic review of Virginia laws and to disallow many that seemed to contradict metropolitan notions about the proper mode of colonial governance, and this experience inspired London officials to recommend similar revisions to ten other royal colonies, including Jamaica. No doubt well aware of the Virginia experience, however, the legislatures of no other colonies complied with this recommendation. In Jamaica, as Knowles reported in January 1754, the Assembly simply ignored it. Metropolitan officials finally withdrew it altogether in 1761. Evidently, American assemblies had no intention of permitting such codifications to become a vehicle for restricting their scope for legislative action. More immediately important, Knowles, in the same speech, called upon the Assembly to "pay that dutiful regard to his majesty's instructions to me, in framing all your bills, as I may be able readily to give my assent to them."[34]

For its part, however, the Assembly ignored the implicit threat in this announcement and proceeded to frame its supply bills in its customary manner. When in mid-October 1753 it presented Knowles with several bills, he discovered that two bills, an additional duty bill and a measure to prevent frivolous arrests, had been framed without regard to his instructions. While the former appointed a commissioner to receive and issue public money "in derogation of the officer appointed by the crown" for that purpose, the latter had been passed "for a limited time, and without a suspending clause." These measures, Knowles

Trade to Knowles, May 16, 1753, CO 138/19, ff. 468–69, 475–76; Francis Delap to [Peter Forbes], February 13, 1751, Sharpe Papers, Manuscript 366, National Library of Jamaica, Kingston; Petitions of Thomas Graham, 1753, CO 137/25, ff. 265–66, 360–61.

34. *Assembly Journals*, September 18, 1753, 4:401; Board of Trade to Knowles, June 3, 1752, CO 138/19, pp. 258–59; Labaree, *Royal Instructions*, 1:167; Knowles to Board of Trade, January 12, 1754, CO 137/27, f. 18.

announced, were "so contrary to the tenor of his majesty's instructions to me, that I cannot pass them." Accordingly he rejected them and prorogued the Assembly for a day so that it might have "another opportunity of re-considering and altering those bills" in such a way that they would not be "liable to those objections."[35]

When Knowles convened a new session the following day, he again entreated it "to comply with the demands of your sovereign, who hath upon all occasions, extended the most distinguished marks of his royal favour to this colony" and to pass legislation in a form agreeable to his instructions. In this standoff with the Assembly, Knowles thought that he had a trump card: the Board of Trade's July 1753 report on twelve Jamaica acts passed in 1751 and 1752 during the final years of Trelawny's governorship. Prepared for the Privy Council, this report left little doubt that London officials would thenceforth subject Jamaican laws to a very strict review and disallow any measures that were contrary to the royal instructions. Laying this report before the Assembly, Knowles asked its members to consider whether in view of the Board's harsh line it would be of any benefit to "you or the people of this island" to continue to refuse to include suspending clauses in its bills.[36]

The report represented a wholesale condemnation of a pattern of behavior on the part of the Jamaica Assembly that, as the Board implicitly suggested, seemed bent upon aggrandizing its own authority at the expense of that of the Crown. In the Board's opinion, most of the laws it reviewed constituted a serious violation of the royal instructions. It condemned four revenue acts which appointed commissioners to receive and disburse public monies as "an open breach and violation of the" governor's seventeenth instruction forbidding him to pass any revenue measures that did not put the money to be raised under the control of the Crown's receiver general. To an act granting all supreme court judges tenure during good behavior, a measure that would have brought Jamaican practice into conformity with the English as it had been established at the time of the Glorious Revolution, the Board objected that "the Situation and Circumstances in which the said Island

---

35. *Assembly Journals*, October 18, 1753, 4:418.
36. *Assembly Journals*, October 19, 1753, 4:419.

or other American Plantations stand" made it "[in]adviseable, either for the Interest of the Plantations themselves, or of Great Britain, that the Judges in the former should hold their places" during good behavior rather than, as had been the case in Stuart England, at the pleasure of the Crown. It denounced a law to use ballots in elections as a "great . . . Innovation" that was contrary to both English practice and "long usage" in all the colonies except South Carolina. It objected to an act to appoint commissioners to hear debt cases on the grounds that it made "an extensive a Change in the Constitution of Government with respect to the administration of Justice" and represented a "great . . . incroachment on Your Majesty[']s Prerogative to which the establishing Courts of Justice belongs." It criticized an act excluding Crown officers from sitting in the Assembly and acting in the Council in a legislative capacity as "extraordinary and unprecedented" in that it barred the Crown's servants in Jamaica "from Privileges which they ought to enjoy, in Common with the rest of Your Majesty's Subjects." Finally, it found defective this law and four others of "an extraordinary nature" because they had been passed without a suspending clause in violation of the governor's twenty-second instruction. "Obedience to" that instruction, it declared "has been always thought most necessary to be secured, and can be no way so effectually secured, as by constantly denying the Royal approbation to every Act passed in contradiction to it." With this declaration the Board signaled its intention to seek disallowance of all such laws in the future.[37]

But the Assembly was not to be intimidated by the Board of Trade's threats. This was the body which two years earlier had been daring enough to resolve that the Board had "no right to take notice" of any Jamaica affairs that were "not a public act of the legislature of this island, or represented to them by their agent in London,"[38] and Knowles subsequently reported to the Board of Trade that since "the arrival of Your Lordship[']s Representation to His Majesty against the 12 Acts passed here in 1750 and 1751" Chief Justice Rose Fuller, a lead-

37. Board of Trade to Privy Council, July 19, 1753, CO 138/19, pp. 481–99. This report is reprinted in James Munro and W. L. Grant, eds., *Acts of the Privy Council of England: Colonial Series*, 6 vols. (London: His Majesty's, 1908–12), 4:215–23.

38. *Assembly Journals*, October 26, 1750, 4:259.

ing member of the Assembly, had "with others of the same turbulent Spirit been endeavouring to propagate amongst them [the contention] that your Lordships and the Ministry intend to take away their Priviledges as Englishmen."[39] Instead of backing down, the Assembly went on the offensive, Speaker Charles Price evidently reminding Knowles of the principles of the association earlier formed by Trelawny and various leading men and informing him that if he "intended to Govern quietly," he should follow the advice of not the Board of Trade but the members of the association.[40] When Knowles made it clear that he would not submit, the Assembly, in response to Knowles's speech at the opening of the new session, adopted on October 29 a set of seven resolutions that directly challenged the constitutionality of the assumptions underlying the Board's report as well as its emerging policy for imperial governance.

These resolutions focused on the two most prominent constitutional issues: the Assembly's right to appoint revenue officers and the suspending clause requirement. The first resolution dealt with the former issue, the Assembly declaring without equivocation that it was "the undoubted right of the representatives of the people, to raise and apply monies for the services and exigencies of government, and to appoint such person or persons for the receiving and issuing thereof, as they shall think proper," a right, it asserted, that "this house hath exerted, and will always exert, in such a manner as they shall judge most conducive to the service of his majesty, and the interest of his people." The six remaining resolutions dealt with the suspending clauses. No such clause, the Assembly declared, "hath ever been inserted in any act of a public nature, passed by the legislature of this island." Such clauses, it announced, could only function to prevent the application of expeditious "remedies . . . against evils or inconveniences" and, had they been required in the past, might actually have prevented the colony from defending itself "against its foreign and intestine enemies." Arguing that the existing system whereby all laws were subject to review and disallowance by the Crown was "agreeable to the prerogative of the crown of England, and of the rights and privileges of

39. Knowles to Board of Trade, January 14, 1754, CO 137/27, ff. 130–31.
40. Knowles to Board of Trade, January 12, 1754, CO 137/27, ff. 1–20.

the people of that kingdom, to which the people of this island are undoubtedly entitled," it denounced the suspending clause requirement as "a very great alteration of the known and established constitution of this island" and "derogatory to the undoubted right the subject hath of proposing laws to the crown." For that reason, the Assembly resolved, it could not "consent to the insertion of such clause[s] in public bills, without giving up the rights of the people, their own liberties, and the happy constitution which they have enjoyed under his present most gracious majesty, and his royal predecessors, for above seventy years."[41]

With these resolutions the Assembly again emphatically defended its conception of the Jamaica constitution as an instrument that gave its members, as the guardians of settler rights and privileges, absolute independence in the passage of provincial laws. If it willingly conceded that those laws were liable to subsequent review and disallowance in England, it wholly rejected the contention that the Jamaica legislature might be subject to any prior metropolitan restrictions as a constitutional innovation and an abridgement of its historic autonomy to which it was determined never to submit.

In transmitting these resolutions to Knowles the next day, the Assembly expressed its "readiness" to comply with royal commands "in every instance consistent with the trusts reposed in us by the people, and those rights which we do most humbly apprehend ourselves entitled to, under the happy influence of his majesty's mild government." Caught in the middle between the intransigence of the Board of Trade and that of the Assembly, Knowles could only respond weakly that he would take the resolutions "into consideration, and compare [them] with his majesty's instructions, whose command I am in duty bound to obey."[42]

Although Knowles subsequently informed the Board of Trade that he regarded the Assembly's resolutions as the "most extraordinary . . . ever entered into by any Assembly in His Majesty[']s Colonies" and shrewdly pointed out that they "sufficiently shew[ed] the sense they have of being Independent here," he ignored the resolutions, swal-

41. *Assembly Journals,* October 29, 1753, 4:431.
42. *Assembly Journals,* October 30, 1753, 4:432.

lowed his pride, and continued to try to cajole the Assembly into passing legislation. The bankruptcy of the Crown's receiver general Benjamin Hume revealed that he could not repay £20,000 of the public
money, nearly all the money in the treasury, and Knowles tried to work
with the Assembly to prevent such an unfortunate development in the
future. For its part the Assembly agreed not to forego the appointment
of revenue officers but to appoint the receiver general as its collector,
thus preserving the principle that it had the right of appointment. But
it altered the custom of the receiver general's receiving a commission
based on a percentage of taxes by insisting that he be paid a salary instead. By this action, Knowles complained, the Assembly was endeavoring "even to make the Crown[']s Officers dependent upon them."[43]

This situation significantly increased tension between the Assembly and Knowles, who tried with only modest success to persuade the
Assembly to raise the receiver general's salary. When the Assembly
proved recalcitrant, Knowles, growing more and more impatient, insisted on November 14 that the Assembly resolve this problem before
it "proceed[ed] to any other business." In response the Assembly asserted its "undoubted right . . . to proceed in such business as is before
them"; declared Knowles's request "a direct violation and breach of the
liberties and privileges of this house, and a high infringement of the
liberties of the people"; announced that it "would not proceed in any
business, until" it had been "righted in" its "liberties and privileges";
and demanded from Knowles "a reparation." When the governor denied that he had meant to disturb the Assembly "in the exercise of
their rights and privileges" and charged it with misconstruing his expressions, that body denounced him further for thereby abridging its
"right of applying to his excellency for reparation" and asserted that
his denial constituted "a great reflection on the honour of the house,
and a new violation of their liberties and privileges." When the House
continued to refuse to do any business, an exasperated Knowles twice
more prorogued the Assembly for a day, reconvening it on November 20 and 22. At his wits' end, Knowles finally apologized to the As-

43. Knowles to Board of Trade, January 12, 1754, CO 137/27, ff. 1–20; Brief
against Charles Knowles upon a Complaint lodged against him by Wm. Beckford
in the House of Commons [February 12, 1757], Fuller Family Papers, Bundle 18,
7a, East Sussex Record Office, Lewes, England.

sembly when he reconvened it again on November 22, and he subsequently sought to dampen animosities by giving "an Entertainment at his Farm to many of the Gentlemen of the Assembly," thereby restoring some degree of political harmony with the Assembly which eventually passed five bills that Knowles could sign.[44]

As it proceeded back to business, however, the Assembly entered upon its journals a sworn copy of Charles II's 1661 proclamation for encouraging immigration to Jamaica. According to Knowles, Rose Fuller had obtained this document from London for the specific purpose of stirring up opposition to the Parliamentary inquiry into the state of Jamaica lands. In 1752 the House of Commons had directed the Board of Trade to prepare a report on what had been done over the past two decades "toward peopling, strengthening, and improving the Island of Jamaica." Laid before the House of Commons in February 1753, this report became the basis for a printed bill "for coming at a knowledge of the Titles by which the present occupyers of Lands [in Jamaica] hold them." Although the session ended before the bill had been passed, the Jamaican lobby in London, several of whom, including William Beckford, a member of Parliament, had titles to vast uncultivated acreage in Jamaica, endeavored to head off the bill. Originally, Fuller's objective in obtaining Charles II's 1661 proclamation, according to Knowles, was to distribute it about the island to let people "see the Conditions or Terms on which they held their Tenures, in order to prepare them to oppose the methods intended by the Printed Bill offered by the House of Commons last Year . . . in Case the same should pass into a Law."[45]

In the political climate of Jamaica in the fall of 1753, however, this document quickly came to serve another purpose. With "the arrival of Your Lordship[']s Representation to His Majesty against the 12 Acts passed here in 1750 and 1751," Knowles reported, Fuller had "with others of the same turbulent Spirit been endeavouring to propagate

44. *Assembly Journals,* November 3, 6–8, 14–17, 19–20, 22, 1753, 4:440–43, 448–51, 454–56; Brief against Charles Knowles [February 12, 1757], Fuller Family Papers, Bundle 18, 7a, East Sussex Record Office.

45. *Assembly Journals,* November 22, 1753, 4:455; Knowles to Board of Trade, January 12, 1754, CO 127/27, f. 16; *A Short Account of the Interest and Conduct of the Jamaica Planters* (London: M. Cooper, 1754), 13–14.

amongst" the public the idea "that your Lordships and the Ministry in-tend[ed] to take away their Priviledges as Englishmen." Emphasizing the clause in the proclamation declaring all children born in Jamaica to be "naturall borne subjects of England" and "free denizens of En-gland" with "the same privileges, to all intents and purposes, as our free borne subjects of England," Fuller allegedly presented this docu-ment "as a Magna Charta for this Island." No doubt, as Knowles sug-gested, Fuller and his colleagues had this document read in the As-sembly and inserted in the Assembly minutes to underline its status as fundamental law—"a Magna Charta" that provided a legal basis for Jamaica's claims for English rights and local autonomy as exhibited in part by the Assembly's resolutions of October 29.[46]

While political storms raged in Jamaica, the wheels of London ad-ministration were moving slowly but inexorably in a direction that gave Knowles even less scope for maneuver. In November 1753, John Sharpe, Jamaica's London agent, petitioned against the Board of Trade report on the 1751 and 1752 laws in terms that made it clear that Jamaica's conception of imperial governance differed markedly from those of the Board of Trade. Defending the acts as being "of great and publick Utility and calculated for the ease and benefit of the Subjects" of Jamaica, he denied that any of them encroached upon the pre-rogative. Arguing that the royal instructions did not "affect the Rights of the Assembly," he contended that the Assembly's appointment of revenue officers followed logically from the principle that "the same Power which gives and raises the Money . . . hath a right to give the Collection of it to whom they please" and pointed out that this right was "exercised by the Assembly in all the other Sugar Islands," add-ing that "it would be extream hard to deny it to Jamaica." Because many of the measures contained "nothing in the least" that affected the royal prerogative but related "wholly . . . to Regulations touch-ing their own Property and within themselves," he stated, they were "within the discretion and power of that Legislature." Acts that related solely "to the Domestick Management of the Affairs of Jamaica," did not "prejudicially affect the Royal Prerogative of the Mother Country

46. *Assembly Journals*, November 22, 1753, 4:455; Knowles to Board of Trade, January 12, 14, 1754, CO 1377/27, ff. 19, 130.

or Sister Colonies," and were "approved of and desired by all His Majesty's Subjects in that Island," he declared, should be confirmed, not disallowed. Representing the views of the Jamaica legislature, Sharpe could scarcely have been more explicit in his enunciation of the doctrine that the domestic affairs of Jamaica were the province of the Jamaica Assembly and that metropolitan officials ought not to interfere unless Jamaican laws somehow violated the royal prerogative or affected the welfare of other polities within the empire.[47]

When the Privy Council took up the Board of Trade's report in February 1754, however, it took little heed of Sharpe's arguments. Rather it thoroughly endorsed the report, confirming only two of twelve acts, disallowing seven, and authorizing the issuance of an additional instruction to Knowles to deal with the suspending clause and issues relating to the three short-term acts that had already expired. This instruction censured Knowles and threatened to remove him from office if he did not "pay a due Obedience and Regard for the future to your Commission and Instructions by constantly refusing your Assent to any Bills of an unusual or extraordinary Nature and Importance wherein Our Prerogative or the Property of Our Subjects may be prejudiced or the Trade or Shipping of this Kingdom any way Affected untill" he had sent them home for approval. The instruction followed this endorsement of suspending clauses with an admonition never to give his "Assent to any Law for raising Money . . . by which it is not expressly declared that such Money shall be put into the Hands of our Receiver General" and, by implication, not under the control of any Assembly-appointed officers.[48]

IV

In Jamaica in the meantime, Knowles, desperate to break the impasse between himself and the Assembly, took measures that

47. John Sharpe, Extract of a Petition [November 1753], Sharpe Papers, Manuscript 367, National Library of Jamaica, Kingston.

48. Minutes of the Privy Council Committee, February 5, 14, 26, Privy Council Papers, Public Record Office, 4/1, pp. 945–49, 951; Grant and Munro, *Acts of the Privy Council*, 4:215–23; Privy Council Minutes, February 28, 1754, Privy Council Papers 104, pp. 40–41; Board of Trade to Privy Council, February 27, 1754, CO 138/20, pp. 10–14; Labaree, *Royal Instructions*, 1:150–51.

brought constitutional conflict in the island to an entirely new level when he seized upon a January 1754 petition from Kingston merchants to the Crown as a device that would enable him to govern the island on the terms demanded by his London superiors. This action stimulated an internal controversy within Jamaica that lasted almost five years and went through several distinct phases. Bringing Knowles into fierce political struggles with the island's entrenched political leadership, it eventually cost him his job.

The first phase of this controversy, lasting for the first six months of 1754, involved a vigorous round of petitioning in which the antagonists laid out their case for or against the Kingston petition. Emanating principally from the colony's overseas merchants, most of whom resided in Kingston, the Kingston petition requested the removal of the colony's capital from Spanish Town to Kingston on the grounds of Kingston's superior size, its importance as Jamaica's chief port and urban center, and the inconvenience of having to go seventeen miles inland to Spanish Town to conduct one's legal business. Immediately throwing his support behind this petition, Knowles recommended it to his London superiors as an instrument by which "the Planters' Pride & Power" could be lowered and the "Trade[,] strength & Revenue of the Island" increased.[49]

In letters to the Duke of Newcastle, who had succeeded his brother Henry Pelham as chief minister, and the Earl of Holdernesse, who as secretary of state for the southern department had nominal authority over colonial affairs, Knowles explained the benefits that would flow from the success of this petition. "Since the first appointment of Assemblys in this Island," he told Holdernesse, "the Planters have constantly composed that Body" because "the Seat of Trade was too remote from the Seat of Government for the Merchants, & Burghers of Port Royal & Kingston to attend a session without Manifest loss and detriment to their Affairs." The result was that "the Planters have engross'd that House to themselves & by their Oppulency & high Spirit have constantly obstructed the Governours of this Colony from carry-

49. Privy Council Memorial to the King, January 1754, Egerton Manuscripts 3490, ff. 19–32, British Library; Knowles to Duke of Newcastle, January 29, 1754, Newcastle Papers, Additional Manuscripts 32734, ff. 86–88.

ing on His Majesty's Instructions, and all [other] Measures . . . calculated for whatever good purposes unless they tended purely to their own Interest." Thus, he explained to Newcastle, had "these powerful princes" been able to acquire "vast Tracts of Land" and to screen from metropolitan eyes both the extent of their holdings and "the Slender (nay wicked) titles some of them hold these lands by," with the result that they had been able to keep the price of sugar high by preventing their extensive uncultivated lands from "being improved into Sugar Plantations" or being occupied by new white settlers. Neither the amount of sugar produced nor the white population, he predicted, would ever be increased "till some of the Vast Tracts of Land belonging to these Mighty-Men" were "resumed by Law and Vested again in the Crown." Considering trade "a mean Vocation," the planters had, Knowles charged, for "a long time supported an Interest against the Merchants with the verry Money they borrow from them," a practice that the merchants were "determin'd to submit to . . . no longer, but to gett into the Assembly, if the Government is removed to Kingston, as their business will admitt of their attending the House there which it wou'd not do in Spanish Town," thus "destroying the [planters'] Power, & creating a country balance for the future."[50]

Holding "the greatest part of the Property of the Country in their hands," the merchants, Knowles explained, were "Men of Interest in the Island," who would not fail to operate as "a Check upon the Planters['] insolence and [to] enable a Governour to carry on His Majesty['s] Service with . . . great ease and certainty." Whereas the planters had always been the "constant Contemners and Opposers" of government who on every occasion and on every issue had betrayed their determination to "govern without Controul," the merchants had "a constant reliance on the Government," were always the governor's "hearty Friends," and could thus be depended upon to support all metropolitan measures intended to add "Strength & Security to the Island," including uncovering the "flagrant . . . scene of Deceit" surrounding the planters' land engrossment. Knowles called upon Newcastle, Holder-

50. Knowles to Holdernesse, February 5, 1754, CO 137/60, f. 69; Knowles to Newcastle, January 29, 1754, Newcastle Papers, Additional Manuscripts 32734, ff. 86–88.

nesse, and the "rest of the King's Ministers" to act favorably upon the Kingston petition and thereby seize upon such a favorable opportunity for establishing metropolitan authority in the colony. "The late behav[i]our of the Assembly," he added darkly, made it absolutely "necessary that something shou'd soon be done, or there will be an End of all Regal Authority here."[51]

His sanguine expectations notwithstanding, Knowles through his support of the Kingston petition only succeeded in intensifying his political problems within Jamaica. Led by Rose Fuller, Speaker Charles Price, and Richard Beckford, three of the most prominent political figures in the colony, the Spanish Town interest soon mounted a counterpetition aimed at keeping the capital in Spanish Town. To oppose the Kingston petition, Fuller organized a rally of a few hundred people in Spanish Town on January 31, 1754, just a few yards away from the building in which Knowles was holding a session of the court of chancery. According to Fuller's subsequent defense of his behavior, this meeting included some town inhabitants who were not freeholders but principally consisted of a combination of people "in eminent Stations," including seven judges and court officials, six assembly members, several justices of the peace, the rector of the parish church, eight barristers, "several Gentlemen of Estates, and many Freeholders and Housekeepers of the said Town and Neighbourhood thereof." But Knowles, regarding the gathering as a mob and Fuller's action in calling it as a blatant attempt at intimidation, summoned a company of troops from Kingston to keep order and charged Fuller with inciting a riot. Although no riot occurred, local residents quickly began to make life in Spanish Town miserable for the governor and his family, "huzzaing and singing . . . impudent songs" as they passed by the King's House, his residence, insulting his wife while he was away on a tour of the island, preventing his servants from buying meat in the market, and breaking into the King's House, taking the island's mace, shattering it, and strewing the pieces before the governor's door. The local doctors even refused to treat his sick child. This harassment effectively drove the governor out of Spanish Town. Fearing for his family's safety, he moved to Kingston into a house provided by some of the Kingston

51. Ibid.

petitioners. Unless the capital itself was removed to Kingston or "something of that kind . . . done now to create a Ballance in the Assembly," he excitedly told his London superiors, "I do apprehend the King will have no share in the Government of this Island long, without force to support it."[52]

Along with the Kingston petition, these events stimulated an intensive contest for the support of the island's rural parishes. The result was an extraordinarily extensive political mobilization, the scale of which was certainly unprecedented in Jamaica and probably also in any of the other American colonies. In January 1754, 591 people had signed the original Kingston petition, and 545 people, only 11 of whom had not signed the original petition, signed a second one a few weeks later.[53] Most of the parishes in eastern Jamaica drew up and signed petitions to support the Kingston proposal: 87 people from the town and parish of Port Royal, 69 from the parish of St. Andrew, 78 from the parishes of St. Mary and St. George, and 188 from the parish of St. Thomas in the East. Altogether, these petitions contained 1,024 signatures from 975 different people.[54]

Galvanized into action by these petitions, the supporters of Spanish Town drew up three separate petitions between February 1 and June 24, 1754, that included 529 signatures from 506 different people.[55] The parishes immediately surrounding and to the west of Spanish Town also produced petitions in support of the existing capital, with the signatures of 13 people from the parish of Clarendon, 7 from the parish of St. John, 12 from the parish of St. Catherine, 11 from the parish of Vere, and 221 from the parishes in Jamaica's westernmost

52. Knowles to Board of Trade, February 15, 1754, CO 137/26 and May 7, 1754, CO 137/27, ff. 196–98; Rose Fuller's Answer to Charles Knowles's Complaint, September 1754, CO 137/28, ff. 70–74.

53. Memorial of the Merchants and Factors of Kingston to the Board of Trade, January 1754, CO 137/26, ff. 176–87; Petition of Kingston Merchants to the King [February 1754], CO 137/27, ff. 453–56.

54. Port Royal Petition [February 1754], CO 137/27, f. 162; St. Andrew Petition, ibid., ff. 157–58; St. Marys and St. George Petition, ibid., f. 161; St. Thomas in the East Petition, ibid., ff. 159–60.

55. Spanish Town Petition, February 1, 1754, CO 137/27, ff. 184–87; Spanish Town's Answer to the Kingston Petition [February 1754], CO 137/27, ff. 139–53; Spanish Town Petition, June 24, 1754, CO 137/28, ff. 52–57.

county, Cornwall.[56] In total, these petitions contained 801 signatures of 747 different people. Thus, at least 1,722 people, perhaps 20 percent of Jamaica's total free population including women and children, participated in this contest by signing their names to petitions. Slightly more than half, 56.6 percent were on the Kingston side; 46.4 percent supported Spanish Town.

During the spring and summer of 1754, rival Jamaican interests thus flooded London with petitions for and against removal of the capital to Kingston, but the Spanish Town interest did not stop with sponsoring petitions. In early April an anonymous writer, perhaps Thomas Frearon, a learned and much respected judge who had never been out of Jamaica, writing under the pseudonym Veridicus, or truth teller, took the contest to another level with the production of a substantial pamphlet. With some additions from an anonymous London lawyer associated with Gray's Inn, this pamphlet was published in London in September 1754 under the title *The Respondents Case*. Whereas the initial Kingston petition and all the petitions that later supported it had stressed the utilitarian arguments for removal, *The Respondents Case* following the lead of the Spanish Town petition not only sought to demonstrate the inutility of removal but also to set forth "the *juridical Case*" against it. In the process of constructing "the Law State of the Case," Veridicus, exhibiting substantial learning in history, law, and languages, laid out the intellectual underpinnings of the Assembly's aggressive defense of settler liberties as they had taken shape in the colonies over the previous century and a half.[57]

In colonies, as in larger polities, wrote Veridicus, the function of government was largely protective. That is, it secured the lives, prop-

56. Clarendon Petition [February 1754], CO 137/27, f. 210; St. John Petition, ibid., f. 211; St. Catherine Petition, ibid., f. 212; Vere Petition, ibid., f. 213; Cornwall County Petition [June 1754], CO 137/28, ff. 62–64. The small number of signatories from Clarendon, St. John, St. Catherine, and Vere, most of whom were local justices of the peace, suggests the haste with which these petitions were assembled.

57. Veridicus, *The Merchants, Factors and Agents Residing at* Kingston *in the said Island, Complainants, Against The Inhabitants of* Spanish-Town, *and of the four adjacent Parishes, and against the Members of the honourable Assembly, annually and constitutionally held at* saint jago de la Vega, *and against the Planters, Freeholders, Settlers, and chief Body of the People of the Island of* Jamaica: *The Respondents Case* (London, 1754), ix.

erties, and liberties of the inhabitants. No less than the metropolis, however, the colonial polity was socially exclusive and unequal. As he explained, laws were "principally made for the Protection and Security of the Freeholders, Settlers and staid Inhabitants of a Colony," and the "staid" inhabitants by no means included everyone who resided there. They did not, for instance, include "transient Persons, mere Merchants, Factors, Agents, or any other set of Transients, having no Plantations, or what is among us called Settlements, and who have only a momentary Residence, and Habitations for the Time being in this Island." Such people were but "Under-strappers, the mere Factors and Agents of his Majesty's Planters . . . and . . . only to be looked upon as the *Carnalia* of this Country, and the mere *Turba Rhemi* of *Kingston*." Neither did the staid inhabitants include the many "Ruffians, Sailors, and other transient Persons, who frequently resort[ed]" to the port of Kingston "in mighty numbers." They emphatically did not include the many thousands of slaves, many of whom were eager "to change Conditions with their Masters." "In all Countries of the World," declared Veridicus, such transients or, in the case of slaves, disenfranchised people, had "little or nothing to do with the Policy and publick Laws" and no "Right to interfere with the Policy of the State" or to apply for "the Repeal of publick Laws," the "Honour of Obedience to the Laws in being" operating as the only right to which they were entitled (20, 23, 30, 50, 55–56).

The organs of government were thus, according to Veridicus, all the instruments of the staid population. Thus was the Assembly, the lawmaking body of the colony, composed of members who were "not only the greatest Proprietors of and in the Country" but also had been "severally chosen out of the best people by all the Freeholders of the respective Parishes in this Island." Precisely because they were thus representative of the "staid Families" in the colony, such people knew "best the true Interest of this Country, which is certainly blended with their own, as well as with that of their Constituents." With this statement Veridicus implicitly endorsed the position the Jamaica agent John Sharpe had taken in his presentation to the Privy Council the previous November: that the Jamaica Assembly also knew better how to legislate for their country than did distant officials in London. Invariably, as well, the actions of the Assembly represented—and embodied—"the legal sense of this whole Island as to all and singular Matters in question." If the Assembly made the laws, the courts enforced them and adjudicated disputes arising out of them—with the security of the lives, liberties, and properties of the colony's staid inhabitants primarily in mind. As the repository of all the statutes, court decisions, land records, and wills and inventories of the staid inhabitants, the island record office was thus "the Charter-Chest of all the Titles to every individual Plantation, as well as to all the opulent Estates on this Island" (14, 31, 51–52).

Perhaps because it had so recently and repeatedly been called into question by the actions of London officials, Veridicus took special pains to spell out the legal foundations of colony governance. Authority in British colonies, legislative and all other kinds, depended in his view upon a variety of supports. These included, in the first instance, the original and fundamental laws promulgated coeval with or soon after the initial settlement. Citing Sir Edward Coke's commentaries on Magna Charta in his *Institutes,* Veridicus argued that "any By-laws, Acts, Orders or Concessions made contrary to" these fundamental laws were actually "against law" because they were "against the general Liberty of the Subject" and were therefore "void and ineffectual as being against Law." Indeed, he concluded, because "all His Majesty's Planters, or the greatest Part of them," had become "staid Inhabitants, and very considerable Settlers in this Island" on the basis of "the public Faith flowing from these fundamental Laws," they "ought never to be altered; and indeed . . . never [could] be altered, without renting all Order, and breaking all Unity, without sapping the very Foundation of the Constitution of this Country" (7–8, 12–13).

The English inheritance was a second source of authority for colonial governance. Veridicus cited Charles II's 1661 proclamation that Jamaicans would have the same status as "free Denizens of *England*" with the "same Privileges to all Intents and Purposes as his Majesty's free born Subjects of *England*" to show that "the Laws of *England*" were "their *Birth-right*" and that "the People of Jamaica" had "just the same legal Rights to the Possession of their own Freeholds" and to other inherited rights including consensual government and due process of law "as the People of England have to theirs." Indeed, in making this case, Veridicus took the usual colonial line that Charles II's proclama-

tion, like other similar documents issued in connection with the establishment of civil government in other colonies, was "in Truth of the
Nature of Declaratory Laws, for they gave no new Right, but only declared an old one." Even without such an instrument, he contended,
those "brave *Britons* who made the Conquest of Jamaica" would automatically have taken their inheritance—"all the old and valuable Laws
of *England*"—with them. That inheritance, he insisted, was "truly the
Birthright of the People of this Island." By adding such "a valuable
Jewel" to the English Crown and opening up such "a fine large Ave-
nue to the Wealth of the World," he argued, the conquerors of Jamaica
could not possibly "be supposed to have forfeited" that birthright (4,
8, 10–11).

A third source of authority in colonies was metropolitan judicial
rulings. Veridicus cited several cases at Westminster adjudging, as he
put it, "that the Benefit of all the Laws of *England* preceding the Conquest of this Island, did of Right appertain to the Conquerors." Chief
among these laws, he wrote, was "the uncontroverted *Magna Charta*
of *England*," which, according to these judicial rulings, endowed "the
People of *Jamaica*" with full entitlement "to all and singular the Benefits, Privileges, Protection and Immunities conceded [to the metropolitan English] by that Law or Charter" (10–11).

A fourth source of authority for Jamaica governance explored by
Veridicus was explicit contract. The 1728 Jamaica Revenue Act, which
provided a perpetual revenue for the island's civil establishment, declared all English laws as had "been at any time esteemed, introduced,
used, accepted or received as Laws in this Island . . . to be and continue Laws of this his Majesty's Island of *Jamaica* for ever." Confirmed
by the Crown, this act, wrote Veridicus, constituted "a fair, honest
and mutual Contract between the King and People," by which, in return "for a valuable Consideration," the King acknowledged that "all
the Privileges, Immunities, Freeholds and Possessions" of Jamaicans
would become "perpetual." Though, like Magna Charta, it gave "no
new Right" but only "ratified and confirmed existing ones," this act,
Veridicus emphasized, was "in Truth, the *modern Magna Charta of Jamaica*," a "*Charter of Confirmation*" that further guaranteed that "all our
Liberties, Immunities, Privileges and possessions enjoyed under the
Charter" would be "possessed *Justâ Causâ praecedente*" (8–10).

A fifth and highly important source of authority was colonial custom. Veridicus quoted Coke on the authority of "the *Customs of the Realm*" in England, "the most valuable and significant" of which were those that met the four tests of being "*ancient, universal, uninterrupted, and notorious.*" As inviolable possessions "claim[ed] by Prescription," rights based on such customs were legally sacrosanct, even if there were no other legal foundations for them. Veridicus cited the writings of Secretary of State John Thurlow to prove that any "Possession which surpasseth the Memory of every Man living" could "*be deemed an Immemorial Possession*" that "create[d] an inflexible *legal Title.*" In the case of Jamaica, he argued, "the *tacit Consent* of the King, his Governors and the People" had "effectually operated" to do just that. "'Tis certain," he declared, "that, 99 Years [of] quiet Possession" created "an uncontrol[l]able Prescription of a just right." "Every such antient, uniform, general Custom of the Country," he claimed, "maketh a Part of the Law of the Land," of "the *Laws and Customs* of his Majesty's Island of *Jamaica*" (5, 13, 39–40).

In Veridicus's view the English doctrine of custom was paralleled by still a sixth source of authority for colonial polities: international practice as rooted in Roman and civil law. He cited various provisions from the Justinian Code to show that possession, in some cases for as little as three to ten years, constituted a "sufficient Legal Title," not just to freeholds but also to "Chattels, Franchises, consuetudinary Liberties, incident Privileges, or such like Concomitants of the Freehold." These provisions were in turn the original source of "all the *Possessory Laws of Italy, France, Germany, and Holland*" as well as the customary law of England itself. "Being of almost ten times ten Years Duration," rights based on the doctrines of possession, asserted Veridicus, "should be deemed an uncontrolable Title in *Jamaica,* and in every other *British* Colony that is not sufficiently settled, and that not only in Odium of those who rashly and unjustly attempt to disturb the peaceable Possession of the *veteres Colonii;* but also, lest by a constant Uncertainty, the Settlers of Colonies being as diffident as unsecure, might be thereby induced to neglect the Improvement of what they do possess" (15–20).

A seventh and final source of authority for colonial governance was natural law. Whatever was deducible "from the original and primary Law of Nature," declared Veridicus, was "as much a Rule for Kings, and . . . as just a directory of their Actions, and as solid a Basis for their solemn Determinations in the great Concerns of Mankind, or in the most important Affairs of the World, as any other Law, Act or Statute whatsoever." What was authorized by the "Light of Nature," which Veridicus suggested was equivalent to "natural Sense" and the "Law of Reason," carried as much weight, he argued, as what was sanctioned by positive law and custom. Thus, the principle that the acquisition of a privilege carried with it "all that is naturally incident to that Privilege," he declared, was at once "a Rule in Reason, a Maxim in Law, and a certain and eternal Principle in Nature" (7, 42–43).

In all instances, according to Veridicus, these sources of authority operated to promote four fundamental principles of British governance. The first was the idea of consent. Colonial governance, no less than metropolitan governance, was consensual, all acts requiring the agreement of both governors and governed. This consent could be explicit as, for instance, in the formal promulgation of positive law through statutes, or implicit as in the mutual acquiescence to a long-standing custom, "the *tacit consent* of the King, his Governors and the People," wrote Veridicus, operating "as effectually . . . as their express Concourse doth, or could have done in the making of a positive Act for that very [same] Purpose" (5).

The second principle involved the subordination of the King or his colonial representatives to the law. If "Justice and Reason" dictated to the King what "he ought not to do," law, in the English constitutional system, told him precisely what he could not do. Long consented to by the populace, "the just Prerogative of the Crown" constituted an essential "Part of the Law of the Kingdom," but prerogative, declared Veridicus, could not be extended to the destruction of ancient rights "declared and confirmed by Charters and Laws." Such rights, he asserted, could "never be legally or justly annihilated by mere Prerogative: For to dispense with such perpetual and fundamental Laws" was "against the Petition of Right" and therefore beyond the bounds of prerogative authority" (37–38, 57).

A third principle involved the sanctity of due process of law. Veridicus cited Coke to show that, according to English legal traditions, "no freeborn Briton, or other free Man, shall be ousted of his Possession, or be directly or indirectly attacked or invaded as to any Franchise, customary Liberties, Privileges or Immunities without an open fair Trial, according to the Law of our Land, and the verdict of twelve sworn honest and legal Men, or by a Jury of our own Peers" (14).

The fourth principle involved the sanctity of possessions, a term that extended not just to tangible property but to all fundamental privileges, rights, and liberties. Thus, Veridicus contended, the "constant and uninterrupted possession" of liberties over a period that "surpasseth the Memory of every Man living" had to "*be deemed an Immemorial Possession,*" to which its possessors had "an inflexible *legal Title*" (4–5).

From these principles and the sources of authority on which they were based, Veridicus contended, it followed that colonial "Liberties, Franchises and Privileges," like those of the metropolis, flowed "from positive and perpetual Laws" and were "grounded upon uninterrupted and immemorial Possession" and could not legally be undermined through the application of such illegal, that is, nonconsensual, devices as "a high commission, dormant Powers, obsolete Instructions, and new born Innovations" that sought to "deprive us the People of that sweet and pleasant Security which we enjoy under wise but not fleeting Laws, under an established but not a floating Government" (42, 68). Both "the publick Laws" and "the authoritative Sentiments and the Legal Sense of this whole Island," Veridicus concluded, required that no custom could be abridged through the unilateral actions of the metropolitan government. Rather they could be changed only "in the regular and usual Way by . . . the Representatives of the People elected and legally Assembled" (50, 52, 54).

Implying that Jamaica was not part of a national state but was, rather, a "Lordship" based upon a mutual covenant between the Crown and the freeholders of Jamaica, Veridicus argued that "by disfranchising it's [*sic*] freeholders, and depriving it's [*sic*] antient Possessors and kindly Tenants of their *Dominium utile,* to which they have the same just Right and legal Title that their King Lord hath to his said *Dominium directum,*" the application of such devices would not only destroy the colony's constitution but effectively annihilate "the very Lordship itself, and . . . destroy the *Dominium directum* of this Island" (22).

Declaring that "anticonstitutional Innovations may prove as fatal to

Colonies as Plague, Pestilence, or Famine" and were "the certain Fore-runners of Destruction, Devastation, and Extirpation," Veridicus concluded by demanding "that no Change or Alteration be made use of in the King's Writs, and that there may be no new Modelling or Transmigration of his Majesty's Courts, and that, there may be no intermeddling with our Freeholds, our Records, and our Laws; and that the fundamental Constitution of this Country, it's [*sic*] antient, well-approved Customs, and it's [*sic*] universally received consuetudinary Liberties may not directly or indirectly be *incroached upon,* invaded or innovated: And all this we with Humility and Sincerity do request," he added, "because we know that it is our Right, and because we very plainly do foresee, that a contrary Conduct to what is here desired, may tend to turn Order into Anarchy, Amity into Animosity, and to open upon our Country the Flood-Gates of false Policy, Madness, and Misery!" (49, 65–66).

In a telling passage, Veridicus complained that the Kingston petitioners, instead of going about things "in the regular, and usual Way by a solemn and proper Application to the Representatives of the People elected and legally assembled in Virtue of His Majesty's Royal Writts," had bypassed the Jamaica legislature altogether and applied "to the Sovereign directly and immediately and without any Intervention." With this complaint, Veridicus strongly suggested that the Jamaica legislature was the proper venue for consideration "of such weighty Affairs" as a change in the location of the capital, a matter "in which the Order of his Majesty's Government, the Peace of the People, and the Security of the whole Society" were so deeply concerned, and betrayed his resentment that the petitioners had called the metropolis into a matter that ought to have been left to the provincials. He thereby implied that whether the Crown in Britain should or should not be consulted on any provincial matter was a subject for the determination of the provincial legislature. In the views of the Jamaican political establishment, not the least objectionable feature of the Kingston petition was thus its implicit challenge to the competence of the legislature and to the local autonomy Jamaican settlers had so carefully cultivated for the better part of a century (53).

Whether or not any relevant London officials ever read *The Respondents Case,* the government moved cautiously in its response to the uproar over the proposal to make Kingston the seat of governance for Jamaica. The Privy Council received the initial petitions from the Kingston and Spanish Town interests in late May 1754 and referred them to the Board of Trade two weeks later. Over the next eight months the Board held more than twenty meetings hearing testimony on the merits of these petitions, but it seems to have been reluctant to report back to the Privy Council.

Indeed, the Board's relationship with Knowles continued cool. At the very time he was endorsing the Kingston petition, the Board was denouncing him for having consented to a law excluding royal officers from sitting in the Assembly and admonishing him "for the future [to] act with a due Regard to His Majesty's Rights and those of his Officers and the Welfare of the Government intrusted to your Care."[58] Moreover, the Board infuriated Knowles by seeming to side with Rose Fuller, whose extended family in England was closely allied with the existing ministry, in reference to the alleged riot in Spanish Town on January 31, demanding that Knowles submit proofs for his charges that a riot had occurred and that Fuller had incited it and even providing Fuller with copies of Knowles's official letters to the Board. Knowles especially objected to reports that the Earl of Halifax, the president of the Board, had said that Knowles would be recalled in three months. Insisting that he had done no act of government "without the advice and concurrence of His Council and a due regard to the Royal Instructions (which," he insisted in a telling point, "is the cause of all this uproar and opposition)," he argued that a consideration of all the facts would doubtless exonerate him from any charges of wrongdoing and result in his receiving "that support necessary towards carrying on this Government."[59]

But little support was forthcoming. The Board did support Knowles in his controversy with Fuller, who was chief justice of Jamaica, over the jurisdiction of the judges in the spring of 1754. Whereas Fuller insisted that Jamaica judges could hold courts of nisi prius on the basis of a 1751 Jamaica law that had been recommended for disallowance but

58. Board of Trade to Knowles, January 31, 1754, CO 138/20, pp. 4–8.

59. Knowles to Board of Trade, October 7, 1754, CO 137/28, ff. 95–97. See also Board of Trade to Privy Council, October 15, 1754, CO 138/20, pp. 41–79.

not yet disallowed, Knowles contended that both the impending disallowance of the law and the failure of the judges to obtain a royal commission specifically empowering them to hold such courts prevented the judges from holding them. In defiance of Knowles, Fuller contended that as long as the act was not disallowed, the judges deemed themselves "bound by our Oaths as Judges to regard the said Act as a Publick Law of this Island and to put the same in execution untill a disallowance thereof by the King shall be notified to your Excellency in Form," and congratulated his ally and fellow judge John Morse for actually holding such a court, "taking him by the hand and telling him he had acted like an Englishman and that he had as much right to do what he had done as any Lord Chief Justice of England." According to Knowles, the "sole view" of Fuller and Morse in holding such courts was "to insult his Majesty's Authority." When Knowles dismissed Morse for this behavior, Fuller resigned his commission as chief justice.[60] Similarly, the Board suggested in the fall of 1754 that Knowles's endeavors to defeat the "extraordinary Attempts and Innovations" of the Jamaica Assembly would win royal approval. But it remained wholly noncommittal on the fate of the Kingston petition on which Knowles had pinned his hopes for political survival. Rather, it recommended that he use his "utmost Endeavours to conciliate the unhappy Differences by which the Peace of the Island has been so greatly disturbed, and to avoid all Occasion of future Controversy and Dispute, taking Care at the same time to observe your Instructions and on every Occasion acting with a steady and due Regard to them."[61]

V

Left on his own, Knowles, increasingly aware that settler Jamaicans would never support the removal of the capital to Kingston without a formal legislative enactment by the Assembly, adopted the desperate political strategy of trying to win legislative approval, thereby launching the controversy over the capital into a second and

60. This dispute may be followed in Metcalf, *Royal Government,* 125–27. The quotations in this note are from Knowles to Board of Trade, April 10, 1754, CO 137/27, f. 138, and June 24, 1754, CO 137/28, ff. 21–22; and Fuller to Knowles, June 15, 1754, CO 137/28, f. 33.

61. Board of Trade to Knowles, October 15, 1754, CO 138/20, pp. 85–97.

even more complicated phase, one that would continue through June 1755. To further his new strategy, Knowles sought to gain a majority in the Assembly by manipulating elections. Accordingly, he dissolved the Assembly and called for new elections early in the fall. Between the fall of 1754 and May 1755, he called three successive elections and dissolved two more Assemblies in his effort to achieve this goal.

Held in early October 1754, the first election, hotly contested in many parishes, produced a significant gain for Knowles and the Kingston interest but not a firm majority. His supporters did, in conformity with his instructions, succeed in pushing through a revenue bill without, as he put it, the "Clogg of Commissioners as had been usual for some years past." Taxes were to go directly into the hands of the Crown's receiver general. But Knowles's actions in trying to gain a majority in the Assembly soon embroiled him in a new dispute with that body over legislative procedures and privileges. Bad weather had prevented elections in two eastern parishes expected to return members in the Kingston interest, and, contrary to long-standing procedure, Knowles issued writs to hold new elections in these parishes after the Assembly had convened but before it had requested him to issue such writs. Notwithstanding the presence of many of his supporters, the Assembly invoked the conventional English Parliamentary principle, long since incorporated into Jamaica constitutional practice, that the House was the proper judge of elections and returns of all members and that it had "an undoubted right . . . to void all writs issued by the governor, during the continuance of the assembly, for electing members to serve in this house, when such writ shall be issued without the request of this house." Denouncing these resolves as "extraordinary" and confident that his supporters would do even better in a new election, Knowles dissolved the House after it had sat for just over two weeks.[62]

In his dissolution speech, Knowles seized the occasion to articulate the principles that he hoped would lead to a gubernatorial majority in the Assembly. Contending that their resolutions but "too plain[ly]" manifested a disposition for "carrying things on with so high and

---

62. Knowles to Board of Trade, November 20, 1754, CO 137/28, ff. 154–55; *Assembly Journals*, November 7–8, 1754, 4:484–85.

usurped an authority," he reminded the Assembly that the "prerogative of the crown, and the liberties of the people" were both "your duty
to maintain and preserve, as well as mine," and accused it of "invading
them daily." Seizing upon the association established by Trelawny as an
effort by "some of you . . . to alter the established constitution of your
country" by entering into a secret and "wicked association, destructive to the rights and property of the inhabitants" and the "extraordinary paper . . . sent me the last assembly, by your speaker," as "proofs
of the designs that have been laid, to subvert our happy constitution,
and wrest power out of the hands of the crown," he charged the Assembly with having "for years past lavished away" vast sums of money
"in donations and gratifications to particular favourites" and promised
to make such peculation "publicly known" so that the people might
thereafter "have an opportunity of contributing to their own happiness
. . . by a more proper choice of their representatives." "The sounding
words, *liberty!* and *privileges!,*" he asserted, "convey dangerous ideas;
but the loss of the people's *liberties* may as soon happen . . . through
the *tyranny* of a *decemvirate,*" he declared in a direct reference to the
members of the association, "as under the administration of any single
person." Almost as an aside, Knowles ended his speech by challenging the Jamaican view of the foundations of settler liberties, declaring, in repeating conventional metropolitan theory about the constitutional structure of the Empire, that the Assembly's existence derived
from nothing more than "his majesty's commission, under the great
seal to me directed."[63] In the election contest that followed, Knowles
and his supporters dilated upon these themes. No doubt with the governor's sponsorship, an anonymous writer signing himself Jamaicanus
and claiming to be "a *Native* of this Island" who had formerly opposed
the "Measures of the Government," published early in 1755 a pamphlet that reproduced both the association and Charles Price, Sr.'s advice to Knowles on how to have a peaceful administration. Denouncing these documents as "dangerous Attempts to destroy and subvert
both" the "glorious Constitution and [the] Government (which makes
us envied by all other Countries)," Jamaicanus expressed his "Detes-

63. *Assembly Journals,* November 8, 1754, 4:485.

tation and Abhorrence of all Illegal; Anti-Constitutional and Tyrannical Associations of Ten, Eleven, or let their Number be what it will,"
declared that "only a *groveling wretch*" could possibly "*choose* to set any
one, or more of his Fellow Subjects, to lord it over himself," and called
upon "all *Free Britons* and *honest Men*" to disown those involved in the association.[64] Particularly intense was the campaign to discredit Charles
Price, Sr., his opponents denouncing him as "the ruling Demogogue"
who had "so long Governed this Island that he will not easily give up
his Power." "I appeal to all who know this Island," declared Knowles,
"whether the Laws for these fifteen or sixteen years past, have not been
made by him and two or three of his Colleagues[,] leading Men of the
Assembly for private views and purposes only."[65]

Knowles's tactics so far succeeded as to enable his supporters to win
an equality in the January 1755 election, and in case of yet another dissolution, he predicted that he had "a certainty of a Majority of five."
For that reason he confidently predicted that his opponents would
be forced to give in, and on the day after the Assembly met on January 20, he confidently wrote the Duke of Newcastle in London that he
doubted "not of being able to execute effectually all His Majesty[']s
Instructions & Govern this Island in Peace & quietness. I have had an
arduous task to bring matters this length," he wrote, congratulating
himself on his success, "having had a stubborn race to deal with." But
Knowles's optimism was short-lived. When he endeavored to gain a majority in the Assembly by demanding that it unseat James Dawes, who
in 1748 had been convicted at Westminster for having uttered "trea-
sonable expressions" against George II, the Assembly, by a narrow vote
of nineteen to seventeen, sustained its decision to admit Dawes on the
grounds that by taking all the necessary oaths required of an assembly-
man and thereby pledging his fidelity to the King, he had "obtained a
legal right to sit in the house." No doubt salivating at the prospect of
winning a majority of his own supporters in the House by a new election, Knowles thereupon dissolved the Assembly after it had sat for
just four days, denouncing the actions of the Assembly majority to his

64. Jamaicanus, *Jamaica Association Develop'd*, 25–26.
65. Knowles to Board of Trade, December 31, 1754, CO 137/28, f. 166.

superiors in London as little less than "inviting Traytors to take an Asylum in the Assembly of Jamaica."[66]

In the ensuing elections, Knowles and his party succeeded beyond their wildest expectations, obtaining a majority of nine. First meeting on April 8, 1755, it elected Edward Manning, a merchant and strong supporter of the removal of the capital, as speaker, thus depriving Charles Price, Sr., of the office for the first time in over a decade. Thereafter, it moved quickly to achieve Knowles's agenda, voting on April 17 to bring in a bill to remove the seat of government to Kingston, passing on April 30 that bill, sending it on May 7 to Knowles for his signature, and passing a bill on May 19 to build a house and offices for the governor in Kingston. Knowles signed the measure the same day. By this series of actions, the Assembly rejected the appeals of the inhabitants of Spanish Town to keep the capital there.[67]

Knowles was ecstatic. "Whilst the Governing Power was in the hands of Mr. Price, Fuller, Beckford & their Faction," he wrote Newcastle immediately after he had signed the removal bill, passing such a bill "was always look'd upon [as] next to an impossibility." "The many Arbitrary Acts of Power the Factious opposition to Government here had invested themselves with," he told the Board of Trade in reiterating a complaint he had frequently made, had been a "matter of Complaint for near a Century past, and to divest them of this Usurped Power & open the People[']s Eyes, who had been so long deluded, was no easy task, yet," he exclaimed proudly, "I have the Pleasure to tell Your Lordships [that] I have accomplished this, and will venture to say [that] if the Act for removing the Courts & Records is confirm'd, not only the Peace of the Island will be effectually restored, but His Majesty's just Rights & Prerogative maintain'd in every point." Yet, he had to admit that, in defiance of the Crown's repeated instructions, he had had to pass this unusual bill without a suspending clause in order to

66. Knowles to Newcastle, January 21 and 25, 1755, Newcastle Papers, Additional Manuscripts 32737, ff. 198–99, 248–49; Knowles to Board of Trade, January 21, 1755, CO 137/28, f. 292, and January 25, 1754, CO 137/29, ff. 1–2; *Assembly Journals*, January 22–24, 1755, 4:491–93.

67. Knowles to Board of Trade, April 10, 1755, CO 137/29, f. 17; List of Assembly members, April 8, 1755, CO 137/29, f. 21; *Assembly Journals*, April 9, 17, 22–26, 29–30, May 7, 19, 1755, 4:496–97, 503, 508–14, 519, 531–32.

obtain the Assembly's and the Council's support. Evidently not even his strongest supporters in Jamaica were willing to permit suspending clauses to be introduced into Jamaica legislation! Pleading necessity and "Numberless other Reasons . . . both Provincial and Political," he urged both Newcastle and the Board to seek Crown approval of the removal law. Without such approval, he warned, "I foresee [that] nothing but Anarchy & Confusion will ensue, and Oppression to all those who have assisted me in bringing these Measures to bear."[68]

The removal bill was not the only instance of Knowles's political triumph in the spring of 1755. During the heat of the October 1754 election, Knowles and his party began to suspect that Francis Delap, a supporter of the Spanish Town interest and as provost marshal the person responsible for overseeing elections, might try to deliver the election of three members for Port Royal parish to the Spanish Town interest. Accordingly, just before the election, Knowles, with the Council's approval, replaced Delap and ordered him to return the writs for Port Royal and two other parishes. Because Knowles had neglected to notify Delap of his dismissal and because the writs had not been executed, Delap thought that his compliance with this order might render him, as he later put it, "liable to many Pains and Penalities, contained as well in the Laws of *Great Britain,* as in the particular Acts . . . of this Island" and refused to deliver them to his successor, instead hiding them in chests stored at the houses of Charles Price, Sr., and William Wynter in Spanish Town. Though Price and Wynter immediately handed over the chests containing the writs, Knowles ordered Delap's imprisonment, first in Kingston and then at the fort at Port Royal, where without the government's showing any cause for his imprisonment he was held in irons, debarred from access to counsel or friends, prohibited the use of pen, ink, and paper, and told that he would shortly be dispatched to England "as a State Prisoner." Though Knowles did not carry out this last threat, the courts, now presided over entirely by people of his appointment, consistently denied Delap access to habeas corpus and bail. Indeed, the government brought

68. Knowles to Board of Trade, May 19, 1755, CO 137/29, f. 40; Knowles to Newcastle, May 21, 1755, Newcastle Papers, Additional Manuscripts 32855, ff. 80–82.

no formal action against him until February 1756 when it finally filed three informations charging him with secreting the writs "with an Intention to suspend the Execution of the Writ[s], subvert the Government, and disturb the Peace of the Country." Yet, Jamaica's supreme court showed no hurry to begin proceedings, and Delap continued to languish in jail.[69]

The Delap affair represented an important sidebar to the removal controversy because, as the Jamaican political establishment was aware from the very beginning of Delap's imprisonment, it raised fundamental constitutional questions about the capacity of a desperate and unrestrained governor to manipulate the judicial system in his private interest in violation of traditional English legal safeguards for the rights of individuals. From jail, Delap urged his political allies to "exert themselves" in his behalf "to support the Law, and the Liberty of the Subject" and warned them that if they did not do so the law would be unable to protect any person "from Injury and Oppression" of the sort he had experienced. Through their agents in London, they made sure that this latest instance of Knowles's arbitrary behavior came to the attention of metropolitan authorities. The result was an order from the King and Privy Council commanding Knowles to admit Delap to bail and to show cause for having imprisoned him. Instead of complying with this order, which he received while the Assembly elected in May 1755 was sitting, Knowles laid the case before the Assembly, in which he now had a substantial majority. On May 9 and 10, the Assembly reviewed the case, praised Knowles for having Delap confined, and asked the governor to order the attorney general to prosecute Delap for "his wicked crimes and misdemeanours, with the utmost rigour of the laws." Thus vindicated by the legislature, Knowles quickly sought the approval of the courts. On June 18, 1754, the supreme court, functioning with a jury handpicked to achieve a result favorable to Knowles, found Delap guilty, the jury, despite an effective defense, deliberating for less than two minutes. The chief justice sentenced him to pay a fine of £500 and serve a year and a day in prison "without Bail of Mainprize." Reporting this outcome to Newcastle, Knowles expressed cer-

69. *An Account of the Trial of Francis Delap, Esq; Late Provost-Marshal-General* (London: T. Kinnersly, 1755), viii, ix, 45.

tainty that the result of the trial would "sufficiently Justify my Conduct to His Majesty and His most Honourable Privy Council" as to clear "up my Conduct to the World" and win "the approbation of my Sovereign."[70]

But Knowles's victories came at a high price. The behavior exhibited by him and his adherents deeply alarmed much of the settler population, created profound resentments against them, and stirred manifold apprehensions about the tyrannical potential of delegated government unrestrained by close metropolitan supervision and unchecked by the power of an independent representative assembly. As Knowles's May Assembly was getting on with the passage of the removal bill, an anonymous tract, entitled simply "Grievances," unprinted, perhaps because the governor controlled the Kingston press, circulated in manuscript around the colony. As its title implied, "Grievances" consisted largely of a five-page list of actions by Knowles and his followers that could be construed as "publick Grievances" that gave "great cause of Complaint" and cried "aloud for Redress." Denying the Assembly its privileges and harassing it with prorogations and dissolution, interfering in elections and "new Model[ling] the ways of Elections" for the purpose of giving "a Party all advantages for obtaining a Majority devoted to give a Sanction to" his "unwarrantable" proceedings, suspending laws, intimidating judges and dismissing any who would not heed his commands, replacing public officers with "inferiour Men" whose chief recommendation lay in their willingness to serve as "the Instruments of Faction," obstructing justice, imprisoning people without cause, ignoring petitions, dispossessing men of their estates, and engaging in a variety of acts that showed nothing but contempt for the "antient usage and custom" of the island—these were only the most egregious of many examples of Knowles's "arbitrary Ministration of Power." "Is this treating British Subjects as what they are?," asked the author. "Is it not exercising the most arbitrary Power over a People?[,] & ought the [lives and] Properties of Britons be thus Sported with[?]."[71]

70. Ibid., x, xi, 54, 7, 8; *Assembly Journals*, May 9–10, 14–15, 1755, 4:521–22, 525, 528–29; Knowles to Newcastle, June 30, 1755, Newcastle Papers, Additional Manuscripts 32856, f. 411.

71. "Grievances," Hall Family Papers, MSS 0220/FB226, Folder 44, Mande-

But this document also had two larger points to make about the nature of British colonial governance. The first was that "Subordinate Powers," such as those exercised by colonial governors, included "no authority beyond what is by positive grant & Commission granted to them," no power even of exercising "the prerogative of doing good beyond that grant & Commission, much less of employing it to carry on uncertain projects or to serve private purposes." The second was that the governor's commission directed him "to govern not only according to the Fundamental Laws of the Mother Country but also according to the particular Laws & Customs of that Colony over which it" granted "the governing Power[,] provided the same" were "not repugnant to the Laws of the Mother Country." The "particular oecomony of a Colony" sometimes required its legislature "to make Laws different in some respects from the Laws of the Mother Country." In a colony like Jamaica, the very "being and subsistence of" which required "a permission of holding some of Human kind in perpetual Slavery which by the fundamental Laws of the Mother Country absolutely abhors within itself," the author argued, the "repugnancy so provided against" could "only relate to what is Subversive of that form of Government[,] that Liberty & property established by those fundamental Laws, and what tends to dissolve that dependency of the Colony on the Mother Country, and to lessen that Utility which is necessary for the well being of both, and for which it was first Settled." For that reason, the author contended, "Whatever Customs & Laws of the Colony circumscribed within these bounds are established & have been allowed of, they are the Customs & Laws by w[hi]ch that Colony should be Governed Jointly with the fundamental & General Laws of the Mother Country extending to that Colony." For that reason, the author insisted in an obvious reference to Knowles, "A Subordinate power appointed to govern that Colony by such a limitted Commission who acts Contrary to those Customs & Laws or in Violation of them, Abuses his Authority, is guilty of a breach of Trust[,] and exerts an Arbitrary Sway."[72]

---

ville Special Collections Library, University of California, San Diego, La Jolla, California.

72. Ibid.

When the May Assembly found a copy of this wholesale condemnation of Knowles and his allies tacked to the House door, it branded it "a false, malicious, and scandalous libel, highly reflecting upon the justice and wisdom of his excellency the governor's administration, as also upon the proceedings of the honourable privy-council of this island, and of this house, and tending to create jealousies in, and inflame the minds of the people" and ordered it "burnt in the open street, fronting this house, by the hands of the common hangman."[73]

VI

With passage of the removal bill, the conflict over the location of the capital entered still a third phase, one in which each side desperately sought to persuade metropolitan authorities either to confirm or to reject the bill. Knowles's expectations that metropolitan appreciation for his achievements would insulate him from attacks such as that composed by the anonymous author of "Grievances" and enable him to accomplish the constitutional revolution in Jamaica which his superiors enjoined on him proved to be entirely illusory. In April 1755, well before Knowles had succeeded in getting the removal bill through the Assembly, some London officials had decided that his repeated dissolutions and other tactics had thrown Jamaica "into great Confusion and Disorder, and greatly obstructed the Course of Justice and Government there,"[74] and at the same time, the Crown's law officers concluded that Knowles had no solid legal foundation for dissolving either the October 1754 or January 1755 assemblies. With regard to the former, they ruled that the Assembly's claim that the governor had no right during sessions to issue writs for elections was "analogous to the Law & Practice of England" and depended entirely upon the "Constitution & Usage" of Jamaica; concerning the second they decided that James Dawes's subscription to the oaths of allegiance in Jamaica meant that his English conviction "was no legal Objection to his right or capacity of sitting" in the Jamaica Assembly.[75] In July the

73. *Assembly Journals,* May 1, 1755, 4:515.

74. John Pownall to William Murray and Richard Lloyd, April 25, 1755, CO 138/20, pp. 110–11.

75. Murray and Lloyd to Board of Trade, April 29, 1755, CO 137/28, ff. 7, 9–10.

Board of Trade advised the Privy Council that Knowles's actions in uni-laterally moving the courts and legislative session to Kingston without the consent of the Assembly was "improper."[76]

These actions were a harbinger of the metropolitan reaction to the removal law. The Board of Trade was dismayed by the absence of a sus-pending clause in the bill. As Rose Fuller, just arrived in England from Jamaica, gleefully reported to a correspondent in Jamaica, Knowles "had promised the ministry that he should carry the suspending clause by his supporting ye favourite scheme of ye removal," and the minis-try was therefore deeply "surprised to find those laws passed and exe-cuted without it." As a result, Fuller wrote, the ministry was "heartily displeased" with Knowles, "which I doubt whether they ever were be-fore, the language being that though he was wrong headed, & did ir-regular things yet he was doing the King['s] business, meaning that his proceedings would produce the injection of that clause in our acts." Because Knowles had failed in that grand objective, Fuller reported, the ministry now appeared ready to remove him and "reject ye laws upon account of that clause being omitted." Certainly, as Ferdinand Paris, London agent for the Spanish Town interests, informed Fuller, the removal act was "flat in the Teeth of all the Reports & Orders on the 12 Acts of 1751 & 1752, as well as contrary to the Instructions & without a Suspending Clause."[77]

A month later, Paris wrote Fuller that a leading member of the Board of Trade had told him that the Board had two profound reser-vations about the removal act that would probably prevent its being confirmed. The first was a doubt about whether the Jamaica legislature could by its "sole Authority, enact, & execute, a Repeal of a former Law, confirm'd by the Crown," or whether such an attempt was "not void, & a nullity, for Want of Power" in the legislature. The second was whether "the Commands, in the Instructions to the Gov[erno]r, not to pass unusual & extraordinary Bills, without the Suspending Clause" did "not operate like an Exception, out of the Powers, given in the Commission to the Gove[rno]r & thereby render this Act a mere

76. Board of Trade to Privy Council, July 3, 1755, CO 139/20.

77. Rose Fuller to _____, September 3, 1755; Rose Fuller to John Venn, Sep-tember 3, 1755; and Ferdinand John Paris to Fuller, September 30, 1755, Fuller Family Papers, Bundle 19, No. 3, East Sussex Record Office.

Nullity, ab Initio." Accordingly, when the Board met in late October, it voted to send the removal act to William Murray and Sir Richard Lloyd, respectively attorney general and solicitor general, for an opinion on *"whether the Legislature of Jamaica have a Power by their Constitution, to pass such a Law, to take immediate Effect, without the Crown's Consent, & without inserting in it, a Clause, suspending its Execution,* until the Pleasure of the Crown could be known." A few days later, the Board wrote Knowles expressing its own displeasure that he should have assented to such a law without a suspending clause "after the very positive Instruction you have received from His Majesty upon this Point."[78]

At the same time, Fuller and Paris were endeavoring unsuccessfully to bring Knowles's persecution of Francis Delap before London authorities. In the view of his supporters, Delap's treatment and trial represented a violation of all of the basic principles of English law. Pointing out that "his Judges had before found him Guilty in the Legislative as they have now in their Judicial Capacity," they charged that the vindication of Knowles for his treatment of Delap had required a packed jury, complained that even after his conviction Delap remained a "mark of an outrageous & wanton Fac——n to throw their unruly Darts at," and celebrated him as a genuine "Martyr to Liberty." Judging Delap's petition to the King unsuitable for presentation because of the nature of its prayer, his friends in London urged Delap and their allies in Jamaica to submit a new petition with a "proper prayer." Delap's case was "so flagrant," Fuller wrote, that it afforded such "a fine opportunity which may never again happen of establishing the liberty & property of ye colonies upon a pure & solid foundation and of trying the disposition of ye great men in England to us that I think we should be out of our senses if we did not prosecute it to the utmost." The establishment of "the Liberty of ye Subject in ye colonies upon a just & solid foundation," he wrote to a correspondent in Jamaica, was a matter in which "we are all soe deeply interested" that the case had to be pursued "or we are undone."[79]

78. Paris to Fuller, October 4, 1755, Fuller Family Papers, Bundle 19, No. 3; John Pownall to Murray and Lloyd, October 30, 1755, ibid., Bundle 20, No. 7; Board of Trade to Knowles, November 6, 1755, CO 138/29, ff. 70–71.

79. Edward Clarke to Fuller, September 4, 1755; Fuller to _____, Septem-

In the meantime, Knowles's opponents in Jamaica complained that they lived under "a Scene of Oppression[,] venality & indeed every Species of immorality" and that this "Unhappy Country" had been "Subdued & Chained under a Yoke of Tyranny." They could only hope that when Knowles's "system of Government is detected, & laid open to Publick View" in London, metropolitan authorities would recall him, make him an "Example for all future G——s," and restore all other Jamaica affairs "to their Pristine State." "Our Publick Disorders daily encrease," lamented Thomas Frearon, "so that if there be not a Speedy remove, I can[']t say what the Consequences may be." Without relief from Britain in the form of the disallowance of the removal bill, Edward Clarke warned Fuller, "this Country will languish away by Fraud, Corruption, & Oppression on one Side, and passion, perversity, & futility on ye other." In view of the impending war with France, the "Disorder & Confusion within" Jamaica seemed to its residents especially ominous. Unknown to his opponents, Knowles had indeed, already in July 1755, used the prospect of war to ask the Board of Trade for leave to resign the Jamaica governorship and return to sea.[80]

The disorder about which Clarke and Frearon complained was never more evident than during the first legislative sessions held since passage of the removal bill. Principally called to pass a tax bill to provide funds for metropolitan troops stationed in the island, the Assembly convened in late September 1755 to find the political balance shifting in the opposition's favor. Over the previous few months, the death of two members of the governor's party and the resignation of one member of the opposition had reduced the governor's majority to four, but the defection of two members of the governor's party and the possibility of gaining additional seats in the by-election to fill vacated seats combined to raise opposition hopes for regaining control of the Assembly. Led by former speaker Charles Price, Sr., the opposi-

ber 3, 1755; Paris to Fuller, November 12, 1755, Fuller Family Papers, Bundle 19, No. 3; Fuller to _____, Fall 1755, ibid., Bundle 20, No. 13.

80. Edward Clarke to Rose Fuller, September 3, 1755, October 24, 1755; Thomas Frearon to Fuller, October 15, 1755; Mark Hall to Fuller, October 21, 1755, in Fuller Family Papers, Bundle 19, No. 3; Knowles to Board of Trade, July 25, 1755, CO 137/29, f. 50.

tion came to the opening session with plans, as a later writer charged, to "*purge the House of several of its Members,* regulate all the Courts of Justice and Public Offices upon their own Plan, and carry back the Court and Records to *Spanish-town* again." When the Assembly met, the absence of one member of the governor's party enabled the opposition to gain a majority of one, and it quickly pushed through votes to suspend two members of the governor's party on dubious legal grounds, thereby gaining a working majority of one. This majority enabled the opposition to initiate an investigation of Knowles's dismissal of judges and other public officers. In the debate over the money bills to pay the troops, one opposition member avowed "with the most insolent and indecent Language . . . that His Majesty, or his Ministers, might have *taken warning* by former Resolutions of the House, and have ordered his Governors to recall these Troops, for that they would not provide for them any longer," and the House proceeded to extend the old money bills for just a few months in direct violation of Knowles's instructions not to pass any bill for a shorter term than one year.[81]

But Knowles, having, in his view, finally put "an End" to the power by which "the great Planters . . . had been long used to govern their Governors," was determined, as one of his supporters later remarked, not to "suffer the Reins that had been put into his Hands by his Royal Master to be wrested from him by a Party, which, by a Despotism long usurped and tamely submitted to, has reduced the Substitute of the Sovereign to a mere Instrument of their own Power, and made use of his Name as a Sanction to their Oppression." Accordingly, on October 23 he prorogued the Assembly for an hour, a step that had the immediate effect of readmitting the two suspended members which made the governor's party equal in numbers to the opposition and gave Speaker Edward Manning, one of Knowles's principal supporters, the deciding vote. When opposition members perceived what had happened, they tried to break up the House by leaving en masse, but the governor's party used force to keep three of the opposition in the

81. See for a narrative reflective of Knowles's point of view *An Historical Account of the Sessions of Assembly, for the Island of Jamaica: Which began on Tuesday the 23d of Sept. 1755* (hereafter cited as *Historical Account*) (London, 1757), 9, 16, 54.

House and proceeded, in an election inquiry, to displace an absent member with one of their supporters and to expel another opposition member, thereby regaining a comfortable majority. When the sixteen opposition members who had left the House refused to return, the Assembly expelled all of them as well. With fewer members than were required for a quorum, the Assembly was unable to do further business until late November when the Rump reduced the quorum from twenty-one to nineteen and eventually to fifteen, after which it passed a money bill in a manner "conformable to his majesty's instructions" so that the troops could be supported, albeit many settlers refused to honor it.[82]

From the point of view of the opposition, these machinations represented a new low, even for the Knowles administration. Claiming that the prorogation for an hour and the subsequent expulsion of seventeen opposition members had no other purpose than to screen Knowles from the Assembly's inquiry "into the Abuses in the several Courts of Justice" and other oppressive measures, they saw Jamaica, in the words of Edward Clarke, as "Languishing under ye most Despotic Acts of Government[,] Ruled by ye wanton will of a little Tyrant[,] the weight of whose power began to grow terrible," a veritable "Babel of Power & iniquity" in which "the Ancient Frame of a well-constituted government" had been completely torn "to pieces" by Knowles's "set-[t]ing aside all orders[,] rank[,] & degrees amongst men—Rendering ye Administration of the Government weak & frail in all its branches by turning out fit and introducing unfit persons in all the offices Civil and Military—Making hasty dunces in ye Court of Chancery [and] passionate & petulant Decretal orders to ye manifest injury of good Substantial Men[']s Credit & perhaps at ye Ruin of orphans most certainly to their great Loss—Granting partial Administrations (as ordinary) to favorites no ways entitled there to the prejudice of other persons. In short," Clarke declared, "by every iniquitous Act of G——n——t he has perpetuated a name here to Posterity that will sting in the Nostrils

82. Ibid., 4, 71; "The Prorogation for an hour," March 17, 1756, Fuller Family Papers, Bundle 18, No. 7d; Knowles to Board of Trade, December 1, 1755, CO 137/29, ff. 98–99; *Assembly Journals,* September 23–24, October 23, November 11, 19, 1755, 4:533–35, 540–44, 549–50.

of all Mankind When not one Single Virtue in either Public or a Private will be remembered to his Honor!"[83]

Perhaps sensing that he could no longer keep his coalition together, Knowles reportedly became "a mere Frantic," bolting his doors, remaining in his house for a day or two at a time, becoming "suspicious of Every Body he Speaks to, Jealous of Ye Advice given him even by those he had always Consulted," and having "no reliance . . . but upon himself & even there he is not at peace." Starting in mid-December 1755, he began pressing his request for permission to resign. "For want of proper Support" from London, he wrote the Board of Trade in early 1756, "I find myself driven to a state of desperation . . . and entirely unable to discharge the Duty of the Trust reposed in me."[84]

London authorities soon granted this request. By early January 1756, Knowles's opponents had gotten a petition to London complaining about the "extraordinary and Illegal methods" the governor's party had used "to obtain a Majority" in the October Assembly, and the Board of Trade concluded that "the Minds of His Majesty's Subjects" in Jamaica were so "greatly inflamed, and [such] great Heats and Animosities have prevailed," that Knowles, whether or not he was responsible, should be removed. Perhaps because metropolitan authorities recognized that Knowles's maladroit behavior derived in some major part from their insistence that he not deviate from his instructions, the Privy Council on January 27 did not dismiss him but merely gave him leave to resign.[85]

At the same time, the Board was moving to resolve the dispute over removing the capital to Kingston. On December 27, 1755, Murray and Lloyd, the attorney and solicitor generals, reported, after extensive hearings, that Knowles should not have passed the removal act and two accompanying statutes without suspending clauses, and on Feb-

83. *Historical Account,* 60; Edward Clarke to Rose Fuller, December 20, 1755, Fuller Family Papers, Bundle 19, No. 3.

84. Edward Clarke to Rose Fuller, December 20, 1755, Fuller Family Papers, Bundle 19, No. 3; Knowles to Earl of Holdernesse, December 13, 1755, Egerton Manuscripts 3490, ff. 36–37, British Library; Knowles to Board of Trade, January 2, 1756, CO 137/29, f. 107.

85. Board of Trade to Privy Council, November 4, 1755, January 21, 1756, CO 138/20, p. 137, 150–53; Order in Council, January 27, 1756, CO 137/29, f. 92.

ruary 12 the Board, complaining that "the Practice, which is become too frequent in His Majesty's Colonies, of passing Laws of a Nature not warranted by his Majesty's Instructions, which take immediate Effect and continue in force till His Majesty's Pleasure be signified to the contrary, is productive of Consequences very prejudicial to His Majesty's Service," reported against the removal act and three other statutes passed at the same time. On February 19, 1756, the Privy Council Committee on Plantation Affairs voted to accept the report. Also in February the Crown appointed Henry Moore, a Jamaican with close ties to the ministry, lieutenant governor to succeed Knowles and instructed him to dissolve the Assembly, call new elections, and get the new Assembly's opinion on the wisdom of moving the capital.[86]

With Knowles on the way out and the removal bill in the process of disallowance, the Jamaican lobby in London struck directly at Knowles in the most public way. In late January 1756, William Beckford, Jamaica's most extensive landholder who had become an absentee in England in the early 1750s and was elected to Parliament in 1754, condemned Knowles in the House of Commons for his "tyrannic government of Jamaica" and moved for all the papers necessary for a prosecution. When the ministers tried to head off an inquiry on the grounds that Knowles had already been recalled, William Pitt chastised the ministry for "endeavouring to screen the guilty," and the ministry agreed to call for papers, which minister Henry Fox collected from the Board of Trade and presented to the House over the next two months. But it would be another year before the House formally considered the charges against Knowles.[87]

Knowles did not leave Jamaica until early July, and during the intervening months public life in Jamaica remained embittered. Knowles

86. Murray and Lloyd to Board of Trade, December 27, 1755, CO 137/29, ff. 70–71; Account of the Proceedings before the Privy Council on Removal of the Seat of Government in Jamaica [1758], Privy Council Papers 1/50/45; Board of Trade to Privy Council, February 12, March 9, 1756, CO 138/20, pp. 160–66, 172–76.

87. Horace Walpole, *Memoirs of the Reign of George II*, 2 vols. (London, 1846), 2:152–53; *Journals of the House of Commons* (London, various dates), 27:399, 457, 468–69, 530 (January 23, February 18 and 24, March 17, 1756); Henry Fox to Board of Trade, January 26, 1756, CO 137/29, ff. 82–84.

continued to denounce "the People (the Rebells to All Government I mean)," who, notwithstanding all his efforts, still seemed to be "much in the same disposition of Mind" that had led them to oppose all his measures to shore up royal authority in the colony.[88] On the other side, the opposition found nothing to admire in the Knowles administration, charging that he had appointed Catholics to office[89] and arbitrarily forbidden people to leave the colony.[90] The imprisoned Francis Delap continued to deplore the failure of due process of law in Jamaica under the Knowles regime. Metropolitans should not assume "that we are Free, or in a Condition to State our Grievances, or that our J——s, C——ts, Records &c, are upon the same fair footing . . . as in England. In England," he wrote, "you have Fair-Play," but in Jamaica one could only expect "to be tryd by a Gang of Sh——p——s and P——k P——k——ts, who have first Rob'd you, had afterwards charged you with Robbing them, who could at one and the same Time Act the several parts of Inquistions, accusers, W——t——ss, J——udg——s, and J——rs, all of them Consederate and Unanimous to Punish you first and then to try and find you Guilty." With Fuller, Delap continued to hope that his "unfortunate Case" would "Attract the Attention of all Friends of Truth and Liberty" and "be considered as that of all His Majesty[']s Subjects and Especially of those Residing in the Colonies."[91] Even as Knowles was preparing to leave the colony in June, the opposition feared that he and his allies, still in control of the Assembly, would try to "take some very extraordinary steps," such as passing the removal bill with a suspending clause and thereby at once answering the chief metropolitan objection to the measure and making sure that the capital would remain in Kingston.[92]

88. Knowles to Board of Trade, April 7, 1756, CO 137/29, f. 112.

89. See _____ to Earl of Holdernesse, February 16, 1756, and Samuel Dicker to Holdernesse, February 19, 1756, Egerton Manuscripts 3490, ff. 38–41.

90. Knowles to John Gregory, June 30, 1756; John Gregory to Charles Knowles, July 2, 1756; and John Gregory to Stephen Fuller, July 7, 1756, Fuller Family Papers, Bundle 19, No. 3.

91. Delap to Ferdinand J. Paris, February 4, April 19, 1756, Fuller Family Papers, Bundle 19, Nos. 12A, 12B.

92. John Gordon to Rose Fuller, June 15, 1756, Fuller Family Papers, Bundle 19, No. 3.

Although Knowles reportedly "continued his Mad Rash Conduct to the very last day," his departure in early July filled the opposition with optimism. "After such a Series of Injustice[,] Tyranny & Confusion," said Delap, who had recovered his freedom only a week before Knowles's departure, Jamaica, in the words of Spanish Town resident Charles White, now had "a noble Prospect, of Tranquility being once more restored to this so long distracted Country." The "Dog Star is set and no more rages amongst us," White said, "and all his pestiferous influence ceases." "Everything has been done for us at home[,] as the phrase is[,] that our hearts could wish," White declared in expressing his gratitude to metropolitan authorities for removing Knowles, and the Spanish Town interest looked forward to Knowles's receiving his final comeuppance in London. It was impossible, wrote William Nedham, "that the Ministry will Protect & Support a Man of his Stamp."[93]

VII

When Henry Moore, newly appointed lieutenant governor, succeeded Knowles in July 1756, the contest over the removal of the capital entered a fourth and final phase marked by relative political tranquility and the eventual resolution of this bitter dispute. Moore gained the instant applause of the Spanish Town party when he "immediately dissolved Our Oxhead Assembly of P——k P——kets," issued writs for a new Assembly to meet in Spanish Town in mid-August, and announced his intention to live in the King's House at Spanish Town. Moore himself was remarkably sanguine about his prospects for "reconciling the Animosities which have reign'd so long among us." Unlike Knowles, he made no attempt to interfere in elections, and he wrote his English patron, the Earl of Holdernesse, that the Kingston interest had been so discredited through its association with Knowles that it would be unable "to return more than eleven Members," the "inclination of the People" tending hugely toward the people who had had no association with Knowles's party. Expressing confidence that

93. William Nedham to Rose Fuller, July 24, 1756; Francis Delap to Ferdinand J. Paris, July 8, 1756; and Charles White to Rose Fuller, July 30, 1756, Fuller Family Papers, Bundle 19, No. 3.

the Assembly would "set forth the real Sentiments of the People, in regard to" the location of the capital, he confidently predicted that "in a very short time all odious distinctions will be laid aside, & we shall unite again for the Public Service."[94]

Thomas Pinnock, a Jamaican who had supported Knowles for most of his tenure, was not so sure. Doubting that Knowles's presence was in itself the real "Obstacle to harmony" in Jamaican public life, he expressed the fear that "Contention" was "the darling passion of this Community." "This Island is healthy, pleasant, and fruitfull, and affords the Industrious Man a genteel and agreeable living for his labour" so that "he may live Comfortably & Enjoy his little in great cheerfulness, provided he can curb his Ambition," he declared, "but as our Government over Slaves is allmost Absolute, so it intoxicates the brain, and creates in us a most notorious Desire to Lordity over our Equalls, from whence great men can Bear no Controle, nor have they any bounds to their passions. I have been here from England [since] the entrance of 1731, and I have seen little or no alteration in the minds of people for as the Old ones have dropt of[f], the like principles have been in their Successors."[95]

For the short term at least, Pinnock could scarcely have been more accurate. In the election for the new Assembly, just nine of thirty-two members adhered to the Kingston party, and when that body met on August 17, it immediately signaled its political colors by electing Charles Price, Sr., speaker. As the long-term speaker, Price was the nominal leader of the Spanish Town party. At Moore's request, the Assembly quickly set to work responding to the metropolitan call for the "unprejudiced and dispassionate sense of the legislature" upon the issue of the location of the capital. On September 3, it sent an address to the King in which it expressed its view that Spanish Town was the "proper place" for the capital. At the same time, it condemned Knowles's removal bill as "an unjustifiable and unconstitutional" attempt to render "the prerogative subservient to the purposes of a few,

94. Francis Delap to Ferdinand J. Paris, July 8, 1756, Fuller Family Papers, Bundle 19, No. 3; Moore to Holdernesse, June 29, July 9, July 26, 1756, Egerton Manuscripts 3490, ff. 42–47.

95. Thomas Pinnock to _____, June 26, 1756, Miscellaneous Manuscripts, 490, National Library of Jamaica.

instead of following the royal example of your majesty, by making it the protection of your subjects in general." Offering to satisfy the legitimate grievances of Kingston merchants by establishing circuit courts to be held in Kingston and ports of entry in other parts of the island, the Assembly prayed that "your loyal subjects will be restored to the full enjoyment of their rights and privileges" as they had existed before Knowles undertook his nefarious schemes to rig elections and subvert the wishes of a majority of the island's inhabitants.[96]

Although Moore predicted that this address and his own "perseverance and moderation" would produce a reconciliation, subsequent events proved that he was far too sanguine. The Jamaica Council was still controlled by Knowles's appointees, and its behavior demonstrated that Jamaica was yet a long way from political quietude. Not only did it refuse to join in the Assembly's address to the King, it sent an address of its own reaffirming its commitment to the removal bill and the principles that lay behind it.[97]

At the same time, the Assembly began to move aggressively to investigate what it referred to in a letter to Jamaica's London agent as the "unconstitutional methods made use of, to get an assembly to answer the purposes of Mr. Knowles," including the imprisonment of Francis Delap. From late September through mid-November, its committee on the state of the island subjected the behavior of Knowles and his allies to what it referred to as a "parliamentary enquiry." On October 9, it summarized the preliminary results of its findings in an address to Moore. In this address, the Assembly asked Moore to suspend Philip Pinnock, whom the Assembly subsequently denounced as "the principal promoter of all the grievances and uneasinesses" Jamaica had experienced under Knowles, from his seat on the Council and to remove him from the chief justiceship, principally on the grounds that his treatment of Delap had polluted "the fountains of Justice" in the colony. "The unconstitutional, illegal, and cruel treatment, Mr. Delap received" at the hands of Pinnock and his fellow judges, the Assembly

96. *Assembly Journals,* August 17, 19, September 3, 1756; 5:572–75, 575–76, 586–87.

97. Moore to Holdernesse, September 1, October 3, 1756, Egerton Manuscripts 3490, ff. 48–49, 54–55; *Assembly Journals,* September 7, 28, 1756, 4:589, 607–9.

complained, "wants a precedent, unless we look back to the age of the star-chamber," while the condition of his confinement was unknown outside the bounds of "the Turkish dominions." Because Pinnock remained a powerful advocate for the removal bill in the Council and a staunch foe of Moore, the lieutenant governor eagerly granted this request, suspending Pinnock from his seat on the Council and removing him from the chief justiceship. This action put Moore at loggerheads with the majority of the Council, threatened to undermine "his plan of moderation," and ultimately forced him to suspend six additional councillors, a move that brought him the Assembly's hearty approval. With neither the governor nor the Council on its side, the Kingston interest no longer had a power base from which to pursue its claims.[98]

In London during the winter and early spring of 1757, the Jamaican lobby renewed its campaign against Knowles in the House of Commons. With the backing of First Minister William Pitt, William Beckford, who had introduced the subject to the House in January 1756, and Rose Fuller, recently elected to Parliament, among others, prepared an elaborate brief against Knowles in February 1757, listing twenty specific examples to prove that he had "Enterprized many things to divide" Jamaicans "into Parties and Factions contrary to the Established Custom and Laws of the Island," attempted "to destroy the Freedom of Elections and Privileges of the Members of the Assembly," thereby seeking to intimidate "the Legislative Power" of Jamaica, interfered with judicial proceedings, and "wantonly exercised an Arbitrary and tyrannical Power ag[ain]st such of the Judges, Counsellors, Members of Assembly and Officers of the Crown as had Courage and Integrity to represent against his unlawful and dangerous proceedings." Six resolutions rehearsed in detail and condemned Knowles's persecution of Francis Delap.[99] In his defense, Knowles's supporters

---

98. *Assembly Journals,* September 7, 22, 25, 29–30, October 2, 7, 9, 20, 29, November 3, 6, 10, 13, 1756, 4:590, 599, 603–5, 610–13, 616–33, 641, 661–66, 669–77, 683–86, 689–715, 717–20; Moore to Board of Trade, November 4, 1756, CO 137/29; Moore to Lord Granville, November 4, 27, 1756, Privy Council Papers 1/58/3; Moore to Holdernesse, November 27, 1756, Egerton Manuscripts 3490, ff. 58–59; Zachary Bayly to Rose Fuller, January 20, 1757, Fuller Family Papers, Bundle 19, No. 3.

99. Brief on the Charge against Charles Knowles Esqr. Late Governor of Ja-

produced an elaborate pamphlet detailing the history of his administration and arguing that the enmity against Knowles arose entirely
from his determination to put an end to the power by which Jamaican planters "had been long used to governing their Governors." His
only fault, the anonymous writer of this pamphlet claimed, lay in his
refusal to "suffer the Reins that had been put into his Hands by his
Royal Master to be wrested from him by a Party, which by a Despotism
long usurped and tamely submitted to," had "reduced the Substitute
of their Sovereign to a mere Instrument of their own Power, and made
use of his Names as a Sanction to their Oppression."[100]

Although the Jamaicans succeeded in getting the House of Commons to call for additional papers on the Knowles administration, Pitt's
resignation on April 4 derailed their efforts, and by the time that Pitt
returned to office on June 18, the Knowles matter had been settled—
and in a way far from congenial to Jamaican settler interests. Not only
did the House fail to condemn Knowles, it resurrected the Board of
Trade's adverse October 1754 report on the Jamaica Assembly's de-
fiant resolutions of October 29, 1753, and—for the very first time in
the history of British imperial governance—intervened in the domestic internal affairs of an American colony by passing on May 23, 1757,
three resolutions denouncing the Assembly's resolutions of October
1753. The first and second of these resolutions declared the Assembly's claim to exclusive control over public funds and to the right to
appoint officers to handle those funds to be "Illegal, repugnant to the
terms of his majesty's commission to his governor of the said island,
and derogatory of the Rights of the Crown & people of Great-Britain."
The third denied that the Crown's demand for suspending clauses in
unusual Jamaica legislation represented any "alteration of the constitution of that island" or was in any way "derogatory of the rights of"
the king's "subjects there."[101]

maica, to be heard before the Committee of the whole House, 22 February 1757,
Buccleuch Muniments, SRO/GD/224/299/4, Dalkeith, Scotland; Proposed resolutions against Knowles, n.d., Fuller Family Papers, Bundle 20, No. 14. A preliminary version of the brief, dated February 27, 1757, may be found in Fuller
Family Papers, Bundle 18, No. 7f.

100. *Historical Account*, 4, 71.

101. See *Journals of the House of Commons*, February 1, 7, 22–24, March 1, 28,

The high point of the initial phases of the metropolitan effort to tighten the reins of empire, these resolutions—emanating from the metropolis's highest power—seem to have carried little weight in Jamaica. So that "his majesty's subjects in" Jamaica might "be fully apprized of the sense of" the House of Commons upon the Jamaica Assembly's "extraordinary claims," Board of Trade Secretary John Pownall transmitted the resolutions to Lieutenant Governor Henry Moore just eleven days after they had passed, and Moore duly transmitted them to the Assembly when it met in November 1757. Although the Assembly entered the resolutions in its minutes and voted that they "lie upon the table, for the perusal of the members," it took no further notice of them, neither acknowledging their receipt nor challenging their validity.[102] As William Lewis reported to Rose Fuller just two months later, "most of the Gentlemen" in the island, seemed to have had "a surfeit of Contention, and" were "willing to pass over some defects rather than continue to deserve the Character of [a] turbulent ungovernable people, which in England 'tis said is given to us."[103]

The same sentiments probably also accounted for the dropping of the Delap affair. Delap, unsatisfied with the Assembly's investigation of the previous fall, which he denounced for its failure to get "to the Bottom of the principal Matters, the great Abuses of power under the late Adm[inistratio]n especially those relevant to the Freedom of Elections, the Privileges of the Assembly, & other Fundamental points," continued to press his case for another two years. Reminding Jamaica's principal political leaders in both Jamaica and England that his case was not that "of a Single Man, that had been ill treated . . . but took in the freedom of the People, the Whole Matter of Elections, & indeed

---

31, April 4–6, 25, 27, 29, May 4, 10, 12, 17, 18, 20, 23, 1757, 18:674, 683, 725–27, 733, 743, 800–21, 825, 833, 836–39, 854–55, 858, 864, 883, 889, 898, 900, 902–3, 910–11. The resolutions are on pp. 910–11. See also Pitt to Board of Trade, February 17, 19, March 21, April 4, 20, 1757, CO 137/29, ff. 235–52; List of Papers laid before House of Commons, April 5, May 9, 1757, CO 138/20, pp. 200–3, 207. The Board of Trade's original report of October 15, 1754, may be found in CO 138/20, pp. 41–79. See also, Metcalf, *Royal Government*, 135–36.

102. *Assembly Journals*, November 8, 1757, 5:28–29.

103. Lewis to Rose Fuller, January 17, 1758, Fuller Family Papers, Bundle 19, No. 3.

the very fundamentals of our Constitution," he argued that "a better Opprtunity could not happen, for getting our Rights & Liberty's & those of the Colony's in general fixed and Ascertained" and urged his supporters to push "Mr. Knowles, both at Law, & in the House of Commons" for "the Acts of Tyranny & Oppression they have been guilty of towards me" and "to leave no Stone unturned" to vindicate him and to "Support . . . the common cause of Liberty and of the Colonies." But his ministrations were of little avail. As late as October 1758, he was still complaining of "the Shamefull Neglect of the Assembly or Principal Gentlemen" in not avidly pursuing his case and of their "scandalous . . . Desertion of the Cause." "Strange!," he declared, "that such an opening Should be lost" for "Getting our Rights & Libertys better Settled and Secured."[104]

The Jamaican political establishment exhibited a similar spirit of accommodation in its appointment of a new London agent. When Lords Holdernesse and Halifax both recommended Lovel Stanhope for the Jamaica agency, Ferdinand J. Paris, solicitor for the Spanish Town interests, pointed out that Stanhope was a mere "Creature of" the "Courtiers" and warned against the dangers of being "drawn into such a Snare." If "the Gentlemen of Jamaica" give way to "one single application of this Sort," he cautioned, "they may rest assured, they'l never be free Agents Themselves, nor have a free Agent for them, hereafter; but their Agency will be lookt upon, as a Court Perquisite, to be always insisted on, as a Thing usual, & of course; for some great Man's poor Relation, or Dependant." Thus forfeiting control over the agent, Paris predicted, would make "certain, that all their Purposes & Designs & Instructions, would be instantly communicated to & as instantly defeated by the Ministers unless they perfectly quadrated with their own Schemes." Declaring that the colony agent "sho[u]d be very faithful, & desirous to serve his Jama[ica] Ma[ster]s," Paris called upon the Jamaica Assembly, which he referred to as "a Body of People, over whom no Courtiers have any coercive Authority, *as yet,*" to insist upon its right

104. Delap to Charles Price, Sr., April 21, 25, 1757, Fuller Family Papers, Bundle 18, No. 12c; Delap to Stephen Fuller, October 8, 1758, Fuller Family Papers, Bundle 19, No. 3.

to be "free in the Choice of so high a Trust" and thereby "keep Themselves free, & not bind Themselves, their Posterity, & their Country, in Fetters, to any Court Minion, whatever."[105] But, as planter William Gale reported to Rose Fuller, the recommendations of Holdernesse and Halifax, "to whom we are so immediately indebted for the Late Change" in the governorship, "had such Weight, that, as soon as they were known, to have spoke their Inclinations in the Affair, the Election [of Stanhope] was Unanimous."[106]

No doubt, the Assembly's failure either explicitly to challenge Parliament's resolutions or to pursue the Delap case also had much to do with the fact that the fate of the capital removal bill was still pending in London. On this complicated issue, the wheels of the administration moved slowly. On February 8, 1757, the Board of Trade held a hearing to which it invited representatives of both Spanish Town and Kingston interests. At this meeting the Board outlined a plan whereby the removal act would be disallowed, the repository of records and the supreme court would remain in Spanish Town, the governor's residence and the site for Assembly meetings would be left to the governor's discretion, and circuit courts and ports of entry would be established in Kingston and elsewhere in Jamaica "for the Ease & Conveniency" of suitors, witnesses, jurors, and masters of vessels. The attorney and solicitor generals, Robert Henley and Charles Yorke, took more than three months to approve this plan, with the provision that the Crown should not establish new courts without "an Act of the Legislature in Jamaica, or by the Parliament of Great Britain." On May 25, 1757, the Board of Trade finally laid the plan before the Privy

105. Paris to Stephen Fuller, November 16, 1756, Fuller Family Papers, Bundle 19, No. 1, emphasis added.

106. Henry Moore to Holdernesse, February 27, March 20, 1757, Egerton Manuscripts 3490, ff. 77–78, 85–86; Edmund Hyde to Rose Fuller, May 2, 1757; William Gale to Rose Fuller, May 3, 1757; James Prevost to Rose Fuller, May 4, 1757; Samuel Whitehorne to Rose Fuller, May 7, 1757; John Venn to Ferdinand J. Paris, May 21, 1757; John Morse to Rose Fuller, June 5, 1757; William Lewis to Rose Fuller, June 6, 1757; Thomas Frearon to Rose Fuller, June 25, 1757; William Wynter to Rose Fuller, June 25, 1757; and William B. Ellis to Rose Fuller, August 28, 1757, Fuller Family Papers, Bundle 19, No. 3.

Council, which on June 15 asked for further details on port locations and suitable circuit court districts. The Board took nearly a half year to produce this information.[107]

In the meantime, public life in Jamaica remained outwardly calm. Moore peppered his London superiors with letters, claiming to have succeeded in "restoring Peace to this distracted Country"—without violating his instructions.[108] Some members of the Jamaican political establishment wished for the appointment of "a Man of Family and Spirit" to succeed Knowles as full governor, while others distrusted the "new Politicians" who seemed to want to become "Great Men" without attending to "the business of the Country." "Poor Jamaica," lamented the planter William Lewis, "hath lately been deprived of so many Gentlemen of Capacity and Fortune, that it seems to be on its last Legs." Still others continued to hope that justice would "be administered to" Knowles, "that late Disturber of our Peace and perverter of our constitutional Rights." Except for the Kingston partisans, however, everyone agreed with Moore that Jamaicans "enjoy[ed] perfect Tranquility under the present mild Administration." As William Gale wrote Rose Fuller, there was no longer in Jamaica any "such thing as Delaping or Dragooning a Man out of his Liberty or Estate."[109]

Yet, they also agreed that the "Minds of the People" could never "be at rest . . . as long as the Fate of" the removal bill was "in Suspense." "As soon as this affair is determined," Thomas Frearon wrote Rose Fuller in June 1757, "the Heats & Animosities in this Country will subside & . . . we shall again become a united People, an Event much to be de-

107. Stephen Fuller to Charles Price, Thomas Frearon, and John Ellis, February 9, 1757, and Stephen Fuller to Gentlemen of Jamaica, February 9, 1757, Fuller Family Papers, Bundle 19, No. 3; Account of Proceedings before the Council on Removal of the Seat of Government in Jamaica, n.d., Privy Council Papers PC, 1/50/45; Henley and Yorke to Board of Trade, CO 137/30, ff. 1–3; Board of Trade to Privy Council, May 25, 1757, CO 138/20, pp. 205–25.

108. Moore to Holdernesse, January 18, June 29, October 31, 1757, February 12, 1758, Egerton Manuscripts, 3490, ff. 67–68, 99–100, 103–4, 107–8.

109. Zachary Bayly to Rose Fuller, January 20, 1757; John Venn to Rose Fuller, May 22, 1757; William Lewis to Rose Fuller, June 6, 1757, and January 17, 1758; Charles White to Rose Fuller, March 19, 1757; William Gale to Rose Fuller, May 3, 1757, Fuller Family Papers, Bundle 19, No. 3. See also *Assembly Journals*, September 27 and 30, 1757, 5:1–2, 5.

sired by all good Men, especially in this Time of War with a potent Enemy." As the decision dragged on through 1757, however, they became increasingly concerned as to "whether we shall be restored to our Rights, or not," and they became more and more worried when they heard that the merchants of London, Bristol, and Liverpool had petitioned Parliament in favor of the removal bill. "We wait with the highest Impatience for the decision at home," William Lewis wrote Rose Fuller in January 1758, "and with great Astonishment that it is so long in Agitation, from whence arise some fears and Apprehensions."[110]

Finally, in December 1757, the Board of Trade completed its plan to establish three new ports in Jamaica and divide the island into three counties that would double as circuit court districts. On the grounds that "the Intervention of Parliament here in Matters which relate to the peculiar Police and private Oeconomy of particular Colonys has not been usual, and may therefore if introduced in this Case excite Jealousy and Uneasiness in the Minds of His Majesty's Subjects in that Island," the Board opted to leave this piece of legislation in the hands of the Jamaica Assembly.

But it did recommend that the attorney and solicitor generals prepare a draft of a bill to establish circuit courts and counties to be sent to Jamaica, not as a piece of legislation that the Jamaica Assembly had to pass, but merely "as an Instruction to the Governor . . . for his Guidance and Direction [in] passing such Law." Accepting this report, the Privy Council's committee on colonial affairs directed the preparation of this draft legislation. But it took another six months for the attorney and solicitor generals to complete this work. On June 29, 1758, more than four years after it had first taken up the matter on May 29, 1754, the Privy Council formally disallowed the removal law and sanctioned the Board of Trade's proposals for settling the Jamaican dispute. A week later, the Board transmitted this outcome to Jamaica.[111]

110. Moore to Holdernesse, April 27, 1757, Egerton Manuscripts 3490, ff. 87–88; Frearon to Rose Fuller, June 25, 1757; James Prevost to Rose Fuller, May 4, 1757; William Wynter to Rose Fuller, June 25, 1757; William Lewis to Rose Fuller, January 17, 1758, Fuller Family Papers, Bundle 19, No. 3.

111. Account of Proceedings before the Council on Removal of Seat of Government in Jamaica, n.d., Privy Council Papers 1/50/45; Board of Trade to Privy Council, December 8, 1757, CO 138/20, pp. 228–36; Privy Council Minutes,

Reaching the island in late September, this news set off elaborate celebrations in Spanish Town, where local residents burned effigies of Knowles, his flagship, and "an eminent merchant" of Kingston, probably the then-deceased merchant Edward Manning. Moore duly laid notice of the disallowance of the removal bill and associated acts before the Assembly, then in session, and recommended passage of the draft act dividing Jamaica into three counties, complete with circuit courts. Overjoyed, the Assembly immediately prepared an address of thanks to the King, expressing its great sense of gratitude and "duty to your majesty and *your people*," a phrase that hinted at a separate political status and identity, and then set to work on the draft act. The Assembly made a number of small modifications to meet local circumstances but essentially accepted the draft act in the form submitted to it. Moore ecstatically reported that the Assembly had passed the bill "with no more Opposition to it than will barely shew the Efforts of a Faction Allmost extinguished."[112] The long constitutional crisis in Jamaica was seemingly over.

When George Haldane, the newly appointed governor of Jamaica, arrived in the colony in April 1759, Moore was able, as he later reported, to deliver "the Government in perfect tranquility." Haldane did nothing during his short tenure to alter this situation. Some Kingston inhabitants offered him a house and pen to reside in Kingston, but he "politely refused" the offer, evidently intent upon not repeating Knowles's mistakes. When he met the Assembly on May 1, he was delighted to hear it praise the settlement of the previous year as a set of regulations "justly calculated to give proper relief to one part of" the Crown's "dutiful subjects" in Kingston while "at the same time, preserving the legal rights of the other" in Spanish Town. He was especially pleased when the Assembly, in an obvious move to make sure that the governor would continue to reside in Spanish Town, voted £12,000 to purchase lands near the capitol for the governor's use "and to be

June 28 and 29, 1758, Privy Council Papers, 2/106, pp. 179–83, 186–90; Board of Trade to Henry Moore, July 5, 1758, CO 138/20, pp. 408–9. See also Ferdinand J. Paris to Rose Fuller, December 2, 1758, Fuller Family Papers, Bundle 19, No. 2.

112. *Assembly Journals*, October 3–4, 18, 1758, 5:68–70, 78; Moore to Board of Trade, October 3, November 12, 1758, CO 137/20, ff. 135, 145.

annex'd forever to the Crown." Though he did not himself expect to profit much from this measure, Haldane predicted that within a few years it would provide a substantial revenue that would put "governors forever afterwards out of the power of the people."[113]

Haldane's sudden death, on July 26, 1759, returned Henry Moore to the governorship which he held for more than two years until the arrival of Haldane's replacement, William Henry Lyttelton, in December 1761. Moore's tenure was hardly placid. In April 1760, the island was wracked by the most general slave uprising in its history. Led by a charismatic slave foreman called Tacky, the rebellion spread rapidly from the north coast eastward and westward and lasted for more than three months. The Jamaica militia managed to suppress it with the help of the British troops stationed in the island and the independent Maroon population, which honored its treaty commitment to hunt down runaway slaves. The rebellion put the Jamaican settler community into a panic, but it also helped to allay political unrest within the colony. As Jamaica's factions united in an appeal to Britain for more troops, Moore's second stint as governor was relatively quiet. The grave constitutional crisis of the 1750s provoked by aggressive metropolitan efforts to trim the authority of the Jamaican settler establishment seemed finally to have run its course.[114]

Whether metropolis or colony had gained most from this controversy and the developments that preceded it could not have been totally clear to contemporaries. Through its extreme claims of October 1754, the Jamaica Assembly had invited the attention and unprecedented intrusion of the British Parliament into Jamaica's internal governance. In the face of metropolitan resistance, moreover, the Assembly had had to back down from its most extreme claim, the authority

113. Haldane to Board of Trade, April 23, May 11, July 20, 1759, CO 137/30, ff. 183–84, 191–93, 233–34; Haldane to Newcastle, April 23, May 20, 1759, Newcastle Papers, Additional Manuscripts 32890, ff. 280–81, 32891, ff. 202–3; Moore to Newcastle, July 29, 1759, Egerton Manuscripts 3490, ff. 133–34; John Venn to Rose Fuller, July 18, 1759, Fuller Family Papers, Bundle 19, No. 3; Edward Clarke to Rose Fuller, April 10, 1759, Fuller Family Papers, Bundle 20, No. 3; *Assembly Journals,* May 1, 3, 5, 1759; 5:115, 118, 120–21.

114. See Metcalf, *Royal Government,* 150–52; *Assembly Journals,* December 15, 1760, 5:244.

to appoint revenue collectors, and maintained a tenuous hold on the principle by naming the Crown's receiver general as collector. By accepting the essentials of the 1758 draft legislation for dividing the colony into counties, the Assembly also opened up the possibility of forfeiting some of its legislative initiative to the metropolitan government. Finally, in the rush to ensure that Jamaica's governors would continue to reside in Spanish Town, the Assembly contributed to make metropolitan governors more independent financially.

On the other hand, the Assembly's control over the island's finances, the foundational source for its extensive authority in the island's governance, remained virtually absolute, and perhaps most important, it had never given way on the metropolitan demand that it include suspending clauses in legislation that either altered already confirmed laws or was of an unusual nature. Finally, the provincial political establishment could interpret the metropolitan government's repudiation of Knowles's efforts to move the capital to Kingston and destroy the political base of the planter establishment as a vindication of Jamaica's customary rights and of the elaborate constitutional arguments constructed by Veridicus to defend those rights. In short, a decade of close attention to Jamaica affairs had left constitutional arrangements almost exactly where they had been when metropolitan authorities undertook to lessen colonial autonomy in the late 1740s.

VIII

How far the Jamaican establishment would go to defend its vision of the Jamaica constitution was revealed early in William Henry Lyttelton's administration. On February 15, 1762, the Privy Council, upon the recommendation of the Board of Trade, disallowed four Jamaica acts passed between 1756 and 1761 having to do with the regulation of imports and the treatment of prize ships during the Seven Years' War. In its long report on these acts, the Board made clear that, notwithstanding its lack of success over the previous twelve years in bending the Jamaica Assembly to its will, it had by no means abandoned the objective of diminishing colonial autonomy and expanding metropolitan authority in the American empire. The report condemned the Jamaica legislature for eliminating duties imposed by a 1728 act confirmed by the Crown and called upon the Crown "to discountenance the irregular practice, which has but too much prevailed in all your majesty's colonies, of setting aside the provisions of perpetual laws confirmed by the crown, by temporary laws made to take immediate effect, without the royal consent." For making general commercial regulations on matters "to which the jurisdiction of the British legislature alone" could "extend," the Jamaica legislature, the Board declared, was guilty of "an arrogant assumption of power" that was "not warranted by the constitution" and "justly" deserved "the severest censure." Regarding an act which established the death penalty for some categories of smuggling, the Board expressed its amazement that "the legislature of Jamaica could have so far departed from the known and established principles of Justice, equity, and reason, and the laws of the mother country, as to have adopted so sanguinary a clause." In closing, the Board called for "such declaration of your majesty's disapprobation and animadversion, as the conduct of the legislature of the island of Jamaica, in passing laws of so extraordinary and unprecedented a nature, shall appear to your majesty to deserve."[115]

When Lyttelton laid this report before the Jamaica Assembly in October 1762, he was appalled by its response. The Privy Council had signified its willingness to assent to a new prize law that was free from the objectionable clauses in the disallowed laws, but the Assembly would have none of it. Rather, as it informed Lyttelton, it had "maturely weighed the purport of the proposition, permitting them to re-enact the provisions of the act passed in 1756, for the regulation of prizes" and decided that it "did not incline to accept the proposition." Boldly asserting that it did not "admit the objection of the board of trade to that act to carry any weight" and that its members were "by no means disposed to submit their sentiments to the determination of that board," the Assembly announced that it would never "at any time, suffer them in any respect to direct or influence their proceedings, by any proposition or proceedings whatever." At the same time, the Assembly went on the offensive against the Board, authorizing a committee to compile a list of the many Jamaica acts passed since 1728 "which appear not to have been reported on by the board of trade, in order to receive his majesty's confirmation or disallowance." This last

115. *Assembly Journals*, October 2, 1762, 5:346–50.

step, Lyttelton told the Board of Trade, was to supply a foundation for bringing "a charge against your Lordship's Board of having neglected to lay many of their Laws before the King."[116]

When Lyttelton expressed "his amazement" that the Assembly would take a report adopted by the King in Council so lightly and called upon it to explain its "extraordinary and unprecedented declaration" and discharge itself "from any intention of treating" the Board "in a contemptuous manner, and thereby affronting his majesty's mild and gracious government," the Assembly denied that it meant to show "the least disrespect to his majesty, or his most honourable privy-council," but saucily expanded upon its denunciation of the Board of Trade. By endeavoring "to represent the legislature of this island in a very disadvantageous light to his majesty, and" mentioning "them as objects of his severest censure," the Assembly told Lyttelton, the Board of Trade had given them adequate grounds to "think themselves ill-treated." Excoriating the Assembly for the "public manner in which you have arraigned the conduct of the king's commissioners for trade and plantations," Lyttelton thereupon prorogued the legislature for a short cooling-off period.[117]

When Lyttelton reconvened the Assembly a week later, it was unrepentant. It considered but rejected a motion to inform Lyttelton that it was "so far from intending to apologize" for its expression "of our resentment of the treatment we have received from the" Board of Trade that it was "unalterably determined to vindicate ourselves to his majesty, from their hard and unjust aspersions." According to Lyttelton, there were two reasons for this rejection: first, because the Assembly decided "that a complaint to His Majesty wou'd not avail them," and second, because it agreed that "it became them better to assert their own Rights & Liberties themselves by Resolutions of the Council & Assembly than to refer them to the decisions of any third party, even of the Crown itself." Accordingly, the Assembly immediately set to work constructing and adopting a set of seven resolutions to which the Council concurred with minor amendments on October 23. The

116. *Assembly Journals,* October 6–7, 1762, 5:351–52; Lyttelton to Board of Trade, October 13, 1762, CO 137/32, ff. 207–11.

117. *Assembly Journals,* October 8–9, 12, 1762, 5:352–54.

Council having, as Lyttelton told the Board, been "comprehended in the censure" of the Board, were "no illwishers to the measures of the House of Assembly."[118]

These seven resolutions represented a reiteration and an elaboration of the constitutional ideas Jamaica's political establishment had been honing for decades in defense of its claims for the predominant role in Jamaica's internal affairs. The first resolution cited Charles II's 1661 proclamation to support the assertion that Jamaican settlers were "intitled to the benefit and protection of the Laws of England and to the rights and Priviledges of Englishmen." The second used the 1728 Jamaica revenue act as the foundation for the claim that all English laws that had "been at any time esteem'd[,] introduced[,] used[,] Accepted[,] or received as Laws of this Island" should "Continue Laws of . . . Jamaica forever." The third resolution declared that Jamaica had "enjoyed without Interruption for upwards of Eighty Years the Use and Benefit of the Laws of England and among others That most essential privilege[:] the power of Enacting Laws for their own Government and Support by a Legislature composed of His Majesty's Comm[ande]r in Chief[,] His Majesty's Council and an Assembly of the Representatives of the People." A fourth resolution cited earlier reports by the Board of Trade to prove that it was "the Constitution of this Colony confirmed by constant and invariable Usage that all Laws of a Publick Nature which" were "not repugnant to the Laws of our Mother Country" were "in full force and Effect after they have been passed by the Gov[erno]r[,] Council and Assembly," albeit they "remain[ed] liable to be rejected by His Majesty in Council." A fifth resolution asserted that Jamaica could "not have made so considerable a Progress in its Settlements . . . with a less Degree of Protection than its Constitution affords." Implicitly calling into question the constitutionality of suspending clauses, the last two resolutions declared that the Board of Trade's recent castigation of the Jamaica legislature for "setting aside the provisions of perpetual Laws confirmed by the Crown" was "a Misrepresentation of the Constitution of this Colony and would if admitted deprive us of some of our most valuable and established Rights[,] abridge

118. *Assembly Journals,* October 22, 1762, 5:359–60; Lyttelton to Board of Trade, October 13 and 24, 1762, CO 137/32, ff. 207–17.

the power of the Legislature and draw this Colony into many inconveniences as well as into a dangerous and unconstitutional Dependance upon that Board."[119]

In two probing letters to the Board of Trade, Lyttelton sought to spell out for his metropolitan superiors the meaning of the legislature's stand on this question. No friend to the constitutional pretensions of American assemblies, Lyttelton would later deplore the fact that late seventeenth-century English authorities had given up on their efforts to establish "in Jamaica the *Irish Constitution*" after "they had shown so much *firmness* and *resolution* to support the *rights* of the *Crown*." In the case at hand, he explained, the resolutions "fully shew[ed] the sense which the Assembly & Council have of what they judge to be their Rights & Privileges." "Whatever powers" the Assembly "was meant to have by His Majesty's Commission & Instructions to His Governors," he declared, "an Inspection of their Journals" revealed that its members had "for some years last past considered the House of Commons of Great Britain as their Model & have assum'd and exercis'd the powers thereof as nearly as the circumstances of this Country cou'd allow of," assuming that whatever they "found upon consulting the Journals of the House of Commons to have been constitutionally done there" was "a sufficient authority to them to proceed in the same manner here." Moreover, Lyttelton observed, they claimed their authority, not as metropolitan officials had long claimed, "by virtue of His Majesty's Commission to His Governor," but on the basis of their "inherent Right so to do as English Subjects, entitled to the use & benefit of the Laws of England of which the Custom of Parliament makes a part." Of course, this position stood in complete opposition to the House of Commons 1757 resolutions concerning Jamaica, which, as one metropolitan commentator interpreted them in 1763, had declared "in the Case of Jamaica that the Colonies have no Constitution" but "that the Mode of Government in each of them" depended entirely "upon the Good Pleasure of the King as expressed in his Com[m]ission and Instructions to his Governor."[120]

119. Jamaica Council Minutes, October 23, 1762, CO 138/22, ff. 232–33.
120. Lyttelton, "State of the Constitution of Jamaica," n.d., Additional Manuscripts, 12409, f. 25; Lyttelton to Board of Trade, October 24, 1762, CO 137/32,

At the same time, Lyttelton complained, the Council had built a parallel pretension "to exercise the powers of the House of Lords . . . upon the same foundation." Considering itself in its legislative capacity to represent "one of the three Estates . . . of this Island," its members constantly "endeavour'd to assimilate themselves in every thing as nearly as they cou'd to the House of Lords in Great-Britain, whose powers and usages they have, as far as ever the condition of this Country cou'd admit of, consider'd as an Authority & model for them to govern themselves by." No wonder, then, that the Council had "readily . . . concurr'd with the Assembly in asserting a right . . . jointly with the Governor & Assembly to pass laws contrary to the King's Instructions; & in considering your Lordship's Report to His Majesty . . . as a misrepresentation of their Constitution."[121]

Having "already acquired too much force by the toleration it has met with here to be done away with by anything less than His Majesty's Interposition & Declaration against it," the doctrine on which these parallels were founded, Lyttelton believed, was not the grandiose pretensions of the assemblymen and councillors only but was "universal" and "much espous'd by the Inhabitants of this Island in general." Stressing his helplessness in "this difficult Station" and his inability to deal with the situation on his own, Lyttelton entreated the Board "to reflect how extremely difficult it is for the King's Governor to support His Majesty's Authority in this Island with a Council assuming the Powers of the House of Lords, and an Assembly those of the House of Commons of Great-Britain if at any time they shall be possess'd by a Spirit of Faction [or opposition], more especially when it is consider'd that . . . the Assembly shou'd grant annual supplies, without which the King's Troops cannot be subsisted, or many other charges of Government be defray'd."[122]

Notwithstanding the fact that settler Jamaicans offered repeated and "strong assurances . . . of their Loyalty & dutiful attachment to

---

ff. 212–15; "Hints Respecting the Civil Establishment in Our American Colonies," [1763], Shelburne Papers, 48:503, William L. Clements Library, Ann Arbor, Michigan.

121. Ibid.

122. Ibid; Lyttelton to Board of Trade, October 13, 1762, CO 137/32, ff. 207–11.

His Majesty," Lyttelton concluded, they "nevertheless[,] as far as I am able to judge, [displayed] such an eager desire to be freed from those restraints, which the wisdom of His Majesty's Councils has put them under in common with the rest of His Colonies in the great point of Legislation, & such an aspiring endeavour to acquire in their Assemblies & within the Sphere of their activity the same Powers and Privileges as are enjoy'd by a British House of Commons, as, I humbly conceive, may well deserve the consideration of His Majesty's Ministers."[123]

Reminding the Board of the Assembly's "constant & steady refusal to insert a clause, in any Act they pass, suspending the execution thereof until His Majesty's pleasure be known" and of the incompatibility between the Jamaica legislature's resolutions and the House of Commons' 1757 condemnation of the Assembly's October 1753 resolutions "as derogatory of the Rights of the Crown & people of Great-Britain," Lyttelton stressed the point that the Jamaica legislature's defiance of the Board of Trade was neither "accidental [n]or temporary" but rather grew "out of the opinion which the people of this Island have form'd of the Constitution of this Government & of their Rights & Privileges and will therefore be likely to produce similar effects to those I am now contemplating whenever they shall think those Rights infringed either by your Lordships in your Representations to The King or by me in the execution of His Majesty's Instructions concerning the passing of Laws or otherwise." These opinions, he counseled, were "too deeply rooted & founded upon Doctrines & Practises of too high & complicated a nature to be removed or much lessen'd by any Means in my power without His Majesty's special directions & Interposition[,] which are so necessary that either this Country must be thrown into a state of the greatest Confusion & distraction by a denial on my part of the validity of the pretensions of the Council & Assembly, unless that denial be supported by a solemn Declaration of the Crown, not to say the Parliament also, of such a sort as may bring back the Government to its first Principles again, or His Majesty's Authority & the Honour of your Lordship's Office must suffer by an acquiescence

123. Lyttelton to Board of Trade, October 13, 1762, CO 137/32, ff. 207–11.

in me."[124] The dilemma Lyttelton described was precisely the same as the one Trelawny had identified in his letters to Henry Pelham fourteen years earlier, and it was no closer to being resolved.

Through his long analysis Lyttelton hoped, as he wrote George Grenville, both to impress the Board of Trade with "the manner in which I have endeavour'd to do my Duty as His Majesty's Governor on this occasion" and to shift responsibility for dealing with the recalcitrant and bumptious Jamaicans to London. In this last hope he was to be sorely disappointed. The "commotions" in Jamaica merited an article in a London newspaper and, according to the Jamaica agent, Lovel Stanhope, put "the Board of Trade in such a Temper, that I dare not show my head at their Board till their Heat is a little subsided." The Board found the legislature's resolutions to be "of so very extraordinary a nature and Tendency, so injurious to your Majesty's Authority and subversive of the great constitutional Principles of Provincial Government" that, it wrote the Privy Council in February 1763, it immediately sent them to the attorney and solicitor generals for consideration. The challenges represented by the resolutions, it declared, were "of the utmost importance to the Maintenance and support of your Majesty['s] Government, not only in Jamaica, but in all your Majesty's American Colonies." Although the Privy Council held several meetings between March 3, 1763, and December 14, 1764, to consider "the most proper method to be taken by the Government upon this occasion," it seems never to have taken any formal action.[125]

Why the Privy Council should have failed to take some action on a challenge so fundamental is unclear. Perhaps it was overtaken by events. By December 1764, Lyttelton was on the verge of involving himself in an even more intense controversy in Jamaica over the ex-

124. Ibid; Lyttelton to Board of Trade, October 24, 1762, CO 137/32, ff. 212–15.

125. Lyttelton to Grenville, January 11, 1763, Stowe Papers, Box 22 (64), Huntington Library, San Marino, California; Stanhope to Lyttelton, February 23, 1763, Lyttelton Papers, 12 (i), Worcester Record Office, Worcester, England; Board of Trade to Privy Council, February 17, 1763, CO 138/22, ff. 261–62; Privy Council Minutes, March 3, 1763, Privy Council Papers 2/109; Munro and Grant, *Acts of the Privy Council*, March 3, 1763–December 14, 1764, 4:520–21.

tent of the Assembly's privileges, a controversy that would interrupt the normal process of governance in Jamaica for two years and lead to his resignation.[126] Perhaps it was distracted by a variety of other colonial issues posed by the new American territories acquired as a result of the recently concluded Seven Years' War. Or perhaps it simply did not know what to do. The lesson of the immediately previous decade and a half and of the subsequent privilege controversy suggested that settler Jamaicans were a stubborn people willing to go to extraordinary lengths in defense of their liberties and constitution, even if it meant standing up to the might of the metropolis. Without the sanction of the settler community, the pronouncements of the metropolis carried little authority in the de facto settler republic of mid-eighteenth-century Jamaica. And when the metropolitan government repeatedly failed to secure such sanction for its pronouncements, it had little choice but to back off. From the late 1740s through the early 1760s, the Jamaican provincial establishment, operating principally through the Jamaica Assembly, had shown itself, in response to a series of challenges from the metropolis, to be indomitable and, in regard to the colony's provincial affairs, governable only on its own terms.

The Assembly had long enjoyed wide latitude in constructing and presiding over the internal polity of Jamaica, and its stubborn and successful resistance to the new policies emanating from London after 1748 underlined its continuing commitment to the idea of legislative supremacy within the island's government. In the constitutional structure that had evolved in Jamaica, the representative component—what Montesquieu referred to as the republican element in the metropolitan British constitution—was extraordinarily powerful. To suggest, as I did at the outset of this essay, that this development had long since turned Jamaica into a settler republic is emphatically not to argue that Jamaican leaders at any point subscribed to republican political ideology. Rather, it is to restate the familiar point, made by Adam Smith in *The Wealth of Nations* in 1776, that Britain's American colonies were "republican" in "their manners . . . and their governments" long be-

126. See Jack P. Greene, "The Jamaica Privilege Controversy, 1764–66: An Episode in the Process of Constitutional Definition in the Early Modern British Empire," *Journal of Imperial and Commonwealth History* 22 (1994): 16–53.

fore they became formally republican in 1776.[127] The extensive authority of the legislative branch had made Britain's American colonies *functionally republican* long before they became antimonarchical. That is precisely why, during the North American settler revolt that began in 1774–76, the transition from monarchy to republican government was so easy in those polities that had the wherewithal to participate in that revolt and why the revolution it produced was so profoundly conservative.

The colonial case against Britain in the 1760s and 1770s, like the Jamaican responses in the 1750s, was deeply conservative in that it invoked an ancient colonial and, by implication, imperial constitution as a defense against metropolitan innovations in the system of British imperial governance. Until 1776, colonial spokesmen sought, not escape from the British Empire, but the equal enjoyment of British rights and liberties within the empire. Like their Jamaican predecessors, they principally drew their conceptions of liberty from the English jurisprudential tradition articulated over time, first by various metropolitan legal theorists, and then, by whig polemicists, a tradition which generations of colonial leaders had internalized and employed to support colonial claims to traditional English rights and liberties. By incorporating those rights and liberties into the constitutional structures they had built in every colony, they had effectively naturalized them and turned them into Jamaican or Virginian or Pennsylvanian liberties. Without the full possession of these rights and liberties, they had repeatedly professed, they would be little more than slaves. Living in societies that protected slavery by law and, in many cases, had heavily slave populations, they knew at first hand what slavery was like, a point upon which Edmund Burke put special emphasis in his explanation of the American commitment to liberty. The Jamaica conflict of the 1750s may have been exceptional in its duration and intensity, as in the impression that it made upon metropolitan political consciousness, but it was by no means unique. For Britons living outside the bounds of

---

127. Adam Smith, *An Inquiry into the Nature and Causes of the Wealth of Nations,* ed. R. H. Campbell and A. S. Skinner, The Glasgow Edition of the Works and Correspondence of Adam Smith (1776; Oxford: Oxford University Press, 1976), 2:585.

the home island, in Ireland and in America, enjoying British liberty within the larger empire had long required a high degree of provincial self-government.

In 1763, on the eve of the great controversies that led to the secession of the thirteen colonies from the British Empire, that Empire, as illustrated by the experience of Jamaica, remained what it had been in the late 1740s and earlier: a negotiated empire in which the provincial legislatures, ever alert to any threat to the liberties of the colonies, exercised as great a degree of influence in shaping the imperial constitution as did metropolitan authorities. In the ongoing effort to understand the constitutional structure of the early modern British Empire, historians need to be acutely aware of the extraordinary significance of this influence.[128]

128. An elaboration of this point can be found in Jack P. Greene, *Peripheries and Center: Constitutional Development in the Extended Polities of the British Empire and the United States 1607–1788* (Athens: University of Georgia Press, 1986), 1–150.

The Dialectic of Liberty:
Law and Religion in Revolutionary
America

I

Liberty in the English-speaking world of the eighteenth century was simultaneously the most cherished right that a people could possess and the most volatile term of distinction in political debate. In 1776 all parties on both sides of the Atlantic assumed "there is not a word in the whole compass of language which expresses so much of what is important and excellent"; most agreed that "the sound of that single word, *LIBERTY*, should be equal to an army of other words."[1] Liberty, in consequence, emerged as the term of choice in every disagreement, spawning a quite literal army of words in the pamphlet wars of the Anglo-American conflict. Since liberty covered all that was right, it could just as easily be turned into anything that was needed, and the same writer often used the term in a variety of ways without distinguishing between connotations.[2] Liberty could signify an exact or identifiable right, a loose encomium, a term of worship, membership in the British Empire, a personal possession, or the simple enjoyment of property. It also appeared as a badge of virtue, a distinction between peoples, a divine guarantee, a natural law, a political goal, participa-

1. The first quotation is from the radical English Whig, Richard Price, *Observations on the Nature of Civil Liberty, the Principles of Government, and the Justice and Policy of the War with America* (London: T. Cadell, 1776), 5. The second quotation, from the other side of the political spectrum in England, is from Thomas Bernard, *An Appeal to the Public, Stating and Considering the Objections to the Quebec Bill* (London: T. Payne, 1774), 28.

2. In summarizing the problem of the many meanings of liberty for the eighteenth century, Montesquieu observed "There is no word that admits of more various significations and has made more varied impressions on the human mind, than that of liberty." Baron de Montesquieu, *The Spirit of Laws*, trans. Thomas Nugent (1748; New York: Hafner Press, 1949), 149 [bk. 11, no. 2] (hereafter cited as *Spirit*).

tion in government, an affirmation of security and, not least, as the very worst of apprehensions. The eighteenth century made an absolute claim upon liberty as a concept but feared the relative continuum that it contained. Thus in Johnson's *Dictionary* from 1755 the first meaning opposed liberty to slavery while the last raised vague alarms over permissiveness; *to take a liberty* led to "exorbitant liberty" and the danger of "license."[3]

No investigation can hope to clarify the myriad confusions over liberty. Eighteenth-century rhetoricians approached the concept from different directions, deliberately conflated the various possibilities, and allowed the term itself to change under the pressure of events. Many of these confusions are of special interest to historians or philosophers of the period. When, for example, Patrick Henry supposedly proclaimed "give me liberty or give me death" in 1775, the now-famous juxtaposition, liberty or death, already formed a familiar phrase throughout the Anglo-American world. Did Henry actually utter these words or not? Insertion of the sentence may have come later through Patrick Henry's first biographer William Wirt.[4] Debates of this kind

3. Samuel Johnson, *A Dictionary of the English Language* (London: W. Strahan, 1755). For a more substantial catalogue of the distinctions between uses of the term liberty in England and America, see John Phillip Reid, "A Word We Know" in *The Concept of Liberty in the Age of the American Revolution* (Chicago: University of Chicago Press, 1988), 11–21 (hereafter cited as *Concept*).

4. Patrick Henry gave his famous speech on March 23, 1775, over disputed resolutions to prepare for the defense of Virginia, but no record was kept. For the best summary of the uncertain provenance and potential later sources of Patrick Henry's attributed language, see David A. McCants, "The Authenticity of William Wirt's Version of Patrick Henry's 'Liberty Or Death' Speech," *Virginia Magazine* 87 (October 1979), 387–402. See, as well, Christopher Looby, *Voicing America: Language, Literary Form, and the Origins of the United States* (Chicago: University of Chicago Press, 1996), 270–78. Wirt's obvious poetic license can be seen in his own description of Henry's speech. Writing in 1817 and depending utterly on the memory of witnesses forty-two years after the event, Wirt manages to give Henry's facial expressions as well as his final words! "'I know not what course others may take; but as for me,' cried he, with both arms extended aloft, his brows knit, every feature marked with the resolute purpose of his soul, and his voice swelled to its boldest note of exclamation—'give me liberty or give me death.'" William Wirt, *Sketches of the Life and Character of Patrick Henry* (1818; Philadelphia: Claxton, Remsen, and Haffelfinger, 1878), 141–42.

over the historical record are real ones, but they tend to miss a larger problem at the source. Given universal resort to the term, what are the actual roots of discourse on liberty in early America? The eighteenth century experienced a strategic and now largely hidden conflict over the idea of liberty itself—a conflict with significance for the modern body politic. The evolution of liberty in early America involved two main competing sources and the sudden dominance of one over the other, though the competition between them and conflicting use continues to this day. Arguments over liberty still flow from this dialectic over original meanings.

In effect, two competing modes of thought established a republic based on liberty in America. The first mode, new world Protestantism, provided the oppositional platform from which insecure provincials challenged their own mother country. Clergymen were the rhetorical masters of what was still a Bible culture in eighteenth-century America, and they used their knowledge to produce the moral differentiation, the dissenting vocabulary, the prospect of union, and the weekly indoctrination from the pulpit that colonials needed in order to come together against the power and hegemony of the British Empire. Not for nothing did the Loyalist historian Peter Oliver name the ministry "the black regiment" with "so active a Part in the Rebellion."[5] The second contributing mode of thought drew upon the American idea of law. The idea itself came through English common law and the legal treatises of the European Enlightenment, but Americans quickly made these sources their own. Less independent in voice than its religious counterpart, American legal thought was just as vibrant in developing oppositional terms through a language of rights, and it tri-

---

5. Peter Oliver, *Origin and Progress of the American Rebellion: A Tory View,* Douglass Adair and John A. Schultz, eds. (Stanford: Stanford University Press, 1967), 41. [Oliver completed his manuscript in 1781.] For accounts of the ministerial role in rousing the colonists in the 1760s and after, see Alice M. Baldwin, *The New England Clergy and the American Revolution* (Durham: Duke University Press, 1928); Alan E. Heimert, *Religion and the American Mind: From the Great Awakening to the Revolution* (Cambridge: Harvard University Press, 1966); and Richard H. Brown, "Spreading the Word: Rural Clergymen and the Communication Network of Eighteenth-Century New England," *Proceedings of the Massachusetts Historical Society* 94 (1982): 1–14.

umphed in the actual making of the republic. For while ministers gave Revolutionary Americans much of their moral and intellectual courage to fight, lawyers defined the event and capped its directions.

The movement toward legal explanation had concrete manifestations. The touchstones of Revolutionary achievement, 1776 and 1787, took their meaning from the seminal legal documents that lawyers wrote in those years. Another lawyer would then complete this text-oriented basis of achievement by assigning these documents their ultimate place in an American ideology of liberty. Under enormous pressures in the 1860s, Abraham Lincoln took the Constitution of the United States of America, the "*picture of silver*," and made it the frame of an earlier, all-important "apple of gold," the Declaration of Independence.[6] Through this established centrality, the Declaration became the symbol of American liberty. Lincoln's version of it privileged a national understanding of equality and turned its claim about the pursuit of happiness into an opportunity for all in republican life.

In this way, law easily trumped religion in the process of national formations. Wasn't it logical, after all, for *early republican* lawyers to replace *colonial* ministers when it came to shaping the republic?[7] Many have said so, but the chronological argument falters over the issue of origins, and it fails altogether in assessing how liberty is employed as the lynchpin of choice in cultural understanding. When in crisis, the sometimes loosely joined United States of America have needed all of their intellectual resources, one of which has been "In God We Trust."[8]

6. Abraham Lincoln, "Fragment on the Constitution and the Union" [c. January 1861] in Roy Basler, ed., *The Collected Works of Abraham Lincoln,* 8 vols. (New Brunswick: Rutgers University Press, 1953), 4:169.

7. The most frequently quoted summary of this phenomenon is Edmund S. Morgan's. "In 1740 America's leading intellectuals were clergymen and thought about theology; in 1790 they were statesmen and thought about politics." See Morgan, "The American Revolution Considered as an Intellectual Movement," in Arthur M. Schlesinger, Jr., and Morton White, eds., *Paths of American Thought* (Boston: Houghton Mifflin, 1963), 11.

8. Somewhat facetiously, given his detailed analysis of the Supreme Court's established doctrine that government action involving religion must have a secular purpose, Leonard Levy asks "Does the motto 'In God We Trust' have a legitimate secular purpose and effect that conform to the establishment clause [of the first amendment to the Constitution]?" Less facetiously, Levy goes on to say, in

The same lawyer who completed the textual formations of the republic of laws also saw more forcefully than any other leader the need for providence in articulating the promise of America. In the crucible of the Civil War, Lincoln held the nation to religious understandings in his Gettysburg Address and Second Inaugural. One of his last acts would be to urge his cabinet to devise an amendment that would bring God into the fabric of the Constitution.[9]

The recognition that religious explanation joins legal explanation in the construction of American liberty leaves many questions unanswered.[10] If the religious sources of liberty are powerful and signifi-

---

his suggestion of a comprehensive religious dimension in American public life, that the motto would indeed have to be found to be unconstitutional under this doctrine but for the fact that "the Court has enough cunning to avoid rendering such judgments." See Leonard W. Levy, *The Establishment Clause: Religion and the First Amendment* (hereafter cited as *Establishment Clause*) (New York: Macmillan Publishing Company, 1986), x, 123–31, 180–82. See, as well, *Lemon v. Kurtzman,* 403 U.S. 602, 612–13 (1971).

9. Reported in Gideon Welles, *Diary of Gideon Welles, Secretary of the Navy Under Lincoln and Johnson,* 3 vols. (Boston: Houghton Mifflin, 1909–11), 2:190. For fuller analyses of Lincoln's heavy reliance on religious language and imagery as president, see Robert A. Ferguson, "Lincoln: An Epilogue," in *Law and Letters in American Culture* (Cambridge: Harvard University Press, 1984), 305–17, and Dwight G. Anderson, *Abraham Lincoln: The Quest for Immortality* (New York: Alfred A. Knopf, 1982).

10. The assumption that early American thought is dominated by a combination of religious and legal frames of reference has been made previously by Perry Miller, *The Life of the Mind in America from the Revolution to the Civil War* (New York: Harcourt, Brace, and World, 1965), and by J. C. D. Clark, *The Language of Liberty 1660–1832: Political Discourse and Social Dynamics in the Anglo-American World* (Cambridge: Cambridge University Press, 1994) (hereafter cited as *Language*). Clark, in arguing for a variety of denominational refinements and in claiming that the American Revolution must be seen as a "war of religion," overstates his case, but I share his assumptions that "law and religion dominated men's understanding of the public realm," that they were "profoundly related," and that "the language of liberty" in the eighteenth-century Anglo-American world flows from the connection. See 1–45, 296–372. The first observer to note the twin-dominance of religion and law in American thought and action was a contemporary, Edmund Burke, who also called each impulse a "main cause" of a uniquely American attachment to liberty in his noted analysis before Parliament. Edmund Burke, "On Moving His Resolutions for Conciliation with the Colonies, March 22, 1775," in

cant, *why* did they disappear from civil discourse so rapidly in the early republic? *Where,* in the continuing dialectic, are the religious contributions to civil and political liberty in American life? *How* did religious and legal sources of liberty interact to produce a distinct American understanding? *What,* if anything, does a closer look at religious explanation restore to a balanced understanding of American liberty? The next four sections take up each of these questions in turn and in order of difficulty.

II

The abrupt removal of religious voices from republican discourse in the post-Revolutionary era remains one of the neglected stories in American history. How did it happen? There are essentially three reasons for ecclesiastical disenfranchisement, and each reflects a corresponding strength in the legal temperament. First, the rapid rise of the commercial republic undercut the ministry on both financial and rhetorical grounds even as it enhanced the legal profession. Second, the doctrine of separation of church and state—with enforcement by the legal profession—effectively silenced the ministry on a variety of issues crucial to republican formations. Third, secularization in the early republic provided alternatives to what had been dominant religious explanations of human behavior and external phenomena. A variety of disciplines—science, psychology, economics, history, as well as law—all challenged religious exegesis. Even so, legal thought was most crucial in co-opting political interpretation from the pulpit, and it is important to understand why. The "Evangelical Basis" and "The Legal Mentality" were at once compatible and conflicting modes of explanation in the early "life of the mind in America," but how they joined and where they departed, as well as the ongoing struggle between them, remains to be worked out.[11]

Because the three factors undercutting the clergy reinforced each other in the aftermath of the Revolution, the result was more than a

---

The Works of the Right Honourable Edmund Burke, 16 vols. (London: F. and C. Rivington, 1803), 3:52, 54–55.

11. The terminology here and the insistence on their differences come from Miller, *Life of the Mind in America,* 2–155.

simple acceleration of effects. Financially, ministers lost ground while lawyers grew rich on the settlement of wartime disputes and the land transactions of continental expansion. The disestablishment of religion also cost ministers dearly; it eliminated state support, leaving them to their congregations on fixed salaries that dwindled during inflationary cycles.[12] Intellectually, commercialism reduced the power of the pulpit in more obvious ways. The presumed moral superiority of America over England during the Revolution had been the special province of ministers who emphasized American simplicity, public-mindedness, sacrifice, and piety over British materialism, cynicism, and depravity. The byword of warning from every Revolutionary pulpit in the land had been "luxury." Ministers turned luxury into a two-headed monster feeding on corruption and lost spirituality, supreme dangers to a virtuous republic fighting for its God-given rights against a British Empire seeking taxes for its own gain. But if these warnings bolstered the Revolution, they played less well in the increasingly material culture of the early republic. Potent polarities concerning virtue and vice began to blur. Instead of uniting against a common external foe, the theme of luxury as vice came to remind early republicans of growing differences in their own more complicated moral landscape.[13]

The disestablishment of religion also translated into clerical exclusion through enforcement of the doctrine separating church and state. For lawyers like John Adams, the earliest understanding of religious freedom involved more than freedom of conscience; it meant opposing clerical authority in the state in all forms, or, as Adams put the mat-

12. Disestablishment of religion in America must be understood in terms of financial support for religion by government rather than in terms of a single established church though it was not until 1834 that the last established church lost its position. See Levy, "State Establishments of Religion" in *Establishment Clause*, 25–62, and Michael W. McConnell, "The Origins and Historical Understanding of Free Exercise of Religion," *Harvard Law Review* 103 (May 1990): 1436–37. For an account of the original power and dwindling status of the clergy in Revolutionary America, see Emory Elliott, "The Dove and Serpent: The Clergy in the American Revolution," *American Quarterly* 31 (Summer 1979): 187–203.

13. For the centrality of a rhetoric against luxury in the Revolution and subsequent problems in applying that rhetoric to post-Revolutionary America, see Edmund S. Morgan, "The Puritan Ethic and the American Revolution," *William and Mary Quarterly*, 3d ser., 24 (1967): 3–43.

ter himself, it meant "deriding . . . the ridiculous fantasies of sanctified effluvia from episcopal fingers."[14] Lawyers like Adams and Thomas Jefferson worked ceaselessly to implement their suspicion of ecclesiastical authority by insisting on the exclusion of religious leaders from all governmental questions.[15] By the Federal Constitutional Convention of 1787, the lawyers who framed the republic regarded the prospect of an official chaplain with disdain.[16] The pattern of exclusion did not end there. With the doctrine of separation of church and state firmly in place, American law would eventually displace or qualify most vestiges of public religious explanation. American courts today restrict religious expression in the civic sphere whenever the secular interest of the state is thought to be present.[17]

14. John Adams, *A Dissertation on the Canon and Feudal Law* [1765], in Charles Francis Adams, ed., *The Works of John Adams* (hereafter cited as *Works*), 10 vols. (Boston: Little, Brown, 1850–56), 3:451–53, 462.

15. Jefferson, for example, fought a life-long battle and largely established a test, subsequently taken up in the twentieth century by the Supreme Court, that called for "building a wall of separation between church and state." See Thomas Jefferson to the Baptist Association of Danbury, Connecticut, January 1, 1802, in *The Writings of Thomas Jefferson,* ed. Albert E. Bergh, 20 vols. (Washington, D.C.: Thomas Jefferson Memorial Association, 1907), 16:281–82. See, as well, *Everson v. Board of Education,* 330 U.S. 1, 15–16 (1947), in which Justice Hugo Black for the majority explicitly adopts Jefferson's language and intent. For a detailed account of how early republican lawyers use the doctrine of the separation of church and state to exclude the ministry from active involvement in republican discourse, see Robert A. Ferguson, *The American Enlightenment* (Cambridge: Harvard University Press, 1994), 73–79.

16. The Framers regarded Benjamin Franklin's formal motion for a chaplain to help ease their disputes as so unnecessary and embarrassing that they kept it from receiving so much as a formal vote on the convention floor. See Max Farrand, ed., *The Records of the Federal Convention of 1787,* rev. ed., 4 vols. (New Haven: Yale University Press, 1966), 1:450–52. For a full account of the determination of the Framers to separate off religion from the state, including "the significance of the absence" of references to providence in the Federal Constitution itself, see Walter Berns, "Religion and the Founding Principle," in Robert H. Horwitz, ed., *The Moral Foundations of the American Republic,* 2d ed. (Charlottesville: University Press of Virginia, 1979), 157–82.

17. For just a few of the recent decisions by the Supreme Court of the United States that have construed the Establishment Clause of the First Amendment to limit severely government recognition of religion and to restrict religious expres-

Nothing proves the rivalry between legal and religious thought in America more conclusively than the continuing clumsiness of American law in dealing with religious issues. With some exasperation, Justice Byron White complained in 1973 that "one cannot seriously believe that the history of the First Amendment furnishes unequivocal answers to many of the fundamental issues of church-state relations. In the end," he added defensively, "the courts have fashioned answers to these questions as best they can."[18] Their best, however, has not been good enough for most critics. Leading legal commentators describe an "Alice in Wonderland" quality in Supreme Court interpretations of the religious provisions of the First Amendment of the Federal Constitution. As Leonard Levy has observed, "the Court exercises a freedom almost legislative in character, bringing us close to the intolerable, a Humpty Dumpty Court."[19] Others find "little doctrinal stability," an "ahistorical manner," "inattention to original meaning," and willful inconsistencies in the judiciary's methodological approaches to the different religion clauses of the First Amendment.[20] Recently, both legal confusion and cultural acrimony achieved new heights when in June of 2002 the United States Court of Appeals for the Ninth Circuit decided

---

sion in aspects of the public sphere, see *Lemon v. Kurtzman*, 403 U.S. 602 (1971) (forbidding "an excessive government entanglement with religion"); *County of Allegheny v. American Civil Liberties*, 492 U.S. 573 (1989) (holding unconstitutional a free-standing display of a nativity scene on the main staircase of a county courthouse); *Wallace v. Jaffree*, 472 U.S. 38 (1984) (forbidding a one-minute period of silence in public schools "for meditation or voluntary prayer"); and *Lee v. Weisman*, 505 U.S. 577 (1992) (forbidding the offering of prayers as part of an official school graduation ceremony).

18. *Committee for Public Education v. Nyquist*, 413 U.S. 756, 820 (1973).

19. As Levy explains, "Humpty Dumpty told Alice scornfully that when he used a word it meant just what he chose it to mean, neither more nor less. 'The question is,' said Alice, 'whether you can make words mean so many different things.'" *Establishment Clause*, 180–81. Philip B. Kurland, using a different section of Lewis Carroll's *Alice's Adventures in Wonderland*, comes to the same conclusion about the court's confusion and willful shifts in direction. See Kurland, "The Religion Clauses and the Burger Court," *Catholic University Law Review* 34 (Fall 1984): 14.

20. See Jesse H. Choper, "A Century of Religious Freedom," *California Law Review* 88 (December 2000): 1741, and McConnell, "Origins and Historical Understanding," 1410–15.

that reciting the Pledge of Allegiance in public schools was unconstitutional because the Pledge includes the phrase "one nation under God."[21] The trouble, of course, is never over religion per se but over the use of religious expression in public discourse, and even these difficulties belong to a long-standing dialectic in which law and religion have shared the national arena and intellectual affinities within it.

Indeed, harder to appreciate but much more decisive in the rivalry have been the linguistic homologies that allowed eighteenth-century law to subsume religious thought. Law took the place of religion in early republican civil discourse through structural equivalencies. A guiding providence could be found in nature as "Nature's God" and, therefore, in something called "the law of nature." It followed that fundamental rights once sacred because "antecedent to all earthly government" and "derived from the great Legislator of the universe," could enter legal lexicons instead as inalienable rights or as natural rights or even as man-made rights—as long as they began before recorded time, literally from time immemorial or time out of memory.[22] Eighteenth-century religious understandings found little to fault in these easy transitions. Patriots, most of whom were also believers, welcomed the progress in their legal rights as part of a divine plan. Intellectually and methodologically, they saw significant and comforting correspondences in the forms of presentation: Scripture to precedent, dogma to doctrine, liturgy to procedure, sin to crime, the voice of God to the voice of the people. And there were good reasons for their presumed familiarity. Each parallel and resemblance referred back to Western legal origins in religious thought, and every lawyer's use of them took

21. *Newdow v. Elk Grove Unified School District*, quoted in *New York Times*, June 27, 2002.

22. Adams, *A Dissertation on the Canon and the Feudal Law*, in *Works*, 3:449, 462. In 1788 in his *Defence of the Constitutions of the United States of America*, Adams would confirm his ongoing attachment to natural law by proudly proclaiming that "The United States of America have exhibited, perhaps, the first example of governments erected on the simple principles of nature" (ibid., 4:292). For tracing the story of how legitimizing gestures of longevity, "time out of memory," lend credence to Anglo-American law, see J. G. A. Pocock, *The Ancient Constitution and the Feudal Law: A Study of English Historical Thought in the Seventeenth Century* (1957; reprint, New York: W. W. Norton, 1967), 30–55, 232–33, 241, and Pocock, *The Machiavellian Moment: Florentine Political Thought and the Atlantic Republican Tradition* (Princeton: Princeton University Press, 1975), 506–52.

the form of professional instinct. European law carved its own independent place out of medieval Christian conceptions of authority and
organization. The law took what the church could give it—often a great
deal—and it continued to take at every available opportunity.

The many parallels remind us that the shift towards legal explanation in the early republic should not be overstated. Ministers remained
extremely active in celebrating "the sacred cause of liberty," in shaping "visions of a republican millennium," and in crafting the so-called
Second Great Awakening, a revivalist event that reached many Americans in the 1790s.[23] Religious fervor may even have increased within
the general culture. Nevertheless, religious discourse had much less
to do with civic identity in the early republic than it did in the colonial period, and it fell increasingly under the rhetorical sway of natural
legal rights.[24] One can go further. The proficiency with which the law
superseded religion in republican formations has created something
of a conceptual divide in the history of ideas.[25] On the one hand, religious displacement from civic discourse has made it harder to determine how early Americans actually thought about the public sphere.
On the other hand, the ease with which the law supplanted its philosophical rival has made it just as difficult to differentiate what remains
from what has been displaced in public understandings.

23. For good accounts of these activities in the Second Great Awakening, see
Nathan O. Hatch, *The Sacred Cause of Liberty: Republican Thought and the Millennium
in Revolutionary New England* (New Haven: Yale University Press, 1977) (hereafter
cited as *Sacred Cause*), and Donald G. Mathews, "The Second Great Awakening as
an Organizing Process, 1780–1830," *American Quarterly* 21 (Spring 1969): 23–43.

24. See *Language*, 44–45. Publishing records in early America also support
the notion of a switch in emphasis. As Charles Evans, the comprehensive bibli-
ographer of early American literature has noted, "heretofore [before the 1770s]
the periods of growth into a national literature had been distinctly religious," but
beginning in the 1770s, publishing entered "a period of a complete and radical
change in its character, now distinctly political." See Charles Evans, "Preface to
Vol. 3," in Evans, ed., *American Bibliography: A Chronological Dictionary of All Books,
Pamphlets, and Periodical Publications Printed in the United States of America, 1639–
1800* (Chicago: Blakely Press, 1905), 3:vii.

25. For analyses that accept the premises of this conceptual divide but with
different interests in mind, see *Sacred Cause*, 15–20 and Barry Alan Shain, *The
Myth of American Individualism: The Protestant Origins of American Political Thought*
(Princeton: Princeton University Press, 1994), 167–240.

A minor incident within a major historical event can at least signal the dimensions of the problem. The most daring American military campaign in the course of the Revolution—a campaign doomed to failure from the outset—involved the American invasion of Canada in 1775 with the conquest of Quebec as its goal. The Reverend Samuel Spring, chaplain of the Revolutionary brigade that marched on Quebec, tells us that just before the expedition set off he gave a rallying sermon to the massed troops over the grave of George Whitefield, the leading revivalist and acknowledged firebrand of the Great Awakening in the 1740s. But Spring did more than preach. Eyewitness accounts reveal that he descended into the grave to remove the collar and wristbands of Whitefield, who had died five years before, and that he solemnly distributed pieces from the articles of clothing to the officers of the expedition in a pledge and guarantee of their righteous cause.[26]

Quebec had been targeted in the first place because of negative colonial reactions to the Quebec Act of 1774 in which Parliament validated Roman Catholicism in Canada. Many American patriots saw the Quebec Act as a jesuitical plot and their own responses as the struggle of liberty against arbitrary power and papal tyranny. To take Quebec would mean to secure the continent for a Protestant vision of this world—and the next![27] Whitefield, the great itinerant preacher

26. For the most complete account of Samuel Spring's descent into the grave of George Whitefield with relevant primary sources, see Charles Royster, *A Revolutionary People at War: The Continental Army and American Character, 1775–1783* (Chapel Hill: University of North Carolina Press, 1979), 23–24, 383. See, as well, J. T. Headley, *The Chaplains and Clergy of the Revolution* (New York: Charles Scribner, 1864), 92–93. The earliest printed account of the incident may well have been by the Loyalist minister, Samuel Peters, in "Genuine History of Gen. Arnold, by an Old Acquaintance," *Political Magazine* [London] 1 (November–December 1780): 746, reprinted in Kenneth Walter Cameron, ed., *The Works of Samuel Peters of Hebron, Connecticut* (Hartford: Transcendental Books, 1967), 164.

27. A full account of this mentality appears in *Sacred Cause,* 74–79. Samuel Sherwood, in perhaps the most influential single sermon from 1776, would draw particular attention to "jesuitical emissaries, the tool of tyrannical power." See *The Church's Flight into the Wilderness: An Address on the Times,* in Ellis Sandoz, ed., *Political Sermons of the American Founding Era* (Indianapolis: Liberty Fund, 1991), 512. See, as well, Stephen J. Stein, "An Apocalyptic Rationale for the American Revolution," *Early American Literature* 9 (Winter 1975): 211–25. For a variety of reasons, this fear of the Jesuits remained a permanent part of the political land-

who won converts in mass revivals all over America, stood for three other useful propositions: first, the inter-colonial character of the Great Awakening and, hence, the projected unity of the new Revolutionary brigade; second, God's imminent involvement in a colossal American destiny, which certified the connection between political and religious rights; and third, the power of the religious voice in American thought, which made ministers guardians of political liberty in America. Not the least officer to receive the talismanic touch of Whitefield's clothing was Aaron Burr. It would be difficult to find a more secular mind in the early republic than that of Burr, who fought bravely in the Revolution but resisted religious conversion at all points in a long and tempestuous life. Even so, Aaron Burr was the grandson of Jonathan Edwards, the greatest of American divines, and he would have known the relevance of Samuel Spring's conviction and the reasons for it.

There is a balance within the dialectic to be struck here. Religious fervor reached unusual heights in Revolutionary America, levels that no culture could maintain indefinitely, but the larger point in raising the Spring incident should not be missed. Early Americans had no choice but to think through a religious frame of reference; it was the mental equipment that people brought to daily life, and it was the ordering device for larger conceptions of history and communal well-being. Furthermore, the root of this conception required the thinker to accept a premise that Samuel Adams, the organizer of Boston mobs, gave most succinctly. In words that came from many lips throughout the crisis, Adams claimed "The Religion and public Liberty of a People are intimately connected; their interests are interwoven, they cannot subsist separately; and therefore they rise and fall together." [28]

---

scape. As late as 1817, John Adams was warning Thomas Jefferson of the danger: "Do you know that The General of the Jesuits and consequently all his Host have their Eyes on this Country?" Adams to Jefferson, May 18, 1817, in Lester J. Cappon, ed., *The Adams-Jefferson Letters: The Complete Correspondence Between Thomas Jefferson and Abigail and John Adams*, 2 vols. (Chapel Hill: University of North Carolina Press, 1959), 2:515.

28. Samuel Adams, "Article Signed 'Valerius Poplicola'" [*Boston Gazette*, October 5, 1772], in *The Writings of Samuel Adams*, ed. Harry Alonzo Cushing, 2 vols. (1906; New York: Octagon Books, Inc., 1968), 2:336.

III

What did it mean to think that public liberty and religion would rise or fall so certainly and precipitously together? Although the first radical dissenters in religion colonized America for a variety of reasons (including commercial gain), their eighteenth-century descendants gave priority to one motivation only. By 1765 the first settlements in America stood for a single-minded quest for religious liberty, installing a vital *first* freedom on the American strand. In this eighteenth-century narrative, while "the first place is due religion," it was "a love of universal liberty" that supplied the real motivation for settlement, thereby joining the first Puritans to the Sons of Liberty a century and a half apart. The connection, however artificial, was ideologically momentous; it created an account that was at once legally correct (based on historical precedent) and religiously sound (part of God's plan). John Adams summarized the premises involved: "I always considered the settlement of America with reverence and wonder, as the opening of a grand scene and design in Providence for the illumination of the ignorant, and the emancipation of the slavish part of mankind all over the earth."[29]

The same narrative conveniently put the colonies, not to mention the colonial speaker, at the center of human history. John Adams assumed that Americans knew the most about the inevitable spread of liberty because either a new kind or a special degree of liberty—they amounted to the same thing for Adams—had been born in America. Colonials of all persuasions easily accepted this flattering account, although it was a European, Hector St. John de Crèvecoeur, who offered up the most graphic expression. Reshaping an ugly image to explain how religion worked to the unique benefit of America, Crèvecoeur thought he knew why religious belief would lead to harmony instead of persecution in "the most perfect society now existing in the world." Religion resembled gunpowder. In Europe, where it was confined, it tended to explode; in America, spread to the four winds, the gun-

29. Virtually every leading Revolutionary pamphlet that treated the subject claimed that the Puritans' first priority in settlement, a century before, was religious liberty and that this priority kindled other forms of liberty. The actual accounting in the text is paraphrased and quoted from John Adams, *A Dissertation on the Canon and Feudal Law,* in *Works,* 3:445–64.

powder of religion burned harmlessly but with a glorious flame for all to enjoy.[30]

As secular statements, the claims of Adams, Crèvecoeur, and many others sound like naive exercises in self-aggrandizement, and so they were. They allowed everyone who believed them to feel important. But the same claims were also central to national formations, and behind them was a religious fervor that lent sincere conviction to mere assertion as well as place to provincialism. In 1742 Jonathan Edwards, the greatest philosopher of early America, supplied an elaborate rendition of the free society in America and what it meant for the world and beyond. The earthly fulfillment of this society added an electrifying dimension to divine promise. "The days are coming when the saints shall reign on earth," observed Edwards in a direct appeal to civic leaders. All Americans were meant to unite in "a strange revolution" that would "renew the world of mankind." For Edwards, "the *New Jerusalem* . . . has begun to come down from heaven," and it would come down first in America. Since "*America* was discovered about the time of the reformation," and since "[only] *America* has received the true religion of the old continent, the church of ancient times," it followed from both Scripture and history that "God intends it as the beginning or forerunner of something vastly great." "This work will begin in *America*," Edwards insisted, and he already saw "the first fruits of that glorious day."[31] Elsewhere, he drew intricate analogies between church and community, calling upon both "visibly to unite, and expressly to agree together, in prayer to God for the *common prosperity;* and above all, that common prosperity and advancement, so unspeakably great and glorious, which God hath so abundantly promised to fulfil in the latter days."[32]

One did not have to be a revivalist to emphasize the intrinsic connection of religious and civil liberty in the organization of society. In *A Discourse on the Christian Union* from 1760, Ezra Stiles, a more

30. J. Hector St. John de Crèvecoeur, "Letter III: What Is an American?" in *Letters from an American Farmer* (1782; New York: E. P. Dutton, 1957), 36, 47.

31. Jonathan Edwards, *Some Thoughts Concerning the Present Revival of Religion in New England,* in Peter N. Carroll, ed., *Religion and the Coming of the American Revolution* (Waltham, Mass.: Ginn-Baisdell, 1970), 2–9 (hereafter cited as *Religion*).

32. Edwards, *An Humble Attempt to Promote Explicit Agreement and Visible Union of God's People, in Extraordinary Prayer* [1746], in *Religion*, 14.

conservative minister and also president of Yale College, called on all Americans to "stand fast in the liberty wherewith the gospel has made us free." Stiles drew explicit analogies between "the *equality* and *independence* of every congregational apostolic church" and a corresponding freedom in harmony of "the thirteen provinces on this continent." What were churches if not little colonies? Stiles argued that "the same principles may take place in confederating a multitude of lesser bodies, as in confederating larger bodies, such as provinces, cantons, and kingdoms."[33] The American Revolutionaries of the 1770s learned how to translate the confederating premises of religious liberty into direct political action. The premise they shared with Edwards and Stiles left no need for disagreement: a religious people deserved to be free.

Thus far, the religious components of liberty in eighteenth-century America can be traced with some assurance. But how many eighteenth-century Americans listened to ministers who preached like Jonathan Edwards and Ezra Stiles? Even if they listened and even if churchgoing was the major social activity of the time, did Americans act upon such statements? Was New England the main source of such language or did the revivalism in other sections, particularly in the western areas of every colony where few sermons were printed, also trigger visions of an America that challenged European hegemony? In the absence of available evidence, historians tend to disagree over these issues and take the debate into the intricacies of denominational, class, and regional differences. If, however, the investigation turns less on levels of belief and more on the formation of general political understandings, a broader connection can be seen. The radical dissenting basis of religion in America, roughly seventy-five percent of the population as opposed to less than ten percent in England during the eighteenth century, made a difference in the approach to politics.[34] How much of a difference? That is the obvious question that remains.

33. Ezra Stiles, *A Discourse on the Christian Union*, in *Religion*, 69–70.
34. Edmund S. Morgan argues that "from the resistance against Parliamentary taxation in the 1760's to the establishment of a national government in the 1790's, [the Revolution] was affected, not to say guided, by a set of values inherited from the age of Puritanism" and that "Americans of the Revolutionary period in every colony and state paid tribute to the Puritan Ethic and repeated its injunctions." See Morgan, "The Puritan Ethic and the American Revolution,"

A good answer must carry beyond the articulation of religious liberty as such and toward a more general and philosophical conception of liberty from a religious perspective. One of the shrewdest observers of the times, Edmund Burke, gave a celebrated summary of the American situation before Parliament in 1775:

> Religion, always a principle of energy, in this new people, is no way worn out or impaired; and their mode of professing it is also one main cause of this free spirit. The people are protestants; and of that kind, which is the most adverse to all implicit submission of mind and opinion.[35]

A great deal lay behind Burke's assertions and recognition of a "free spirit" and "principle of energy," particularly in his related implication that both characteristics flowed from religion and toward a political stance about authority. Burke saw the religious temperament that would attach certain ideas about liberty to republican inceptions.

Dissenting Protestantism in America—"adverse to all implicit submission of mind and opinion"—measured temporal authority in severe terms. Worldly leaders were suspect, and that suspicion led toward expansive notions of civil liberty for the subject and an implied equality of consequences for all. American ministers never seemed to tire of noting that kings and counselors went down in the end just like ordinary people. Three of the most renowned rejoinders to authority in

---

William and Mary Quarterly, 3d ser., 24 (1967): 3–7. See, as well, Sacvan Bercovitch, "How the Puritans Won the American Revolution," *Massachusetts Review* 17 (1976): 597–630, and *Language.* "American exceptionalism," concludes Clark, "if it is to be a viable explanation, has to be relocated on the territory of American religious experience," and he points with others to "that profound shift in the composition of the colonial population which meant that while less than a tenth of Englishmen in 1776 were Dissenters, more than three quarters of Americans were enlisted in other denominations" (13).

35. Edmund Burke, "On Moving His Resolutions for Conciliation with the Colonies, March 22, 1775," in *The Works of the Right Honourable Edmund Burke,* 3:52. Alexis de Tocqueville would later offer a similar summary in tracing "the origin of the Anglo-Americans." "It [the character of Anglo-American civilization] is the result . . . of two distinct elements. . . . I allude to *the spirit of religion* and *the spirit of liberty.*" Alexis de Tocqueville, *Democracy in America,* trans. Phillips Bradley, 2 vols. (1835, in French; New York: Vintage Books, 1958), 1:45.

colonial America took this route, all from ministers who raised conceptions of liberty through the deaths of kings: they were Benjamin Colman's *Government the Pillar of the Earth* in 1730, Jonathan Mayhew's *A Discourse Concerning Unlimited Submission and Non-Resistance to the Higher Powers* in 1750, and Samuel Davies's *On the Death of His Late Majesty, King George II* in 1760.

Benjamin Colman, pastor of the prestigious Brattle Street Church in Boston, preached his greatest sermon before the civil authorities of Massachusetts. He began by proclaiming that any speaker filled with the Spirit had the right to address "nobles and rulers, captains and the mighty men" in order to "lay 'em low before God." He finished by boldly denouncing all temporal authority as ephemeral and suspect in the best of circumstances. Colman took his text from 1 Samuel: "For the Pillars of the Earth are the Lord's, and He hath set the World upon them." The leaders in front of him were God's earthly pillars, but every one of these leaders would soon "moulder into dust"; that is, if God's "pleasure" didn't actively destroy them first ("he disposes of them as he pleases"). The godly ruler was to be obeyed, but what of the ungodly ruler? Colman placed his own trust in Samson, the warrior who tore down the pillars of the Philistines. "*Put not your Trust in Princes,*" he thundered. "We must not look too much at the loftiness of any, nor lean too much on any earthly pillar."[36] The rhetorical power in Colman's challenge had several prongs. Clearly, a minister in colonial America could use the veil of Scripture to say what no secular speaker would dare to utter, and this level of freedom of speech belonged, at least by implication, to any one of God's vessels when properly inspired. Then too and even when trivialized, civil authority had no rhetorical counter to a minister who questioned the secular world through the guiding hand of providence.

Jonathan Mayhew took up the problem of the ungodly ruler with a vengeance. The gist of Mayhew's position in *A Discourse on Unlimited Submission* came in a single sentence where he announced the right to "speak freely" in America. Speaking freely for Mayhew meant choos-

36. Benjamin Colman, *Government the Pillar of the Earth: A Sermon Preached at the Lecture in Boston, Before His Excellency, Jonathan Belcher, Esq; Captain General and Commander in Chief, August 13th, 1730* (Boston: T. Hancock, 1730).

ing between polar opposites. True Protestants lived "on the side of liberty, the Bible, and common sense, in opposition to tyranny, priest-craft, and nonsense." Common sense was the unusual term in May-hew's otherwise conventional Protestant understanding of the Refor-mation, and he wielded it much as Thomas Paine would twenty-six years later. For a leader of the liberal reform clergy in Massachusetts like Mayhew, common sense clarified Scripture *and* liberty; both came directly from Heaven and reached all of the way down to the people's earthly capacity, enabling them to act as proper judges when a ruler oppressed them. The execution of Charles I was Mayhew's announced theme, but it served in *Discourse* to claim a general liberty for over-throwing ungodly rulers. Liberty, in this sense, defined the people's right to rebel when their reason told them it was just. In Mayhew's words, "for a nation thus abused to arise unanimously and resist their prince, even to the dethroning him, is not criminal, but a reasonable vindication of their liberties and just rights." *Discourse* provided a stun-ning reversal of ordinary political implications. Suddenly, not the at-tempt to resist but the failure to resist constituted "treason"—treason not just "against the whole body politic" but "against God."[37]

Samuel Davies's eulogy for George II in 1760 applied the patterns of Colman and Mayhew to another aspect of liberty, one that would figure prominently in Revolutionary rhetoric. The Virginia evangelist and new president of the College of New Jersey carefully chose an ambiguous text from 2 Samuel for his sermon, "How are the Mighty fallen!" George *was* mighty, but he *had* fallen. Davies used the phrase first to dance a little over the body of George, reminding his auditors, much in the way that Benjamin Colman had, of the triviality of earthly power: "a throne is only a precipice, from whence to fall with greater noise and more extensive ruin into the grave." Everyone knew that George II had been a good monarch. Davies noted the fact but cleverly turned his catalogue of the dead King's virtues to other purposes. The real question was whether a successor, George III, could rise to the same level, and this uncertainty, like the ambiguity in the scriptural text, supplied another opening. The people, Davies observed, had the

---

37. Jonathan Mayhew, *A Discourse Concerning Unlimited Submission and Non-Resistance to the Higher Powers* [1750], in *Religion*, 30, 41.

right to judge between a good and a bad king; for only a king who preserved liberty and the Protestant religion together would find willing obedience in America. In a remarkable addition, he then turned to the subject of *how* the people would exercise their judgment.

Davies's description of the people's solid happiness under George II allowed him to take the logical step toward a *right* of happiness. George II had known "the generous, disinterested, god-like pleasure of making multitudes happy." The colonies by enjoying his success, "a long and delightful experience" in a "happy reign" of thirty-four years, also had grown accustomed to it. Again and again, Davies emphasized the happiness of the people. "Happy!" he warbled, "thrice happy, to live under a reign so gentle and auspicious!" Obviously, no one could raise a circumstance of life so intensely without contemplation of the opposite condition. What if the people were *not* happy? Repeating the many virtues that George III would have to live up to in George II, Davies raised new worries that would soon become a refrain in America. There was always the danger of "evil counsellors" and "mischievous influence." He closed on an ominous note that would be long remembered. "We can be certain," Davies warned, "of almost nothing but what is past." The gloom in this cautionary note brought the subject of liberty to the edge of a curious inversion. The pursuit of happiness as a positive right would prove most immediately useful to experts on unhappiness.[38]

Gad Hitchcock, pastor of Pembroke Church in Boston, would be that expert in 1774 when he preached what he called his "moving ser-

---

38. Samuel Davies, *On the Death of His Late Majesty, King George II*, in *Religion*, 17–23. For the development of the assumption of happiness into a full-blown *right* to happiness by 1768, see Daniel Shute, *An Election Sermon* [1768], in Charles S. Hyneman and Donald S. Lutz, eds., *American Political Writing During the Founding Era, 1760–1805*, 2 vols. (Indianapolis: Liberty Fund, 1983), 1:109–36 (hereafter cited as *American Political Writing*). In this Congregationalist minister's version, happiness is "the end of creation" and the central feature of God's plan. Happiness as a *British* right merely confirmed a divine plan already in existence. "The happiness of THIS PEOPLE in the enjoyment of their natural rights and privileges under providence is provided for by their being a part of the *British* empire, by which they are intitled to all the privileges of that happy constitution; and also by the full and ample recognition of these privileges to them by character" (1:110, 131).

mon." The performance was moving because his nominal host, General Thomas Gage, the new military governor of Massachusetts, stalked out in the middle of it with retinue in tow. Hitchcock copied other ministers by carefully cloaking himself in the veil of Scripture. His text came from Proverbs 29:2: "When the righteous are in authority, the people rejoice: but when the wicked beareth rule, the people mourn." In a performance filled with suspense, Hitchcock steadfastly clung to the sorrows of his people, leaving to his audience the implied conclusion of evil rulers. "The people mourn!" he repeated over and over again in tones of drawn out sadness. "It is, however, certain that the people mourn!"[39] The adroitness in this strategy lay in the impossibility of a response. If the people were the best judges of their own happiness and if the people were *supposed* to be happy and they were *not* happy, who but their leaders could be at fault? Unhappiness became its own sufficient indictment.

The pursuit of happiness as part of liberty had many logical philosophical sources, but Christian theology offered the prospect of something more, *complete* happiness. Its radical Protestant variants in colonial America added both the certitude of typological verification (biblical Scripture carried into contemporary historical parallels) and millennialism (the conviction that God's plan included a thousand-year reign of happiness on earth). Put another way, religion in America knew what to do with happiness as a realizable social goal. The relevant biblical quotation that appeared everywhere on Revolutionary lips came from the fourth chapter of the book of Micah. The passage in question began with a still acclaimed notion of peace ("They shall beat their swords into plowshares"), but the emphasis in eighteenth-century understandings fell upon the personal happiness that would result therefrom: "They shall sit every man under his vine and his fig tree; and none shall make *them* afraid; for the mouth of the Lord of hosts hath spoken *it*."[40]

39. Gad Hitchcock, *An Election Sermon* [1774], in *American Political Writing*, 1:281–304.

40. The biblical phrase from the book of Micah appears over and over again as a standard formulation in the period. For just a few of the more prominent uses, see John Dickinson, "Letter V," in *Letters from a Farmer in Pennsylvania* [1768], in Forrest McDonald, ed., *Empire and Nation: Letters from a Farmer in Pennsylvania,*

The passage offers an interesting example of the dialectic of liberty at work in American understandings. The farmer secure on his own land conflated Lockean, common law, and religious notions. Inasmuch as security through the right of property appealed to every commonwealth theory of government and law, the passage welcomed recognition on both sides of the Atlantic.[41] That said, a more expansive reading necessarily put the emphasis in the quotation squarely on "every man," not just the landowner, and this more general vision of propertied ease played better in boundless America where the religious context of the passage also added to that significance. The figure who sat under his own vine and fig tree was important because he was *unafraid.* He had achieved *tranquillity.* Montesquieu gave the popularly cited legal version of the definition in *The Spirit of the Laws.* "The political liberty of the subject," he wrote, "is a tranquillity of mind arising from the opinion each person has of his safety."[42] There was, nonetheless, a paradox in the definition that only a religious perspective could solve. In a legal or political frame of reference, the notion of tranquillity vied directly with a contrary impulse, the constant need for vigilance. How could anyone be tranquil in the enjoyment of liberty while remaining ever alert against the many dangers that threatened?

Although a religious temperament also required eternal vigilance, the focus of attention involved more manageable sources and a different mechanism of control. The secular lover of liberty worried about a plethora of external pressures on liberty—tyranny, faction, luxury,

---

John Dickinson, and Letters from the Federal Farmer, Richard Henry Lee (Indianapolis: Liberty Fund, 1999), 29; George Washington to the Hebrew Congregation in Newport [August] 1790, in W. B. Allen, ed., *George Washington, A Collection* (Indianapolis: Liberty Fund, 1988), 548; Paul F. Boller, Jr., "George Washington and Religious Liberty," *William and Mary Quarterly,* 3d ser., 17 (October 1960): 486; and Silas Downer, *A Discourse on the Dedication of the Tree of Liberty* [1768], in *American Political Writing,* 1:98.

41. Scholarly debates over how important Locke's actual writings were to American understandings seem pointless in the light of general dissemination of those ideas through newspaper and other popular accounts, but for a recent summary of these debates, see *Language,* 24–27.

42. *Spirit,* 151 [bk. 11, no. 6]. Perhaps the best known of many uses of the same definition in the American Revolution was that of the Continental Congress in its *Appeal to the Inhabitants of Quebec* in 1774, in *American Political Writing,* 1:235–36.

the ignorant multitude, minority interests, Indian attack, imbalance in government, economic failure, foreign invasion, civil war, incompetent leadership, dissident groups, individual traitors, and so on. The list was endless and largely beyond the observer's control. True, the enlightened observer could turn embattled participant, but then all sense of ease and tranquillity would be lost. By way of contrast, a religious temperament lumped every difficulty into one comprehensive category: *sin*.[43] The category itself was large but ideologically under control. The first directive against sin asked each person to look within; only then did one reach for the external world and blame it for one's troubles. The message from the pulpit was simple. Solve the inner problem of sin and everything would follow in combinations of the godly people of America. In the crisis of the Revolution, minister after minister intoned with the tranquillity of conviction, "If God be for us, who can be against us?"[44]

In America the new-found biblical man who sat unafraid under his own vine and fig tree became a comprehensive symbol of liberty because "God hath spoken it." Here again, civil or legal and spiritual liberty were inseparable but with primacy given to a religious frame of reference. Nathaniel Niles, minister and lawyer, displayed just how this conflated conception of liberty would operate in a crisis with *Two*

43. The two most famous Revolutionary sermons of 1776, by Samuel West and Samuel Sherwood, both adopted this tactic. "Our cause is so just and good that nothing can prevent us but only our sins," cried West. Pointing to "awful backslidings and declensions in this land" as the real cause of the Revolution, Sherwood was confident that "a godly remnant" could be united to sustain God's covenant with America and prevent it from being "given up to desolation and ruin." See, Samuel West, *A Sermon Preached Before the Honorable Council, and the Honorable House of Representatives of the Colony of the Massachusetts Bay, May 29th, 1776*, in *Religion*, 146, and Samuel Sherwood, *The Church's Flight into the Wilderness: An Address on the Times* [1776], in Sandoz, *Political Sermons of the American Founding Era*, 523–25.

44. For good examples of ministerial exploitation of the phrase, see Samuel Langdon, *Government Corrupted by Vice, and Recovered by Righteousness, A Sermon Preached Before the Honorable Congress of the Colony of the Massachusetts-Bay in New England . . . the 31st Day of May, 1775*, and David Jones, *Defensive War in a Just Cause* SINLESS, *A Sermon Preached on the Day of the Continental Fast* [1775], *Religion*, 141, 146.

Discourses on Liberty, a sermon delivered in the North Church of New-buryport, Massachusetts, just after the British closed Boston Harbor in 1774. Liberty was the highest earthly good, but Niles substantiated the claim by proving that civil liberty depended on spiritual liberty: "The former without the latter, is but a body without a soul." Because the civil and spiritual elements were inseparable and the blessings of heaven, liberty was a duty as well as a right: "It is a loan of heaven, for which we must account with the great God." The individual Christian was to unite with the whole in a cosmic vision of America's struggle with England. Niles's constitutive metaphor for union made the individual a drop in the river of God. "The smallest particles have their influence," he observed. God would take care of the whole if each of his servants exercised a part in proper godliness. If you accepted God, then it was spiritual liberty that united America.[45]

It is almost impossible to exaggerate the confidence with which the religious view of liberty celebrated itself, galvanized colonial Americans, and clarified each stage of America's uncertain struggle with England. The vast majority involved in that struggle still believed that cosmic forces dictated the nature and degree of civic well-being. Specific historical events contained an equally specific spiritual significance—all pointing in Revolutionary rhetoric toward the spread of liberty. "This was from God," ran a typical explanation from the pulpit when Parliament repealed the Stamp Act, "that God who made us free, who gave us our birth-right *liberty.*"[46] Ministers regularly bolstered their anxious flocks with declarations that only authentic religion could make a citizen bold or a soldier brave; only such a person would grasp the true nature of liberty.[47] Similar assumptions held sway in both the rank and the file of the Revolutionary Army.[48]

45. Nathaniel Niles, *Two Discourses on Liberty,* in *American Political Writing,* 1:258–59, 270–74.

46. Joseph Emerson, *A Thanksgiving-Sermon Preach'd at Pepperrell, July 24, 1766 . . . On Account of the Repeal of the Stamp-Act,* in *Religion,* 89–90.

47. For examples, see Samuel West, *On the Right to Rebel Against Governors* [1776], and Simeon Howard, *A Sermon Preached to the Ancient and Honorable Artillery Company in Boston* [1773], in *American Political Writing,* 1:432, 200.

48. Soldiers painted the word "liberty" with the number of their regiment

Above all, the religious voices in America could boast a comprehensible arrangement of liberty. God's plan of happiness had been designed specifically for godly communities, and that plan could be known.[49] Knowing it and then speaking it was the best assurance of communal happiness in the very near future. Revivalist Joseph Bellamy's sermon on the coming millennium established a trend of thought for thinking about the future. It was so immensely popular in the 1760s and after because, in resorting to biblical parallels, it guaranteed the completion of God's plan of happiness despite the uncertainties of history. The Bible clarified the history to come when read with proper expertise before a believing community. Bellamy carefully charted the prophecies, and they made it "perfectly rational to conclude, that all things are only preparatory, as an introduction to the glorious day."[50]

What happened to this confidence and control of American destiny as seen through a religious conception of liberty and collective happiness? After the Revolution, ministers maintained the spiritual-keeping of their congregations, but they lost the capacity to represent the gathered community in political thought. Benjamin Colman's crumbling pillars in *Government the Pillar of the Earth* back in 1730 gave a clue as to what would occur. The confidence of the ministry to speak on civil affairs came from a premise that Colman rendered there with

---

on their bullet boxes. When Ethan Allen, elected leader of the Green Mountain Boys of New Hampshire, formally demanded the surrender of Fort Ticonderoga of its British commander in 1775, he did so "in the name of the Great Jehovah and the Continental Congress." Common soldiers shaped their own accounts of events with the words "Remember that it is ye hand of God," and "I trust that All-wise being who has protected me will still protect me." The battle slogan "The Lord is on our side" was a frequent one, and providence was invariably the source "for the many battles we have won." See, George F. Scheer and Hugh F. Rankin, eds., *Rebels and Redcoats: The American Revolution Through the Eyes of Those Who Fought and Lived It* (New York: World Publishing Co., 1957), 66, 51, 40, 339, 428, 433.

49. Shute, *An Election Sermon* [1768], in *American Political Writing*, 1:109–12.

50. Joseph Bellamy, *The Millennium* [1758], in Alan Heimert and Perry Miller, eds., *The Great Awakening: Documents Illustrating the Crisis and Its Consequences* (Indianapolis: Bobbs-Merrill, 1967), 609–10, 620–23.

great precision. "As government is the pillar of the earth," he preached then, "so religion is the pillar of government."[51] Americans stopped believing that statement in quite the same way as they went about the formation of republican institutions. Religion remained a concern and for many a central concern, but it was no longer the pillar, no longer the explanatory tool, no longer the primal articulator of liberty. Ministers had ceased to be the guardians of social well-being. The keeping of liberty, once a joint responsibility, had passed rather suddenly to the legal mind in America. Something, however, had been lost in the process, and at crucial moments, communal sense of that loss would lead to resurgence in the religious side of the dialectic. Religion spoke to the people in a way that law never can. For while the law possesses many virtues, it smells of the lamp, of calculation and reason, of an elitest response; none of these elements ever tells the wistfully searching subject much about happiness.[52]

IV

What difference did passage to a more secular discourse on liberty really make? Legal rhetoric had its own place in colonial oppositional politics, and each of the freedoms just noted in religious discourse—freedom of religion, freedom of speech, the emerging ideal of equality, even the pursuit of happiness—were entrenched in careful legal argument well before the Revolution. Moreover, lawyers quickly inscribed each liberty in the republican framework. The seventeen state constitutions written during the Revolution along with the Articles of Confederation, the Northwest Ordinance of 1787, and the Federal Constitution from the same year represented the greatest collective intellectual accomplishment of the age and an achievement in lawmaking that has not been surpassed by any other.[53] The question,

51. Colman, *Government the Pillar of the Earth*, 22.

52. For the best-known discussion of distrust of the law in just these terms, see John Hart Ely, *Democracy and Distrust: A Theory of Judicial Review* (Cambridge: Harvard University Press, 1980), 56–59.

53. See, Ferguson, "The Literature of Public Documents," in *The American Enlightenment 1750–1820*, 124–49. Between 1776 and 1787 every state except Rhode Island and Connecticut wrote and adopted a new constitution, and a number of states wrote more than one.

then, remains a serious one. What, if anything, has been lost to discussions of liberty by removing religious voices from civic discourse?

Religion and law were competing frames of reference in the eighteenth century because they thought very differently about common conceptions of authority and legitimacy. If religion demanded a higher faith and the truth of revelation, the law placed its own narrower faith in human artifice and the power of argument. Religion, particularly in its revivalist mode, touched the affections and called on heaven; law insisted on reason and sought answers in human behavior. Religion assumed divine protection; law protected the rights of those who held proper standing within its rules and who knew how to complain when those rights were infringed. Religion ordered the cosmos; law decided individual cases in dispute. Religion sought all-or-nothing answers; the watchword in every legal answer was balance. Religion searched for the spirit in the word; law classified words for use. These and other distinctions can be exaggerated, but even as approximations they led eighteenth-century proponents of each framework to regard civil liberty in different ways.

Although eighteenth-century law agreed with religion in making liberty an absolute value, it approached the subject in more instrumental ways. Civil liberty and social happiness in a legal understanding depended less on abstractions like virtue and righteousness and more on a well-made constitution and a proper set of laws.[54] The degree of civil liberty to be sought became, in consequence, less a cosmic aspiration and more a calculation of what a culture could bear to receive within its available conformities and conventions. Liberty could thrive in a legal understanding only in keeping with existing communal customs.[55] Philosophically, the legal notion of civil liberty rested on a cau-

54. In the "Preface" to the most complete and influential theory of constitutionalism of the day, his three-volumed master work, *Defence of the Constitutions of the United States of America* [1787–88], John Adams was quite certain that a proper constitution created virtue rather than virtue creating a proper constitution. *Works*, 4:284–87, 292–94, 298.

55. In the most pointed version of the premise, Montesquieu wrote "*It is necessary People's Minds should be prepared for the Reception of the best Laws*" and also "Liberty itself has appeared intolerable to those nations who have not been accustomed to it." *Spirit*, 292 [bk. 19, sect. 2].

tious, virtually redundant foundation. Liberty existed where it could be tolerated; it depended on a rule of law, which is to say on the degree to which ruler and ruled agreed to be governed.[56]

All of these tactical considerations meant in practical terms that the law recognized civil liberty through a strict enumeration of values in context, and the context in colonial America was English common law. As Englishmen, eighteenth-century Americans claimed the right to life, the right of habeas corpus, the right of free speech, the right to a public trial before a jury of one's peers, the right of property, and the related protections of the British constitution. They also understood that these rights extended somewhat vaguely to a larger right to resist oppression. But this last right remained abstract, and it was further qualified by uncertainty over the meaning and import of the term oppression and by the assumption that the British constitution provided the perfect vehicle of liberty for those subjects fortunate enough to fall under its sway.[57] Oppression was what would now be called a float-

---

56. E. P. Thompson, "The Rule of Law," in *Whigs and Hunters: The Origin of the Black Acts* (New York: Random House, 1975), 258–69. Two of the most important characteristics that Thompson identifies here as crucial to the agreement that makes a rule of law possible are, first, a level of imbrication of law within the basis of productive relations to the point where the language of law is unavoidable to all concerned in their actions and thoughts, thereby providing an underlying basis in language for agreement to take place between ruler and ruled, and second, a structure of accessibility to legal remedies for the ruled so that mechanisms of agreement can be created out of a rhetoric that protects nonrulers.

57. The clearest justification for resisting oppression in eighteenth-century Anglo-American culture comes from the one nonlawyer to contribute greatly to an English concept of law, John Locke, though even here, at the end of *The Second Treatise of Government* [1689], matters are not all that clear. Locke sharply qualifies resistance and is unusually tentative in his conclusions. Moreover, he achieves his level of resistance by deliberately eschewing all argument based on English common law and the ancient constitution, an extraordinary absence in the political theory of the times. The basis of Locke's claim begins in natural law: "*Self-defense is a part of the Law of Nature; nor can it be denied the Community, even against the King himself.*" But when does self-defense allow rebellion? Locke is unsure. "[H]ow they [the people] will be hindered from resisting illegal force, used against them, I cannot tell," he writes in addressing this delicate subject. He believes that the people should *not* "mutiny or murmur" even after "*Great mistakes* in the ruling part, many wrong and inconvenient Laws, and all the *slips* of humane

ing signifier in the legal rhetoric of the eighteenth century. The point on the continuum between unwarranted intrusion, which called for redress, and oppression, which might justify resistance, could be identified in very different ways. In the English-speaking world of the eighteenth century, it might also be treason to talk too much about the distinction or to define the line too finely. The American Sons of Liberty would try to handle the problem by removing all middle ground between the polarities of liberty and slavery in justifying their rebellion.[58] Here, of course, was the answer to Samuel Johnson's celebrated jibe: "how is it that we hear the loudest yelps for liberty among the drivers of negroes?"[59]

The two greatest discursive productions of the legal mind in America during the Revolutionary period were John Dickinson's *Letters from a Farmer in Pennsylvania* and the collaboration of Alexander Hamilton, James Madison, and John Jay in *The Federalist*.[60] The two-pamphlet

---

frailty." Only "a long train of Abuses," language repeated in the American Declaration of Independence, should rouse them. Even then, Locke distinguishes resistance from rebellion and prefers to speak in circumlocutions about "dissolution of government" and "Cases, whereby a King may Un-king himself." In such a case, "how to *strike with Reverence,* will need some Skill to make intelligible." Over all, Locke proclaims one greater certainty. "This I am sure, whoever, either Ruler or Subject, by force goes about to invade the Rights of either Prince or People, and lays the foundation for *overturning* the Constitution and Frame of *any Just Government* is guilty of the greatest Crime, I think, a Man is capable of, being to answer for all those mischiefs of Blood, Rapine, and Desolation, which the breaking to pieces of Governments bring on a Countrey." John Locke, *Two Treatises of Government,* student ed., ed. Peter Laslett (Cambridge: Cambridge University Press, 1988), 405, 418–22. See, as well, Peter Laslett's introduction (ibid., 76–79) in which he discusses Locke's "extraordinary" refusal to argue through common law and his "instinct in leaving the whole historical and constitutional controversy on one side."

58. For the best summary of American legal understandings and their relation to the concept of liberty, see *Concept,* 1–84.

59. Samuel Johnson, *Taxation No Tyranny: An Answer to the Resolutions and Address of the American Congress* [1775], in Donald J. Green, ed., *Political Writings,* vol. 10 of *The Yale Edition of the Works of Samuel Johnson* (New Haven: Yale University Press, 1977), 454.

60. The claim of discursive preeminence for *Letters from a Farmer in Pennsylvania* and *The Federalist* can be justified in three ways. First, these writings were easily

series—twelve letters by Dickinson in 1767 and 1768 and eighty-five by Hamilton, Madison, and Jay in 1787 and 1788—illustrated the propositions noted above, but they also did more. Written at the beginning and the end of the Revolutionary period, they reflected the problems and the continuities of American legal attitudes toward liberty. As Dickinson's letters awakened the colonies to a qualified but sustained spirit of resistance, so *The Federalist* formalized the final accomplishment of republican formations in the ratification fight over the Federal Constitution. Dickinson, though unwillingly, brought Americans to the edge of rebellion; *The Federalist,* quite willingly, capped the Revolution in the name of a new order.[61] Together, they were central in placing legal restraints on the concept of liberty in contradistinction to the more open-ended avowals of religious thought.

Dickinson was "the penman of the Revolution," centrally involved in every major formal intercolonial document of law from 1765 to 1787 (including the Congressional Resolution against the Stamp Act in 1765, the Declaration of Independence, the Articles of Confederation, and the Federal Constitution). Nevertheless, he was known best in the eighteenth century for *Letters from a Farmer in Pennsylvania.* His *Letters* galvanized American opposition against "taxation without representation" as no other writing. The first of many American pamphleteers to assume an agrarian guise, Dickinson wielded the persona with such success that he was known thereafter as "The Farmer," though in life he was a dynamic lawyer and leading cosmopolite in Philadelphia.[62]

---

the most influential examples of pamphleteering by lawyers in context. Second, they were the longest, best organized, and most carefully constructed pamphlets by lawyers (or any other American writer) of the day. Third, Dickinson and Jay were generally acknowledged to be of the two or three best-educated lawyers in America as they wrote. In turn, Alexander Hamilton was a very successful practitioner of law in New York in the 1780s, and *The Federalist* was largely his production both in organization and in number of contributions. James Madison, who alone of the four never practiced law, can still be included in the category as a leading legal theoretician and lawgiver in the Federal Convention of 1787.

61. For a full account of the calculation of conservatizing elements in capping the Revolution, see Gordon Wood, *The Radicalism of the American Revolution* (New York: Alfred A. Knopf, 1992).

62. For the identification of Dickinson as "the penman of the Revolution," for the immediate influence and continuing importance of *Letters from a Farmer*

Letters offered the best technical legal explanation of the colonial right to resist taxation imposed by British authority. Dickinson could accurately boast that he possessed "a greater knowledge in history, and the laws and constitution of my country than is generally attained by men of my class."[63] He then confirmed it by festooning his arguments with detailed footnotes from acts of Parliament and leading authorities in English and continental law. But this legal erudition, based on four years of study at the Middle Temple in London, would prove a straitjacket as well as a resource on the subject of liberty.

Dickinson's commitment to liberty came through the British constitution and common law, and that commitment restricted him to a theory of resistance *within* the comprehension of the British Empire. Although every letter from the Farmer summoned Americans to resist British encroachments, he insisted first, that "the cause of *liberty* is a cause of too much dignity to be sullied by turbulence and tumult" (No. 3, 17), and second, that resistance by force could be justified only when "the people are FULLY CONVINCED that any further submission will be destructive to their happiness" (No. 3, 18). Even then, Dickinson refused to contemplate formal rupture between England and her colonies: "We are as much dependent on *Great Britain,* as a perfectly free people can be on another" (No. 2, 8). "Where shall we find another *Britain* to supply our loss?" he asked, deploring the possibility of sepa-

---

in Pennsylvania, and for Dickinson's clever manipulation of the persona of the simple farmer even though in real life he was one of the wealthiest men in Pennsylvania and an influential gentleman-lawyer with close connections to the commercial and political circles of Philadelphia, see Carl F. Kaestle, "The Public Reaction to John Dickinson's *Farmer's Letters," Proceedings of the American Antiquarian Society* 78 (1969): 323–59; Pierre Marambaud, "Dickinson's *Letters from a Farmer in Pennsylvania* as Political Discourse: Ideology, Imagery, and Rhetoric," *Early American Literature* 12 (1977): 63–72; and Stephen H. Browne, "The Pastoral Voice in John Dickinson's First *Letter from a Farmer in Pennsylvania," Quarterly Journal of Speech* 76 (February 1990): 46–56.

63. John Dickinson, "Letter No. 1," *Letters from a Farmer in Pennsylvania to the Inhabitants of the British Colonies* [1767–68], in Forrest McDonald, *Empire and Nation: Letters from a Farmer in Pennsylvania and Letters from the Federal Farmer,* No. 1, 3. All further references to *Letters from a Farmer in Pennsylvania* in the text will be to this readily available edition and, as above, will be identified first by letter number and then page number in this edition.

ration. "Torn from the body, to which we are united by religion, liberty, laws, affections, relation, language, and commerce, we must bleed at every vein." For Dickinson, only "the constitutional modes of obtaining relief" applied (No. 3, 19–20). "Let us behave," he concluded, "like dutiful children, who have received unmerited blows from a beloved parent" (No. 3, 20).

The Farmer's reliance upon Anglo-American law held him to a balance that he realized might become impossible. He pleaded for a spirit in which "it will be impossible to determine whether an *American's* character is most distinguishable for his loyalty to his Sovereign, his duty to his mother country, his love of freedom, or his affection for his native soil" (No. 3, 18). Liberty was Dickinson's overriding concern, but the exercise of freedom was only one of a number of variables to be factored into an equation. Later, this balancing act would help to prepare early republicans for the concept of dual sovereignty; in the moment, circumstance and legal theory were already pushing Dickinson and his readers off the intellectual tightrope that he had designed so carefully. As English commentators like Samuel Johnson would point out, the rights of Englishmen came with legal obligations: the assertion of the former included accountability to the latter. "It seems to follow by consequence not easily avoided," wrote Johnson, "that [our colonies] are subject to English government, and chargable by English taxation." By resorting to English rights and English law to support their right to object, the colonies remained under those laws and could not pick and choose between them. In Johnson's withering summary, "These lords of themselves, these kings of *Me*, these demigods of independence, sink down to colonists, governed by a charter."[64]

Acceptance of English law left Dickinson with another problem. Over and over, *Letters from a Farmer in Pennsylvania* posed a leading question to which there was no answer. Where was colonial unity when it was most needed (No. 2, 14; No. 4, 24–25; No. 6, 36; No. 8, 46–47; No. 10, 65–67; No. 11, 77)? Dickinson complained that the colonies in 1767 were not opposing Parliament's newest incursions against colonial liberties with anything like the unified zeal that led them to thwart

64. Samuel Johnson, *Taxation No Tyranny*, in Green, ed., *Political Writings*, 424–25, 429.

the Stamp Act just two years before, and this was true even though the new Townshend Act of 1767 (with its duties on glass, paper, and other imports) and the equally new Declaratory Act (insisting on Parliamentary supremacy over the colonies in all matters) were as dangerous to American liberties as the Stamp Act had been.[65] He feared that "*We have already forgot* the *reasons* that urged us with unexampled unanimity, to exert ourselves two years ago*" (No. 12, 81). Americans needed to recover what had been lost. They had to realize anew that their liberty could only be secured through unified opposition (No. 10, 67–68).

Not surprisingly, communal unity proved much harder for Dickinson to project than it was for reformist ministers, who orchestrated continental harmony through their vision of a religious liberty peculiar to the new world. For the Farmer, the politically unified opposition to the Stamp Act had been "unexampled." Colonial solidarity of any kind was a rarity and hardly the norm in a British Empire where colonies dealt with the mother country far more frequently than with each other. Dickinson's stress upon chartered membership in that Empire only underlined the issue. The British constitution secured English liberties everywhere in the Empire but *through* Britain, *through* British government. Dickinson could call for colonial unity all he wanted, but his own theories forced him to admit "These colonies are dependent on *Great-Britain*" and "[Britain] has a legal power to make laws for preserving that dependence." He also accepted that Parliament possessed the legal right and the political duty "to preserve [colonial] dependence, and the connection of the whole in good order" (No. 5, 27–28).

An orientation in common law gave strength to legal resistance but undermined more radical assertions of liberty. A telling simile exposed Dickinson's predicament. "The *legal authority* of *Great Britain*," he wrote

65. Parliament had suspended the New York Assembly's legislative powers as of October 1, 1767, because of New York's refusal to supply British troops in accordance with the provisions of the Quartering Act. The Townshend Acts of 1767 in response to repeal of the Stamp Act placed new duties on paper, glass, and other commodities as they were exported to the colonies. The Parliamentary Declaratory Act of the same year claimed the power of Parliament to bind the American colonies in all cases whatsoever. *Letters from a Farmer in Pennsylvania* sought chiefly to prove that these new impositions were as bad or even worse than the Stamp Act.

at the end of *Letters from a Farmer in Pennsylvania,* "may indeed lay hard restrictions upon us; but like the spear of *Telephus,* it will cure as well as wound" (No. 12, 81).[66] Dickinson's legal cures contained such a wound. The common law revealed the nature of Parliamentary abuse, but it could not be used to challenge the supremacy of British authority under the constitution.

The dilemma for the colonial legal mind in the act of resistance can best be seen in the controlling legal text of the era, a text that had a phenomenal impact on American culture generally.[67] William Blackstone's *Commentaries on the Laws of England* (1765–69) unified law, nation, and history around a proposition taken from Montesquieu's *Spirit of the Laws,* a source that doubled the credibility of the basic claim in Anglo-American legal circles. In Blackstone's words, "A learned French authority [Montesquieu] . . . hath not scrupled to profess, even in the very bosom of his native country, that the English is the only nation in the world, where political or civil liberty is the direct end of its constitution." All of English history in Blackstone's view had to be read as the recovery of ancient liberties and rights through the evolution of a proper constitution that had achieved final perfection in the Glorious Revolution of 1688. That constitution had achieved permanence—"ESTO PERPETUA!"—because it *was* proper and perfect for all concerned. No matter how dire the problem, every grievance could be resolved by constitutional remedy. "The vigour of our free consti-

66. In classical mythology, Telephus can only be healed by the rust of the spear that wounded him. *The Oxford Classical Dictionary,* 3d ed. (Oxford: Oxford University Press, 1996), 1480.

67. Daniel J. Boorstin argues that William Blackstone's *Commentaries on the Laws of England* ranks second only to the Bible as a literary and intellectual influence on the history of American institutions. See Boorstin, "Preface to the Beacon Press Edition," in *The Mysterious Science of the Law: An Essay on Blackstone's Commentaries Showing How Blackstone . . . Made of the Law at Once a Conservative and a Mysterious Science* (Boston: Beacon Press, 1958). For the specific but seminal influence of Blackstone on colonial and early republican notions of authority and therefore of liberty, see Bernard Bailyn, *The Ideological Origins of the American Revolution* (Cambridge: Harvard University Press, 1967), 200–201, and Gordon Wood, *The Creation of the American Republic, 1776–1787* (1969; New York: Norton Library, 1972), 10, 260–64, 350–54, 599.

tution," Blackstone explained, "has always delivered the nation from these embarrassments [attacks on liberty], and as soon as the convulsions consequent on the struggle have been over, the balance of our rights and liberties has settled to its proper level."[68] Always? The common law tied everyone to its common solution: remonstrance, yes; rebellion, no.[69]

Lawyers more radical than Dickinson worked to solve this legal dilemma. As resistance mounted, they found it expedient to tie English rights to natural rights, and they were helped by the fact that natural law functioned as a parallel source of liberty in the eighteenth century, rendering the connection to English liberties plausible.[70] James Otis, the lawyer whom John Adams termed "the earliest and the prin-

68. William Blackstone, *Commentaries on the Laws of England* [1765–69], facsimile of the first edition, 4 vols. (1765–69; Chicago: University of Chicago Press, 1979), 1:140–41, 123 (hereafter cited as *Commentaries*). In the quotation, Blackstone refers to book 11 ("Of the Laws Which Establish Political Liberty with Regard to the Constitution") of Montesquieu's *The Spirit of the Laws*. For Blackstone's optimistic overview of English history paraphrased in the text see "Chapter the Thirty Third: Of the Rise, Progress, and Gradual Improvements, of the Laws of England," *Commentaries*, 4:400–436.

69. In keeping with this disregard for rebellion, Blackstone's summary of the progress of English common law dismisses the Puritan Revolution in a single sentence as the work of "insolent and ungovernable" popular leaders "joining with a set of military hypocrites and enthusiastics" in "the murder of their sovereign." Oliver Cromwell's revolutionary regime is the one episode to receive no treatment in Blackstone's four volumes on the annals of English law: "I pass by the crude and abortive schemes for amending the laws in the times of confusion which followed." Even the so-called Glorious Revolution of 1688 is a dubious precedent for Blackstone. Writing of "the law of redress against public oppression," Blackstone tepidly acknowledges the "abdication" of James II and "new settlement of the crown" on William of Orange, but James II's decision to "withdraw himself out of the kingdom" is a crucial ingredient in Blackstone's acceptance of the situation, and he adds "it is not for us to say" what legitimates such action then or in a future situation. Uncomfortable with the whole idea of popular redress, Blackstone drops the subject with the words "since law and history are silent, it becomes us to be silent too." Ibid., 4:431; 1:238.

70. See *Concept*, 25–28; also, Daniel T. Rogers, "Natural Rights," in *Contested Truths: Keywords in American Politics Since Independence* (New York: Basic Books, 1987), 45–66.

cipal founder" of the Revolution, showed the way in *The Rights of the British Colonies Asserted* (1764).[71] Otis realized that a guarantee of rights through the colonial charters would always remain unstable. Parliament could revoke the charters of colonial rights whenever it wished to do so; that was what Parliamentary supremacy meant. It could not, however, touch English rights deemed natural, and Otis used the distinction to declare "Every British subject born on the continent of America or in any other of the British dominions is by the law of God and nature, by the common law, and by act of Parliament (exclusive of all charters from the crown) entitled to all the natural, essential, inherent, and inseparable rights of our fellow subjects in Great Britain."[72]

Much of the subsequent success of Revolutionary rhetoric depended on how well lawyers manipulated Otis's grab bag of legal authorities on liberty. There were legal rights, they began to insist, that didn't need to be written out. As the Massachusetts Stamp Act Resolves argued in 1765, these rights were "founded in the Law of God and Nature," and they were "the common Rights of Mankind."[73] Matters came to a head in 1774 when Congress debated whether to rely on natural law as well as British law in its responses to the Crown, and John Adams, who often saw farther than others in the 1770s, came up with the winning argument. Asked "whether we should recur to the law of nature, as well as to the British constitution," Adams announced himself "very strenuous for retaining and insisting on it, as a resource to which We might be driven by Parliament much sooner than We were aware."[74] The balance would tilt toward natural law and away from

71. John Adams to William Tudor, June 1, 1818, *Works,* 10:317.

72. James Otis, *The Rights of the British Colonies Asserted and Proved* [1764], in Bernard Bailyn, ed., *Pamphlets of the American Revolution, 1750–1776* (Cambridge: Harvard University Press, 1965), 426, 442–44. For a parallel interpretation of this pamphlet, see Robert H. Webking, "James Otis," in *The American Revolution and the Politics of Liberty* (Baton Rouge: Louisiana State University Press, 1988), 16, 25.

73. Quoted from Edmund S. Morgan, ed., *Prologue to Revolution: Sources and Documents on the Stamp Act* (Chapel Hill: University of North Carolina Press, 1959), 56.

74. John Adams, Diary, 8 September 1774, and Autobiography, in L. C. Butterfield, ed., *Diary and Autobiography of John Adams,* 4 vols. (Cambridge: Harvard University Press, 1961), 2:128–30, 3:309.

British rights in the Revolution. But while Adams and other Revolutionary lawyers raised natural law in defense of liberty at each turn in the contest, every use carried them back to a rival frame of reference. Arguments based on natural law turned in the end on a religious conception of liberty and that conception, based on the order of the universe rather than on contextual exposition, would force lawyers to be more open-ended and vague about liberty and claims of rights than the legal mind could long accept with comfort.[75]

To the extent that a benevolent natural world was essential to the concept of inalienable or inherent liberty, it depended on the presence of a design antecedent to human society. Somewhere, somehow, there had to be an earlier force in the universe that sustained natural rights for those rights to have universal validity beyond a British frame of reference. There was, in fact, no real alternative for an eighteenth-century American who wanted to sustain challenges to British authority. If the universal order proved to be arbitrary in its treatment of individual human beings, then who could argue against the presence of arbitrary authority in England or, more particularly, against the exercise of that authority elsewhere? The rights of Englishmen in America meant so much more if the British sovereign who professed to rule by divine law was concurrently bound by God's will in a way for anyone to observe through the design of nature. Accordingly, ministers confirmed the design of nature as part of God's plan, while lawyers made it visible and practical with the claim that natural law constrained civil law. The Reverend Samuel West, among others, affirmed that the law of nature prevented "anything that is immoral, or contrary to the will of God, and injurious to their fellow-creatures." Natural law remained as "unchangeable as the Deity himself, being a transcript of his moral perfections."[76] For James Otis, who thought "*A lawyer ought never to be without a volume of natural or public law, or moral philosophy, on his table or in his pocket,*" the same hold of natural law over human action in society opened an argument that many would use. Since government had "an

75. In eighteenth-century legal practice, natural law was rarely if ever a viable response to the strictures of positive law in either civil or criminal context. See *Concept*, 23–27.

76. Samuel West, *On the Right to Rebel Against Governors,* in *American Political Writing*, 1:414.

everlasting foundation in the *unchangeable will of God,* the author of nature, whose laws never vary," violations of natural law were illegal. "If such a proceeding is a breach of the law of nature," Otis wrote, "no law of society can make it just."[77]

These arguments, endlessly repeated in a variety of forms, served the Revolution well, but they raised substantial problems in the peace that followed. The right of the people to turn natural law against positive law applied just as easily to political authority under the Articles of Confederation as it had previously under the British Crown. The new rulers in America soon found that open-ended ideas of liberty under natural law were hard to control, and they were especially alarmed by the exaggerated sense of rights that followed therefrom. A reallocation by the legal mind was already evident in 1778, when Theophilus Parsons penned his criticisms of a proposed constitution for Massachusetts. *The Essex Result,* written by a man who would become Chief Justice of the Supreme Judicial Court of Massachusetts and who would be known throughout New England as "the giant of the law," prefigured much that would happen in the Federal Convention nine years later, right down to a first articulation of the theory of checks and balances and the naming of an ideal bicameral legislature as "the house of representatives" and "the senate."[78]

The Essex Result sought to curb domestic unrest, the unfortunate by-product of Revolutionary zeal. Parsons worried about the rise of "The artful demagogue, who to gratify his ambition or avarice, shall, with the gloss of false patriotism, mislead his countrymen." Why were the people in danger of being so easily misled? Caught up in the rhetoric of the times, they tended to exaggerate their own role when "the

77. John Adams quotes Otis here on a lawyer's preferred reading, Adams to Hezekiah Niles, January 14, 1818, *Works,* 10:275. For Otis's own quotation, see Otis, *The Rights of the British Colonies Asserted and Proved,* in Bailyn, *Pamphlets of the American Revolution,* 423, 447. See, as well, *Language,* 100, 117–18.

78. Theophilus Parsons, *The Essex Result* [1778], in *American Political Writing,* 1:494, 510–11. For Parsons's eminence and the epithet that confirmed it, see Theophilus Parsons, Jr., *Memoir of Theophilus Parsons, Chief Justice of the Supreme Judicial Court of Massachusetts; with Notices of Some of His Contemporaries* (Boston: Ticknor and Fields, 1859), 156–57, 166, 206–8.

voice of the people is said to be the voice of God. No man," Parsons observed, "will be so hardy and presumptuous, as to affirm the truth of that proposition in its fullest extent." A "false patriotism" had grown from inflated conceptions of liberty, and the combination was preventing a proper legal balance from emerging in the new order. "The idea of liberty has been held up in so dazzling colours," Parsons complained, "that some of us may not be willing to submit to that subordination necessary in the freest States." In short, the people had lost their proper sense of place under the restraints of wise leadership ("gentlemen of education, fortune, and leisure"). Constitutions and the law were *for* the people but not *by* them. "We are to look further than to the bulk of the people," Parsons wrote, "for the greatest wisdom, firmness, consistency, and perseverance." Direction had to come from above if the laws were to be "wisely and consistently framed," and Parsons was direct about what this meant. A further enumeration of constraints had to regulate civil liberty.[79]

The authors of *The Federalist* agreed with Theophilus Parsons's assumptions in *The Essex Result* and wrote in 1787 to implement them through the ratification of the Federal Constitution. Like Parsons, they roundly condemned "a zeal for liberty more ardent than enlightened."[80] They feared the passions of the people, planned to have those passions "controlled and regulated by the government" (No. 49, 331), deplored the loss of a "spirit of moderation" in public discourse (No. 37, 225), and wanted to establish a new "requisite stability and energy in government" against "the inviolable attention due to liberty" (No. 37, 227). Like Parsons, they found their answers in the proper design

79. *Essex Result,* in *American Political Writing,* 1:486, 490–91.

80. The quotation is from Alexander Hamilton, "The Federalist No. 26," *The Federalist: A Commentary on the Constitution of the United States* (New York: Modern Library, 1937), 26:159, but similar sentiments abound elsewhere in the text. See, for example, "Federalist No. 10" in which James Madison writes, "Liberty is to faction what air is to fire" (No. 10, 55) or Hamilton again in "Federalist No. 1" when he writes that "the noble enthusiasm of liberty is apt to be infected with a spirit of narrow and illiberal distrust" (No. 1, 5). For convenience, all future references to *The Federalist* in the text will be to this edition and will be noted there, as here, first by the number of *The Federalist* paper in which the reference appears and then by page number to the Modern Library edition.

of strong government: "the genius of the whole system; the nature of just and constitutional laws" (No. 57, 373; No. 1, 5).

The intellectual affinities between *The Essex Result* and *The Federalist* flowed from a mutual source, the legal temperament of the period. Alexander Hamilton, James Madison, and John Jay can be distinguished from each other, but they shared this temperament to an extraordinary degree in *The Federalist*. They agreed that a stronger legal union would be necessary to "repress domestic faction and insurrection" (No. 9, 51); also that their legal knowledge had prepared them to design "the more perfect structure" or "proper structure" so definitely needed (No. 9, 48; No. 10, 62). Abstractions like republican virtue, enlightened reason, and natural law were dangerous enthusiasms not to be trusted in the business of forming "a more perfect union" (No. 10, 53–58; No. 49, 329; No. 51, 340).

The Revolution had been a success but mistakes had been made in the aftermath. "Is it not time," Hamilton sneered, "to awake from the deceitful dream of a golden age, and to adopt as a practical maxim for the direction of our political conduct that we, as well as the other inhabitants of the globe, are yet remote from the happy empire of perfect wisdom and perfect virtue?" (No. 6, 33). Madison made it equally clear that anyone who trusted to "reverence for the laws" and "the voice of enlightened reason" as constraints was dreaming of "a nation of philosophers . . . as little to be expected as the philosophical race of kings wished for by Plato" (No. 49, 329). Only a strong government "framed with singular ingenuity and precision" could hope to hold the passions of the people in place (No. 49, 332). "If men were angels," cautioned the ever-practical Publius, or "if angels were to govern men, neither external nor internal controls on government would be necessary." Fortunately or unfortunately, there were no angels in human affairs. "In framing a government which is to be administered by men over men," strict design and meticulous controls were the essential ingredients. A careful balance of "opposite and rival interests" with an even more careful "subordinate distribution of powers" had to supplant "the defect of better motives" (No. 51, 337). Republican lawgivers could not afford to trust to the ideals of the day. They were to remember instead that "the ordinary administration of criminal and civil justice" formed the "great cement of society" (No. 16, 103) and that a government for the people had better be "tolerable to their prejudices" before it could hope to be "best suited to their happiness" (No. 38, 234).

The legal temperament behind *The Federalist* espoused such views with an assurance born of the secular enlightenment in American thought. Hamilton, Madison, and Jay wrote with extraordinary confidence. Faced with the unprecedented prospect of a continental republic, they nonetheless believed that they personally held the important answers to the problem at hand.[81] Indeed, the intellectual quality of their self-assurance is easy to miss because, as men of affairs, they appeared impatient of theoretical assertion and moral abstraction.[82] The combination, an impatience based upon practical certitude, meant two things. First, the authors of *The Federalist* were quick to dismiss their primary intellectual competitors in eighteenth-century thought, the clergy. To be sure, all three authors of *The Federalist* paid lip service to the "Almighty hand" that guided them, but they were adamant in linking religious zeal to faction and in discounting moral and religious arguments as a source of political definition.[83] Second, they were just

81. Each of the writers of *The Federalist* expressed anxieties, but they feared mostly failure, not their inability to understand what needed to be done. Hamilton spoke for all three in the last *The Federalist* paper with an assertion that is implicit everywhere in their prose. "I shall not dissemble," he wrote, "that I feel an entire confidence in the arguments which recommend the proposed system to your adoption, and that I am unable to discern any real force in those by which it has been opposed. I am persuaded that it is the best which our political situation, habits, and opinions will admit, and superior to any the revolution has produced" (No. 85, 570).

82. Publius repeatedly claimed that "Theoretic reasoning, in this as in most cases, must be qualified by the lessons of practice" (No. 43, 284), and he was dismissive of those who had not had that practice (No. 2, 11; No. 37, 231; No. 85, 573). He was particularly impatient in dealing with abstract theoretical assertions against the federal plan (No. 9, 49–50; No. 47, 313–15). Both Hamilton and Madison were quick to challenge anti-Federalist arguments based on "the celebrated Montesquieu."

83. Madison invokes "a finger of that Almighty hand" to explain "the unanimity almost as unprecedented as it was unexpected" in the Federal Convention (No. 37, 231), but he traces faction to religious zeal and rejects the adequacy of

as quick to propose the legal temperament as the best guide of republican destinies. "The Federalist No. 35," ostensibly on taxation, gave several pages to "the man of the learned profession" as the best arbiter and most objective leader in a political dispute (No. 35, 214–15).[84]

In sum, *The Federalist* did more than cap the Revolution by calling for the ratification of the Federal Constitution; it confirmed, once and for all, the dominance of legal over religious explanation in civic discourse. Learned contrivance, practical artifice, and hard-headed institutional planning were the keys to a new mental adventure where those engaged knew they were neither angels nor under the control of angels. Philosophically, in dismissing the relevance of angels, Publius expressed the shift in a single sentence. "But what is government itself," he asked, "but the greatest of all reflections on human nature?" (No. 51, 337). The priorities established here reached well beyond *The Federalist*. What were the implications of calling government "*the greatest of all reflections on human nature*"? By insisting that the best focus of human endeavour belonged to the study of institutions and worldly behavior, Publius carried Americans toward a new balance in the conception of liberty. Henceforth, liberty would appear more in the guise of governmental prescription, enactment, and protection and less forcibly as an assertion of abstract, inalienable right.

V

The priorities of *The Federalist* bring the inquiry back to the original question of this essay. If the eighty-five letters of Hamilton, Madison, and Jay represent the nation's most influential exposition of constitutional protections, they also remain the touchstone text in placing liberty under the constraints of government.[85] What then, if

---

religious and moral arguments as political controls (No. 10, 55, 58). Hamilton and Jay use similar references to providence but within the same spirit of restriction (No. 1, 5; No. 2, 9).

84. Here, in "The Federalist No. 35," "learned professions" becomes "the man of the learned profession," and, although the legal profession is not singled out, the context makes it clear that Hamilton is not speaking here of clergymen or academicians so much as he is identifying men of affairs, where lawyers predominated, just as they had in the Federal Convention.

85. Most famously on the significance of the work itself, Thomas Jefferson

anything, has been lost—or gained—in the conception of modern liberty? The benefits achieved in contemporary liberal society are perhaps too obvious to list; prosperity and the legal emphasis on individual rights have granted the majority of American citizens the freest opportunity in history to pursue their happiness.[86] It follows that the general idea of gain should be kept in mind to protect the inquiry about loss from misrepresentation. The corresponding idea of loss, in turn, should be approached with caution. The primary question— "What then, if anything, has been lost?"—has nothing to do with nostalgic impulses or with a projected act of recovery or rescue. Meaningful responses must concentrate instead on the historical construction of liberty as an idea and its relation to ongoing American understandings.

The farthest reaching eighteenth-century definition of liberty in America came from an English source. Blackstone's *Commentaries on the Laws of England* declared that "liberty, rightly understood, consists in the power of doing whatever the law permits." Taken by themselves, these words implied that legal enactment defined the scope of lib-

---

argued that *The Federalist* was "the best commentary on the principles of government which ever was written." Letter from Jefferson to James Madison, November 18, 1788, in James Morton Smith, ed., *The Republic of Letters: The Correspondence Between Thomas Jefferson and James Madison 1776–1826*, 3 vols. (New York: W. W. Norton, 1995), 1:567. On the contrasting issue of constraints on liberty, consider that Alexander Hamilton took up the subject of why a Bill of Rights was not necessary in the Federal Constitution only as an afterthought in "The Federalist No. 84." In one of the most telling indications of his marked indifference to concerns about safeguarding liberty, Hamilton openly admits his tardiness in dealing with the subject: "[These concerns] either did not fall naturally under any particular head [of his organization of *The Federalist*] or were forgotten in their proper places" (No. 84, 555).

86. Whatever the limits and exclusions in American culture, even its critics admit that the edifice of governmental structures created and explained in 1787 has been successful. The American rule of law has long since answered in the affirmative Hamilton's famous opening question in *The Federalist:* "It has been frequently remarked that it seems to have been reserved to the people of this country, by their conduct and example, to decide the important question, whether societies of men are really capable or not of establishing good government from reflection and choice, or whether they are forever destined to depend for their political constitutions on accident and force" (No. 1, 3).

erty, and the writer of them was notoriously quick to reconfigure personal rights as civil obligations.[87] Still, Blackstone necessarily thought in eighteenth-century terms. He *automatically* assumed a fundamental law prior to all human intervention, accepting what critics now call "a preinterpretive concept of law."[88] As he put the matter himself, "The principal aim of society is to protect individuals in the enjoyment of those absolute rights, which were vested in them by the immutable laws of nature. . . . Hence it follows, that the first and primary end of human laws is to maintain and regulate these *absolute* rights of individuals."[89]

Blackstone agreed with John Locke in presenting "the natural liberty of mankind," and, like Locke, he had little difficulty in finding liberty "posterior to the formation of states and societies," mediate to common human understanding, and traceable to God. "This natural liberty," Blackstone wrote, "consists in a power of acting as one thinks fit, without any restraint or control, unless by the law of nature: being a right inherent in us by birth, and one of the gifts of God to man at his creation, when he endued him with the faculty of free will."[90] Eighteenth-century participants, whether governors or governed, made these assumptions facts by applying simple reason to the law of nature. In Lockean terms, "Reason, the common Rule and Measure, God hath given to Mankind" unlocked the secrets of a natural order that defined acceptable human behavior and formed discernible law ("It is certain there is such a Law, and that too, as intelligible and plain to a rational Creature, and a Studier of that Law, as the positive Laws of Common-wealths, nay possibly plainer").[91] Much followed

87. *Commentaries*, 1:6, 119.

88. For a recent discussion and application of preinterpretive concepts of law, see Anthony J. Sebok, *Legal Positivism in American Jurisprudence* (Cambridge: Cambridge University Press, 1998), 246–51 (hereafter cited as *Legal Positivism*). Blackstone's own preinterpretive concept is stated quite clearly: "Upon these two foundations, the law of nature and the law of revelation, depend all human laws; that is to say, no human laws should be suffered to contradict these." *Commentaries*, 1:42.

89. *Commentaries*, 1:119–20.

90. Ibid., 120–21.

91. John Locke, "Of the State of Nature," *The Second Treatise*, in Laslett, *Two Treatises of Government*, 275 [ch. 2, sect. 11–12].

therefrom. As long as such premises on natural law remained in place, liberty as a basic conception was inalienable or, to use Blackstone's language, it belonged to "absolute rights . . . which every man is intitled to enjoy whether out of society or in it."[92]

But what if nature turns out *not* to be mediate? What if human reason fails to discern a liberty prior to formal institutions? What if law rests entirely on its own language and protest against it must be mounted through its own enactments? If these revocations become accepted truth, then Blackstone's definition—liberty consists in the power of doing whatever the law permits—takes on some negative connotations and the user of it comes perilously close to the predicament that John Dickinson faced in *Letters from a Farmer in Pennsylvania.* You cannot defy a legal regime if you accept its values as your restrictive gauge of meaning. You must be able to stand outside to rebel against. You need a preinterpretive concept of law to challenge legal interpretation.[93]

It should be clear that American law has reached most if not all of the positions raised in the interrogatives of the last paragraph. Few observers today, with a vastly extended and complicated conception of the universe before them, regard nature as mindful of (or patterned for) specific human needs. Neither philosophers nor lawyers celebrate common reason now. In the words of a frequently cited contemporary source, "Technically, of course, reason alone can't tell you anything; it can only connect premises to conclusions."[94] Even less modern credence has been given to a concept of liberty based on a prior state of nature. Contemporary theorists generally discount natural law as the undergirding force in legal thought. We now live in an age of rampant legal positivism. Most legal systems in the world today accept an exclusive hegemony of their own devising and turn to their own empirical structures for the solutions to even epistemological problems. Legal positivism projects its own morality, resisting all other criteria: "At the very heart of its case, [it] affirms the reality of legal obligation, based on nothing more than the actual law in effect."[95]

92. *Commentaries,* 1:119.
93. *Legal Positivism,* 251.
94. Ely, *Democracy and Distrust,* 56.
95. The quotation is from Lloyd W. Weinreb, *Natural Law and Justice* (Cam-

Does one need an external gauge to justify and safeguard fundamental rights? An argument in response must remember the balances involved. Legal positivism protects fundamental rights vigorously and with great accuracy through the formal stipulations of its own system. Many fundamental rights—for instance, the right to life, to a prompt public trial, to a jury of one's peers, to free speech, to protection from false imprisonment, to freedom of religion, and to a free press— welcome in their tangibility the specificity of statute and case law. As long as one accepts the proposition that positive law coincides with a just social order—a proposition that most Americans have been willing to acknowledge through their history, the problem of articulating and safeguarding fundamental rights remains internally consistent and manageable. From the other side of the coin, natural law as a preinterpretive concept of law hardly represents a panacea in any discussion of rights. In the eighteenth century at the height of its intellectual legitimacy, natural law came into play as a legal remedy only in extreme cases or in a time of crisis. Lawyers had many reasons even then for not trusting to its loose constructions and potential excesses.

But none of these considerations quite reaches the interactive complexity of American law and religion over the idea of liberty, and there remains the question of how origins now lost or diminished must figure into the equation. Within American law, liberty is a very different kind of fundamental right than others. Less tangible and hardly ever a legal remedy on its own, liberty functions rather as a comprehensive reminder of all legal remedies. When modern legal interpreters talk

----

bridge: Harvard University Press, 1987), 125 (hereafter cited as *Natural Law*). My definition of legal positivism derives from Weinreb and the classic first study of this subject, Lon L. Fuller, *The Law in Quest of Itself* (Chicago: The Foundation Press, 1940), 4–5, 16. For the predominance of legal positivism in modern law, see Heinrich A. Rommen, "The Victory of Positivism," in *The Natural Law: A Study in Legal and Social History and Philosophy*, trans. Thomas R. Hanley (1947; Indianapolis: Liberty Fund, 1998), 109–13. Fuller provided the original definition of legal positivism that all later discussions have had to cope with when he wrote "By legal positivism I mean that direction of legal thought which insists on drawing a sharp distinction between the law *that is* and the law *that ought to be.*" I rely here and in the next four paragraphs on the above sources for the philosophical differences between natural law and legal positivism; also on the recent defense of legal positivism in *Legal Positivism.*

about liberty, they instinctively employ a language that pulls them beyond the specificity of legal determination. For instance, when Justice Brandeis articulates a right of privacy as intrinsic to liberty in *Olmstead v. United States,* he discusses "conditions favorable to the pursuit of happiness" and "the significance of man's spiritual nature, of his feelings and of his intellect."[96] When liberty comes up in another context, Brandeis's colleague Justice McReynolds admits that the Supreme Court cannot really "define with exactness the liberty thus guaranteed," but he knows that "without a doubt, it denotes not merely freedom from bodily restraint, but also the right of the individual to contract, to engage in any of the common occupations of life, to acquire useful knowledge, to marry, establish a home and bring up children, to worship God according to the dictates of his conscience, and generally to enjoy those privileges of happiness by free men."[97] The striking fact about both comments is that they assume and depend on a spiritual level of explanation. These and other courtroom formulations of liberty need the kind of terminology—happiness, feelings, conscience, spirituality—that they would otherwise reject as insufficiently analytical or vague. They assume the individual worth and desirable well-being that religion supplies.

The value of natural law in eighteenth-century discussions of liberty resided largely in its integrative evaluative function on this ethical plane of explanation. It was ethical in its assurance of the harmonies that correct human behavior could be expected to reach. It was integrative in that it supplied a standard against which the legal system of that day could be tested.[98] The cultural power of that standard should not be underestimated. Revolutionary Americans regarded small intrusions as absolute challenges to liberty through their immersion in natural law norms. They were not prepared to obey a law of the state contrary to reason or against the ordained consent of the governed.[99]

96. *Olmstead v. United States,* 277 U.S. 438, 478 (1927). [Justice Louis Brandeis is dissenting in this opinion.]

97. *Meyer v. Nebraska,* 262 U.S. 390, 399 (1923).

98. The terminology, though not the application, in this sentence comes from *Legal Positivism,* 226.

99. Concern about the fragility of liberty and the need for special vigilance in protecting it is everywhere in Revolutionary rhetoric. Once again John Dickin-

How would contemporary Americans respond to a similar intrusion today? Surely not with the rubrics of natural law. The quiescent response of public opinion and political opposition in 2002 to the Federal Government's antiterrorist policies—"sweeping claims of unbridled executive authority to hold secret deportation hearings, label and incarcerate 'enemy combatants' without access to lawyers or judges"—offers a case in point. What might have formerly led to general protest against the invasion of the fundamental right of habeas corpus has been fought out instead on the highly technical level of a federal judiciary that asks the government to show the courts what it is doing.[100] The nature of protest has changed to match a larger shift in the understanding of what law has become.

The philosophical problem raised in the loss of natural law as a viable resource for objection to positive law has been stated quite simply: "No intrinsic quality of law ensures its morality in the manner of natural law."[101] The loss is significant because acts of resistance demand a moral imperative. To resist the overwhelming authority of the state requires a special cognizance on the part of an actor who undergoes an unknown level of risk. "Why am I willing to hazard this much?" a resisting person must ask in order to achieve the inner coherence

---

son presents the most articulate example of a general phenomenon. The Farmer opens his letters with the observation, "From my infancy, I was taught to love *humanity* and *liberty*. . . . Benevolence towards mankind, excites wishes for their welfare, and such wishes endear the means of fulfilling them. *These* can be found in liberty only, and therefore her sacred cause ought to be espoused by every man, on every occasion, to the utmost of his power." He adds later, "Here then, my dear countrymen, Rouse yourselves, and behold the ruin hanging over your heads. If you Once admit that *Great Britain* may lay duties upon her exportations to us . . . the tragedy of *American* liberty is finished." Or again, "A Free people therefore can never be too quick in observing, nor too firm in opposing the beginnings of *alteration* either in *form* or *reality,* respecting institutions formed for their security." Dickinson, *Letters from a Farmer in Pennsylvania,* No. 1, 3; No. 2, 14; No. 6, 36.

100. Both the quotation and the description of how the administration of George W. Bush "has encountered few obstacles from Congress or public opinion" while facing technical and highly contextual challenges from "federal judges, across the ideological spectrum" are from Linda Greenhouse, "The Imperial Presidency vs. the Imperial Judiciary," *New York Times,* September 8, 2002.

101. *Natural Law,* 103.

necessary to perform against a far more visible establishment. That coherence requires an element of inner spirit. Significantly, the patterns of resistance against state imposition in American history have tended to pit religious morality against established law. The abolitionist movements of the antebellum period, the right-to-vote protests after the Civil War, the prohibition movement in the first decades of the twentieth century, the antiwar and civil rights movements of the 1960s, and the anti-abortion protests of contemporary times have all relied heavily on religious impulses to make their cases. Are the alternative explanations that religion has always given to the concept of liberty still available? Yes, they are. In a crisis, belief in a secured collective happiness appeals at least as much as the protected conditions that allow the individual pursuit of it. As the remarks of Justices Brandeis and McReynolds have just demonstrated, the language of religion remains a resource.

Even so, the dialectic of liberty is not the same. Legal positivism has become profoundly secular in its impulses and trajectory, and there are severe limits to what it will allow itself to receive from outside its frame of reference. On its own terms, positive law cannot go beyond the experience of freedom within its immediate domain, and it rejects ethical challenge to its carefully reasoned internal coherence.[102] The basis if not the dimensions of this intransigence began almost in the same moment that Publius wrote *The Federalist.* Alexander Hamilton and his colleagues sought to strengthen the uncertain normative footing of positive law in their own time. In practical terms, their orientation required them to present the Federal Constitution in an attractive enough stance to secure moral sanction through the consent of the people. In legal terms, it meant preserving while curbing individual liberty in order to increase the ability of the state to make law.[103]

---

102. Ibid., 125. Lon Fuller's version of the same point runs as follows: "The illusion characteristic of natural law is the belief that there is no limit to what human reason can accomplish in regulating the relations of men in society. The illusion characteristic of positivism is the belief that reason can deliberately set itself a limit and stop at this limit." See *The Law in Quest of Itself,* 110.

103. In this, Hamilton, Madison, and Jay are no different than other political theorists of their day and ours. For a general explanation of the phenomenon in these terms, see *Natural Law,* 67.

Since then, the power and authority of the state to make and enforce law have increased a hundredfold while acceptance of liberty as a rhetorical guide to action has dwindled.

Liberty today is all too often an abstraction taken for granted in American discourse. Success has not bred contempt, but it has discouraged articulation in the face of change. Liberty is the lightly tongued given, like the air we breathe. Vigilance in protecting it is no longer a communal calling card. After all, the problem of preserving liberty while guarding the authority of the state can seem hopelessly abstract as long as the state is understood to be just. But what if the state grows unjust or wrong or simply misinformed? To what extent would the legacy of Revolutionary leaders who spoke a vaguely familiar but very different language more than two hundred years ago suffice in response? Somewhere in the dialectic of liberty, a republic defined by the right of revolution has been replaced by a modern nation-state where the test of membership has become loyalty.[104] The members of that nation-state should think more about what this institutional metamorphosis means in practice, and the intricate eighteenth-century root system in the liberty tree is a good place to begin. The suggestion here is not of return but of useful realization. Liberty, always a vexed value, is best protected by knowledgeable debate over its many meanings and applications.

104. George Fredrickson traces this shift from revolution toward loyalty and toward a "new respect for nationalism and the positive state" through the ideological formations of the Civil War. "The Civil War, by making the very concept of 'revolution' or 'rebellion' anathema to many Northerners, had widened the gulf that separated nineteenth-century Americans from their revolutionary heritage." See George M. Fredrickson, *The Inner Civil War: Northern Intellectuals and the Crisis of the Union* (New York: Harper and Row, 1965), 135, 184, 187, 191. I argue here that some of the conditions enabling that shift came earlier. Movement away from religious understandings and natural law and toward legal positivism in the early republic had already begun the process and prepared the way.

Religious Conscience and Original Sin: An Exploration of America's Protestant Foundations

One of the central questions of continuing interest to students of the American Founding concerns the nature of the ideas and values that guided Americans into and out of their war of independence. Some, like Michael Zuckert, contend that it was primarily a "natural-rights philosophy" which was and "remains America's deepest and so far most abiding commitment" and that this is what shaped Americans' understanding of things political. Moreover, he holds that this understanding was carefully embraced and found its inspiration in the political writings of the late-seventeenth-century English philosopher John Locke.[1] Other scholars find that a particular slice of pagan thought, known as civic humanism or classical republicanism, inherited from Greece and Rome, shaped most Americans' political and social views. And still others argue that the central organizing principles of American social and political life were derived, either immediately or indirectly, from varying and changing forms of Protestant Christianity.[2]

Largely in accord with the last group of authors, I argue in what follows that, at its revolutionary Founding, America was a nation of mostly British Protestants and Protestant communities whose culture was controlled by varying and contending Protestant categories of thought embedded in an inherited English legal culture. Although in the limited space at my disposal I am able to explore only a select number of features of American life and thought which support this position, I nonetheless hope to suggest ways by which Protestantism proved fundamental in shaping the ground upon which American po-

---

1. Michael P. Zuckert, *The Natural Rights Republic: Studies in the Foundation of the American Political Tradition* (Notre Dame: University of Notre Dame Press, 1996), 95, and see 175.

2. For their survey of these varying literatures, see Joseph P. Viteritti and Gerald J. Russello, "Community and American Federalism: Images Romantic and Real," in *Virginia Journal of Social Policy & the Law* 4 (Spring 1997): 691–96.

litical and social thought came to rest. Accordingly, I explore two key, if tension-ridden, facets of the Protestant inheritance that molded America's cultural landscape for well over a century before the Founding and thereafter continued to powerfully influence it. First is the American elevation of the freedom of religious conscience to a hallowed and inalienable individual right. Its persistent influence on the American political and religious culture resulted from the transformation of one of eighteenth century's most traditional and dominant meanings of liberty, spiritual or Christian liberty, into the form of a right. And second is the formative role played by Americans' acceptance of the Reformed Protestant understanding of original sin and its ubiquitous deformation of each and every human being. Only through a proper recognition of original sin's centrality do key features of American political thought, such as America's localism and hostility towards long chains of hierarchy, become readily understandable.

Few historians of the period disagree that Revolutionary-era Americans were a British Protestant people who wished to be guided not by reason alone, but rather by revelation and/or inner illumination.[3] For example, Henry May, the preeminent student of the Enlightenment in America, believes that this religious description accurately captures "most people who lived in America in the eighteenth and

3. Ironically, given the broad agreement concerning the Protestant character of Americans, this fact is often set aside and otherwise overlooked by students of the period. See Stanley N. Katz, "The Legal and Religious Context of Natural Rights Theory: A Comment," in *Party and Political Opposition in Revolutionary America,* ed. Patricia U. Bonomi (Tarrytown, N.Y.: Sleepy Hollow Press, 1980), 36–37, who observes that "curiously, however, neither the 1920's nor the 1960's interpretations took *religious* ideas seriously as a component of American opposition ideology . . . in what was, after all, still an intensely religious society"; Michael Novak, *On Two Wings: Humble Faith and Common Sense at the American Founding* (San Francisco: Encounter Books, 2002); James H. Hutson, *Religion and the Founding of the American Republic* (Washington, D.C.: Library of Congress, 1998); and Norman Hampson, *The Enlightenment: An Evaluation of its Assumptions, Attitudes and Values* (1968; reprint ed., New York: Penguin Books, 1986), 131, who writes of the eighteenth century that "it is something of an historical impertinence to consider the century as the age of Enlightenment since religion exercised a far greater hold over most sections of every society than it does today."

nineteenth centuries."[4] Nor were they Christians in name only, for "the majority of inhabitants continued to go to church . . . [and] the preaching colonists heard most of the time—remained consistently otherworldly."[5] Critical legal theorist Mark Tushnet further observes "it was not 'religion in general' that the framers saw as the basis of secular order. Rather, it was Christianity and, more specifically, Protestant Christianity."[6] And for eighteenth-century Americans, as it had been for Christians for almost two millennia, it was not a perfected society, as counseled by European adherents of the Enlightenment, which was necessary for individual and political well-being, but the intercession of Christ and the Holy Spirit, for only They could free man from sin— above all his disfiguring selfishness, lusts and passions.[7]

Such aspirations, contrary to the claims of those who would relegate Christianity to the backwaters of American life, are readily discoverable in American legal codes and social practices. For example, only one of the thirteen states, Virginia, failed to require a religious test for those wishing to hold public office. All other states required that state officeholders, including federal senatorial electors, be Protestant (Connecticut, Rhode Island, Georgia, Massachusetts, New Hampshire, New Jersey, North and South Carolina, and Vermont), Trinitar-

4. Henry F. May, *The Enlightenment in America* (New York: Oxford University Press, 1976), xiv, and see 45–46, where he continues that "for most inhabitants of the American colonies in the eighteenth century, Calvinism was . . . in the position of laissez-faire in mid-nineteenth-century England or democracy in twentieth-century America."

5. Harry S. Stout, *The New England Soul: Preaching and Religious Culture in Colonial New England* (New York: Oxford University Press, 1986), 6.

6. Mark Tushnet, "The Origins of the Establishment Clause," in *Georgetown Law Journal* 75 (April 1987): 1515.

7. See Perry Miller, *The New England Mind: From Colony to Province* (Cambridge: Harvard University Press, 1953), 2:69, who follows Augustine's *Confession* where it is argued that "Whenever God converts a sinner, and translates him into the state of grace, he freeth him from his natural bondage under sin, and by his grace alone inables him freely to will and to do that which is spiritually good"; and Augustine, "On Grace and Free Will," 1:771, and "On the Predestination of Saints," 1:779–85, in *Basic Writings of Saint Augustine,* ed. Whitney J. Oates (New York: Random House, 1948).

ian Christian (Delaware), accepting of the truthfulness of Scripture (Pennsylvania and Vermont), Christian (Maryland), or non-Catholic (New York). Moreover, Delaware's constitution demanded of office-holders that they "profess faith in God the Father, and in Jesus Christ His only Son, and in the Holy Ghost." And, at the time of the Revolution, "only three colonies allowed Catholics to vote. They were banned from holding public office in all New England colonies save Rhode Island. New Hampshire law called for the imprisonment of all persons who refused to repudiate the pope, the mass, and transubstantiation. New York held the death penalty over priests who entered the colony; Virginia boasted that it would only arrest them. Georgia did not permit Catholics to reside within its boundaries; the Carolinas merely barred them from office."[8]

During the war, it behooves us to take note of what James Hutson calls the "deeply religious men in positions of national legislative leadership." For example, Hutson, in his admirable *Religion and the Founding of the American Republic,* argues that the secretary of the Congress, Charles Thompson, "retired from public life to translate the Scriptures from Greek to English" and that the famous pamphleteer, John Dickinson, "also retired from public life to devote himself to religious scholarship." Much the same was true of three of the Congress's presidents: Elias Boudinot, Henry Laurens, and John Jay.[9] Under their leadership, thirteen times Congress unapologetically, via proclamations for days of fasting and humiliation, sought on behalf of the young nation the intervention of Jesus Christ and, at other times, that of the Holy Ghost. Indeed, the Continental Congress on March 14, 1781, had even appointed James Madison to serve on a committee of three "to prepare a recommendation to the states for setting apart a day of humiliation, fasting and prayer" which was delivered on March 20, 1781, for May 2. Like Jefferson in Virginia in the 1770s and 1780s,[10] Madison too was involved in the close working together of church

8. Derek H. Davis, *Religion and the Continental Congress, 1774–1789: Contributions to Original Intent* (Oxford: Oxford University Press, 2000), 153.

9. Hutson, *Religion and the Founding of the American Republic,* 49.

10. See Daniel L. Dreisbach, "Another Look at Jefferson's Wall of Separation: A Jurisdictional Interpretation of the 'Wall' Metaphor," Witherspoon Fellowship Lectures, Family Research Council, August 2000, 5.

and state in late-eighteenth-century America. Not surprisingly then, this same Congress consistently acted in support of Christianity in its daily prayers, its appointment of military chaplaincies, its collective attendance at worship services as a body, its ordering that an American Bible either be imported or published, and its persistent efforts to bring American Indians to Christ.[11] All this was to be done while America's first central government was frantically trying to organize new state governments, negotiate various treaties, and manage a war against the world's greatest power.

Yet, in still other ways the early national and state governments displayed an ample willingness to patronize Protestantism in eighteenth-century America. Thus, "officials donated land and personalty for the building of churches, religious schools, and charities. They collected taxes and tithes to support ministers and missionaries. They exempted church property from taxation. They incorporated religious bodies. They outlawed blasphemy and sacrilege, [and] unnecessary labor on the Sabbath and on religious holidays."[12] Well into the nineteenth century, states and localities were comfortable in "endorsing religious symbols and ceremonies," crosses were common on statehouse grounds, holy days were official holidays, chaplains continued to be "appointed to state legislatures, military groups, and state prisons," thanksgiving prayers were offered by governors, subsidies were given to Christian missionaries, the costs of Bibles were underwritten, tax exemptions were provided to Christian schools, "public schools and state universities had mandatory courses in the Bible and religion and compulsory attendance in daily chapel and Sunday worship services . . . [and] polygamy, prostitution, pornography, and other sexual offenses . . . were prohibited. Blasphemy and sacrilege were still prosecuted . . . and other activities that depended on fate or magic were forbidden."[13] According to Justice Story, a most highly respected jurist, Harvard professor of law, and Supreme Court justice, "It is impossible for

---

11. See, for example, Worthington Chauncey Ford, ed., *Journals Of The Continental Congress, 1774–1789* (Washington, D.C.: Government Printing Office, 1904–), November 11, 1775, 3:351.

12. John Witte, Jr., *Religion and the American Constitutional Experiment: Essential Rights and Liberties* (Boulder: Westview Press, 2000), 53.

13. Ibid., 97–98.

those who believe in the truth of Christianity as a divine revelation to doubt that it is the especial duty of government to foster and encourage it among all the citizens and subjects."[14] Protestant Christianity was simply an accepted and protected part of American life and law.

Yet, in spite of Christianity's ubiquitous presence in law and culture, not all Protestants, let alone Christians, adhered to the same views regarding the proper relationship between church and state. Indeed, many pious Christians are doctrinally opposed to too intimate a relationship between them. It must be remembered, therefore, that secular liberals are not unique in defending a sharp separation of the functions of church and state. Augustinian Catholics, Christian humanists of all varieties, and various Protestant pietists and members of the "Free" churches, most without the intervention of any form of secular philosophy, have done so as well. Accordingly, it is a mistake to assume that a politics of church-state separation is by necessity a reflection of Lockean liberalism or any other secular philosophy.[15] It is just as likely, and in America more likely, that such positions are a reflection of pietistic or humanistic Christianity. Most Americans, therefore, who endorsed a politics of church-state separation in the late eighteenth century, are likely to have done so with authentically Christian not secular concerns in mind. Yet, holding to a reductionistic and dualistic logic (i.e., if not Calvin, then necessarily Locke), Zuckert defends

> a Lockean conquest, or at least assimilation, of Puritan political thought. . . . Before Locke, the Puritans said one sort of thing about politics; after Locke, they said quite different sorts of things, which

14. Joseph Story, *Commentaries on the Constitution of the United States,* ed. Thomas Cooley (1833; 4th ed., Boston: Little, Brown, and Company, 1873), 2:603, and see 2:602–9 where Story writes that "The right of a society or government to interfere in matters of religion will hardly be contested," for "the great doctrines of religion . . . never can be a matter of indifference in any well-ordered community." Indeed, "the real object of the First Amendment was not to countenance, much less to advance, Mahometanism, Judaism, or infidelity, by prostrating Christianity; but to exclude rivalry among Christian sects." See also James McClellan, *Joseph Story and the American Constitution: A Study in Political and Legal Thought* (Norman: University of Oklahoma Press, 1971), 118–59.

15. This is a central assumption of Zuckert, *Natural Rights Republic,* 121, and 146–47.

turns out to be the same things Locke said, in more or less the language of Locke. . . . Doesn't this sort of thing, especially when conjoined with the observation that the Puritan forebears were committed to no doctrine of religious toleration at all, impel a strong conclusion of Lockean influence?[16]

But couldn't the changes, even if correctly reported, have resulted from other forces in addition to, in lieu of, or that share a common ancestor with Locke, ones that were carried within Anglo-American Protestantism itself?[17] Zuckert, in his reductionistic, either/or intellectual universe, fails to consider this or any other possibility.[18]

Admittedly, though, by the end of the eighteenth century, American Protestantism had changed in important ways. As James Hutson observes, "Evangelicalism emerged from the Awakening as the force of the future in American religion; those groups on the wrong side of it were driven to the sidelines."[19] Membership in Protestant congregations was steadily growing, not declining, in the late eighteenth century,[20] and we have every reason to believe that this change in theology resulted from internal dynamics within Protestantism rather than from a hypothesized alien secular conquest. Although by the century's end, Reformed theology no longer provided "the moral and religious background of fully 75 per cent of the people who declared their inde-

16. Ibid., 172, and see 175.

17. See Frederick C. Beiser, *The Sovereignty of Reason: The Defense of Rationality in the Early English Enlightenment* (Princeton: Princeton University Press, 1996), and J. C. D. Clark, *The Language of Liberty, 1660–1832: Political Discourse and Social Dynamics in the Anglo-American World* (Cambridge: Cambridge University Press, 1994) for their insightful explorations of the development of rationalistic approaches within Anglicanism.

18. See Zuckert, *Natural Rights Republic,* 40, in particular but more generally throughout.

19. Hutson, *Religion and the Founding of the American Republic,* 35.

20. See Hutson, ibid., who writes that "The assumption that church membership steadily declined in the last three decades of the century is totally inaccurate" (21). Furthermore, he supports estimates that "Between 1700 and 1740, between 74.7 and 80 percent of the population attended with some frequency" (24) and "that in 1776 between 71 and 77 percent of Americans may have filled the pews on Sunday" (32).

pendence in 1776."[21] Protestantism in its many guises continued to thrive. Indeed, in recognizing that Socinians, Arians, Arminians, and various other Protestant pietists and humanists gave vent to legitimate expressions of the Christian mind, the universe of Protestant-inspired thought and practices is greatly broadened and made more fully co-extensive with American-Revolutionary-era culture.

Americans, then, were predominantly Protestants, though certainly not all of one piece. And for all Protestants, the most important form of liberty was not the instrumentally critical liberty of communal self-government or that of liberal natural rights but instead the liberty through which Christ could make them free, that is, spiritual liberty. Like other prevalent eighteenth-century understandings of liberty, it defended an objective set of ethical standards that rested more on duties than on rights. In the words of George Haskins, "This was not liberty in the modern sense, a freedom to pursue individual wishes or inclinations; it was a freedom from any external restraint 'to [do] that only which is good, just and honest.' Christ had been sacrificed and resurrected to set men free, but the liberty so given was a freedom to walk in the faith of the gospel and to serve God through righteousness."[22] It was a "positive" form of liberty which carried within its meaning the only ends for which it could be legitimately exercised. More concretely, H. Richard Niebuhr notes that spiritual liberty is "the freedom from the rule of Satan, sin, and death; from the compulsions of obedience to superpersonal forces of evil; from domination by self-interest and the passions . . . freedom for faith and hope and goodness, rather than a negative liberty from external control."[23] According to

21. Sydney E. Ahlstrom, *A Religious History of the American People* (New Haven: Yale University Press, 1972), 124; and see George Lee Haskins, *Law and Authority in Early Massachusetts: A Study in Tradition and Design* (Lanham, Md.: University Press of America, 1960), 223–24; Patricia Bonomi, *Under the Cope of Heaven: Religion, Society, and Politics in Colonial America* (New York: Oxford University Press, 1986), 3; and David Hackett Fischer, *Albion's Seed: Four British Folkways in America* (New York: Oxford University Press, 1989), 1:423, who reports that of approximately 3,000 congregations in 1775, only 500 or 18 percent were Anglican (Episcopal) and the vast remainder were Reformed congregations.

22. Haskins, *Law and Authority in Early Massachusetts*, 17.

23. H. R. Niebuhr, "The Protestant Movement and Democracy in the United

Niebuhr's insightful account, spiritual liberty was markedly unlike the liberal "negative" sense of liberty correctly associated with a natural-rights philosophy.

In America this traditional Protestant sense of liberty was understood to eschew all claims of worldly liberation at the individual level while consistently and enthusiastically promoting and conflating a mixture of spiritual and political liberty at the corporate level. The result was that, among most Americans, spiritual liberty was used to defend the freedom of the community while simultaneously limiting that of the individual. In the illuminating words of Robert Wiebe, "The basic rights of a group—religious liberty, moral autonomy, academic freedom—became the crime of any individual who demanded a personal version of them."[24] And it was this Protestant localist understanding of corporate rights which was preeminent in eighteenth-century America rather than the individualistic vision of rights today associated with Locke (whatever he may have argued himself).[25] Yet, the equally Protestant right of religious conscience would provide an intellectual and moral foundation from which to challenge this.

FREEDOM OF RELIGIOUS CONSCIENCE

There was one freedom in America that was natural and uniquely individual and, by the middle of the eighteenth century, beyond challenge—the freedom of religious conscience. But it is useful to remember that at the beginning of the Revolutionary years, religious conscience was unique in being the only freedom that almost all Americans agreed was an unalienable individual right that could not be legitimately surrendered to or confiscated by society upon entering

---

States," in *The Shaping of American Religion,* ed. J. W. Smith and A. L. Jamison (Princeton: Princeton University Press, 1961), 31, 33, and 36.

24. Robert H. Wiebe, *The Segmented Society: An Introduction to the Meaning of America* (New York: Oxford University Press, 1975), 44. He continues, "If the hypothetical individual—sinful man, citizen of the republic, economic man— was a commonplace in American discourse, that terminology was used in the service of conformity, not individual freedom."

25. See Barry Alan Shain, *Myth of American Individualism: The Protestant Origins of American Political Thought* (Princeton: Princeton University Press, 1994; 3d reprint with corrections, 1996).

it. Curiously, however, even this hallowed right did little to limit the local community's exercise of its corporate religious responsibilities. And such responsibilities required that the local community insist on attendance at the preaching of God's word, that respect be paid to the Sabbath and God's revealed dictates and commandments (even forbidding inappropriate travel and leisure activities), that the rights of political participation be limited, and that one be taxed, church member or not, to retain a teacher of the community's (often established) Protestant faith. In many areas of life, communities were accordingly willing to encroach on matters of personal choice well beyond matters of conscience such as forbidding theater attendance, balls, masques, dice playing, cock fighting, and horse racing.[26] It was clearly an absolute or perfect (and ultimately revolutionary) right, but obviously initially not as extensive as is often believed today.

The Protestant freedom of religious conscience was thus clearly separate from the panoply of personal rights that its defenders, in the main, unintentionally helped create via their war efforts. Intentional or not, the most revolutionary fallout of the war was indeed the universalization, secularization, and extension of unalienable individual rights. Here, Zuckert and others, even if wrong in their historical reconstruction of the reasons and influences which produced this particular outcome, are right in closely associating the rise of the language of natural rights and the American Revolution.[27] In fact, Ernst Troeltsch, when asked "Whence comes the idea of the rights of the individual?" answered that "It is derived from the Constitutions of the North American States . . . from their Puritan religious principles . . . It was only in virtue of being thus put on a religious basis that these demands became absolute, and consequently admitted of and required a theoretical legal exposition. It was thus that they first passed into Constitutional Law."[28] But such extensive rights were neither intended by

26. See Ann Fairfax Withington, *Toward a More Perfect Union: Virtue and the Formation of American Republics* (New York: Oxford University Press, 1991), 184, who describes the Continental Congress's embrace of such prohibitions.

27. See Zuckert, *Natural Rights Republic*, 146–47.

28. Ernst Troeltsch, *Protestantism and Progress: A Historical Study of the Relation of Protestantism to the Modern World* (1912; reprint ed., trans. W. Montgomery, Boston: Beacon Hill Press, 1958), 119–20; and see Karl Holl, *The Cultural Significance of the*

the majority of elite political actors (to say nothing of the people) nor initially derived from a well-entrenched, secular foundation as Zuckert claims. The long-term, destabilizing consequences of rights claims being widely promulgated during and after the war for independence, however, are another matter and are difficult to dispute.

Like in much of Western Christendom,[29] in colonial America the freedom of religious conscience was not viewed positively during the seventeenth and the early decades of the eighteenth century. And according to one of the most celebrated students of that period, Perry Miller, "The Puritans were not rugged individualists . . . [and] they abhorred freedom of conscience."[30] It was only toward the end of the seventeenth century that elite colonial spokesmen began reluctantly to embrace this understanding of liberty. But in 1673, Urian Oakes, the president of Harvard, without great enthusiasm for either, argued for an extremely narrow understanding of the freedom of conscience and even less for the merits of toleration when he held that freedom gives

> men liberty to destroy themselves. Such is the liberty of Conscience, even a liberty of Perdition, that some men so unconscionably clamor

---

Reformation (1911; reprint ed., New York: Meridian Books, Inc., 1959), 72, who writes that individual rights "achieved world significance through the Constitution of the United States and the French Revolution." Curiously, early twentieth-century German scholars showed great interest in exploring this late eighteenth-century American-inspired transformation. However, also see Sheldon S. Wolin, *Politics and Vision: Continuity and Innovation in Western Political Thought* (Boston: Little, Brown and Co., 1960), 338, who writes that "The great transformation was effected whereby 'individual interest' was substituted for individual conscience . . . It was invested with many of the same sanctities and immunities, for, like conscience, it symbolized what was most valued by the individual and what was to be defended against the group or society."

29. See Troeltsch, *Protestantism and Progress,* 66–67, who reminds us that in classic Protestant thought "the modern problem of the relation of Church and State simply did not as yet exist" as it saw in each "two distinct functions in a body which is indivisibly one and the same, the *Corpus Christianum.* The applicability of religious standards to the whole body, the exclusion or, at least, the disenfranchisement of unbelievers and heretics, the principle of intolerance and infallibility, are for it also self-evident necessities."

30. Perry Miller, "Jonathan Edwards and the Great Awakening" in *Errand into the Wilderness* (Cambridge: Harvard University Press, 1956), 160–61.

for. But remember, that as long as you have liberty to walk in the Faith and Order of the Gospel, and may *lead quiet and peaceable lives in all Godliness and Honesty,* you have as much Liberty of Conscience as *Paul* desired under any Government.[31]

The extensive defense of a loosely defined liberty would not be easily drawn from America's Protestant inheritance, but from the defense of freedom of conscience, it would come.

Importantly, then, this transformation in New England to a greater acceptance of the freedom of religious conscience resulted initially from the colonies' loss of political autonomy that attended the Andros administration of the Dominion of New England (1686),[32] rather than from internal liberal intellectual or social forces pushing colonial religious and secular leadership toward a more tolerant stance. As Craven has written, only after this period did leaders of the colony "embrace the doctrine of toleration as a defensive weapon" and become increasingly sympathetic to freedom of religious conscience and "religious liberty—not the liberty they had understood, which was the liberty to do God's will and to require that all others in their midst conform, but the liberty John Locke suggested was the natural right

31. Urian Oakes, *New England Pleaded With, And Pressed to Consider the Things which Concern her PEACE at least in this her Day* (Cambridge, Mass., 1673), 53, and he continued, "I look upon an unbounded Toleration as the first born of all *Abominations* . . . it belongs to the *Magistrate* to judge what is *tolerable in his Dominions* in this respect. And the Eye of the *Civil Magistrate* is to be to the securing of the way of God that is duly established" (54–55).

32. See Christine Leigh Heyrman, *Commerce and Culture: The Maritime Communities of Colonial Massachusetts, 1690–1750* (New York: W. W. Norton, 1984), 118. In the South as well, it was England that constantly pressured the provincial governments to show greater tolerance toward religious dissenters, most particularly toward Catholics in Maryland. See Rhys Isaac, *The Transformation of Virginia, 1740–1790* (Chapel Hill: University of North Carolina Press, 1982), 151–52, who recounts how the British Board of Trade had advised the Virginian government that "A free Exercise of Religion is so valuable a branch of true liberty, and so essential to the enrichening and improving of a Trading Nation, it should ever be held sacred in His Majesty's Colonies"; and Clinton Rossiter, *Seedtime of the Republic: The Origin of the American Tradition of Political Liberty* (New York: Harcourt, Brace & World, Inc., 1953), 78, who notes that the Board had "disallowed two Maryland anti-Catholic laws as tending 'to depopulate that profitable colony.'"

of men."[33] However, I would note that this resolution was one which Americans embraced only reluctantly, and that it is not clear whether any eighteenth-century Americans understood Locke as having advocated, in his defense of the natural freedom of religious conscience, irreligiosity and/or unlimited religious freedom. Rather, in light of Locke's express strictures against atheism, Catholics' religious allegiance to a foreign prince, and his stipulation in his plan of government for Carolina that anyone who was not an active member of a religious body stood "outside of the protection of the law," it is more likely that he was believed to be legitimately concerned with protecting the freedom of conscience for largely heterodox Protestant groups like America's Presbyterians rather than secular or irreligious ends.[34]

This first and most important of the fully unalienable personal rights, that of religious conscience, enjoyed its unimpeachable standing in America only because Protestant Americans attached such enormous importance to the soteriological goal it putatively served. In 1901, Georg Jellinek observed that in eighteenth-century America

> there arose the conviction that there exists a right not conferred upon the citizen but inherent in man, that acts of conscience and expressions of religious conviction stand inviolable over against the state as the exercise of a higher right. This right so long suppressed is no "inheritance," is nothing handed down from their fathers, as the rights and liberties of Magna Charta and of the other English enactments, — not the state but the Gospel proclaimed it.[35]

And clearly, the right of religious conscience did not countenance any freedom devoid of a defining Christian higher end any more than any

33. Wesley Frank Craven, *The Legend of the Founding Fathers* (Ithaca: Cornell University Press, 1956), 25.

34. See Francis Canavan, *Freedom of Expression: Purpose as Limit* (Durham: Carolina Academic Press and the Claremont Institute for the Study of Statesmanship and Political Philosophy, 1984), 54, who cites Leonard Levy to this effect, and John Dunn, *The Political Thought of John Locke* (Cambridge: Cambridge University Press, 1982), 31–32, 245–46.

35. Georg Jellinek, *The Declaration of the Rights of Man and of Citizens: A Contribution to Modern Constitutional History,* trans. Max Farrand (1901; reprint ed., Westport, Conn.: Hyperion Press, Inc., 1979), 74.

other respected understanding of liberty, even secular ones, did at the time.[36] But the defense of religious conscience that emerged in the eighteenth-century West, regardless of its deeply religious foundations, did introduce a new appreciation of the inviolable nature of the personal space surrounding an individual.

In 1744 the socially and politically prominent minister, Connecticut Supreme Court justice, legislator, and former president of Yale, Elisha Williams, cut to the essence of the American and Protestant understanding of the religious purposes served by the freedom of conscience.[37] One of the earliest serious students of Locke in America, Williams followed Locke's striking logic set forth in the *Second Treatise* and *A Letter Concerning Toleration,* but used it to defend state financial support of religion (a point overlooked by many) and attack a Connecticut statute punishing established preachers with the loss of their income for preaching as an uninvited itinerant in another's congregation.[38] He wrote that nothing of equivalent value, not even life itself, could be offered in place of freedom of religious conscience, and that

> the Rights of Conscience are sacred and equal in all, and strictly speaking unalienable. This *Right of judging every one for himself in Matters of Religion* results from the Nature of Man. . . . A Man may alienate some Branches of his property and give up his Right in them to others; but he cannot transfer the *Rights of Conscience,* unless he could . . . substitute some other to be judged for him at the Tribunal of God.[39]

36. For example, see *Civil Liberty Asserted and the Rights of the Subject Defended Against the Anarchical Principles of the Reverend Dr. Price* (London: J. Wilkie, 1776), 44–45.

37. See Thomas J. Curry, *The First Freedoms: Church and State in America to the Passage of the First Amendment* (New York: Oxford University Press, 1986), 97, who writes that this "pamphlet was the only eighteenth-century pamphlet—until the eve of the American Revolution—that addressed itself specifically to the question of liberty of conscience."

38. See Glenn Weaver, "Elisha Williams: The Versatile Puritan," in *The Connecticut Historical Society Bulletin* 53 (Summer–Fall 1988): 119–233.

39. Elisha Williams, *Essential Rights and Liberty of Protestants . . . Being a Letter from a Gentleman in the Massachusetts-Bay to his Friends in Connecticut* (Boston: Kneeland & Green, 1744) 8; see Alan Heimert and Perry Miller, eds., *The Great*

The same theme was also defended in the press. An anonymous author writing in 1748 in the *Pennsylvania Journal* held that "private judgement was 'one of those sacred and original rights of human nature which the Gospel had revived and re-established.' . . . Thus the rights of conscience were sacred and equal in all men."[40] Yet, clearly, this high valuation of the right of conscience was not for these authors a reflection of a secular spirit, but of the development of an inherent feature of Protestantism.

Accordingly, even those who were not pious continued to defend this right on openly Christian grounds. It was, after all, the Christian content that made this new individual right inalienable and protected it from serious challenge. Thus, the humanist and future Loyalist, William Smith, Jr., in the *Occasional Reverberator* argued for the immeasurable worth of this freedom, which could not be exchanged for any other social value. From a Christian humanist foundation, he noted

> various Restraints arise upon this natural Liberty, when Men enter into civil Associations; which, nevertheless, must be by the voluntary Consent of the Party Submitting. But moral Liberty, or a Liberty of Conscience, is of another Nature and cannot be transferred. It claims an entire Exemption from all human Jurisdiction: because its Ends, Offices, and Interests, are superior to all the Ends of Civil Association; and subjecting it to the Power of Man, is inconsistent with the very Being of Religion.[41]

Awakening: Documents Illustrating the Crisis and Its Consequences (New York: Bobbs-Merrill Co., 1967), 324; and John Locke, "A Letter Concerning Toleration," in *Treatise of Civil Government and A Letter Concerning Toleration* (New York: Irvington Publishers, Inc., 1979), 173, who earlier had written that "No man can so far abandon the care of his own salvation as blindly to leave to the choice of any other, whether prince or subject, to prescribe to him what faith or worship he shall embrace." Quite possibly, if Americans were Lockean, it is here in their following his lead in legitimating individual rights by exploiting Protestant categories of thought.

40. Lawrence H. Leder, *Liberty and Authority: Early American Political Ideology, 1689–1763* (Chicago: Quadrangle Books, 1968), 68–69. He is here citing from the "Right of Private Judgment," *Pennsylvania Journal*, January 5, 1748.

41. Smith, *Occasional Reverberator*, October 5, 1753 (the last of four issues) in

By invoking soteriological ends, religious conscience found itself uniquely privileged.

By the beginning of the imperial crisis, freedom of religious conscience had become such a mainstream belief that Edward Dorr in the Connecticut Election Sermon of 1765 could argue in its defense while ignoring any potential concerns regarding this right's elastic potential. An anonymous pamphleteer that year listed it as one of the most important mainstays of happiness, and like spiritual liberty in general, American ministers tied the freedom of religious conscience to their respective colonies' claims for political liberty.[42] The conservative elite's exuberance for this newly energized right ended only when its utility for defending the war for independence was no longer needed and its difficult-to-limit character began to become apparent.[43]

During the war, however, such concerns were rarely raised outside of New York and Pennsylvania, and following Locke even more closely than had Elisha Williams thirty-five years earlier, Samuel Stillman, the

---

Leder, *Liberty and Authority*, 73–74. Note both his acceptance of the telos shared with Christianity and his unusual avoidance of the actual language of Christian devotion. Taking a more Christian though still very "progressive" and unusually ecumenical view for 1761 was Ezra Stiles, *A Discourse on the Christian Union* (Boston: Edes and Gill, 1761), 28, who argues that "the right of conscience and private judgment is unalienable; and it is truly the interest of all mankind to unite themselves into one body, for the liberty, free exercise, and unmolested enjoyment of this right."

42. Edward Dorr, *The Duty of Civil Rulers: A Connecticut Election Sermon* (Hartford: Thomas Green, [1765]), 13; see *Liberty, Property, and No Stamps* (New York: n.p., 1765) which argues that "The British Constitution is of all others confessedly calculated to procure whatever constituted Happiness, namely Liberty of Conscience, the peaceful Possession of Property and a Method of obtaining Justice with Security."

43. See Daniel T. Rodgers, *Contested Truths: Keywords in American Politics Since Independence* (New York: Basic Books, 1987), 66, who notes that "the notion of a reserve of *extralegal* rights had been a tool for the occasion, a crowbar to throw in the tracks of the empire. . . . But in formalizing rights, the consolidators of the 1780s had done their best to close down the style of argument most fertile of further rights production. Men were to be induced to think, once more, soberly and legally. The state of nature, only recently discovered, was already being abandoned."

first (and up through the Revolution, the only) Baptist to be invited to deliver a Massachusetts election sermon, would argue that "some of the natural rights of mankind are unalienable, and subject to no control but that of the Deity. Such are the SACRED RIGHTS OF CONSCIENCE." He then went on to rehearse again for his auditors the revolutionary logic inherent in Protestantism's insistence on salvation being achieved through faith alone by citing at length from Locke's *Letter Concerning Toleration* that

> "the care of souls is not committed to the civil magistrate any more than to other men . . . because no man can so far abandon the care of his own salvation, as blindly to leave it to the choice of any other. . . . All the life and power of true religion consists in the inward and full persuasion of the mind; and faith is not faith without believing."[44]

Here, once more, we witness in late-eighteenth-century American thought the potentially individualist elements in Americans' absolute defense of the freedom of religious conscience.

The most numerous and vociferous claims defending the freedom of conscience, however, are not found in New England election sermons but rather in the instructions of the towns and villages of Massachusetts to their delegates to the state constitutional convention of 1780. In these, one not surprisingly discovers that in almost all cases the right of conscience was the only one defended as unalienable. When it was not the only one, it was invariably still held as the most important. The town of Pittsfield in its instructions to its representatives holds first that "Every man has an unalienable right to enjoy his own opinion in matters of religion and to worship God in that manner that

---

44. Samuel Stillman, *Massachusetts Election Sermon* (Boston: T. J. Fleet, 1779), 11, 23; and see Carl L. Becker, *The Declaration of Independence: A Study in the History of Political Ideas* (1922; reprint ed., New York: Random House, 1958), 79, who in 1922, well understood, though too simplistically, that one could describe the evolution of American political thought by arguing that "The lineage is direct: Jefferson copied Locke and Locke copied Hooker." And, if he were to push back two or three steps more, he might well have discovered that it terminates in the incipient humanism present in the thinking of Aquinas.

is agreeable to his own sentiments." Similarly, the town of Stoughton instructed its delegates to endeavor that "a Bill of Rights be in the first place compiled, wherein the inherent and unalienable Rights of Conscience and all those aleinable [sic] rights ar [sic] not necessary to be given up in to the hands of government together with the equivalent individuals ought undoubtedly to Recive [sic] from Government for their relinquishing a part of their natural and alienable rights for the necessary Support of the Same."[45]

And after having one constitution rejected two years earlier (1778), the members of the 1780 Massachusetts convention were attentive to the wishes of their constituents. They explained in an opening address to them that "We have, with as much Precision as we were capable of, provided for the free exercise of the *Rights of Conscience:* We are very sensible that our Constituents hold those Rights infinitely more valuable than all others."[46] But many of their constituents rejected the third article (concerning religious taxation) of the introductory Declaration of Rights because, as pietistic Protestants, they held that it infringed on their unimpeachable right of religious conscience and their desire to separate the still closely linked goals of church and state in Congregationalist Massachusetts. The residents of the town of Westford, for example, offered an alternative to the third article, one by which their "religious Freedom and the Unalienable Rights of Conscience may be better secured and established." Their motivation, we should remember, was not in any manner secular, but fully Protestant, even if not true to the Christian commonwealth tradition of their Massachusetts Bay forebears.[47] Too often and too easily, nonspecialists conflate liberal opponents of religious establishment with pious Protestants who fought for similar public policy ends but from

45. Reported by Oscar Handlin and Mary Handlin, eds., *The Popular Sources of Political Authority: Documents on the Massachusetts Constitution of 1780* (Cambridge: Harvard University Press, 1966), 410–11, 423.

46. Ibid., 436, and see Articles I–II of the proposed constitution, and the highly controversial third article, 442–43.

47. Ibid., 683, but see 32 where Handlin writes that "General professions of belief in religious liberty therefore were not incompatible with demands for guarantees of a Protestant Christian state."

strikingly different foundations. And, thereby, inattentive authors are apt to draw unwarranted conclusions regarding an imagined secularization in Revolutionary America.[48]

During the years surrounding America's war for independence, then, freedom of religious conscience had become a well-accepted understanding of liberty, frequently still viewed as the only truly unalienable *individual* right (as well, there were *corporate* ones that were viewed as unalienable) in comparison to many of the political rights that governments or communities could "ask" citizens to surrender on appropriate occasions.[49] Accordingly, with the sole exception of the right to religious conscience,[50] over two-thirds of the states made no mention of natural *individual* rights in their constitutions.[51] Delaware's

48. See Hutson, *Religion and the Founding of the American Republic,* 19, who writes that too many scholars have errantly claimed that "by the time of the American Revolution, an indifferent population is seen as acquiescing in the program of leaders, nominally Christian, but committed to the agenda of the Enlightenment, who proceeded to send religion to the sidelines of American life." In reality though, "Religion in the eighteenth century was actually in the 'ascension rather than the declension,'" or even "in a state of 'feverish growth.'"

49. See the Federal Farmer, "Letter VI," in Herbert J. Storing, ed., *The Anti-Federalist: Writings by the Opponents of the Constitution,* selected by Murray Dry from *The Complete Anti-Federalist* (Chicago: University of Chicago Press, 1985), 70, who writes that "Of rights, some are natural and unalienable, of which even the people cannot deprive individuals: Some are constitutional or fundamental; these cannot be altered or abolished by the ordinary laws; but the people, by express acts, may alter or abolish them—These, such as the trial by jury, the benefits of the writ of habeas corpus, etc. . . . and some are common or mere legal rights, that is, such as individuals claim under laws which the ordinary legislature may alter or abolish at pleasure."

50. Five of the original thirteen state constitutions had no declaration of rights: Connecticut (1776), Georgia (1777), New York (1777), Rhode Island (1663), and South Carolina (1778). Four others, Delaware (1776), New Hampshire (1784), North Carolina (1776), and Maryland (1776), had declaration of rights but failed to make any mention of individual natural rights.

51. This is not true of the Declaration of Rights of Virginia (1776), Pennsylvania (1776), Vermont (1777), or Massachusetts (1780). That of Virginia famously begins that "All men are by nature equally free and independent, and have certain inherent rights, of which, when they enter into a state of society, they cannot by any compact, deprive or divest their posterity." Often overlooked, though,

Declaration of Rights, for example, begins by holding that "All government of right originates from the people, is founded by compact only, and [is] instituted solely for the good of the whole." Only the right of conscience is then described as a possession of "all men." The Maryland Declaration follows that of Delaware and begins with the exact same communal rather than individualistic rights language, but in its description of the right of conscience, it is more restrictive still. Only those "professing the Christian religion, are equally entitled to protection in their religious liberty." Not only atheists are excluded from enjoying this most basic right, but all non-Christians as well.

North Carolina's constitution too begins with a declaration of popular sovereignty and then claims "that the people of this State ought to have the sole and exclusive right of regulating the internal government and police thereof." And as one might expect, the only individual right which is described as natural and unalienable is that of conscience (sect. 19). All other rights, taken as they are from the English common law, are couched as recommendations and described in the language of "ought" and are wholly subject to the vagaries of popular will. Finally, New Hampshire's late constitution of 1784, borrowing its language from earlier ones, reminds its citizens that when "men enter into a state of society, they surrender up some of their natural rights to that society, in order to insure the protection of others." However, "Among the natural rights, some are in their very nature unalienable, because no equivalent can be given or received for them. Of this kind are the RIGHTS OF CONSCIENCE."[52] Clearly then the right of religious

─────

is that this formulation is a traditional usage of natural-rights language in that it stipulates the just relationship between generations (one of three conditions under which natural law or rights rather than civil law was controlling) and not between an individual and the society at large. Only in regard to the right of religious conscience (sect. 16) is the relationship constrained between the individual and his or her society. Similarly, it is often ignored that the Pennsylvania "Declaration" privileges in all instances, except in regard to conscience (and even then atheists are excluded), the community's needs over those of the individual.

52. In Benjamin Perley Poore, comp., *The Federal and State Constitutions, Colonial Charters, and Other Organic Laws of the United States* (Washington, D.C.: Government Printing Office, 1878), 2:1280–81. New Hampshire then continues without any sense of tension in Article VI to sustain its taxation "for the support and maintenance of public protestant teachers of piety, religion and morality."

conscience enjoyed an unparalleled status in the minds of eighteenth-century Americans in being the only individual right which could not be surrendered or transferred as one moved from a state of "nature" to one of civil society. All other individual rights were viewed as fungible and subject to corporate oversight and restrictions.

In the decades immediately following the close of the war for independence, Americans disagreed whether freedom of conscience also demanded comprehensive religious freedom (rather than simple toleration).[53] This more inclusive freedom, in turn, was subject to a host of different interpretations. On one side were elite Christian humanists, deists, and their popular pietistic supporters who seemingly wished religious freedom to be understood as broadly as possible. In a classic statement of their position, Jefferson made earlier arguments more emphatic when he wrote to a group of Connecticut Baptists that he, too, believed that "religion is a matter which lies solely between man and his God, that he owes account to none other for this faith." He then went on to suggest, however, in ways never fully accepted by American pietistic Protestants and by most other Americans that the First Amendment to the national Constitution had effectively built "a wall of separation between Church and State," that is, between the national government and religious organizations at the state and local level.[54]

Great differences in interpretation thus existed among those most

53. See Philip A. Hamburger, "A Constitutional Right of Religious Exemption: An Historical Perspective," in *George Washington Law Review* 60 (April 1992): 915–48.

54. "Letter to Nehemiah Dodge and Others" in Thomas Jefferson, *The Portable Thomas Jefferson*, ed. Merrill D. Peterson (New York: Penguin Books, 1975), 303. In spite of Jefferson's claim, it must not be forgotten as Edmund S. Morgan, "Popular Fiction," in *The New Republic*, June 29, 1987, 25–36, reminds us "these prohibitions applied only to the federal government. In 1791 most of the states required a belief in Christianity (five of them in Protestant Christianity) for anyone holding public office . . . [and] the last state to give up religious tests was New Hampshire in 1876." In fact, according to Curry, *First Freedoms*, 158, the last state to do so was Maryland that "retained a religious test for office until the middle of the twentieth century." See also Daniel L. Dreisbach, "Thomas Jefferson and the Danbury Baptists Revisited," in *William and Mary Quarterly* 56 (October 1999): 805–16; and Hutson, *Religion and the Founding of the American Republic*, 82–85.

committed to religious freedom.[55] The pietistic Baptists of Virginia, who on several occasions helped elect Jefferson and Madison, certainly did not similarly conceive of religious freedom[56] particularly at the state level[57] as a wall of separation. Instead, they understood that the "struggle for religious freedom meant that all churches were now able to compete on a completely equal basis. They were eager to do so, but in particular against the forces of deism and irreligion" that they found most threatening.[58] From their perspective it would have been more appropriate to describe the "wall" as a one-way permeable membrane (i.e., no state interference in religion would be countenanced due to its corrupting effect on religion), but religious interference in the pub-

55. See LeRoy Moore, "Religious Liberty: Roger Williams and the Revolutionary Era," in *Church History* 34 (March 1965): 67, who argues that the two major groups, the deists and the evangelicals, sought the same end but, for the former "the issue" and "the field of battle" rest on anthropocentric premises, whereas for the latter, on theocentric ones.

56. See James Madison, "James Madison's Autobiography," ed. Douglass Adair, *William and Mary Quarterly* 2 (April 1945): 191–209, who writes of the Baptists that "Notwithstanding the enthusiasm which contributed to render them obnoxious to sober opinion . . . he [Madison] spared no exertion to save them from imprisonment. . . . This interposition tho' a mere duty prescribed by his conscience, obtained for him a lasting place in the favour of that particular sect" (198–99).

57. See "Letter to B. Rush 12 June 1812" in John Adams and Benjamin Rush, *The Spur of Fame: Dialogues of John Adams and Benjamin Rush, 1805–1813*, ed. John A. Schutz and Douglass Adair (San Marino, Calif.: The Huntington Library, 1980), 224, where Adams most interestingly writes that his loss of office resulted from his having recommended a fast at the national level. "The secret whisper ran through all the sects, 'Let us have Jefferson, Madison, Burr, anybody, whether they be philosophers, Deists, or even atheists, rather than a Presbyterian President.' . . . Nothing is more dreaded than the national government meddling with religion."

58. Thomas E. Buckley, "Evangelicals Triumphant: The Baptists' Assault on the Virginia Glebes, 1786–1801," in *William and Mary Quarterly* 45 (January 1988): 68. Commenting on the Northern Evangelicals, Gregory H. Nobles, *Divisions Throughout the Whole: Politics and Society in Hampshire County, Massachusetts, 1740–1775* (New York: Cambridge University Press, 1983), 84, 87, reminds us that it was their greater religious strictness and purity rather than the opposite that frequently led them to break with established churches.

lic actions of the state was sought and frequently achieved during the next two centuries.

At greater distance, however, stood the religious conservatives who defended an older understanding of Christian communalism and who spoke and wrote as if the support given to the freedom of conscience and religious freedom during the Revolution had gone too far and was beginning to serve the forces of infidelity. Delivering the Massachusetts election sermon of 1784, Moses Hemmenway enunciated a central theme of the 1780s when he warned that

> we should take heed that *Liberty of thinking* for ourselves, or the right of private judgment become not an occasion of infidelity, or skepticism. . . . *Liberty of conscience* must not be abused into a pretence for neglecting religious worship, prophaning God's sabbath and ordinances, or refusing to do our part for the support of government and the means of religious instruction.[59]

Five years later in Connecticut, Cyprian Strong emphatically asserted that "it is impossible, therefore, that civil government should take a neutral position, respecting religion or a kingdom of holiness. It must aid and countenance it, or it will discourage and bring it into contempt."[60] These pillars of rural New England Protestantism, following the war, were trying to re-create accepted limits to contain freedom

59. Moses Hemmenway, *Massachusetts Election Sermon* (Boston: Benjamin Edes and Sons, 1784), 33–34. For similar themes which displayed the continuing deference shown to the liberty of conscience, see Howard, "A Sermon Preached . . ." in John Wingate Thornton, ed., *The Pulpit of the American Revolution: Or, The Political Sermons of the Period of 1776* (Boston: Gould and Lincoln, 1860), 373, who writes that the rulers should use their authority to encourage religion, but only "so far as is consistent with the sacred and inalienable rights of conscience"; and Stephen Johnson, *Integrity and Piety the Best Principles of a Good Administration of Government* (New London, Conn.: Timothy Green, 1770), 24–35.

60. Cyprian Strong, *Connecticut Election Day Sermon* (Hartford: Hudson and Goodwin, 1799), 16–17; and see John Mitchell Mason, *The Voice of Warning, to Christians, on the Ensuing Election of a President* (New York: G. F. Hopkins, 1800), 18–19, who ties the cause of infidelity to Jefferson and asks if "no injury" will result from his election and the consequent undoing of "all the chords which bind you to the God of heaven."

of religion practice and that of conscience and, thus, to prevent any further separation of the moral ends jointly fostered by church and state.[61]

What they could only surmise was that the unalienable individual right of religious conscience, expansively extended to broader rights claims by Americans in their support of the prosecution of the war for independence, had created the foundation upon which a new class of rights would be constructed.[62] This class of rights could not be contained easily as it slowly and erratically developed over the next century into a suit of "trump cards" in the rhetoric of American political life. Unexpectedly, Americans had made possible a class of rights that were highly elastic and could at any time be counterpoised to the corporate claims of the sovereign state,[63] in particular the collective will of a nation of Protestants and Protestant communities, as was America until well into the nineteenth century. Yet, according to Jellinek, "This sovereign individualism in the religious sphere led to practical consequences of extraordinary importance. From its principles there finally resulted the demand for, and the recognition of, full and unrestricted liberty of conscience, and then the asserting of this liberty to be a right not granted by any earthly power and therefore by no earthly power

61. Consider the earlier remarks of Samuel Hall, *The Legislature's Right, Charge and Duty in Respect of Religion* (New London: Timothy Green, 1746), 20, in the election sermon of 1746. Opposing those who argued for less religious coercion in the public realm, he held that "What is begun in Force, may end in Choice: What is begun in Fear, may end in Love . . . besides it's no small Advantage to the common Cause of Vertue, that men can be brought to be visibly or externally Good and Vertuous."

62. See Miller, *New England Mind: From Colony to Province,* 171, who argues that this had been a gradual process in which "Protestantism was imperceptibly carried over into the new order . . . by translating Christian liberty into those liberties guaranteed by statute."

63. See Rodgers, *Contested Truths,* 13, who notes that "Natural Rights was the central radical political slogan of the Revolution. . . . The cry of 'rights' has always been double-edged. . . . It was one of the unexpected results of the search for a Revolutionary argument that the subversive edge of the word 'rights' should have been honed so sharply—or joined to so volatile an adjective . . . it was never again fully extinguishable from political argument: a phrase whose very abstractness left it permanently open to new meanings, new grievances, new users"; and again, 223.

to be restrained."[64] Although this intellectual revolution is still to be mapped out in exact detail, it is clear that it occurred largely without forethought and almost imperceptibly during the years following America's war for independence.[65]

During the war, rather desperate statesmen and theorists had unceremoniously stripped the historically based, socially defined, and Parliamentary-deferring traditional English rights and liberties of their English characteristics,[66] because of the inconvenient historical ties of these rights in Whiggish political theory to Parliamentary sovereignty.[67] It is essential, however, if one is to understand correctly this

64. Jellinek, *Declaration of the Rights of Man and of Citizens,* 60.

65. Such consequences, however, were not entirely unrecognized because the middle-colony moderate and Loyalist critics of the Revolution were well aware of the dangers of what they took to be an unnecessarily risky position. For example, see Howard, "A Letter from a Gentleman at Halifax" in Merrill Jensen, ed., *Tracts of the American Revolution: 1763–1776* (Indianapolis: Bobbs-Merrill, 1967), 68–69, who asked "Can we claim the common law as an inheritance, and at the same time be at liberty to adopt one part of it, and reject the other? Indeed we cannot"; Galloway, "A Candid Examination of the Mutual Claims of Great Britain and the Colonies" in ibid., 360; and Rodgers, *Contested Truths,* 56, who reminds us that "not all the champions of colonial resistance were willing to follow this string of conflations all the way down the line. Among those who valued stability, state of nature talk chafed a sensitive nerve. . . . For many of them the state of nature was a synonym for fearsome anarchy."

66. I am staking out a middle ground between two schools of thought, both persuasively argued. On the one hand, Becker, *Declaration of Independence,* 21, argues that the colonists, out of necessity, had shifted their case from a British-constitutional to a natural-law defense. On the other hand John Phillip Reid, *Constitutional History of the American Revolution: The Authority of Rights* (Madison: University of Wisconsin Press, 1986), 5, has written "All rights asserted in the Declaration were English rights, recognized and protected by British constitutional doctrine. Moreover, it is not true that the American argument shifted during the revolutionary debate. Colonial whigs asserted their rights as 'Englishmen' and only as Englishmen."

67. See, for example, *Some Fugitive Thoughts on a Letter Signed Freeman* (South Carolina: n.p., 1774), 15, that argues that all the British legal precedents being offered in their defense by American patriot authors were in fact, milestones toward "the supreme authority of Parliament, not only over all the *British* Dominions, but also over the Crown . . . [and] the Subjection of the Colonies to Parliament cannot be more strongly featured"; and Janice Potter, *The Liberty We*

transformation to recognize the lack of intentionality here. Only in this way can the development of modern individual natural rights in America (and elsewhere) be freed from a tendentious interpretation that cavalierly casts an inaccurate shadow of design and purpose over the historical development of these rights. For as Rodgers has written regarding this important development during the Revolution, "There was, then, very little from which to predict that the Americans would end up talking seriously, heatedly, of rights passed down unimpaired from something so fantastic as a state of nature. The patriot writers groped for their words throughout the 1760s and 1770s under the shift and stress of circumstances, inventing lines of argument and backing away from them."[68] And, it is an awareness of the nature of this fascinating development that is markedly absent in accounts like that of Zuckert and other "natural-rights" apologists who focus only on the theoretical fallout from the war while failing to attend to Americans' early intentions and the historical developments that followed.

And the best evidence of the American stance and their tentative and uncertain embrace of the language of natural rights is the debate reported by John Adams concerning the decision in the First Continental Congress to break precedent with the earlier Stamp Act Congress of 1765 which had rested its claimed rights entirely on "the rights of Englishmen" and the rights of "natural born subjects within the kingdom of Great Britain."[69] As Adams records in his *Diary* and *Autobiography,* there was no issue that so divided the Congress as to whether, in searching for grounds upon which to defend their break with England, they "should recur to the law of nature, as well as to the British Constitution, and our American charters and grants." He writes, "Mr. Galloway and Mr. Duane were for excluding the law of na-

---

Seek: Loyalist Ideology in Colonial New York and Massachusetts (Cambridge: Harvard University Press, 1983), 143, who argues that "Parliamentary supremacy was the issue more than any other which divided them [Loyalists] irreconcilably from the Patriots and led to civil war."

68. Rodgers, *Contested Truths,* 52.

69. See the "Resolutions of the Stamp Act Congress," October 19, 1765, in Richard L. Perry, ed., *Sources of Our Liberties: Documentary Origins of Individual Liberties in the United States Constitution and Bill of Rights,* rev. ed. (Buffalo, N.Y.: William S. Hein & Co., 1991), 270–71.

ture," but that he "was very strenuous for retaining and insisting on it." And why did Adams take this position? Because, as he explains, it was "a resource to which we might be driven by Parliament much sooner than we were aware."[70] According to Adams, then, a "natural rights philosophy" was not a model that led them into their conflict with Great Britain but was a polemical tool to which, lacking recourse to any others, they would surely "be driven."

When one explores Adams's notes of this debate, along with others, again one finds that much of the discussion revolved around which line of argument would prove most efficacious: appeals to nature or, as Mr. Duane (of New York) claimed, to "the laws and constitution of the country from whence we sprung, and charters, without recurring to the law of nature; because this will be a feeble support."[71] In the end though, the Congress in America's first national Bill of Rights, its "Declaration and Resolves" of October 14, 1774, inserted one brief appeal to the "immutable laws of nature" within nearly a dozen to "the principles of the English constitution . . . the several charters or compacts . . . the rights, liberties, and immunities of free and natural-born subjects, within the realm of England . . . the foundations of English liberty . . . [and their claim that Americans were entitled] to the common law of England."[72] It is most difficult, then, fairly to describe such language as emanating from a conscience and purposeful design to create a "natural rights Republic."

The traditional rights of Englishmen that Americans had vaunted for decades were under the pressures of a constitutional crisis and later of a war for independence, replanted in the fertile soil of Christian, ultimately scholastic in origin,[73] natural law. There they blossomed

70. "Extract from Autobiography" in John Adams, *Works of John Adams, Second President of the United States,* ed. Charles Francis Adams (Boston: Little, Brown, 1850–56), 2:374.

71. Adams, *Diary* for September 8, 1774, ibid., 371.

72. "Declarations and Resolves" in Perry, *Sources of Our Liberties,* 286–89.

73. See Beiser, *Sovereignty of Reason;* Barry Alan Shain, *Man, God and Society: An Interpretive History of Individualism* (London: University of London, 2000); Brian Tierney, *The Idea of Natural Rights: Studies on Natural Rights, Natural Law and Church Law, 1150–1625* (Atlanta: Scholars Press, 1997); and, in agreement, Zuckert, *Natural Rights Republic,* 157.

handsomely and provided legitimacy and cover for the creation of modern universal individual natural rights.[74] Americans no longer sought their rights solely in the *Magna Charta* for they no longer were an English people, and henceforth they exploited their standing as dissenting Protestants and were "a people [who] derive their Liberty from God, the Author of their Being."[75] The relatively young felt most comfortable wielding the weapon of Christian "natural rights" unmodified by any reference to their English historical grounding in common law. One such patriot was the thirty-year-old radical, John Adams, who in 1765 wrote that Americans have

> RIGHTS, for such they have, undoubtedly, antecedent to all earthly government — Rights that cannot be repealed or restrained by human laws — Rights derived from the great Legislator of the universe . . . [which we are told] "is an offensive expression"; "that the king, his ministry, and parliament, will not endure to hear Americans talk of their rights."[76]

American authors during the Revolution further embellished the soul-centered logic that had been used so successfully to defend the individual's claims for freedom of religious conscience, now recast into the language of traditional Catholic natural law, and added to this potent

74. See Leo Moulin, "On the Evolution of the Meaning of the Word 'Individualism,'" in *International Social Science Bulletin* 7 (1955): 184–85, who writes, "The foundations of Anglo-Saxon individualism are essentially of a religious, ethical and moral character, whereas continental individualism is primarily legal and political in France, and philosophical in Germany." Cf., Schmitt (below, n. 87) who argues that the religious origins of individual rights is necessarily a universal phenomenon. Also see Donald S. Lutz, "Studying the Early State Constitutions: A Re-Evaluation of American Political Theory," manuscript copy in my possession, 6, who writes that "The evolution of American constitutions was thus essentially a secularization of covenants into compacts."

75. [John Dickinson], "The Centinel. No. VII" in *Pennsylvania Journal; and the Weekly Advertiser*, May 5, 1768. Cited by Richard J. Hooker, "John Dickinson on Church and State," in *American Literature* 16 (May 1944): 89.

76. "Dissertation on the Cannon and Feudal Law" in John Adams, *The Political Writings of John Adams: Representative Selections*, ed. George A. Peek, Jr. (Indianapolis: Bobbs-Merrill, 1954), 5, 17. He wrote this work while a member of a radical club of young lawyers. Later in his life, sobered by his experiences in France, he described this work as a "lamentable bagatelle."

mix their traditional rights as Englishmen. Jellinek is a sure guide, and he writes that

> the inherited rights and liberties, as well as the privileges of organization, which had been granted the colonists by the English kings or had been sanctioned by the colonial lords, do not indeed change in word, but they become rights which spring not from man but from God and Nature. To these ancient rights new ones were added. With the conviction that there existed a right of conscience independent of the State was found the starting-point for the determination of the inalienable rights of the individual.[77]

And this transformation of the logical grounds of American personal and corporate rights from an amorphous-mixed English historical basis to a natural-rights foundation, Christian in its joining of Catholic natural-law elements and Protestant concerns with personal inwardness and communal localism, occurred remarkably rapidly during the Revolutionary years.[78]

It occurred with such speed that the English historical origins of most claimed right were forgotten, so much so that by the end of the century, moderates like James Wilson actually looked back on the

77. Jellinek, *Declaration of the Rights of Man and of Citizens*, 80. Jellinek's remarks gave birth to a small intellectual industry in Germany that continued to debate these issues for another thirty years. This scholarship deserves to be treated at length. For references, see Roland Bainton, "The Appeal to Reason and the American Constitution," in *The Constitution Reconsidered*, ed. Conyers Read (New York: Columbia University Press, 1938), 126–27, who lists many of the pertinent works in a two-page footnote.

78. American spokesmen frequently joined proscriptive English rights and natural or unalienable rights with a seamless continuity. See *Considerations upon the Rights of the Colonists to the Privileges of British Subjects* (New York: John Holt, 1766), 12, 17, in which the author writes that "No man will deny that the provincial Americans have an inherent, *unalienable Right* to all the Privileges of British Subjects"; and William Henry Drayton, *A Letter from Freeman of South Carolina* (Charles-Town: Peter Timothy, 1774), 30, 37, who writes that "in the same degree with the People of England, are the Americans . . . who enjoyed the benefits of the Common Law of England, and ascertained their ancient and unalienable Rights and Liberties . . . And therefore are the Americans, equally with the people of England, entitled to those liberties of Englishmen. And from such a title, does America derive her freedom."

"historicism" of Blackstone's understanding of the origin and basis of English rights with contempt. Wilson found it incredible that Blackstone could have been so "primitive" in his thought that he would have agreed with Burke, whom Wilson held in still lower regard.[79] Wilson notes that Blackstone argued for

> "the right of personal security, of personal liberty, and of private property"—not as natural rights, which I confess, I should have expected, but—as the "civil liberties" of Englishmen . . . [thus] civil privileges, [are] provided by society, in lieu of the natural liberties given up by individuals. Considered in this view, there is no material difference between the doctrine of Sir William Blackstone, and that delivered by Mr. Burke.

The almost amnesiac yet unusually well-educated Scot drew out perfectly the logical inferences of the traditionalist social ethics of Blackstone, a historically grounded approach to political rights that in America had gone unquestioned before the beginning of the imperial crisis in the early 1760s.

Adhered to as it was by Blackstone whose *Commentaries* was the second-most-cited written work in America during the late eighteenth century,[80] Wilson drives home his point. Accordingly, he continues by arguing that

> if this view [Blackstone's and Burke's] be a just view of things, then the consequence, undeniable and unavoidable, is, that under civil

79. See Edmund Burke, *Reflections on the Revolution in France,* ed. J. G. A. Pocock (Indianapolis: Hackett Publishing Co., 1987), 29, who proves himself to be similarly one-sided in his description of the normally accepted grounds upon which English rights were said to rest (he ignored the natural or universal character of them). Burke held, to the contrary and much closer to the American norm, that "It has been the uniform policy of our constitution to claim and assert our liberties as an *entailed inheritance* derived to us from our forefathers, and to be transmitted to our posterity—as an estate specially belonging to the people of this kingdom, without any reference whatever to any other more general or prior right."

80. See Donald S. Lutz, "The Relative Influence of European Writers on Late Eighteenth-Century American Political Thought," in *American Political Science Review* 78 (March 1984): 189–97.

government, the right of individuals to their private property, to their personal liberty, to their health, to their reputation, and to their life, flows from a human establishment, and can be traced to no higher source. The connexion between man and his natural rights is intercepted by the institution of civil society . . . [thus under civil society, man] is nothing but what the society frames: he can claim nothing but what the society provides.[81]

In opposition to this theory of traditional, socially bound rights that he found indefensible, especially when mixed with unlimited popular oversight, Wilson offered his understanding of unalienable presocial individual rights, granted by the God of nature and now extended beyond religious conscience to political and moral claims, as a superior alternative.[82] Fearing the power of the majority, Wilson paradoxically sought to protect the prerogatives of wealth, through boldly embracing the language of national rights.

Not all men, however, were equally forgetful, creative, or willing to countenance the changes Wilson proposed. Many remembered that the original political ends pursued by the Revolutionary generation had been similar to those ridiculed by Wilson.[83] For example, Rev. William Emerson, delivering Boston's "Fourth of July Oration" in

81. James Wilson, *The Works of James Wilson*, ed. Robert Green McCloskey, reprint of 1804 ed. (Cambridge: Harvard University Press, 1967), 588–89.

82. James Wilson, *The Works of James Wilson*, ed. James DeWitt Andrews (Chicago: Callaghan and Company, 1896), 105, 125.

83. See Louis Hartz, "American Political Thought and the American Revolution," in *American Political Science Review* 46 (June 1952): 329, who writes, "Most liberals of the eighteenth century, from Bentham to Quesnay, were bitter opponents of history, posing a sharp antithesis between nature and tradition. And it is an equally familiar fact that their adversaries, including Burke and Blackstone, sought to break down this antithesis by identifying natural law with the slow evolution of the past. The militant Americans, confronted with these two positions, actually took the second. . . . Blackstone . . . was the rock on which they relied"; and John M. Murrin, "The Great Inversion, or Court Versus Country: A Comparison of the Revolutionary Settlements in England (1688–1721) and America (1776–1816)," in *Three British Revolutions: 1641, 1688, 1776*, ed. J. G. A. Pocock (Princeton: Princeton University Press, 1980), 391, who writes that "In fact, most of the colonists' leading spokesmen in 1765–1766 . . . skillfully employed legal-constitutional arguments rather than Country rhetoric."

1802, held that late-eighteenth-century Americans had decidedly fought "not to create new rights, but to preserve inviolate such as they had ever possessed, rights of the same sort by which George III then sat, and still sits, on the throne of England, the rights of prescription."[84] Similarly, looking back from 1809 at the Revolutionary period, Edmund Randolph recalls that when some objected in the Virginia Convention of 1776 to the natural rights language of the proposed Virginia Bill of Rights, "perhaps with too great an indifference to futurity," others responded "that with arms in our hands, asserting the general rights of man, we ought not to be too nice and too much restricted in the delineation of them" and, more particularly, the "slaves not being constituent members of our society could never pretend to any benefit from such a maxim." Clearly, then, the language chosen in 1776 Virginia had more to do with the polemical work it could do and less with the exacting demands of a refined political theory. And, however these rights were understood, from the perspective of America's first attorney general, the claimed rights should not be understood as universal ones but rather as belonging only "to constituent members of our society."[85] Emerson, thus, was right; Americans had valued their rights but primarily as inheritances embodied in their colonial charters and the common law of England, not as universal abstract rights belonging to all men (to say nothing of women).

The eloquent and intoxicating rhetoric of individual natural rights, born of mixed Christian parents (Protestant ecclesiology and legalism and Catholic natural law) in Revolutionary America, initially enjoyed the briefest of lives.[86] Nevertheless, these Christian-derived and legitimated presocial rights of the individual did not disappear. Instead, in

84. William Emerson, "Fourth of July Oration, 1802," *Old South Leaflets* (Boston: Directors of the Old South Work, n.d.), 6:189.

85. Edmund Randolph, "Edmund Randolph's Essay on the Revolutionary History of Virginia, 1774–1782," in *Virginia Magazine of History and Biography,* 44 (1936): 45.

86. See Becker, *Declaration of Independence,* 233–34, who writes that after the French Revolution "in very few of the innumerable constitutions of the nineteenth century, in few if any of the constitutions now in force [including the French], do we find the natural rights doctrine of the eighteenth century reaffirmed."

both Europe and America they remained available to legitimate the opposition claims of dissident minorities and individuals to various state institutions and national practices in the name of a blossoming set of unalienable individual rights. For as noted by Schmitt:

> That the freedom of religion represents the first of all the funda-mental rights, without regard to any historical details of develop-ment in a systematic sense is unconditionally correct . . . the indi-vidual as such carries an absolute value and remains with this value in his private sphere. His private freedom is therefore something principally unlimited while the state is only a means and therefore relative, and it follows that each realm of state authority is limited and controllable by private concerns.[87]

Yet, it was only after an interlude of some 150 years, late in the twen-tieth century, that this language became hegemonic and Americans were fully affected by the enormous revolution in thought that their Revolutionary forebears had inadvertently given birth to in the late eighteenth century.[88] And whatever its lasting effects may prove to be, the origins of individual natural rights in the Christian-inspired values of Revolutionary-era Americans must be recognized. This Christian in-heritance, along with many others pulling Americans in not always a

---

87. Schmitt, *Verfassungslehre* (Munchen, 1928), 158–59, my translation. And see Bainton, "Appeal to Reason," 127, from which the German original citation was taken, who describes the above as "the best commentary on the whole con-troversy" concerning the origin of individual universal natural rights. Also see Carl Schmitt, *Political Theology: Four Chapters on the Concept of Sovereignty,* trans. George Schwab, reprint ed. (Cambridge: MIT Press, 1985), 36, where Schmitt argues that "All significant concepts of the modern theory of the state are secu-larized theological concepts . . . [and that] only by being aware of this analogy can we appreciate the manner in which the philosophical ideas of the state de-veloped in the last centuries."

88. See Rodgers, *Contested Truths,* 220, who writes that "Nothing in the eigh-teenth- or nineteenth-century past matched this avalanche of multiplying rights claims [in the late 1960s] . . . In the last quarter of the twentieth century, the lan-guage of rights has proved to be the most volatile, flexible language of protest we have"; and Dorothy Fosdick, *What Is Liberty?: A Study in Political Theory* (New York: Harper & Brothers Publishers, 1939), who details the relatively weak position en-joyed by the natural-rights perspective on liberty in the 1880-to-1930 period.

singular direction, is truly one of the formative elements that has fundamentally shaped the character of the American people and their political institutions.

ORIGINAL SIN

But the enduring influence of the hallowed status attached to the individual right of conscience is not the only lasting Protestant presence that continues to shape American culture and politics. For in any attempt to understand late-eighteenth-century American thought and its continuing influence, one must take note not only of the freedom of religious conscience and those natural rights which followed in its train but of the American conception of the controlling power over society and men of the Christian understanding of original sin. For as Princeton's humanistic Witherspoon held, "Nothing can be more absolutely necessary to true religion than a clear and full conviction of the sinfulness of our nature and state."[89] And politically this demanded that governments help the individual in mastering his otherwise uncontrollable passions, lusts, and in particular his selfishness. In opposition, thus, to varying streams of Christian humanism, certain strands of Catholic scholasticism and the adherents of the Enlightenment who would follow them, most Americans adhered to an understanding of man in need of corporate oversight and rebirth in Christ if he was to flourish.

This teaching, an Augustinian Orthodox Christian perspective, particularly a Reformed Protestant one, holds that man's apostate condition makes it impossible for him to live a life of ordered freedom, one that he would have been able to enjoy eternally if not for his Fall from Grace as described in Genesis. It was exactly this strong sense of limits derived initially from the Christian concept of original sin that largely determined, even if not quite as openly as it had in seventeenth-century America,[90] the understanding of things both religious and

89. John Witherspoon, *The Dominion of Providence over the Passions of Men* (Philadelphia: R. Aitken, 1776), 7–8.

90. See Miller, "Religion and Society in the Early Literature of Virginia" in *Errand into the Wilderness,* 129, 132, who writes that in both Virginia and Massachusetts "Political doctrine was founded on the premise of original sin" and that

political in the eighteenth century. And according to Morgan, even during the era surrounding the Revolution "The intellectual center of the colonies was New England, and the intellectual leaders of New England were the clergy, who preached and wrote indefatigably of human depravity and divine perfection . . . and the purpose of government was to restrain the sinfulness of man, to prevent and punish offenses against God."[91] Thus, it is from these two different Protestant-derived elements, the absolutely hallowed freedom of religious conscience and the inescapable deformation of original sin, that so much of the American Founding political culture follows, though in their interface, not without serious tensions.

Somewhat unexpectedly, the case for the centrality of original sin is nearly as strong in American political culture as in its religious history. For example, the anachronistic (by comparison to advanced Enlightenment standards) attachment of eighteenth-century Americans to Christian communalism and intrusive involvement in the life of the individual only becomes understandable when one recognizes that the most local group must "walk" with a fellow sinner and help him or her to lead a more godly life.[92] Similarly, American antipathy toward political and ecclesiastic hierarchy, so characteristic of Reformed Protestant thought, becomes comprehensible when it is realized that no sinful man, no matter how socially elevated, could be trusted with corrupting power. In 1753, Livingston captured this particularly American distrust of hierarchy and fear of empowering necessarily sinful individuals when he wrote that "It is unreasonable to suppose, that Government which is designed chiefly to correct the Exorbitancies

---

the authoritarian character of their governments was "the logical consequence of a theology of depravity and enslavement of the will."

91. Edmund S. Morgan, "The American Revolution Considered as an Intellectual Movement," in *Essays on the American Revolution,* ed. David L. Jacobson (New York: Holt, Rinehart and Winston, Inc., 1970), 29.

92. See Nathan O. Hatch, *The Sacred Cause of Liberty: Republican Thought and the Millennium in Revolutionary New England* (New Haven: Yale University Press, 1977), 125, who writes that "The primary purpose of government" for the Standing Order of New England, "was to restrain the corruptions of human nature"; and Michael Zuckerman, *Peaceable Kingdoms: New England Towns in the Eighteenth Century* (New York: Alfred A. Knopf, 1970), 116–17.

of human Nature, should entirely consist in the uncontroulable Dictates, of a Man of equal Imperfections with the Rest of the Community, who being invested with the Authority of the Whole, has an unlimited Power to commit whatever Exorbitancies he shall think fit."[93]

Also made comprehensible through recognition of eighteenth-century Americans' continued adherence to the Protestant dogma of original sin was the extreme dedication of Americans to political and economic personal independence or autonomy. For them, no man could be trusted with undue influence over one's most precious possession, one's spiritual life, which only an independent man had the wherewithal to guard. For eighteenth-century Americans, man's ability to enjoy unfettered freedom, no matter how attractive it might seem, was prevented by his passionate, egotistical, and unruly nature. Thus, as a result of the Fall, man was destined to live always under the restraints of government. For as the unusually progressive and enlightened James Madison had written, "If men were angels, no government would be necessary."[94] Even the still more progressive Jefferson believed that "The human character . . . requires in general constant and immediate control, to prevent its being biased from right by the seduction of self-love."[95] In fact, Howe has recently argued in a persuasive fashion that for Publius and men of his generation "The idea of inevitable evil in human nature did not surprise [them as they] . . . were well acquainted with the Christian doctrine of original sin and

93. William Livingston, et al., *The Independent Reflector or Weekly Essays on Sundry Important Subjects More Particularly Adapted to the Province of New York,* ed. Milton M. Klein (Cambridge: Harvard University Press, 1963), 329. Also see Bernard Bailyn, *The Ideological Origins of the American Revolution* (Cambridge: Harvard University Press, 1967), 59–60, who writes that in eighteenth-century America "What turned power into a malignant force, was not its nature so much as the nature of man—his susceptibility to corruption and his lust for self-aggrandizement. On this there was absolute agreement. . . . But it was not simply a question of what the weak and ignorant will do. The problem was more systematic than that; it concerned 'mankind in general.'"

94. Publius, "Essay #51," Alexander Hamilton, John Jay, and James Madison, *The Federalist: A Commentary on the Constitution of the United States,* ed. Edward Mead Earle (New York: Modern Library Edition, 1937), 337.

95. "Letter of 24 April 1816," in Thomas Jefferson, *Writings,* ed. Merrill D. Peterson (New York: Literary Classics of the United States, 1984), 1386.

its secularized versions in eighteenth-century faculty psychology."[96] Or in the words of Andrew Eliot, "The necessity of government arises wholly from the disadvantages, which, in the present imperfect state of human nature [Fallen], would be the natural consequence of unlimited freedom."[97]

The most important political implication of their Calvinist-inspired belief in the sinful nature of all men, however, might have been the imperial crisis itself. By passing the Declaratory Act on March 18, 1766, and demanding from Americans "unlimited submission" in "all cases whatsoever," the British Parliament had created a situation that most Americans as Reformed Protestants were obligated to resist.[98] For, as Calvin's teacher Butzer had written in his *Lectures on the Book of Judges*, "Wherever absolute power is given to a prince, there the glory and the dominion of God is injured. The absolute power, which is God's alone, would be given to a man liable to sin."[99] By demanding unlimited submission, Parliament, an external body of sinful men, had effectively "set itself alongside God's Word as a competing sovereign."[100] The Americans' response as a Reformed Protestant people, theologically and historically committed to submitting only to local self-control and through this medium to God and His word "and only God's word —in all aspects of life and faith," should have been predictable.[101] Par-

96. Daniel Walker Howe, "The Political Psychology of *The Federalist*," in *William and Mary Quarterly* 44 (July 1987): 502, and see his *Making the American Self: Jonathan Edwards to Abraham Lincoln* (Cambridge: Harvard University Press, 1997), 108.

97. Andrew Eliot, *Massachusetts Election Sermon* (Boston: Green and Russell, 1765), 8–9.

98. See Max Weber, *The Protestant Ethic and the Spirit of Capitalism*, trans. Talcott Parsons (New York: Charles Scribner's Sons, 1958), 255–56, who has written of the "sinfulness of the belief in authority, which is only permissible in the form of an impersonal authority, the Scriptures, as well as of an excessive devotion to even the most holy and virtuous of men, since that might interfere with obedience to God. . . . It is also part of the historical background of that lack of respect of the American which is, as the case may be, so irritating or so refreshing"; and Zuckerman, *Peaceable Kingdoms*, 248–49.

99. Cited by Hans Baron, "Calvinist Republicanism and Its Historical Roots," in *Church History* 8 (1939): 37.

100. Here, I am largely following Stout, *The New England Soul*, 7.

101. Ibid., 259.

liament had framed the debate in such a way that most Americans immediately understood it in quasi-millennial terms as a struggle between eternal life and perpetual damnation.[102] Accordingly, American pastors could effectively use the themes of spiritual liberty, freedom of religious conscience, and human sinfulness for wartime mobilization.

More generally, the concept of original sin, rather than a dedication to human perfectibility, makes Americans' beliefs about liberty, political and religious, comprehensible. Without understanding its dominating presence, poorly prepared contemporary readers are likely to misinterpret the often libertarian-sounding praises made by late eighteenth-century pamphleteers and ministers concerning the beauties of natural freedom. Or they may forget that the regard paid to "natural liberty" in late-eighteenth-century America could not function as a powerful social solvent because it was effectively mooted by their simultaneous continued belief in man's inherent sinfulness and Fall from Grace.

When we examine, then, American-Revolutionary-era pamphlets and sermons that explicate their social, religious, and political thought, we frequently confront the importance of the concept of original sin that can be seen holding together the tension-filled and inherently fragile balance between the antinomian Christian demands for absolute freedom of conscience and the equally authentic demands for social stability and a Christian cultus consistent with the doctrine of original sin. For example, in the 1776 Massachusetts election sermon, even a rationalist Unitarian like Samuel West, far from being an Orthodox Calvinist,[103] did not equivocate in arguing "The highest

102. See Keith Thomas, "Politics Recaptured," review of *The Foundations of Modern Political Thought,* by Quentin Skinner, in *New York Review of Books,* May 17, 1979, 28, who writes "Lutherans and Calvinists alike continued to represent resistance to unsatisfactory rulers as a religious duty rather than a political right."

103. Here, and elsewhere, in his reductionistic dualism, Zuckert and likeminded political theorists consistently confuse heterodox Unitarian ministers with Orthodox Trinitarian ones and hold that the former were highly regarded by the majority of Orthodox ministers. Compare, then, the evaluation and use of New England ministers made by Zuckert, in every instance (with the exception of Elisha Williams), to the canonical evaluations provided by William B. Sprague, *Annals of the American Pulpit . . . of Distinguished American Clergymen of Various Denominations* (New York: Robert Carter & Brothers, 1859), vols. 1 and 8. Included

state of liberty subjects us to the law of nature and the government of God. The most perfect freedom consists in obeying the dictates of right reason, and submitting to natural law." But he then limits the boundaries of "liberty" reminding his auditors of their sinful condition and that

> The law of nature is a perfect standard and a measure of action for beings that persevere in a state of moral rectitude; but the case is far different with us, who are in a fallen and degenerate estate. We have a law in our members which is continually warring against the law of the mind, by which we often become enslaved to the basest lusts, and brought into bondage to the vilest passions. The strong propensities of our animal nature often overcome the sober dictates of reason and conscience, and betray us into actions injurious to the public. . . . This makes it absolutely necessary that societies should form themselves into politic bodies, that they may enact laws for the public safety.[104]

For late-eighteenth-century Americans, even Christian humanists like West, descriptions of the joy of natural unfettered freedom were depictions of a paradise lost which could be recovered only through death and the loss of their worldly self in Christ.[105] Man was born free but, as a result of his inherently sinful nature, must live in self-imposed societal chains.

---

among those whom Zuckert tendentiously treats as Orthodox but whom Sprague shows to be Unitarian, are West and others like Charles Chauncy and Jonathan Mayhew. And another minister, Abraham Williams, who Zuckert describes as "memorable chiefly because of his 'illustrativeness'" (173), is described as "the Grand Hertick Williams," in Clifford K. Shipton, ed., *Sibley's Harvard Graduates: Biographical Sketches of Those Who Attended Harvard College* (Boston: Massachusetts Historical Society, 1960), 11:498.

104. West, "On the Right to Rebel Against Governors" in Charles S. Hyneman, and Donald S. Lutz, eds., *American Political Writing during the Founding Era, 1760–1805* (Indianapolis: Liberty Fund, 1983), 415.

105. See George M. Marsden, *Fundamentalism and American Culture: The Shaping of Twentieth-Century Evangelicalism, 1870–1925* (New York: Oxford University Press, 1980), 74, who writes that for Presbyterians and other Calvinist sects "Perfection would never be attained in this life. . . . The Christian's life was a warfare, with many setbacks that taught humility and dependence on God's grace."

Peter Powers, in Vermont's second election sermon in 1778, similarly might be seen as arguing for a regime of individualism and natural rights. In reality, a close reading discloses that he too was arguing for a quite different position. He begins by abstractly describing man's natural freedom, that is, his rights and liberty before the Fall. Here he holds that "All men, indeed, are by nature equal: and all have, most certainly, an equal right to freedom and liberty by the great law of nature. No man or number of men, *has* or *can* have a right to infringe the natural rights, liberties or privileges of others." Later, he returns to the theme of liberty and reins in his briefly liberated auditors by reminding them that

> It is a very plain case that many people of the present day, have very absurd notions of Liberty, as if it consisted in a right for every one to believe, do, or act as he pleases in all things civil and religious. This is a *Libertine* principle. No man has any right, before God, to believe or practice contrary to scripture. And Liberty consists in a freedom to do that which is right. The great law of nature, the moral law, is the rule of right action. Man's fall has taken away his freedom of right action; for *whosoever committeth sin is the servant of sin.*[106]

As these two examples help illustrate, for eighteenth-century Americans, even among the most progressive of Christian humanists, it was sin, not their necessarily imperfect society, which stood between them and true freedom.

In an instructive fashion, Nathaniel Whitaker delineated that as a result of the Fall, man's political possibilities were also necessarily severely limited. He began his sermon as was the custom by discussing natural liberty and by citing Locke, which was also quite usual. He went on to argue then, in a fashion not emphasized by Locke but common for American authors, that the state of nature is in fact of little interest to man "since the corruption of nature by sin, the lusts and passions of men so blind their minds, and harden their hearts, that this perfect law of love is little considered . . . [and the] state of nature

---

106. Peter Powers, *Jesus Christ the True King and Head of the Government* (Vermont Election Sermon) (Newbury-Port, Mass.: John Mycall, 1778), 10, 40.

. . . is a state of war, rapine and murder."[107] Sin, original sin, was the implacable foe of man, and it alone prevented him from enjoying the absolute freedom consistent with their idealized state of nature.

Whitaker continued by boldly indicating who should decide how much natural liberty is to be surrendered for the public good in civil society. He writes that

> perfect civil Liberty differs from natural, only in this, that in a natural state our actions, persons and possessions, are under the direction, judgment and controul of none but ourselves; but in a civil state, under the directions of others . . . In the first case, private judgment; in the second, the public judgment of the sense of the law of nature is to be the rule of conduct.

He protected himself against the charge of supporting tyranny by continuing "When any laws are enacted, which cross the law of nature, there civil Liberty is invaded, and God and man justly *offended*."[108] Even under this condition, the basic stricture of who is to decide (i.e., the community still continued to obtain), man and God simply were left potentially offended.

In Revolutionary America, not only fully Orthodox New England Congregationalists but almost all who have left records of their beliefs concurred. The freedom to live a life directed by lusts and passions, a selfish life of sin, a broad grouping of Protestant adherents and a handful of relatively secular rationalists almost universally condemned.[109] And concerning the elite leadership, Morgan has written that "The

107. Nathaniel Whitaker, *An Antidote Against Toryism* (Newburyport, Mass.: John Mycall, 1777), 10–11.

108. Ibid., 11–12.

109. See Gordon S. Wood, *The Creation of the American Republic, 1776–1787* (Chapel Hill: University of North Carolina Press, 1969), 115–16, who notes that "Everywhere the clergy saw 'Sins and Iniquities.' . . . And the sins were the same vices feared by a political scientist—infidelity, intemperance, profaneness, and particularly 'pride and luxury in dress'"; and Eric Foner, *Tom Paine and Revolutionary America* (New York: Oxford University Press, 1976), 90–91, who writes that "Inherent in the Commonwealth ideology which shaped the American Whig mind was a view of human nature as susceptible to corruption, basically self-interested and dominated by passion rather than reason."

men who steered Americans through the Revolution . . . started from a conviction of human depravity,"[110] as is found in the thinking of New England Federalists like Jeremiah Atwater, the first president of Middlebury College, and David Daggett, United States senator and chief justice of Connecticut's Supreme Court. According to Atwater, "Liberty, if considered as a blessing, must be taken in a qualified sense" in which "unbounded liberty" was nothing "other than the liberty of sinning, the liberty of indulging lawless passions."[111]

Many of the New England supporters of the new Federal Constitution in 1787 and 1788 also believed not only that man was sinful but that "The civil power has a right . . . to prohibit and punish gross immoralities and impieties. . . . For this reason, I heartily approve of our laws against drunkenness, profane swearing, blasphemy, and professed atheism."[112] And as Curry has shown, this understanding was not a minority Federalist belief, but one held by "the vast majority of Americans" who agreed that the "government should enforce the sabbath and respect for the scriptures, limit office to Christians or Protestants, and generally support the Christian Protestant mores that entwined both state and society."[113] Thus, we should not be surprised to discover that even under Jefferson's administration, religious services continued to be regularly held on Sunday in the Capitol, in various

110. Morgan, "American Revolution Considered as an Intellectual Movement," 36, and see Hatch, *Sacred Cause of Liberty,* 92–93, who writes that their "suspicion of human nature found deep roots both in the seventeenth-century [Puritanism they inherited] . . . and in the opposition heritage, which like *Cato's Letters,* suggested that men are controlled by their passions . . . [which] 'are always terrible when they are not controlled.'"

111. Atwater, "Vermont Election Day Sermon" in Hyneman and Lutz, *American Political Writing,* 1172; and see David Daggett, "Sunbeams May Be Extracted from Cucumbers, But the Process Is Tedious: An Oration Pronounced on the Fourth of July, 1799," in *American Forum: Speeches on Historic Issues, 1788–1900,* ed. E. J. Wrage and B. Baskerville (New York: Harper & Brothers, 1960), 41–42.

112. Oliver Ellsworth, writing under the pseudonym of "A Landholder" in Paul L. Ford, ed., *Essays on the Constitution of the United States: Published During Its Discussion by the People, 1787–1788* (1892; reprint ed., New York: Burt Franklin, 1970), 171; and see Josiah Whitney, *The Essential Requisites to Form the Good Rulers Character* (Connecticut Election Sermon) (Hartford: Elisha Babcock, 1788), 11.

113. Curry, *First Freedoms,* 190.

executive offices, and in the Supreme Court, and that Jefferson him-self attended such services and provided "financial support during his presidency for at least nine local churches."[114]

Similarly, John Witherspoon, president of Princeton, long-serving member of Congress, and a man of the moderate Scottish Enlight-enment who was deeply influenced by the moral-sense teachings of Francis Hutcheson, demonstrated a firm rejection of a late Enlighten-ment optimism in human goodness. "The Enlightenment image of a virtuous society seemed extremely cloudy. 'Others may, if they please, treat the corruption of our nature as a chimera: for my part,' said John Witherspoon . . . 'I see it everywhere, and I feel it every day.'"[115] Such relatively modest assertions concerning human depravity are best appreciated when compared both on the one hand to bolder claims made concerning man's absolute depravity by America's ubiqui-tous eighteenth-century Orthodox Calvinist denominations—Congre-gational, Presbyterian, and some Baptist—and on the other to the rare American radical Enlightenment figures like Elihu Palmer and Ethan Allen,[116] and their more plentiful European brethren who argued in defense of human perfectibility.[117]

The American humanistic elite, both republican and Christian, to say nothing of the more pious Protestant and in some ways more con-

114. Hutson, *Religion and the Founding of the American Republic*, 93–96. Hutson further claims that Jefferson was the most theologically involved of America's presidents.

115. Wood, *Creation of the American Republic*, 114–15.

116. To gauge better the moderate character of these stances, consider Philip Greven, *The Protestant Temperament: Patterns of Child-Rearing, Religious Experience, and the Self in Early America* (New York: New American Library, 1977), 65–66, the author's description of the centrality of "the doctrine of original sin and of innate depravity" to the thought of eighteenth-century American Evangelical Christians and that for them "Human nature was corrupt, not in part but totally. Sinful men, said Jonathan Edwards, 'are totally corrupt, in every part, in all their faculties. . . . There is nothing but sin, no good at all.'"

117. See May, *Enlightenment in America*, 231, who discusses the few radical deists in America, like the blind preacher Elihu Palmer who adhered to the be-lief that man was perfectible and that "This great truth, the new deists tirelessly explained, had been hidden from mankind by the sinister alliance of priests and kings, whose chief reliance had always been the absurd doctrine of original sin."

servative average American, rejected the most optimistic elements of the Enlightenment and instead adhered to some version of the Protestant (and earlier Catholic) axiom of original sin. Even according to the celebrated liberal apologist Louis Hartz, "Americans refused to join in the great Enlightenment enterprise of shattering the Christian concept of sin, [and] replacing it with an unlimited humanism."[118] At the end of the century when indeed the advocates of the French Revolution widely championed ideas of human perfectibility, the moderate pillars of American provincial society continued to distance themselves from any rejection of the concept of original sin. And, according to a leading student of the Enlightenment, Norman Hampson, the rejection of the concept of the Fall was the central tenet of the liberal and anti-Christian Enlightenment.[119] Thus, already in 1798 Israel Woodward compared the world views of the French and the American elite, so different in their relationship to Christianity, and found that

> The *liberties* of the American and French nations, are grounded upon totally different and opposite principles. In their matters of civil government, they adopt this general maxim, that mankind are virtuous enough to need no restraint; which idea is most justly reprobated by the more enlightened inhabitants of the United States, who denominate such liberty, licentiousness.[120]

This rejection of secular optimism in human perfectibility in favor of Christian pessimism was and would long continue American orthodoxy.

Even those nonpious leaders we expect to have held the most en-

---

118. Hartz, "American Political Thought and the American Revolution," 324.

119. See Hampson, *Enlightenment*, 102–3; and see Carl L. Becker, *The Heavenly City of the Eighteenth-Century Philosophers* (New Haven: Yale University Press, 1932), 102–3, who writes that "The essential articles of the religion of the Enlightenment may be stated thus: (1) man is not natively depraved . . . (3) man is capable, guided solely by the light of reason and experience, of perfecting the good life on earth."

120. Israel B. Woodward, *American Liberty and Independence: A Discourse* (Litchfield, Conn.: T. Collier, 1798), 8.

lightened views of man, such as the "founding fathers,"[121] or particularly the "four ex-presidents still alive in 1826," continued to believe "That evil in human nature and in world affairs was indelible, and that the hardships of life spring from 'basic nature,' not from custom or 'second nature.'"[122] Recent students of the late eighteenth century have even argued that two of the most secular of American authors, Tom Paine and Ben Franklin, adhered religiously to the concept of original sin.[123] Paine's theism, according to this analysis, becomes particularly evident when his thought is compared to even relatively conservative French Revolutionary thinkers. De Prospo notes that

> What nobody seems willing to consider is the possibility that Paine is no kind of modern humanist whatsoever . . . [and that] the basis of Paine's position on representative government and kingship is the onto-theological status of man . . . [that is] the Creation of an imperfect, natural creature by a perfect, supernatural Creator. . . . The only other application of the doctrine of imputation in eighteenth-century American letters that compares with Paine's thoroughness

121. See Hamilton, "Essay #15," *The Federalist*, 92, who writes that the moral assumptions underlying the Articles of Confederation "betrayed an ignorance of the true springs by which human conduct is actuated, and belied the original inducements to the establishment of civil power. Why has government been instituted at all? Because the passions of men will not conform to the dictates of reason and justice, without constraint."

122. Ralph Ketcham, *Presidents Above Party: The First American Presidency, 1789–1829* (Chapel Hill: University of North Carolina Press, 1984), 144. See Ralph Ketcham, "James Madison and the Nature of Man," in *Journal of the History of Ideas* 19 (January 1958): 66; and Paul Merrill Spurlin, *The French Enlightenment in America: Essays on the Times of the Founding Fathers* (Athens: University of Georgia Press, 1984), 126–27, for American reaction to claims of human perfectibility. In particular, Spurlin writes that "The philosophical notion of indefinite perfectibility bothered the religious-minded Adams no end," while Jefferson took a more intermediate position.

123. See William Pencak, "Benjamin Franklin's *Autobiography*, Cotton Mather, and a Puritan God," in *Pennsylvania History* 53 (January 1986): 13, who notes that Franklin "begins with a description of how the world is ruled by the minions of Satan . . . [and that] such a negative view of human nature, is found throughout the *Autobiography*."

and sophistication is that of Jonathan Edwards, who uses it in *Original Sin*.[124]

And even if such an account is not wholly convincing, it is in keeping with the overtly Protestant climate within which Paine wrote.

John Diggins also reminds us that even the most enlightened of eighteenth-century Americans, including even Boston's ubiquitous Unitarian humanists and the tidewater South's Anglican gentlemen, were on this question of innate humane depravement and subsequent personal and social limitation remarkably Protestant by comparison to European Enlightenment figures.[125] He thus castigates his fellow historians for having "focused almost solely on political ideas" while slighting "religious convictions." He impresses on his readers that "The conviction that man was cursed by the 'Fall'" and that "the unspoken imagery of sin and evil" were the beliefs of the Founding Fathers and are found in "the pages of the *Federalist* and the *Defense.*"[126] In particular, for John Adams, Diggins holds, "Man had lost his reason through the Fall, the Christian account of alienation that stood as a lesson to the pretensions of classical politics." He reminds us that Adams had argued that "The heart is deceitful above all things and desperately wicked . . . [for] it must be remembered, that although reason ought always to govern individuals, it certainly never did since the Fall, and never will till the Millennium."[127] Regarding the Madisonian and puta-

---

124. R. C. De Prospo, "Paine and Sieyes," in *Thought* 65 (June 1990): 195–97.

125. See also Carl Bridenbaugh, *Mitre and Sceptre: Transatlantic Faiths, Ideas, Personalities, and Politics 1689–1775* (New York: Oxford University Press, 1962), xi, who writes that "No understanding of the eighteenth century is possible if we unconsciously omit, or consciously jam out, the religious themes just because our own milieu is secular . . . in England's American colonies the most enduring and absorbing public question from 1689 to 1777 was religion."

126. John P. Diggins, *The Lost Soul of American Politics: Virtue, Self-Interest, and the Foundations of Liberalism* (New York: Basic Books, 1984), 7, 67, 83; see Robert E. Shalhope, "Republicanism and Early American Historiography," in *William and Mary Quarterly* 39 (April 1982): 350–51, who also notes that "The republican temperament that emerged during the Revolution drew on basic evangelical values."

127. Diggins, ibid., 84–85, 94. He is citing Adams, *Defence*, 3:289, 479. Cf., Thomas Pangle, *The Spirit of Modern Republicanism: The Moral Vision of the American*

tively liberal First Amendment, Tushnet has similarly concluded that the "Normative understanding of the establishment clause cannot be translated directly into contemporary constitutional law without a substantial shift in our current intellectual universe, a shift that would somehow have to retrieve the assumption that this is a Protestant nation in a normatively attractive form."[128]

This is not to say, however, that there were no differences between Christian humanists and Orthodox Calvinists regarding their views of man's debased condition. As a predominantly Reformed people, most Americans held that the wages of original sin could not be eradicated through the efforts of individual will and appropriate moral education.[129] And it was here, concerning the means, anthropocentric or theocentric, whereby man's sinful nature might be combated, that the battle lines were drawn between Christian and secular humanists and Reformed Protestants (at least until the rise of Methodism). For in America, even a leading "specimen of the radical temperament" like Benjamin Rush, a scientist and an ardent republican, was simultaneously "a lifelong believer in original sin, divine grace, and the Christian millennium."[130] Even for those men who, at best, had a lukewarm

---

Founders and the Philosophy of Locke (Chicago: University of Chicago Press, 1988), 21, who disagrees with Diggins's understanding of the "Founders." Pangle, like Zuckert, finds that "As for the claim that 'sin' is a major motif, or a key to the thought of *The Federalist Papers,* Diggins himself all but admits that he has been able to find no evidence for this outlandish characterization."

128. Mark Tushnet, "Should Historians Accept the Supreme Court's Invitation?" in *Organization of American Historians Newsletter* 15 (November 1987): 13. Of course, this is largely a problem for elite sectors of American society. Most nonelite Americans are still Christian and in most cases still Protestant if not Evangelical.

129. See May, *Enlightenment in America,* xv, xviii, who cautions his readers that "A great many people believed throughout the period that the religion of the Bible, understood best by simple people, was the safest foundation for all essential truths . . . the Enlightenment developed among the middle and upper classes of European cities, spread mainly among similar groups in America, and failed to reach the agrarian majority. On the whole, various forms of Protestant Christianity served the emotional needs of most Americans better." And on the lack of support, even among the elite in America for the new subjectivist understanding of reason, see 250–51.

130. Ibid., 211.

attachment to the dogmas of Calvinism embodied in the Five Points of the Synod of Dort, the Westminister Confession, or the 39 Articles of the Anglican Church,[131] original sin continued to be understood as a permanent human condition that demanded that society be framed in recognition of this deforming limit on human potential. Members of the radical Enlightenment who were "freethinkers," thus, were scorned in eighteenth-century America.[132]

Particularly difficult for the modern reader to accept, given the misleading historiography of contemporary liberal apologists, is that even the leading lights of late-eighteenth-century America were simultaneously unwilling to countenance the self-development of the uniquely individualistic features of the self.[133] Although arguing powerfully and in a modern fashion against uncontrollable political and religious hierarchy and authority as well as most forms of tradition, early modern American rationalists generally abhorred those aspects of the individual that were alienated from the "objectively right" ordering of the cosmos (that society and man were to reflect in any just and rational society). Their hostility toward emerging individualism, in particular, reflected this.[134] Even American adherents of the moderate Enlightenment believed that society at the most fundamental level was a forum in which the individual was to develop his quasi-divine rational perfection, in a manner strikingly reminiscent of Christianity—at the very least of Thomistic Catholicism.[135] But, from this

131. The five central holdings of the Synod of Dort were the total depravity of man, unconditional predestination and reprobation, limitation of Redemption to the elect, the irresistibility of divine grace, and its perseverance in those saved.

132. See Herbert W. Schneider, *A History of American Philosophy* (New York: Columbia University Press, 1946), 67–72, 83–85, for his discussion of the short list of the few and ill-reputed "freethinkers" writing and living in late-eighteenth-century America.

133. See Shain, *The Myth of American Individualism*.

134. See Fosdick, *What Is Liberty? A Study in Political Theory*, 46, who writes that for Kant, "Liberty is to be one's reasonable self. . . . It is acting in conformity with one's good will which is at once the inevitable and universal expressions of the rationality of the individual"; and Howe, "Political Psychology of *The Federalist*," 488–500.

135. See Troeltsch, *Protestantism and Progress*, 35–36, who notes that "Modern

now equally antiquated perspective, the individual was only free from social constraints so that he could voluntarily accept his absolute obligation to act as he must, that is, in an objectively rational fashion.[136] For the moral agent, knowledge of what was rationally prescribed was determinative, creating an ought and inalienable right that could only be abrogated by the abnegation of one's unique moral standing as a free rational human being. To ignore this rational self-direction was evidence that one was either not truly free or not acting rationally.[137]

From the perspective of eighteenth-century American Reformed Protestants however, the human-centered norms embraced by elite rationalists for overcoming the sinful self were woefully inadequate. Like their forebears in the Reformation, their American descendants staked out an unequivocal position in opposition to such relative optimism concerning man's unaided ability to follow his reason and to will moral behavior. For example, the Southern Evangelical minister from Virginia, David Thomas, held that

> Sin and Satan, and the world, and the flesh have an absolute dominion over them. . . . Nor has any man power to deliver himself out of this woeful condition. . . . The dead as soon might leave their tombs, or dry bones, awake and live, as natural men by any virtue in them, repent and turn to GOD. . . . For without faith it is impossible to please him. And that faith . . . is to be obtained but by the operation of the HOLY-GHOST.[138]

---

individualism" is based "on the idea, which is essentially Christian," that "the destination of man [is] to acquire perfected personality through the ascent to God."

136. See Isaiah Berlin, "Two Concepts of Liberty," in *Four Essays on Liberty* (New York: Oxford University Press, 1969), 147, who writes that "If the universe is governed by reason, then there will be no need for coercion; a correctly planned life for all will coincide with full freedom—the freedom of rational self-direction—for all. This will be so if, and only if, the plan is the true plan."

137. See Berlin, ibid., 141–42, who writes of this understanding that "The only true method of attaining freedom, we are told, is by the use of critical reason, the understanding of what is necessary and what is contingent. . . . What you know, that of which you understand the necessity—the rational necessity—you cannot, while remaining rational, want to do otherwise."

138. David Thomas, *The Virginian Baptist: A View and Defence of the Christian Religion as it is Professed by the Baptists of Virginia* (Baltimore: Enoch Story, 1774), 9–10.

This understanding of sinful man and his crying need for undeserved grace was thundered from pulpits and meetings in the South, as well as the North.

Ministers like Thomas as well as Hugh Alison of South Carolina reminded their listeners that they were freed by "the operation of the blessed spirit! Their bondage is at an end, and their obedience is a *perfect freedom.*"[139] Before the provincial Congress of Georgia, John Zubly warned the legislators in an often-reprinted sermon that "No external enemy can so completely tyrannize over a conquered enemy as sin does over all those who yield themselves its servants . . . till the grace of GOD brings salvation, when he would do good, evil is present with him: in short, instead of being under a law of liberty, he is under the law of sin and death."[140] In sermon after sermon, one confronts an understanding of man that, following Calvin's demanding theology, leaves no room for any confidence in man's natural ability to control his selfish passions and lusts. From this perspective, natural man could gain a vague and imperfect view of the good but, without the aid of Christ and justification through faith, natural man was wholly incapable of fully knowing or willing the good. The heroic view of the free will, unencumbered by original sin, popular among elite Unitarian circles in the nineteenth century, had not yet gained open adherents in the eighteenth-century South.

And in the North, Baptist and Presbyterian ministers and even some of the more "enlightened" Anglicans[141] repeated the same message

139. Hugh Alison, *Spiritual Liberty: A Sermon* (Charleston: Hugh Alison, 1769), 14–16, who began, holding that "All men, being by nature the children of wrath and disobedience, lie exposed to the penalty of a broken law. . . . But believers in Christ are already freed from the condemning sentence of the law, and delivered from the guilt of sin."

140. John Joachim Zubly, *The Law of Liberty . . . Preached at the Opening of the Provincial Congress of Georgia* (Philadelphia: J. Almon, 1775), 27, who continues, "but whenever he feels the happy influence of the grace of the gospel, then this 'law of liberty makes him free from the law of sin and death.' Rom viii. 2."

141. See the Lyme, Connecticut, pastor, Stephen Johnson, *Some Important Observations, Occasioned by . . . the Public Fast* (Newport, R.I.: Samuel Hall, 1766), 52, who reminds his listeners in Newport that "Sin kindles a fire in the divine anger, which (without repentance and pardon in the blood of Christ) will burn to the lowest hell."

of man's unaided inability to fend off the wages of original sin. According to Hatch, even radical political activists like the Baptist Isaac Backus held that the "Definition of true liberty was premised much more on human depravity than on rationality or inalienable rights, and reflected John Winthrop's sermon on Christian Liberty and Jonathan Edwards's definition of true virtue."[142] Further exemplifying this outlook, Dartmouth's president reminded his auditors "In CHRIST's kingdom—there is no such thing as a natural right in this spiritual kingdom. None has right so much as to be, or do, or enjoy the least thing in this kingdom, but by grant from Christ."[143]

Even as progressive a minister as the Unitarian Simeon Howard maintained man's woeful inadequacy through individual effort to overcome his inherent sinfulness. In 1780 he asked his audience "to reflect with shame upon the selfishness and corruption of our species, who, with all their rational and moral powers, cannot otherwise be kept from injuring and destroying one another."[144] According to Stout, even with humanistic ministers like Howard this was the norm because "a purely natural theology was unacceptable even to the most liberal and open-minded New England ministers. . . . It was a truism of New England pulpit teaching that the natural man—no matter how wise and enlightened—was incapable of reconciling himself to God. This reconciliation could be accomplished only through the intervention of the Holy Spirit."[145] Combating sin demanded the action of the Holy Spirit and that of brethren joined together in community and congregation.[146]

142. Nathan O. Hatch, "In Pursuit of Religious Freedom: Church, State, and People in the New Republic," in *The American Revolution: Its Character and Limits*, ed. Jack P. Greene (New York: New York University Press, 1987), 393.

143. Eleazar Wheelock, *Liberty of Conscience; or, No King But Christ, in his Church* (Hartford: Eben. Watson, 1776), 16.

144. Howard, "A Sermon Preached . . . May 31, 1780" in Thornton, *Pulpit of the American Revolution*, 382–83, who goes forward to argue that "This is a very humiliating consideration; and, so far as we know, there is no other order of creatures throughout the boundless universe who, if left to their natural liberty, would be so mischievous to one another as man."

145. Stout, *New England Soul*, 135–36.

146. See David H. Flaherty, "Law and the Enforcement of Morals in Early America," in *Perspectives in American History* 5 (1971): 211, who writes that "The

Most Revolutionary-era Americans thus accepted that one of the responsibilities of local political, social, and religious communities was aiding the individual sinner in his or her quest for freedom in Christ.[147] Therefore, in the late eighteenth century, it still continued to be held that

> Most men instinctively chose the Puritan vision of the state of nature—after the fall. They believed that hard work and harsh laws were needed to curb man's innately sinful nature, so they sought to bind themselves into a society as a defense against the terrors of sinfulness within . . . [and] to fetter their unruly natures in a web of reciprocal obligations, an entangling network of laws. . . . In the ideal, everyone watched over everyone else and did not hesitate to intervene if another got off the track.[148]

Nevertheless, during this period there existed a small number of influential elite Christian humanists and a smaller group of secular rationalists who were moving toward the tenets of classical liberalism. This demanded, of course, that they reject that one of the still important functions of public bodies was their efforts to help reform the individual. Accordingly they did not assign the same priority to spiritual and moral concerns as did their more Orthodox Protestant peers. But, in considering this caveat to the previous discussion, two considerations must be borne in mind.

First, the soon-to-be liberal elite was still during the Revolutionary years as publicly committed to religion and the dogma of original sin as any of the pastors or publicists cited above.[149] Although many of

---

enforcement of the moral law became one of the primary obligations of colonial governments. . . . The civil authorities in every colony made a regular effort to establish and uphold high standards of conduct."

147. See Curry, *First Freedoms,* 103, who writes that "The idea that government should promote a Christian society persisted" because "most Americans tended to assume that the common elements of Protestantism equated with natural religion."

148. Richard Lingeman, *Small Town America: A Narrative History 1620–The Present* (New York: G. P. Putnam's Sons, 1980), 61.

149. The early modern rationalists shared in common with their more religious brethren a belief in objective moral truth and rational ethical standards. They no more countenanced arbitrary, in effect, sinful behavior than the more

these men, particularly some of those described as the "Founders," understood Christian religiosity in a wholly instrumental fashion, this does not vitiate the power of their commitment to "religion." "Men like Jefferson and Madison," according to Pangle who frequently ridicules defenders of America's Protestant character, "did honor religion" but "not for its theological richness or theoretical insight, but for its moral value."[150] Other students of the period, like "Miller, Levy, and Curry" have demonstrated that the Founders understood religion to be "an essential precondition of social order and a crucial prop for the novel sort of government they were creating." Elite forces supported establishment in many of the new states, assuming it to be necessary. Nonetheless, they did so more often in terms of bourgeois morality than godly ends.[151] But this realization does not imply that the vast majority of Americans, who most certainly were not privy to the private thoughts of the elite, would have understood that the "religion" that the "Founders" so vociferously supported was, in fact, strikingly different from that preached by their Protestant pastors and regularly asserted by themselves.[152]

---

religious members of the elite. See Gordon S. Wood, "Introduction," in *The Rising Glory of America, 1760–1820* (New York: George Braziller, 1971), 17, who writes that "Although nature had been important to Revolutionary Americans, it was not the wilderness or landscape they had sought to celebrate, but the natural order of a Newtonian universe."

150. Pangle, *Spirit of Modern Republicanism*, 81.

151. See May, *Enlightenment in America*, 257, who writes that "All the New England High Federalists [in the main Unitarians] believed morality essential . . . and religion essential to morality"; James H. Hutson, "'The Great Doctrine of Retribution': The Founders' Views on the Social Utility of Religion," paper presented to the John Courtney Murray Seminar, American Enterprise Institute, June 6, 2000; Daniel L. Dreisbach and Jeffry H. Morrison, "George Washington and American Public Religion," paper delivered at the American Political Science Association Annual Meeting, August 31–September 3, 2000, Washington, D.C.; and Shain, *Myth of American Individualism*.

152. See May, ibid., 274, who writes that "It is almost impossible to find any Republican, from Jefferson down who defended or admitted the deist views of the Republican candidate"; and Mason, *Voice of Warning, to Christians on the Ensuing Election of a President*, 8–9, who, in great frustration, attempts to offset the propaganda efforts of the republicans so that the electorate would believe, what we now know to be true, that Jefferson would not have been considered an Ortho-

The majority could not have known, as subsequent scholars would, that some of the most influential of the Founders, slowly moving toward Unitarian Christianity, were not believers in such Orthodox dogmas of Reformed Protestantism as original sin and the necessity of justification by faith in Christ. Indeed, they were careful about keeping their personal views private and were not hesitant to advise others to do the same. For example, the English philosopher and Unitarian Richard Price, in responding to such a request from the American patriot Benjamin Rush, refused and added "You observe that in writing to the citizens of America it would be necessary that I should be silent about the disputed doctrines of Christianity, and particularly the Trinity. I am afraid that were I to write again, I should find this a hard restraint. . . . I hope your countrymen will learn not only to bear but to encourage such discussions."[153] Clearly, in the view of Price, most Americans did not welcome heterodox views on the Trinity and, according to Rush, one should avoid making such offensive pronouncements. To most Americans, then, the elite's embrace of "religion" must have seemed to be more of the same: a Protestant recognition of original sin and damnation that could only be overcome through faith in Christ, self-examination, and God's freely given and wholly undeserved grace which with His blessing led to spiritual liberty, godly living, and finally, sanctification and eternal life in Christ.

Thus, late-eighteenth-century Americans learned from almost every public source, Christian humanist, secular rationalist, Reformed Protestant, and pietistic separatist (theologically Calvinist) that a life of liberty rather than license demanded that passions, lusts, and selfishness be tightly controlled through communal living.[154] From many

---

dox Christian. He draws attention to how well kept this secret was at the time. See also Benjamin Hale, *Liberty and Law: A Lecture* (Geneva, N.Y.: Ira Merrell, 1838), 23, who writing in 1837 could boldly claim, without embarrassment, how different the irreligiosity of men believed to be infidels like Paine was from the "true founders of our national independence [who] were religious men."

153. Price, "Letter to Rush, 30 September 1786" in Bernard Peach, ed., *Richard Price and the Ethical Foundation of the American Revolution: Selections from His Pamphlets, with Appendices* (Durham, N.C.: Duke University Press, 1979), 337.

154. See Perry Miller, "The Moral and Psychological Roots of American Resistance," in *The Reinterpretation of the American Revolution, 1763–1789,* ed. by Jack P.

of the same figures, they were led to believe that their inherent sinful natures could only be overcome by surrendering themselves to Christ and seeking spiritual liberty and rebirth in Him. Recent scholarship has given us little reason to believe that the vast majority of common Americans were not listening to these appeals.[155]

It would only be with the birth of the new world of the 1780s, which was to witness a decline in confidence among elites in their willingness to accept Scriptural claims, that there would be in America a willingness of the elite to embrace the dictates of liberalism and correspondingly to abandon the effort to bend recalcitrant sinful human nature to accord with the dictates of the guiding force of Reformed Protestantism. The predominantly Protestant faith in a divinely ordered cosmos which had for 150 years legitimated and guided Americans through their break with Britain was in fact during the next century to die slowly at the elite level and still more slowly, if at all, at the popular level.

And if one goes outside the confines of Reformed Protestantism in search of additional Protestant standards, as dissenting pietistic and separatist Protestants have done from the first moment of European settlement in North America and resurgent Anglican humanism did during much of the eighteenth century, one quickly discovers that Protestantism and its ancillary teachings encompass a terrain with impressively far-reaching borders. Indeed, in almost every public debate in American history that occurred before the end of the nineteenth century, each side could and did legitimately claim that it was invoking the truest and purest form of Protestantism.[156] It seems safe to suggest, then, that Christianity in America, which until the end of the eigh-

---

Greene (New York: Harper & Row, 1968), 259, who writes that "For Americans, the exercise of liberty becomes simply the one true obedience to God. This is not license, but resistance to sin."

155. See for example Gordon S. Wood, "Ideology and the Origins of Liberal America," in *William and Mary Quarterly,* 3d ser., 44, no. 3 (July 1987): 637, who writes, "when we talk about the great importance of Christianity at the time of the Revolution, we are talking for the most part about ordinary people. Religion was the way such people usually made meaningful the world around them."

156. See John G. West, *Politics of Revelation and Reason: Religion and Civic Life in the New Nation* (Lawrence: University Press of Kansas, 1996).

teenth century meant Reformed Protestant, is a political and cultural resource that is central to a correct understanding of American historical political thought and institutions but one that was capable of supporting an impressively wide array of political alternatives. It is wrong to confuse Christianity even in its most humanistic or pietistic modes with secular liberalism that at best shares with it certain political and social goals. The heart of America's Revolutionary-era's political culture and aspirations was Reformed Protestantism and thus America was born neither secular nor liberal.

Today, Protestant design and conceptions continue to shape many of our inherited political and cultural institutions; if you will, they are active cultural artifacts. Americans, clearly the most religious of any modern industrial people, continue to live within a world subtly formed by the shadows of our Protestant foundations. Most importantly, we continue to live in the shadow of the hallowed freedom of religious conscience and the delimiting consequences of belief in the Christian dogma of original sin. The former, knowing no natural limits, has proven to be a superb solvent of all societal boundaries, while the latter has often served societal aims that stand in opposition to such individualistic and antinomian propensities. Albeit tension-ridden, our political and cultural inheritances are eminently Protestant rather than secular in origin.

Liberty, Metaphor, and Mechanism: "Checks and Balances" and the Origins of Modern Constitutionalism

So famous is the political theory of checks and balances, so well known to Americans, that he is a bold man who tries to say new things about it.
—Stanley Pargellis

My purpose in this essay is to present a new way of thinking about the origins of modern constitutionalism, and in particular about the intellectual origins of the American Constitution. The existing literature on this subject tends to assume that there were two major languages for discussing politics in the second half of the eighteenth century—a rights language, derived from Locke, and a republican language derived from Machiavelli.[1] In recent years the fashion has been to emphasize the importance of the republican language, attacking an older literature which emphasized the importance of rights. My argument here is that this debate fails to recognize that the Founders had a new way of thinking of a constitution as a system, one which could be analyzed in the terms provided by a new "science of politics" (in the

Earlier versions of this paper were given as the keynote address to the annual meeting of the British Society for Eighteenth Century Studies, 2002, and to the Politics, Law and Society Seminar at University College, London; and an earlier version appeared online at www.constitution.org. I am grateful for many helpful suggestions, particularly from Blair Worden and Paul Rahe (who both told me to read Nedham, amongst much else), Harold Cook (who told me to read Mayr), Iain Hampsher-Monk (who told me to read Blackstone), Claude Rawson (who told me to read Ellis), and Richard Samuelson (who drew Otis to my attention).

The epigraph is from Stanley Pargellis, "The Theory of Balanced Government" in Conyers Read, ed., *The Constitution Reconsidered* (New York: Columbia University Press, 1938), 37. I have modernized spelling and punctuation of quotations and most of the titles in the text but not the footnotes.

1. For a recent survey see Alan Gibson, "Ancients, Moderns and Americans: The Republicanism-Liberalism Debate Revisited" *History of Political Thought* 21 (2000): 261–307.

words of *The Federalist* No. 9). It has long been recognized that David Hume provided the Founders with an important example of how to engage in political analysis. I argue here that Madison, Hamilton, and Hume were all the beneficiaries of a conceptual shift which had taken place around 1700, one which expressed itself through the adoption of a new mechanistic language. It is, I maintain, the mechanical metaphor which lies at the origins of modern constitutionalism. This metaphor was used to argue that constitutions are interacting systems in which, as Hume put it, "Effects will always correspond to causes," and that consequently what matters is not the moral quality of the rulers but the structure of the institutions within which the rulers operate. Given this understanding the new mechanists believed it was possible to design a political system in which good government would be established by, as *The Federalist* puts it, "reflection and choice." This new way of thinking did not render the old rights and republican languages irrelevant; rather it assigned them specific roles within the new science of politics. Where we see the languages of rights and republics as being in competition with each other, and even directly at odds with each other, contemporaries saw them as complementary. In order to understand how this could be we need to explore a series of topics that have seemed of little importance to scholars working within the existing paradigm but which were in fact central to the new science of politics.

1. MECHANICAL SYSTEMS

My first subject is a topic which has been almost invisible to historians of political theory, the history of the concept of "checks and balances."[2] The phrase is widely used in contemporary discussions of

2. Invisible is a slight, but only a slight, overstatement. In addition to Bernard Manin's chapter (on which see below, p. 235), there is Pargellis, "Theory of Balanced Government," and E. P. Panagopoulos, *Essays on the History and Meaning of Checks and Balances* (Lanham, Md.: University Press of America, 1985). Also relevant to the subject of this paper is [Anon.], "Organic and Mechanical Metaphors in Late Eighteenth-Century American Political Thought," *Harvard Law Review* 110 (1997): 1832–49, and (an essay which I unfortunately read after this paper was written) Richard Bellamy, "The Political Form of the Constitution: The Separation of Powers, Rights, and Representative Democracy" in *Political Studies* 44 (1996): 436–56. But the work which most closely touches on the topics I address

power and its regulation, and it is precisely because it has become so commonplace that historians and theorists have found it entirely un-problematic, treating it as if it were not a technical language (with all that that implies in the way of intellectual preconditions and hidden presuppositions) but a mere manner of expression. For Garry Wills, for example, it is, when used by the Founding Fathers, simply "an old con-cept borrowed from mixed government theory."[3] There is a marked contrast here with the idea of the separation of powers, whose history has been carefully and intelligently studied.[4]

To study the phrase, one must make some straightforward distinc-tions. First, there is the history of the phrase itself, first used by Hugh Blair in a sermon published in 1777 (and frequently reprinted there-after): "It is wisely ordered in our present state, that joy and fear, hope and grief, should act alternately, as checks and balances upon each

---

here is chapter 2 of A. O. Lovejoy, *Reflections on Human Nature* (Baltimore: Johns Hopkins University Press, 1961), "The Theory of Human Nature in the Ameri-can Constitution and the Method of Counterpoise," 37–65. Lovejoy there offers a reading of *The Federalist* No. 10 with which I agree: I think this "static" reading [which takes Madison's argument on factions to be the equivalent of Locke's on religious sects in the *Letter Concerning Toleration*—cf. John Locke, *Political Writ-ings*, ed. D. Wootton (Harmondsworth: Penguin Books, 1993), 429] is compat-ible with but distinct from the "dynamic" reading of *The Federalist* No. 51 which I offer at the end of this essay. It is important to note a difference between the logic of *The Federalist* No. 10 and No. 51: No. 10 is about ensuring that no fac-tion has a majority in the legislature, while No. 51 is about ensuring there is a balance of power between the various institutions and officers established by the Constitution. No. 10 is consequently about *overbalance;* No. 51 about *equilibrium.* Overbalances are static; equilibria, because they have to be constantly reestab-lished, are dynamic.

3. Garry Wills, *Explaining America: The Federalist* (Garden City: Doubleday, 1981), 117. Others err in the opposite direction, e.g., Roger Scruton, *A Dictionary of Political Thought* (London: Pan Books, 1985), s.v. "checks and balances," which suggests the phrase derives from Thomas Jefferson's *Notes on the State of Virginia* (written 1784; first American edition 1787) in *The Portable Thomas Jefferson,* ed. Merrill D. Peterson (New York: Viking Penguin, 1975).

4. See M. J. C. Vile, *Constitutionalism and the Separation of Powers,* 2d ed. (India-napolis: Liberty Fund, 1998) and W. B. Gwyn, *The Meaning of the Separation of Powers,* Tulane Studies in Political Science, no. 9 (New Orleans: Tulane Univer-sity, 1965; hereafter cited as *Meaning*).

other, in order to prevent an excess in any of them, which our nature could not bear"; and then by Joseph Galloway in *Historical and Political Reflections on the Rise and Progress of the American Revolution* (1780).[5] It was popularized by John Adams (1735–1826, the second president of the United States) in his *Defence of the Constitutions of the United States* in 1787 (the first usage known to the second edition of the *Oxford English Dictionary*).[6] Then there are the histories of the words out of which it is composed for, I will argue, "check" and "balance" have separate histories in political theory. But the history of words and phrases is an empty thing if it is not a way of studying the history of concepts, and any study of the concept of checks and balances needs to include a wider family of words (such as "control," "clog," "counterpoise," and "equilibrium") which were often used to discuss the same or similar ideas. What all these words take for granted, I will maintain, is the idea that a political system can be usefully compared to a machine. Indeed the language I am concerned with here is entirely metaphorical. Nietzsche said that truth is "a mobile army of metaphors, metonyms, and anthropomorphisms," and the scientific revolution serves as a useful illustration of his claim: it is impossible to imagine what has been called the mechanization of the world picture without the metaphors of clock, machine, and automaton, without the metonymic (or perhaps rather synecdochic) distinction between primary and secondary qualities which lies at the heart of the mechanists' enterprise, and without the anthropomorphic conception of God as a clockmaker.[7] And this new mechanical world picture provided in its turn a series of metaphors for talking about political constitutions.

This paper will thus demonstrate the need for a more careful attention to language in the history of political theory. Despite the fact that the Cambridge School has always stressed the importance of linguistic change, only a rather narrow range of terms such as "state" and "liberty" have been studied historically; part of my purpose here is to show that words that apparently have nothing to do with politics, words

5. Hugh Blair, *Sermons* (Edinburgh: William Creech, 1777), 425; Joseph Galloway, *Historical and Political Reflections* (London: G. Wilkie, 1780), 32.

6. *Oxford English Dictionary*, 2d ed., CD-ROM, s.v. *check*.

7. Friedrich Nietzsche, "On truth and lie in an extra-moral sense" in *The Portable Nietzsche*, trans. Walter Kaufman (London: Chatto and Windus, 1971), 46.

such as "system" and "machine," can be central to the history of political theorizing.[8] Indeed a study of the history of a phrase like "checks and balances" may give us a different understanding of its range of possible meanings. The Cambridge School has often claimed that the history of ideas can contribute something to normative moral and political philosophy.[9] The conclusion of my argument is that contemporary references to "checks and balances" miss the most interesting of the ideas that have been embodied in the phrase.

I began with a complaint about the history of political theory, so my first obligation is to show that historians of political theory have failed to think about checks and balances. One example can stand for many. Few texts in the history of political thought have been more widely influential than John Pocock's 1977 introduction to James Harrington's *Political Works*. There he argues that classical republican theory (a term of art including ancient Romans such as Cicero, Renaissance theorists such as Machiavelli, and English Civil War republicans such as Harrington) had, since Polybius in the second century B.C.E., been preoccupied with the idea of how to achieve political stability through balancing monarchy, aristocracy, and democracy. This problem became central to English-language political theory a few weeks before the start of the Civil War, when Charles I issued *His Majesty's Answer*

8. The term "Cambridge School" has become a conventional way of referring to the work of John Dunn, John Pocock, Quentin Skinner, and their pupils. On linguistic change see, for example, Q. Skinner, "Language and Social Change" [1980] in James Tully, ed., *Meaning and Context* (Princeton: Princeton University Press, 1988), 119–32. I should stress that my own efforts here are rather primitive in that I made little use of electronic texts until this essay was in press. A pioneering example of what can be done with modern technology is provided by Nicholson Baker, "Lumber" in *The Size of Thoughts: Essays and Other Lumber* (London: Chatto and Windus, 1996), 207–355. For another study of linguistic change, see David Wootton, "The True Origins of Republicanism: the disciples of Baron and the counter-example of Venturi," in Manuela Albertone ed., *Il repubblicanesimo moderno: L'idea di repubblica nella riflessione storica di Franco Venturi* (Naples: Bibliopolis, 2005), 225–57.

9. E.g., R. Tuck, *Natural Rights Theories* (Cambridge: Cambridge University Press, 1979), 1; Q. Skinner, *Liberty Before Liberalism* (Cambridge: Cambridge University Press, 1998), 107–20 (on which see the review by Blair Worden, *London Review of Books* [1998]: 3).

to the Nineteen Propositions of Parliament, which stated that "There being three kinds of government among men, absolute monarchy, aristocracy and democracy, and all these having their particular conveniences and inconveniences, the experience and wisdom of your ancestors hath so molded this out of a mixture of these as to give to this kingdom (as far as human prudence can provide) the conveniences of all three, without the inconveniences of any one, as long as the balance hangs even between the three estates. . . ."[10] With these words Charles abandoned any claim to absolute rule and provoked what Pocock calls "a true revision of paradigms," a revision embodied in Philip Hunton's *A Treatise of Monarchy* (1643): "Hunton assumed that England was a mixed government, a balance of the independently subsisting forces of monarchy, aristocracy and democracy, just as described in the *Answer to the Nineteen Propositions;* and he further pointed out that in a true balance, each power checked, but none controlled, the other two, with the consequence that no human authority was above the balance or was competent to command once it had broken down." Hunton, we are told, "had employed the republican vocabulary," and it would seem natural to assume that that vocabulary was one of balances, checks, controls.[11] It comes as something of a surprise to turn to Hunton and discover that Hunton uses none of these words, either in the *Treatise* or in its subsequent *Vindication* (1651). I think it is reasonable to complain that Pocock has read the concept of checks and balances back into the *Treatise,* where it is not (or is barely) to be found.

It is true that Hunton once addresses the idea of the balanced constitution, though in his own language:

> In such a composed state [i.e., a monarchy mixed with aristocratic and democratic elements], if the monarch invade the power of the other two, or run in any course tending to the dissolving of the constituted frame, they ought to employ their power in this case to preserve the state from ruin; yea that is the very end and fundamental

10. J. P. Kenyon, ed., *The Stuart Constitution, 1603–1688* (Cambridge: Cambridge University Press, 1966), 21, unreliably quoted in James Harrington, *Political Works,* ed. J. G. A. Pocock (Cambridge: Cambridge University Press, 1977), 19.

11. Harrington, *Political Works,* 20, 22, referring to Philip Hunton, *A Treatise of Monarchy* (London: John Bellamy, 1643), 23, 69.

aim in constituting all mixed policies: not that they by crossing and jarring should hinder the public good; but that, if one exorbitate, the power of restraint and providing for the public safety should be in the rest: and the power is put into divers hands, that one should counterpoise and keep even the other: so that for such other estates, it is not only lawful to deny obedience and submission to illegal proceedings, as private men may, but it is their duty, and by the foundations of the government they are bound to prevent dissolution of the established frame.[12]

Restraint and counterpoise, one might argue, are terms strictly analogous to checks and balances. But restraint is a virtue as well as being a metaphor about limitations on freedom of action. Hunton's own summary of this passage, in the *Vindication*, is "My third argument for mixture was from its end, which was restraint from excess."[13] "Excess" is clearly a normative concept—indeed, in an Aristotelian world, where virtue is defined as a mean, "excess" is by definition a vice. Hunton has no interest in pursuing the concept of a balance beyond this passing remark because he is interested in authority and right, public good, and private duty. To think seriously about checks and balances one has to start thinking about political systems in value-free terms and to see them, indeed, as *systems* which can usefully be compared with mechanical systems.

It would be surprising indeed if Hunton were interested in doing this because the vocabulary he would have needed would have been as much mechanical as republican. In 1648 we find the first reference to the science of *mechanics:* it is followed in 1662 by *mechanism;* and in 1673 the word *machine* is first used to mean an apparatus for applying mechanical power—*engine* had been the English translation for the Latin *machina* until then. John Evelyn, the diarist, is credited with being the first to introduce into English another word with a related meaning, but with a Greek origin, *automaton* (1645).[14] In all the early usages the standard example of a machine or automaton was a clock, and like clocks before them, machines and automata soon became powerful

12. Hunton, *Treatise*, 28.
13. Hunton, *Vindication* (London: John Bellamy, 1651), 44.
14. OED CD-ROM, s.v. *mechanics, mechanism, machine, engine, automaton.*

metaphors for thinking of God, thinking of God as a clockmaker and the universe as a giant clock: as early as 1587, in a translation of the leading French Protestant, Philippe de Mornay, we find the heart described as a divinely constructed clock.[15]

The idea of a system of checks and balances implies an idea of a constitution as a mechanical system, and that implies an interest in mechanism. The idea (if not the language) of political machinery is certainly present in the opening pages of *Leviathan,* where both the human body and that "artificial man," Leviathan, are compared to "*Automata* (Engines that move themselves by springs and wheels as doth a watch)," but having formulated this mechanical model, Hobbes does not seem to know quite what to do with it. The earliest reference to a "political machine"[16] that I have been able to find is in John Dryden's edition of Plutarch's *Lives* (1683), in the life of Lycurgus:

> When he perceived that his laws had taken deep root in the minds of his countrymen, that custom had rendered them familiar and easy, that his commonwealth grew apace daily, and was able to go alone, he had such a calm joy and contentation of mind, as Plato somewhere tells us the Maker of the World had, when he had finished and set this great machine a moving, and found everything very good and exactly to answer his great Idea; so Lycurgus, taking an unspeakable pleasure in the contemplation of the greatness and beauty of his work, seeing every spring and particular of his new establishment in its due order and course, at last he conceived a vast thought to make it immortal too, and, as far as human forecast could reach, to deliver it down unchangeable to posterity.[17]

Here *machine* translates the Greek word *cosmos.*

Within a few years such usages of the word were common. Here the key figures are John Trenchard, his friend Walter Moyle, and their as-

15. Otto Mayr, *Authority, Liberty and Automatic Machinery in Early Modern Europe* (Baltimore: Johns Hopkins University Press, 1986), 47–48 (hereafter cited as *Authority, Liberty*). Mayr's excellent book fails to note the republican use of mechanical imagery.

16. John Trenchard and Thomas Gordon, *Cato's Letters* (1720–23), ed. Ronald Hamowy, 2 vols. (Indianapolis: Liberty Fund, 1995), No. 69, 497.

17. Plutarch, *Lives,* introduction by John Dryden, 5 vols. (1683), 1:195–96.

sociate John Toland, the three of whom played the central role in refashioning the republican intellectual tradition to justify opposition to William III's efforts to build a strong state capable of withstanding attack by the France of Louis XIV. These radicals insisted that a professional army (particularly if kept up during peacetime) was (as republicans had often claimed) a dangerous threat to political liberty. In *An Argument Shewing That a Standing Army Is Inconsistent with a Free Government* (1697), Trenchard and Moyle say that their objective is "to put in motion this machine of our government, and to make the springs and wheels of it act naturally and perform their function."[18] Soon afterwards, Trenchard, in his "incomparable preface" to his *Short History of Standing Armies* (1698), argues that "A government is a mere piece of clockwork, and having such springs and wheels, must act after such a manner: and there the art is to constitute it so that it must move to the public advantage." The secret is "to make the interest of the governors and the governed the same, . . . and then our government will act mechanically, and a rogue will as naturally be hanged as a clock strike twelve when the hour has come."[19] Moyle, writing *An Essay on the Lacedaemonian Government* in the same year, maintained that the best constitution provided "a proper distribution of power into several branches, in the whole composing as it were one great machine, and each grand branch was a check upon the other; so that not one of them could exceed its just bounds."[20] It is not a coincidence that Toland, who may even have collaborated with Trenchard and Moyle in writing the *Argument,* uses the phrase "check and balance" soon after.[21] One of their critics was dismayed by the effectiveness of this new language: "Can you bear smiling at the simplicity of mankind, to find how many

18. Trenchard and Moyle, *An Argument Shewing That a Standing Army Is Inconsistent with a Free Government* (1697), reprinted in *State Tracts,* 3 vols. (London: E. Curll, 1714), 3:566.

19. Reprinted in Gwyn, *Meaning,* 138. Trenchard used both "clog" and "check," 140.

20. Moyle, *The Whole Works* (1727), 59. See Gwyn, *Meaning,* 88. On Moyle see Caroline Robbins, *Two English Republican Tracts* (Cambridge: Cambridge University Press, 1969).

21. Blair Worden, "Whig History and Puritan Politics: The *Memoirs* of Edmund Ludlow Revisited," *Bulletin of the Institute of Historical Research* 75 (2002): 222.

swallow your notions, because you talk so finely for liberty, a militia to defend it, and engineering in your studies?"[22] (This, by the way, is more than twenty years earlier than the OED's first recorded use of "engineering" as a noun.)[23] It is presumably from sources such as these that the language of political machinery found its way into the political essays of the philosopher David Hume, who writes in 1752 of "the political machine" and "the machine of government."[24]

In the light of my earlier reading of Hunton, you will expect me now to argue that this new mechanical language was linked to a rejection of moral categories in political analysis. And this is indeed the case. Trenchard, Moyle, and Toland, former Whigs, found themselves in alliance with former Tories such as Harley in attacking the new party of big government, the court Whigs.[25] They were well aware that those in power shared (at least in theory) many of their principles. And they repeatedly acknowledged that William, as King, was both a legitimate ruler and a man to be trusted—it was essential that their attacks on his policies should have no hint of Jacobitism. But their claim was that good men would eventually be replaced by bad men (it was only a short step, but one they hesitated to take, to claim that power tends to corrupt and turns good men into bad) and that in the long run what counts is not the quality of the men or the rectitude of their intentions but the nature of the political system within which they operate. As Trenchard and Moyle put it, "Let us flatter ourselves as much as we please, what happened yesterday will come to pass again, and the same

22. [Anon.], *A Letter to A, B, C, D, E, F, etc. Concerning Their Argument* (London: D. Brown and R. Brown, 1698), 13.

23. OED CD-ROM, s.v. *engineering*.

24. David Hume, *Essays, Moral, Political, and Literary,* ed. E. F. Miller, rev. ed. (Indianapolis: Liberty Fund, 1987), 370, 372, 529 (hereafter cited as *Essays*). See also for an implicit comparison between constitutions and machines, 273.

25. The best discussion of the debates of 1697–1701 is the introduction to Jonathan Swift, *A Discourse of the Contests and Dissentions Between the Nobles and Commons in Athens and Rome* (1701), ed. F. H. Ellis (Oxford: Clarendon Press, 1967); more recently Blair Worden has published a number of studies which transform our understanding of the politics of Toland and his associates, the most recent being "Whig History and Puritan Politics: The *Memoirs* of Edmund Ludlow Revisited."

causes will produce the like effects in all ages."[26] Moyle, writing to a friend, adopted a more learned language: "Thus you see, as a good author expresses it, *eadem fabula semper in mundo agitur, mutatis duntaxat personis;* which agrees with what Thucydides says in his third book, *eadem accidere, donec eadem hominum natura.*"[27] The casuistical terms in which Hunton and his contemporaries had conducted their debates could thus be dismissed as irrelevant. Trenchard, writing years later as Cato, still dismissed the conventional preoccupation with virtue: "The experience of every age convinces us, that we must not judge of men by what they ought to do, but by what they will do."[28] The task of the political analyst was not to judge moral right and wrong, but to follow the chain of causes at work within a political system. Hume made the same point by taking from Machiavelli the example of Renaissance Genoa. There the very same people who were, when engaged in politics, seditious, tumultuous, and disorderly appeared to demonstrate integrity and wisdom when running the bank of St. George. Forms and institutions were thus seen to be crucial in regulating behavior.[29]

I find it easiest, as you will have noticed, to describe the new political theory by employing the word "system." Hobbes had written a chapter "Of Systems": "By Systems; I understand any numbers of men joined in one Interest, or one Business." Harrington had written of "the system of the government" and "a system of politics," but he seems to have had no immediate successors.[30] Samuel Butler in 1729 was giving the word (which had previously meant little more than an aggregation or grouping) a tightened definition when he wrote "The body is a system or constitution: so is a tree: so is every machine."[31] Once the word was readily available in this new sense it was quickly reemployed in political theory: it appears a year later in the first definition of the

---

26. Trenchard and Moyle, *Argument,* 566.

27. Moyle, *Whole Works,* 53.

28. *Cato's Letters,* 416. In citing *Cato's Letters* and *The Federalist,* I refer to the individual authors who we now know wrote individual sections, rather than to "Cato" (or Trenchard and Gordon) or "Publius" (or Madison, Jay, and Hamilton).

29. *Essays,* 24–25.

30. Harrington, *Political Works,* 286, 834.

31. OED CD-ROM, s.v. *system.*

modern idea of a constitution in its political sense, Bolingbroke's state-ment that "By constitution we mean, whenever we speak with propri-ety and exactness, that assemblage of laws, institutions, and customs, derived from certain fixed principles of reason . . . that compose the general system according to which the community hath agreed to be governed."[32] Indeed he uses it over and over again. The constitution is "a noble and wise system, the essential parts of which are so pro-portioned, and so intimately connected, that a change in one begets a change in the whole." King and people are "parts of the same system, intimately joined and co-operating together, acting and acted upon, limiting and limited, controlling and controlled by one another."[33] But for the pioneers of the new way of thinking in the final years of the seventeenth century, "system" was a word that was too imprecise to serve their purposes. The preferred word to convey the idea of an interacting system was, as in the quotation from Butler, "machine." "Machine" was not a metaphorical term which stood in place of a readily available alternative; at first it was the only available term to convey the idea of complex interaction.

Even when the idea of a system was well-established (and one may note, for example, the use of the word "system" by opponents of the proposed new American Constitution in 1787),[34] the reference to ma-chines remained almost obligatory because the idea of a system re-mained entangled in the idea of a machine. Astronomy had played a key role in reshaping the word "system" because of its use in phrases such as "the Copernican system": Galileo's *Dialogo sopra i due massimi sis-temi del mondo* (1632) had first been published in an English translation in 1661. Thus Adam Smith writes, in the *History of Astronomy* (c. 1749), "Systems in many respects resemble machines. A machine is a little system, created to perform, as well as to connect together, in reality, those different movements and effects which the artist has occasion

---

32. OED CD-ROM, s.v. *constitution.* J. H. Burns, "Bolingbroke and the Con-cept of Constitutional Government," *Political Studies* 10 (1962): 264–76; *Disserta-tion,* Letter X: *Works,* 5 vols. (London: David Mallet, 1754), 2:130.

33. *Dissertation,* Letter XI: *Works,* 2:157; Letter IX: *Works,* 2:125.

34. Bruce Frohnen, ed., *The Anti-Federalists* (Washington, D.C.: Regnery Pub-lishing, 1999), 496, 526.

for. A system is an imaginary machine invented to connect together in the fancy those different movements and effects which are already in reality performed."[35] It was still entirely natural for John Adams, writing in 1765, to compare political constitutions at length with the constitution of the body and with machines such as clocks ("a combination of weights, wheels, and levers, calculated for a certain use and end") before concluding "Government is a frame, a scheme, a system, a combination of powers for a certain end, namely—the good of the whole community."[36] Indeed Sir James Steuart's *An Inquiry into the Principles of Political Oeconomy* (1767) could, when discussing this topic at least, have been written at the end of the previous century:

> It is of governments as of machines, the more they are simple, the more they are solid and lasting; the more they are artfully composed, the more they become useful; but the more apt they are to be out of order.
>
> The Lacedaemonian form may be compared to the wedge, the most solid and compact of all the mechanical powers. Those of modern states to watches, which are continually going wrong; sometimes the spring is found too weak, at other times too strong for the machine: and when the wheels are not made according to a determinate proportion, by the able hands of a Graham, or a Julien Le Roy, they do not tally well with one another; then the machine stops, and if it be forced, some part gives way; and the workman's hand becomes necessary to set it right.[37]

There would seem to be an obvious objection to this line of argument. Is not the concept of a political system or something very like it already present in Polybius? In the words of a mid-twentieth-century

---

35. Adam Smith, *Essays on Philosophical Subjects*, ed. I. S. Ross (Indianapolis: Liberty Fund, 1982), 66. See OED CD-ROM, s.v. *system, solar, Copernican.* My thanks to Johan Sommerville for discussing this with me.

36. *The Political Writings of John Adams*, ed. George W. Carey (Washington, D.C.: Regnery Publishing, 2000), 647 (hereafter cited as *Political Writings*).

37. Sir James Steuart, *An Inquiry into the Principles of Political Oeconomy*, ed. A. S. Skinner, 4 vols. (Chicago: University of Chicago Press, 1998), 2:217; see also 278–79.

translation, Polybius held that Lycurgus, in reforming the constitution of Sparta, understood the perils of a simple constitution, and therefore

> Combined together all the excellencies and distinctive features of the best constitutions, that no part should become unduly predominate, and be perverted into its kindred vice; and that each power being checked by the others, no one part should turn the scale or decisively outbalance the others; but that by being accurately adjusted in exact equilibrium, the whole might remain long steady like a ship sailing close to the wind.[38]

There are two things that are disconcerting about this translation. In the first place, it brings together into the same sentence the words check and [out]balance. Here, though, it simply reflects the magnetic attraction of the modern phrase "checks and balances"—the early translations of Polybius that I have been able to consult do not use the word "check," but rather phrases such as "mutually acted upon by opposite powers" or "each separate power being still counteracted by the rest." Even more alarming is the phrase "like a ship sailing close to the wind." In the first place, Greek ships could not sail close to the wind, so this must be a mistranslation; in the second place, a ship sailing close to the wind implies a complex balance of a number of different forces—wind, sails, ballast, rudder—so if Polybius thought in such terms his notion of equilibrium would imply some sort of complex machine, not the simplest form of a balance, that of two weights in a scale—the sort of balance that has been familiar for millennia.

In fact, Polybius thought only in terms of the simple balance. The passage about a ship remaining in equilibrium while in movement, which might seem to suggest otherwise, has provoked much debate and continues to puzzle scholars because it contains a word found nowhere else.[39] The best interpretation as far as the sense is concerned

---

38. Kurt von Fritz, *The Theory of the Mixed Constitution in Antiquity* (New York: Columbia University Press, 1954), 365 (quoted without demur in James M. Blythe, *Ideal Government and the Mixed Constitution in the Middle Ages* [Princeton: Princeton University Press, 1992], 27).

39. F. W. Walbank, *A Historical Commentary on Polybius,* 2 vols. (Oxford: Clarendon Press, 1957), 1:660–61.

(I am not competent to comment on the technical problems presented by the Greek) is in a French translation of 1792, which assumes quite properly that Polybius is thinking of a galley: if only the rowers on the port side row, the ship turns clockwise; if only those on the starboard side row, it turns anticlockwise; if both row together, an equilibrium is established and it proceeds in a straight line.[40] In other words Polybius is still thinking of a simple balance between two equal forces, not of some complex balance between multiple forces—not of what we would call a "system" which needs to have several interacting parts. The standard modern translation takes Polybius to be talking about loading the cargo in a ship so it remains in trim as it travels along— again a balance of two equal forces.[41] Moreover Polybius assumed that the balancing of forces would be the result of deliberate action, not the unintended consequence of an interactive process. Theorists such as Trenchard and Moyle were interested in the idea that a political system might be constructed so that it would generate outcomes (such as the public good) that none of the participants had intended to achieve.

Thus to describe Polybius as having the idea of a political system is to read systems analysis (itself an aspect of mechanistic thinking) back into a pretechnological culture. When he was first taken up in English, the balance was only one, and not necessarily the preferred, metaphor for the imposition of due limits. Here is *His Majesty's Answer* again: ". . . as long as the balance hangs even between the three states, and they run jointly on in their proper channel (begetting verdure and fertility in the meadows on both sides), and the overflowing of either on either side raise no deluge or inundation."[42] The mixing of metaphors here is testimony to just how little work the idea of the balance was capable of doing before the rise of mechanistic philosophy.

I have chosen a plainly anachronistic translation of Polybius because I want to stress that Polybius is not a fixed quantity but was bound to be read differently at different times. What has become for modern commentators the key passage of Polybius's *Histories* was not

40. *Fragment de Polybe; et quelques extraits de Spelman sur la meilleure forme de Gouvernment possible* (1789?), 27.

41. Polybius, *The Histories,* trans. W. R. Paton, 6 vols. (London: Heineman, 1923), 3:291.

42. Kenyon, *Stuart Constitution,* 21.

always read—it survives only in a fragment and was omitted from those editions which reproduced only the complete books.[43] The middle of the eighteenth century saw what has been called the "rediscovery" of Polybius, and I want to suggest that this was a rediscovery of this particular passage and was linked to the intellectual revolution I am discussing.[44] Even when the passage was translated, its meaning was sometimes far from apparent—a translation of 1634 renders the passage incomprehensible by changing one letter, for instead of saying "Royalty should be restrained from arrogancy by fear of the people," it says, perhaps under the pressure of censorship, perhaps simply through carelessness, "Loyalty should be restrained."[45]

Our own preoccupation with Polybius as the source of the idea of the mixed constitution and of checks and balances is in any case somewhat misleading. Adams, in his *Defence of the Constitutions of the United States,* placed great emphasis on Polybius, and the author of *His Majesty's Answer* also appears to have had Polybius in mind, but for generations of politicians the idea of the balanced constitution would have been familiar, not from an obscure passage in Polybius, but from a far more widely read passage in Plutarch's life of Lycurgus.[46] The significance of this passage has been overlooked, perhaps because mod-

43. It is missing, for example, from the edition introduced by Dryden (1693) and translated by Sir Henry Shears but does appear in the 1698 reprint, where the additions are described as translated by "another hand" (pace English Short Title Catalogue). Its relatively late date means, I think, that this translation of Polybius was not an important factor in the emergence of the new mechanical language. Ellis thinks that this translation was used by Swift (who quotes Polybius) on the grounds that Swift may have known Sir Henry Shears, who he mistakenly thinks is the translator of the whole text, but I see no reason to assume that Shears would have brought this second edition in which he seems to have had no part to Swift's attention, and Swift's own quotation suggests he was translating Polybius himself from either Latin or Greek.

44. Pargellis, "The Theory of Balanced Government," 45.

45. *The History of Polybius,* trans. Edward Grimeston (1634), 287.

46. On Polybius and classical learning in general but with no mention of Plutarch, see Gilbert Chinard, "Polybius and the American Constitution," *Journal of the History of Ideas* 1 (1940): 38–58. I don't deny that Polybius was known—he is referred to by Milton, Moyle, Toland, and Swift—but his relative importance as compared to Plutarch needs assessment.

ern translations do not use the word "balance." Here is the sixteenth-century translation of North:

> In this change of the state, many things were altered by Lycurgus, but this chiefest alteration was, his law of the erection of a senate, which he made to have a regal power and equal authority with the kings in matters of weight and importance, and was (as Plato saith) to be the healthful counterpoise of the whole body of the Commonweal. The other state before was ever wavering, sometime inclining to tyranny, when the kings were too mighty; and sometime to confusion, when the people would usurp authority. Lycurgus therefore placed between the Kings and the people, a Council of Senators, which was as a strong beam, that held both these extremes in an even balance, and gave sure footing and ground to either part to make strong the state of the Commonweal. For the 28 Senators (which made the whole body of the Senate) took sometime the King's part, when it was needful to pull down the fury of the people: and contrariwise, they held sometimes with the people against the Kings, to bridle their tyrannical government.[47]

There is still only one balance here, not a series of checks and balances, but it is worth noting that there are close analogues here to Hunton's language of counterpoise, restraint, and foundation so we can reasonably suspect that it is Plutarch not Polybius that Hunton had in mind.

I have paused over Plutarch's life of Lycurgus partly because Moyle, writing in his *Essay on the Lacedaemonian Government* about Harrington's scheme of government, said, "How nearly this is drawn from Lycurgus's institution you may read with pleasure in his Life writ by Plutarch."[48] This is true to a far greater extent than modern commentators on Harrington have acknowledged. The agrarian; the ballot; rotation of office; the separation between proposing and resolving; the mixture of monarchy, aristocracy and democracy; the idea of a government so constituted that it is capable of surviving forever: all were described by Plutarch and taken up by Harrington. It was ostensibly on the basis of Plutarch and Harrington (and perhaps also on

47. I quote from the 1676 edition, 36.
48. Moyle, *Whole Works*, 56.

the basis of a reading of Nedham) that Moyle developed an account of what we now call the separation of powers, an account which surely influenced both Bolingbroke, whose essays in *The Craftsman* (1730) followed soon after the first publication of Moyle's work (though written in 1698, it did not appear in print until 1727), and Montesquieu (who, like Moyle, writes of the distribution not the distinction—Nedham's term—or separation of power(s) and who, like Moyle, uses a selective account of an existing constitution to describe the maximum amount of liberty possible within civil society).[49] For our purposes Moyle's essay of 1698, not Hunton's *Treatise* of 1643, represents the birth of a new language and a new paradigm: he writes of checks, of controls, of the balance of power (although perhaps not in its modern meaning), of machinery. That new paradigm owed a great deal to Harrington's conceptions of political architecture and political anatomy, but its vocabulary was only in part Harrington's. Harrington had written of checks (in the context of providing political supervision of military commanders) and of the law controlling the Lucchese (in the context of a refutation of Hobbes's views on liberty), but he had made no mention of machines, and when Harrington had written of "the balance," he meant the stable state created by an overbalance, not an equilibrium. The traditional idea of a balanced constitution he dismissed as a mere wrestling match between Kings, Lords, and Commons, and in order to avoid the hated term "balance" when talking of constitutional provisions, he adapted the term "libration" to a novel use.[50]

Harrington, as his description of the constitution of Oceana draws to a close, quotes Plutarch's account of how Lycurgus had admired his own work and aspired to make it permanent. For readers of Moyle's generation, this passage evoked images of machines driven by springs; but Harrington still read it as North had read it, as an account of man imitating God in the construction of an order comparable to that of the heavens: "He conceived such a delight within him, as God is de-

49. On Moyle and the separation of powers see Gwyn, *Meaning*, 87–88; Vile, *Constitutionalism*, while discussing Nedham, Bolingbroke, and Montesquieu, unfortunately contains no discussion of Moyle.

50. Harrington, *Political Works*, 196; OED CD-ROM, s.v. *libration;* Harrington, *Political Works*, 178 (an earlier use). The word occurs twice in *Oceana*, and from there it enters the debates of 1697–1701.

scribed by Plato to have done when he had finished the creation of the world, and saw his own orbs move below him: for in the art of man (being the imitation of nature, which is the art of God) there is nothing so like the first call of beautiful order out of chaos and confusion as the architecture of a well-ordered commonwealth."[51] It is this step from the classical art of political architecture to the modern science of political engineering—which Trenchard called "the art of political mechanism"—that is marked by the new language of checks and balances.[52] It is true that both Nedham and Harrington saw the frequent election of representatives as a key process in politics which Nedham described as "revolution" and Harrington as "rotation," but the whole point of this movement, like the movement of the heavens, was that it kept bringing the political system back to its original starting point, a conformity of interests between government and governed: which is why Harrington can mix astronomical and architectural metaphors in a single sentence. The new emphasis on mechanism, by contrast, made it possible for the first time to think about the political process in noncyclical terms. For later theorists of constitutional machinery, the importance of Polybius and Plutarch and of Nedham and Harrington was that they provided apparent precedents for what was in fact a new way of thinking.

Moyle, tracing the idea of the distribution of power back to Lycurgus, was effectively denying the modernity of the new political theory and the institutions it described. A much more subtle view is implicit in Montesquieu's *Spirit of the Laws* (1748). There Montesquieu writes of moderate governments as requiring the balancing of powers one against another.[53] But mere moderation provides no guarantee of constitutional liberty which exists only where there is a proper separation of powers. Only in England had the separation of legislature, executive, and judiciary (in the English case the "judge" in criminal cases being the jury) come properly into existence, and thus a constitution in which the separate powers provided adequate checks upon each other and political liberty was consequently guaranteed was evidently

51. Harrington, *Political Works*, 341.

52. *Cato's Letters*, No. 61, 421.

53. Montesquieu, *The Spirit of the Laws*, trans. Anne M. Cohler et al. (Cambridge: Cambridge University Press, 1989), 63.

a modern invention.[54] However Montesquieu's account of the English constitution was theoretical rather than historical. Nowhere does he give any indication that he grasped that both the division of powers he so admired and the mechanical language he employed to describe their relationship to each other were scarcely older than he was. (He was born in 1689.)

2. CHECKS AND BALANCES

"Checks and balances" is a phrase now widely employed to describe due process in decision making and has a more precise meaning in descriptions of political constitutions where power is used to check power, of which the American Constitution is the paradigmatic example. Representatives of the New Model Army had claimed the army was a "check and balance" on the Presbyterians in 1647.[55] Nedham had written of a "balance or check" in 1654; Toland had used the phrase "check and balance" in 1701; and Gouverneur Morris had im-

54. Ibid., 155–66.

55. Quoted in John Rushworth, *Historical Collections the Fourth and Last Part,* 2 vols. (London, 1701), 2:746. Here are some other early occurrences of the phrase "check and balance" in chronological order (omitting reprints and quotations in later works): Thomas Madox, *The History and Antiquities of the Exchequer of the Kings of England* (London, 1711), 123; Trenchard and Gordon, *Cato's Letters,* 4 vols. (London, 1723–24), 3:268 [ed. Hamowy, 730]; Clopton Havers, *Osteologia Nova* (London, 1729), 126; Bishop Gibson, *The Bishop of London's Second Pastoral Letter* (London, 1730), 8; Anthony Ellys, *A Plea for the Sacramental Test* (London, 1736), 93; Ephraim Chambers, *Cyclopaedia,* 2d ed. (London, 1738), art. "ephori"; *The Works of Sallust* (London, 1744), 73, 97; Robert James, *Pharmacopoeia Universalis,* 2d ed. (London, 1752), 29; Johann Heineccius, *A Methodical System of Universal Law,* 2 vols. (London, 1763), 2:101, 135; Lauchlan Taylor, *An Essay on the Revelation of the Apostle John* (London, 1763), 153; James Otis, *The Rights of the British Colonies* (London, 1764), 71; *The London Museum of Politics, Miscellanies and Literature* (London, 1770), 266; Arthur Lee, *Answers to Considerations on Certain Political Transactions of the Province of South Carolina* (London, 1774), 62; Lionel Charlton, *The History of Whitby* (York, 1779), 28; *Anglia Rediviva* (London, 1782), 8; Walter Ross, *The Present State of the Distillery of Scotland* (Edinburgh, 1786), 8; Joseph Townsend, *A Dissertation on the Poor Laws* (London, 1786), 50; Robert Hamilton, *The Duties of a Regimental Surgeon,* 2 vols. (London, 1787), 2:79. This list is made possible by Eighteenth Century Collections Online, which became available as this essay went to press; see http://www.gale.com/EighteenthCentury/.

plied a plural form in 1776, writing of "every check and balance," but the phrase we now use was first popularized early in 1787 by John Adams in the opening pages of his *Defence of the Constitutions of the United States,* a work which defended the constitutions of the states and of the Continental Congress, for it was published a few months before the Convention proposed a new constitution for the federal republic.[56] In that same year both John Brooks and Noah Webster used the phrase "checks and balance"; and "balances and checks" was to appear in *The Federalist* that winter. Others quickly took up Adams's terminology: Jonathan Smith, for example, addressing the Massachusetts ratification convention, represented himself as "a plain man and get my living by the plough. I am not used to speaking in public, but I beg you[r] leave to say a few words to my brother ploughjoggers in this house." His few words were about "checks and balances."[57]

It is time now to ask some straightforward, even obvious questions. What are checks? What are balances? What exactly is being checked or balanced? And why do we need both checks and balances? At first, when I began to puzzle over the history of this phrase, my assumption was that the balance was the balance wheel of a clock, that a check might be an escapement mechanism, and that "checks and balances" was a metaphor drawn from clockwork.[58] But this is not the case, and

56. Adams was the author of the Massachusetts constitution of 1780 (*Political Writings,* 498–551) which is often thought to provide the model for the "checks and balances" in the American Constitution and which perhaps best exemplifies what he was defending in 1787: see Alexander Hamilton, John Jay, and James Madison, *The Federalist,* ed. G. W. Carey and J. McClellan (Indianapolis: Liberty Fund, 2001), xxx. There is no occurrence of the phrase "checks and balances" (or any equivalent) in Madison's notes on the Proceedings of the Federal Convention, although there are frequent references to checks and occasional references to balances.

57. OED CD-ROM, s.v. *check;* Adams, *Political Writings,* 110; John Brooks, *An Oration, Delivered to the Society of the Cincinnati in the Commonwealth of Massachusetts, July 4th 1787* (Boston, 1787), 11; *Friends of the Constitution: Writings of the "Other" Federalists,* ed. C. A. Sheehan and G. L. McDowell (Indianapolis: Liberty Fund, 1998), 378; *The Federalist* No. 9, 119; Isaac Kramnick's introduction to *The Federalist* (Harmondsworth: Penguin Books, 1987), 64–65, the edition I cite.

58. I was, at least, in the best company: see Bernard Bailyn, *The Ideological Origins of the American Revolution* (Cambridge: Harvard University Press, 1967), 274.

the prehistory of the phrase proves peculiarly complex; my own efforts here are bound to require correction and modification.

Of the two terms, checks and balances, balance is the older, the one used (if I may so put it, for on this all the translators agree) by Polybius.[59] According to seventeenth-century mechanics, the balance was the first of the six simple forces—the others being the lever, the wedge, the screw, the wheel, and the pulley. (Of these, the most commonly used as a political metaphor after the balance was the screw, as in the following quotation from "A Maryland Farmer": "The aristocracy, who move by system and design, and always under the colorable pretext of securing property, act, as has been frequently said, like the screw in mechanics, always gaining, holding fast what it gains, and never losing."[60] Harrington had compared his principle of rotation to the working of a screw or a vice.[61]) Whatever advances may have been made in the theory of the balance in the seventeenth century, there was nothing new about balances as such.

It is the idea of a balance between two forces that interested those who read Polybius and Plutarch before the eighteenth century. Thus Contarini (1543), as presented in a translation of 1599, praises Venice as embodying the Polybian ideal: "This only city retaineth a princely sovereignty, a government of the nobility, and a popular authority, so that the forms of all seem to be equally balanced, as it were with a pair of weights."[62] After *The King's Answer,* the idea of the balance seems to have ceased to be of any significance in English political debate until it was reintroduced by Trenchard and Moyle in *An Argument Shewing that a Standing Army Is Inconsistent with a Free Government* (October 1697). The term then runs throughout the political debates of the next few years. Of the texts of this period, the one that was best known in later years was Jonathan Swift's *A Discourse of the Contests and Dissentions Between the Nobles and Commons in Athens and Rome* (1701) if only because Swift was so frequently reprinted (he was quoted at length by John Adams in 1787, and had been paraphrased by Benjamin Lincoln in

59. The idea of an equilibrium was of central importance for Greek science: it is a key concept, for example, in Greek medicine.

60. Kramnick's introduction, *The Federalist,* 63.

61. Harrington, *Political Works,* 249.

62. Mayr, *Authority, Liberty,* 143.

1785).[63] Swift, who is writing a satire on contemporary politics under the guise of ancient history, opens with a discussion of the "balance of power," a phrase which first appears in English in 1579 in a translation of Guicciardini and whose usage is said to have become common after the Treaty of Utrecht in 1713.[64] In fact it had already become commonplace during the standing army debate of 1697–1701, being used sometimes in the Harringtonian sense of an overbalance (as in Moyle's "From modern politics we have been taught the name of the balance of power, but it was ancient prudence taught us the thing"), but sometimes also in the modern sense of an equilibrium or near-equilibrium as when an anonymous critic of Trenchard and Moyle writes of "keeping the balance of power in a due libration, turning it sometimes one way, and sometimes another, according to present emergencies."[65] The same idea of an equilibrium was commonplace during these years in discussions of "the balance of Europe." Here is Swift:

> The true meaning of a balance of power, either without or within a state, is best conceived by considering what the nature of balance is. It supposes three things. First the part which is held, together with the hand that holds; and then the two scales, with whatever is weighed therein. Now consider several states in a neighborhood. In order to preserve peace between these states, it is necessary they should be formed into a balance, whereof one or more are to be directors, who are to divide the rest into equal scales, and upon occasions remove from one into the other, or else fall with their own weight upon the lightest. So in a state within itself, the balance must be held by a third hand, who is to deal the remaining power with utmost exactness into the several scales. Now it is not necessary that the power should be equally divided between these three; for the balance may be held by the weakest, who by his address and con-

63. Adams, *Defence*, ch. 4, in *Political Writings*, 132–38; Gordon S. Wood, *The Creation of the American Republic, 1776–1787* (Chapel Hill: University of North Carolina Press, 1969), 577 (which fails to identify the borrowing from Swift).

64. See Mayr, *Authority, Liberty*, 142.

65. Moyle, *Whole Works*, 51; *A Letter to A, B, C, D, E, F, etc. Concerning Their Argument* (1698), 12.

duct, removing from either scale and adding of his own, may keep the scales duly poised.[66]

Two things are very noticeable about this passage—the first is the assumption that a balance must always be a balance between two forces so that if there are three powers they must redivide themselves into two; the second is the conviction that maintaining a balance requires skill, a conscious analysis of the forces at work. One thinks of Halifax's *Character of a Trimmer* (1682)—the art of politics consists in knowing when to change sides, to trim the ship of state in order to restore the balance. This way of thinking implicitly likens the constitutional tension between three different institutions (King, Lords, Commons) to the task of building a coalition of parties within a single chamber. As Montesquieu put it (sliding, as eighteenth-century commentators could not help but do, between the static notion of constitutional equilibrium and the dynamic notion of coalition formation), the three powers of King, Lords, and Commons "should form an equilibrium or a stasis. But since, in the necessary course of events, they are obliged to act, they will be obliged to act in concert."[67] It was natural for John Adams in his influential "Thoughts on Government" of 1776 to assume that to "hold the balance" was synonymous with to "mediate."[68] But it was also obvious that the struggle between two parties might easily degenerate into what Harrington had called a wrestling match. Usbek, in Montesquieu's *Persian Letters* (1721), maintains that "Monarchy is a state of tension, which always degenerates into despotism or republicanism. Power can never be divided equally between prince and people: it is too difficult to keep the balance. The power must necessarily decrease on one side and increase on the other, but usually the ruler is at an advantage, being in control of the armed forces."[69]

How to escape from this bipolar model with its associated stress

66. Swift, *Discourse*, 84–85. Quoted in Mayr, *Authority, Liberty*, 160; see Adams, *Political Writings*, 135.

67. Montesquieu, *Esprit des lois*, 2 vols. (Paris: Garnier, 1961), 1:172 (my translation; compare Cohler translation, 164).

68. *American Political Writing During the Founding Era*, ed. C. S. Hyneman and D. S. Lutz, 2 vols. (Indianapolis: Liberty Fund, 1983), 405; *Political Writings*, 486.

69. Montesquieu, *Persian Letters*, trans. C. J. Betts (Harmondsworth: Penguin Books, 1973), 187.

on compromise, craft, and cunning and its evident risk of instability? Bolingbroke in *The Craftsman* (in a passage published in 1730 which is sometimes said to be a source for Montesquieu's doctrine of the separation of powers) distinguished sharply between the dependency of different parts of the government and their independency. In doing so he is discussing checks and the balance, but he uses the word "balance" coupled with the verb "control": Moyle had followed Nedham in employing the noun "control" in a political context, using it as synonymous with "checks."

> The constitutional dependency, as I have called it for distinction's sake, consists in this, that the proceedings of each part of the government, when they come forth into action and affect the whole, are liable to be examined and controlled by the other parts. The independency pleaded for consists in this, that the resolutions of each part, which direct these proceedings, be taken independently and without any influence, direct or indirect, on the others. Without the first, each part would be at liberty to attempt destroying the balance by usurping or abusing power; but without the last there can be no balance at all.[70]

What was new about this was that it replaced the idea that there must in the end be only two forces in balance with the claim that the three forces must remain independent. A similar view is expressed by Blackstone in his *Commentaries* (1765), only he avoids the word "balance" with its suggestion of stasis. Like Bolingbroke, he starts with a mutual power of veto and then moves on to the interaction of forces which he deftly reinterprets as a dynamic process:

> In the legislature, the people are a check upon the nobility, and the nobility a check upon the people . . . while the king is a check upon both. And this very executive power is again checked and kept within due bounds by the two houses. . . . Thus every branch of our civil polity supports and is supported, regulates and is regulated, by the rest; for the two houses naturally drawing in two directions of opposite interest, and the prerogative in another still different

70. Bolingbroke, in *The Craftsman,* published separately in 1743 in *Remarks on the History of England;* Letter VII: *Works,* 1:341. Quoted in Gwyn, *Meaning,* 95.

from them both, they mutually keep each other from exceeding their proper limits. . . . Like three distinct powers in mechanics, they [people, nobility, executive] jointly impel the machine of government in a direction different from what either, acting by itself, would have done; but at the same time, in a direction partaking of each, and formed out of all: a direction which constitutes the true line of the liberty and happiness of the community.

It is appropriate to think here if not when reading Polybius of a ship sailing close to the wind or (to take the hypothesis of Edward Spelman, in a note to his 1743 translation of Polybius) of a ship which is being rowed and at the same time carried by both the wind and the tide, for we really do have more than two independent forces at work.[71]

Anyone who compares these two passages with the passage I earlier quoted from Swift must recognize that they are talking about different processes. Swift expects the resolutions of one part to influence at least one of the others, for otherwise it will be impossible to bring the scales into balance. Bolingbroke believes that if the different parts pay attention to each other they will necessarily become unbalanced, and Blackstone writes as if each could act independently of the others. A similar argument is made by John Adams in 1787. He maintains that any balance of two weights will be unstable (the whole point of a pair of scales is that the slightest alteration in the weights tips the balance) or tippy, and that three equal and independent weights are needed for stability.[72]

All this would be incomprehensible if the only notion of equilibrium that existed in the eighteenth century was that of a scale in balance. In fact eighteenth-century textbooks on mechanics dealt carefully with the idea of an equilibrium between three independent weights, and we have, for example, Adams's notes on lectures he attended which dealt with this topic.[73] Adams seems to have thought that a three-way balance was inherently more stable than a two-way

71. Quoted in Mayr, *Authority, Liberty,* 163; Edward Spelman, *A Fragment out of the Sixth Book of Polybius* (London, 1743), note to p. 49.

72. I. Bernard Cohen, *Science and the Founding Fathers* (New York: W. W. Norton, 1995), 210.

73. Ibid., 204–10, 218–22.

balance: a mistake perhaps derived from the fact that the experimental apparatus employed in the schoolrooms to illustrate such a system was much less sensitive than a fulcrum balance for it involved a pulley for each weight so that movement would only take place when the friction of all the pulleys had been overcome.

There is a second issue here: need the weights be not only independent but also equal? Bernard Manin, who is one of the few people to have discussed political theories of balance with any care, believes that eighteenth-century theorists always believed that a balance required equal weights, and both Adams and his critics, when talking about the tripartite balance, write as if this were the case.[74] But it would be very strange if everyone made this mistake. We have already seen Swift insisting that "It is not necessary that the power should be equally divided" between the three forces, and the three-way balance would scarcely have been an improvement on the bipolar balance if it had involved the introduction of a new principle of equality. In fact eighteenth-century textbooks showed how to balance three unequal weights in an equal-arm three-way balance by adjusting the angles between the arms.[75]

It is easy to show that not all theorists of multiple balances presumed that the weights must be equal in balances involving three or more forces. This is apparent in Jean-Louis de Lolme's *Constitution of England* (first published in French in 1771, and in English in 1775).[76] De Lolme argues that the legislature naturally outweighs the execu-

---

74. Bernard Manin, "Checks, Balances, and Boundaries: The Separation of Powers in the Constitutional Debate of 1787" (hereafter cited as "Checks") in B. M. Fontana, ed., *The Invention of the Modern Republic* (Cambridge: Cambridge University Press, 1994), 27–62, 59; Centinel in *The Anti-Federalist*, ed. Herbert J. Storing (Chicago: University of Chicago Press, 1985), 15; Adams (writing to Sherman in 1789), *Political Writings*, 449–50.

75. I leave aside a form of the balance which would have been familiar to anyone in the eighteenth century, the steelyard, on the grounds that it employs the principle of the lever to turn unequal weights into equal forces.

76. The literature on de Lolme is thin, but see Jean-Pierre Machelon, *Les Idées Politiques de J. L. de Lolme* (Paris: Presses Universitaires de France, 1969) and Mark Francis with John Morrow, "After the Ancient Constitution: Political Theory and English Constitutional Writings, 1765–1832," *History of Political Thought* 9 (1988): 283–302.

tive with the resulting requirement that the weight of the legislature must be divided and dispersed and the weight of the executive concentrated if a balance is to be achieved. Thus according to de Lolme one of the peculiarities of the English constitution is "its having thrown into one place the whole mass, if I may use the expression, of the executive power," which enables the royal authority to act as a counterpoise to the power of the people. Even so, the two powers are not as a result equal, for it is right that the power of the executive should be in actuality if not appearance the lesser of the two. But the legislative power, if it is not to be excessive, must be limited, and this can only be achieved by dividing it: "The same kind of impossibility is found to fix the legislative power when it is one, which Archimedes objected against his moving the earth"—a rare appeal, one might add, to the principle, if not of the lever, then at least of the fulcrum. Meanwhile, the people as a whole, as a body outside the constitutional system of powers, "at every instant have it in their power to strike the decisive blow which is to level everything," although they are only truly free when they have no need to exercise this unrestrained power. Thus for de Lolme the English constitution consists of a number of independent, separate, and unequal powers (including a judicial power consisting not only of an independent judiciary but also of juries who are judge of law as well as fact) whose "reciprocal actions and reactions produce the freedom of the constitution, which is no more than an equilibrium between the ruling powers of the state."[77] The key to establishing this equilibrium is weakening the legislature and strengthening the executive—the exact opposite of the policies advocated by Trenchard and Moyle.

So, too, for James Madison (who was to become President in 1809 and who had played the key role in the Constitutional Convention of 1787) and Alexander Hamilton (the leading advocate for the construction of a strong American state), the authors (with John Jay) of *The Federalist* (1787–88). Madison and Hamilton believed that since 1776 America had had plenty of experience of overpowerful legislatures. "It is against the enterprising ambition of [the legislature] that the people

---

77. Jean-Louis de Lolme, *The Constitution of England,* rev. ed. (London: Robinson and Murray, 1789), 196, 203–4, 220, 322, 195 (hereafter cited as *Constitution*).

ought to indulge all their jealousy and exhaust all their precautions.
. . . As the weight of the legislative authority requires that it should
be thus divided, the weakness of the executive may require, on the
other hand, that it should be fortified." The result of this division and
fortification is not a balance of equal powers, for the executive is still
the "weaker department," and the legislative authority contains within
itself a "weaker branch" and a "stronger branch."[78] It is these theorists
of politics as the balancing of unequal forces who pioneered what is, I
think, the most important and least recognized aspect of the theory of
checks and balances, and we will return to them shortly, adducing further evidence that there is a close parallel between their arguments.
So far we have seen that by the mid-eighteenth-century there were two
conflicting ways of thinking about a balance of powers—one (Swift's
notion) which stressed the formation of alliances between two powers
in order to balance a third, and the other (Bolingbroke's notion, derived in all probability from Moyle) which stressed the independency
of the powers.

We turn now to the word "check." No one seems to have asked when
the word "check" is first used in a political context. The earliest usage
known to me is in a protest by the New Model Army against the Presbyterians in August 1647 where it is already linked to the word balance.[79] It makes a couple of appearances in Nedham's *A True State of
the Case of the Commonwealth* in 1654. It is probably as a result of Cromwell's reading of Nedham that we find him reported as saying to the
army officers on February 27, 1657, that Parliament was in "need of a
check or balancing power (meaning the House of Lords or a House so
constituted)" to protect the rights of individuals, particularly in matters of religion.[80] But I have not noticed the word "check" anywhere

78. *The Federalist* No. 48, 309; No. 51, 320. See also Jefferson in 1789: "The
tyranny of the legislatures is the most formidable dread at present, and will be
for long years" in *The Portable Thomas Jefferson*, 439–40.

79. Quoted in *The Parliamentary or Constitutional History of England*, 24 vols.
(London, 1751–61), 16:230.

80. *The Writings and Speeches of Oliver Cromwell*, ed. W. C. Abbott, 4 vols. (Cambridge: Harvard University Press, 1937–47), 4:417. This is Burton's report of the
speech; Morgan's version (418) has "You are offended at a House of Lords. I tell
you that unless you have some such thing as a balance you cannot be safe." For

else until the upsurge in radical publication which followed the lapse of the Licensing Act in 1695: we have already seen it used by Moyle in 1698—indeed he uses it repeatedly—and it was used in the same year by Trenchard, by Moyle's friend Hammond, and by Shaftesbury and Toland, the likely authors of *The Danger of Mercenary Parliaments* who write of "a check and curb."[81] In this last example we see it linked to what was presumably an earlier vocabulary in which power was to be bridled (a word we have encountered in North's translation of Plutarch) and curbed.[82] One of the attractions of the word "check" was that it could be used both in a mechanical context and in the context of a human action of surveillance or supervision. We often find it paired with control, which is similarly ambiguous, as in the following passage of Moyle's: "You may observe in every government that when the executive power is transferred to the legislative, there is no control, nor can there be any check upon them; the people in such a case must suffer without redress, they have no resource; because they are oppressed by their own representatives."[83] But there are various types of check or control, and it is worth distinguishing them.

Cromwell's endorsement of Nedham's defense of the Instrument of Government see 3:587. I owe these references to Blair Worden.

81. Moyle, *Whole Works*, 49, etc. The passage on pp. 49–50 ["This wise lawgiver (Lycurgus) made such checks in the executive part of the government that in the administration they reciprocally controlled each other."] is a mystery. It appears, since it is in italics, to be a quotation, but comes, as far as I can see, neither from Herodotus nor Fletcher of Saltoun. If it is a quotation, it would be good to know from what, but its appearance of being a quotation may well be (since the work was published posthumously) a misinterpretation of Moyle's manuscript. Trenchard, *Short History of Standing Armies* (1698), vi; Gwyn, *Meaning*, 140; *State Tracts*, 3:638, 652. Justin Champion tells me Toland reprinted *The Danger of Mercenary Parliaments* in 1721–22 with a new preface for Molesworth's election campaign.

82. E.g., M. Nedham, *The Excellencie of a Free State* [1656] (reprint, London, 1767), 5, 126–27 ("curb"), 65 ("bridle"). The 1767 reprint of Nedham's *Excellencie of a Free State* was widely known in America before the Revolution—more difficult, and more interesting, is the extent of Nedham's influence on the radical Whig tradition in the late seventeenth and early eighteenth centuries: see Worden, "Whig History," n. 58.

83. Moyle, *Whole Works*, 56–57; Gwyn, *Meaning*, 88.

The obvious meaning of "check" was that of preventing an action or exercising a veto: this was its original meaning in Nedham. In 1730, for example, we find James Pitt claiming that the three powers of the government "have a negative on each other"—the Commons being able to exercise a veto over the executive by refusing supply, or in Madison's phrase, employing "the engine of a money bill."[84] Montesquieu, writing in French, talks about each power being able to *empêche, arrête,* or veto the other, and from him there derived a lengthy tradition which assumed that the executive must be able to exercise a veto over the legislature (although in eighteenth-century English constitutional practice, this veto had in fact virtually ceased to exist: Jean-Louis de Lolme could find no case of the King exercising his veto after 1692).[85]

But to *check* might also mean, in Bolingbroke's language, to examine and control. According to the OED, the first use of the word *responsibility* is in Hamilton's and Madison's *The Federalist* (1787).[86] In fact the word can be traced back (in its political usage) to 1762 and was in frequent use in late eighteenth-century English in the context of discussions of ministerial responsibility.[87] (It is one of the more remarkable examples of the power of metaphor that the nineteenth-century notion of moral responsibility has its origin in this notion of ministerial responsibility; although one isolated usage of "responsibility" in a moral context may be noted in 1737.)[88] But the idea, if not the word, goes back before then. The first example the OED gives for the use of *responsible* to mean "accountable" is in Prynne's *Sovereign Power of Parliaments* of 1643 where it is asserted that kings are responsible

84. Gwyn, *Meaning,* 98; *The Federalist* No. 58, 350.

85. Montesquieu, *Esprit des lois,* 1:169–72; de Lolme, *Constitution,* 405.

86. OED CD-ROM, s.v. *responsibility.* The word occurs frequently: *The Federalist,* 370, 405–7, 435–36, 444.

87. Gunnar von Proschwitz, "Responsabilité: L'idée et le mot dans le débat politique du XVIIIᵉ siècle," in *Actes du Xᵉ Congrès internationale de linguistique et philologie romane* (1965), 385–97. The first example discussed by von Proschwitz is from 1766; but see *An Answer to the Observations on the Papers Relative to the Rupture with Spain* (London, 1762), 29.

88. Unpublished paper by Vittoria Franco, "Individuo moderno, responsabilità, frantumazione delle gerarchie sociali." For the exceptional instance, see O. Sedgewick, *The World Turn'd Inside-Out* (London, 1737), 102.

to their kingdoms or parliaments; and this was later extended into a clear doctrine of ministerial responsibility under another name.[89] Thus Trenchard writes in 1698, "The law has always been very tender of the person of the king, and therefore has disposed the executive part of the government in such proper channels, that whatsoever lesser excesses are committed, they are not imputed to him, but his ministers are accountable for them" (although he goes on to complain that in practice this principle of accountability is easily evaded).[90] I am not sure when accountability was first described as a check, but it may well have been during the debates on impeachment of 1697–98. Certainly it is in this sense that Hume wrote (in 1752) of the "particular checks and controls provided by the constitution," checks which make it in the interest of bad men to act for the public good: he is discussing the problem of how a government is to control its administration.[91] For Blackstone, too, it is impeachment which serves as a check on the executive. So important might this idea of accountability seem that it was capable of swallowing up any other concept of checks and balances. According to the OED the first use of the word *accountability* was in *The History of Vermont* in 1794 in a reference to "mutual checks and balances, accountability and responsibility," although in fact the first usage appears to have been in 1784, in Ethan Allen's *Reason the Only Oracle of Man*, and the word is fairly common from 1792.[92]

In the eighteenth century, freedom of the press created a new method of holding those in power to account by summoning them to the bar of public opinion or, to use Bolingbroke's term, "the tribunal of public fame."[93] In general, Anglophone political theory was very slow to recognize the significance of freedom of the press for British liberty. No. 15 of *Cato's Letters*, "Of Freedom of Speech," is perhaps the

---

89. OED CD-ROM, s.v. *responsible*. The need to make rulers accountable is a recurring theme of Nedham's, e.g., *A True State of the Case of the Commonwealth* [1654] (reprint, Exeter: The Rota, 1978), 38, and *Excellencie*, 72–73.

90. Gwyn, *Meaning*, 141.

91. Mayr, *Authority, Liberty*, 162; *Essays*, 15–16.

92. OED CD-ROM, s.v. *accountability;* Allen, *Reason* (Bennington, Vt., 1784), 91, etc. Other examples are now to be found in *Eighteenth Century Collections Online*, see n. 55.

93. *Dissertation*, Letter XVII: *Works*, 2:224.

first sustained defense of free speech, describing it as "the great bulwark of liberty," but I know of no sophisticated analysis of its effects earlier than the one to be found in the Francophone de Lolme. De Lolme, a citizen of Geneva, was impressed by the way a free press can make three kingdoms into one small town. Indeed he maintains public debate in the press has all the advantages and none of the disadvantages of a popular assembly; de Lolme, a former disciple of Rousseau's, was eager to stress the ease with which direct democracy degenerates into tyranny. He is clear, however, that no tyranny can withstand a free press—and the original purpose of his book, first published in Holland for sale in France, was to undermine French absolutism by exploiting this very freedom. De Lolme fully recognized the power of the press as a "mighty political engine," capable of being a check in its own right.[94]

Then there is a third meaning of "check," meaning to interrupt or delay. Here "check" is paired not with "control" but with "clog," a word which originally meant a hobble and had come to mean any obstacle or brake. In 1698–99 there are repeated references to the opposition's desire to "clog the wheels of government."[95] In 1752 we find Thomas Pownall attacking the contemporary working of checks and balances in the British constitution: "Thus it becomes the interest of the democratic part to be a constant clog and check upon the measures of the administering power, and to oppose themselves to every new exertion of its influence."[96] Paine, in *Common Sense,* chose to understand the theory of constitutional checks in this sense:

> For as the greater weight will always carry up the less, and as all the wheels of a machine are put in motion by one, it only remains to know which power in the constitution has the most weight, for that

94. De Lolme, *Constitution,* 291–305, 319–20, 427–28, 439. One may compare de Lolme with Hume, "Of the Liberty of the Press" (1741), particularly in its earlier version: *Essays,* 9–13, 604–5.

95. *A Letter to A, B, C, D, E, F, etc. Concerning Their Argument* (1698), 2; *A True Account of Land Forces in England* (London: J. Nutt, 1699), 1–2; *A Letter to His Most Excellent Majesty* (1698), reprinted in *State Tracts,* 3:633.

96. OED CD-ROM, s.v. *clog;* Mayr, *Authority, Liberty,* 161 (N.B. Mayr's inconsistency on the date of this text); "clog" already appears in close proximity to "check" in Trenchard: Gwyn, *Meaning,* 140.

will govern; and though the others, or a part of them, may clog, or as the phrase is, check the rapidity of its motion, yet so long as they cannot stop it, their endeavors will be ineffectual, the first moving power will at last have its way, and what it wants in speed is supplied in time.[97]

Speed, of course, might be required for good government, and in Massachusetts those who agreed with Paine that there should be only a single legislative chamber complained that senates "have formerly been a check or clog to business of consequence, requiring dispatch."[98] American advocates of bicameralism replied that it was important for one legislative chamber to check another, and since, if both chambers represented the people, the purpose of such a check could not be to balance competing interests, it must be to delay hasty decisions. (Although one did not need to be an American to reach such conclusions —de Lolme had already defended bicameralism in similar terms.)[99] In South Carolina in 1784, for example, it was maintained that the case for two representative bodies was that "the division in the legislative power seems necessary to furnish a proper check to our too hasty proceedings."[100] Benjamin Franklin was arguing in this tradition when he defended the idea of two assemblies, saying it was "like a practice he had somewhere seen, of certain wagoners, who, when about to descend a steep hill with a heavy load, if they had four cattle, took off one pair from before, and chaining them to the hinder part of the wagon drove them up hill, while the pair before and the weight of the load, overbalancing the strength of those behind, drew them slowly and moderately down the hill."[101] There was indeed general agreement

97. Thomas Paine, *Rights of Man, Common Sense and Other Political Writings,* ed. Mark Philp (Oxford: Oxford University Press, 1995), 9–10. On the importance of this passage, see Bailyn, *Ideological Origins,* 285–86.

98. Wood, *Creation,* 224.

99. De Lolme, *Constitution,* 218–28. The Instrument of Government provided a delay of twenty days between the passage of legislation and its taking effect, a provision defended by Nedham (*A True State of the Case of the Commonwealth,* 35) as providing time for reflection.

100. Wood, *Creation,* 239.

101. Adams, *The Works of John Adams,* 6 vols. (Boston: Little, Brown, 1856–61), 4:390 (hereafter cited as Adams, *Works*).

that some mechanism to ensure delay was needed so that, in Madison's phrase, it was the "cool and deliberate sense of the community" which prevailed.[102]

Both checks and balances thus prove to be much more complex notions than one might at first suspect; nor should we be surprised that the linking of the two together presents its own complexities. In Moyle's essay on the constitution of Sparta, the word "check" is frequently used, but "balance" is never used in its Polybian or Plutarchan sense. In Montesquieu the two ideas are kept radically separate: balance is invoked in the context of a discussion of the mixed constitution of the Roman republic as described by Polybius; checks in the context of a discussion of the separation of powers as exemplified by England.[103] Indeed this, I believe, was the general pattern, and modern commentators have been led astray by the fact that it is Adams who first uses the phrase. Manin, for example, concludes that the idea of "checks and balances" develops out of the idea of a mixed or balanced constitution (advocated by Adams) and allows for the active influence of one branch of government on another, while the alternative is the idea of the separation of powers, which provides only for passive or negative "checks."[104] The fact that the idea of a check is here recognized as peculiarly belonging to one tradition while "checks and balances" is supposed to derive from the other suggests confusion in the argument. In fact the idea of checks and balances implies the bringing together of two analytically and historically distinct traditions, that of the mixed or balanced constitution (a tradition in which the word "check" plays no part) and that of the separation of powers (a tradition which makes no mention of balances).

This argument is supported by the second occasion (as far as I know) on which "check" is used as a political term, in Nedham's *True State of the Case of the Commonwealth* (1654) when it is immediately counterposed to "balance." Nedham is formulating the first uncompromising argument for a separation of powers (made possible by the existence of an actual separation in the Cromwellian-written constitu-

102. *The Federalist* No. 63, 371; see Manin, "Checks," 60–62.
103. Compare *Spirit of the Laws,* 162, 182.
104. Manin, "Checks," 30–31.

tion, the Instrument of Government), and complaining that the Rump Parliament's proposal for biennial Parliaments would have placed "the legislative and executive powers in the same persons . . . by which means in effect they become unaccountable for abuses in government. . . . And how easily abuses might have been justified in a parliamentary way, is apparent enough; seeing an opportunity was given in that bill, to the next or any succeeding Parliament (no manner of balance or check being reserved upon them) by claiming an absolute authority to be in themselves, for ever to have continued the power (if they pleased) in their own hands. . . ." At first sight it might seem as if the words "balance" and "check" are here being used as equivalent terms: and indeed when Cromwell linked the terms together in 1657 they seem to have been assumed to be equivalents. But they may equally have been meant as alternatives. By the word "balance" it may be that Nedham meant to invoke the powers of the monarch and Lords within the mixed constitution (which included the monarch's power to dissolve Parliament); by the word "check" he may have meant to invoke the power of the Protector under the Instrument of Government to veto unconstitutional legislation. If so, the word "check" was being put to use to explain how power would be limited within a constitution where powers were separated.[105]

Nevertheless, it was tempting to see the English constitution as embodying both a separation and a balancing of powers, and it was easy to slip into using "check" and "balance" as synonyms. As Toland put it, "All the world knows that England is under a free government, whose supreme legislative power is lodged in the King, Lords, and Commons, each of which have their peculiar privileges and prerogatives; no law can pass without their common authority or consent; and they are a mutual check and balance on one another's oversights or encroachments."[106] (This led directly to an appeal to the authority of Polybius.)

105. Nedham, *A True State of the Case of the Commonwealth*, 10, 33; the word "check" also occurs on p. 22 in the context of a discussion of the danger of an executive power "without check or controll."

106. Toland, *Art of Governing by Partys* (1701), 31. It is possible that Toland is the source of later usages of "checks and balances": this work was twice reprinted (c. 1757, c. 1760). For an example of Trenchard using "check" and "balance" in close proximity and as synonyms, see below, p. 269.

We have seen Bolingbroke also trying to bring together the ideas (but not the language) of both traditions by stressing the constitutional dependency and independency of both branches of government: first published in *The Craftsman* in 1730, his argument was republished in 1743 in *Remarks on the History of England*. In the same year in Spelman's preface to his translation of Polybius's fragment on the balanced constitution, check and balance once again occur in close proximity, as if virtual equivalents.[107]

But why did Toland's phrase not catch on as Adams's did? In 1752 Thomas Pownall attacked those "that talk of balance and counterbalance, of one power being constitutionally a check upon another; and that it is constitutionally the duty of these to pull different ways, even when there is no real matter of difference, yet to preserve the equilibrium of power."[108] Now this is not the old doctrine of the balanced constitution which is under attack, for that had always insisted that the precondition for equilibrium was coalition making and trimming; what is being attacked here is the new Bolingbrokean doctrine, later to be Adams's doctrine, that the three powers can pull in separate, independent directions and yet establish an equilibrium, and it is this new doctrine which brings the idea of the balanced constitution close enough to the idea of the separation of powers for checks to be routinely identified with balances. Blackstone, we have seen, moves seamlessly from a discussion of checks (first the independent capacity of Commons, Lords, and King to veto legislation, and then the capacity of Parliament to hold the King's agents to account) to a discussion of a triangle of forces. But in Blackstone's account the three forces result in movement, not equilibrium. This way of thinking did not lead naturally to a language of checks and balances, or even of "checks and balance," the phrase Noah Webster uses in 1787. In order to understand the power of the phrase, we will need to look more closely at Adams's *Defence*.

We can now see that Adams's phrase involves a further puzzle, beyond the bringing together of two words that belong to very different intellectual traditions: the use of balances in the plural. For most pre-

---

107. Spelman, *Fragment*, iv.
108. Quoted in Pargellis, "Theory," 47–48.

vious writers there had been one balance of forces (as in Polybius and Swift), which trims the ship of state and sustains the mixed constitution, and several checks. What (other than syntactic parallelism) invited the reference to balances in the plural? It seems clear the shift was thought to be particularly appropriate in the context of limits on the power of the legislature: *The Federalist* refers specifically to "legislative [or 'legislature,' in the first printing] balances and checks," in a list of a series of principles to be adopted in any well-constructed constitution, and an exactly equivalent phrase had been used by Gouverneur Morris in 1776: "The authority of magistrates is taken from that mass of power which in rude societies and unbalanced democracies is wielded by the majority. Every separation of the executive and judicial authority from the legislature is a diminution of political and increase of civil liberty. Every check and balance of that legislature has a like effect."[109]

Later Adams was to identify eight balances in the Constitution of 1787: between the states and the federal government, between the House of Representatives and the Senate, between the executive and the legislature, between the judiciary and all the other powers, between the Senate and the president in appointments to offices and treaties, between the people and their representatives, between the legislatures of the states and the senators selected by them, between the people and the electoral college which selected a president. Here some of these balances are clearly what would once have been called checks (between executive, legislature, and judiciary). The result (for Adams was no admirer of the new Constitution) was "all this complication of machinery, all these wheels within wheels, these *imperia* within *imperiis*."[110] I have reproduced these eight in an order of my own, because the first five seem to me a logical consequence of a mixed constitution and a separation of powers within a federal system. But the last three are all cases of a balance between electors and elected, and this involves an idea of balance unknown to Polybius, Swift, and Montesquieu. It is to this idea of balance, central to any account of legislative

109. Quoted in Paul Rahe, *Republics Ancient and Modern* (Chapel Hill: University of North Carolina Press, 1992), 562–63.

110. Cohen, *Science*, 225–26.

balances and checks (including that which appears in *The Federalist*), that I now turn.

There is a simple sense in which at every election the electorate hold their representatives to account and replace those who have failed to give satisfaction. This fundamental check is, we might say, the essence of the liberty to be found in representative government. Peers, Bolingbroke said, are accountable to God, but members of Parliament to their constituents.[111] According to the anti-Federalist author who called himself Centinel, in England "the only operative and efficient check upon the conduct of administration, is the sense of the people at large."[112] But the relationship between the electorate and their representatives is a complex one, and I want to pause over two texts that made a serious effort to analyze it. The first is Edward Spelman's short but incisive introduction to his translation of Polybius on balanced government. Spelman's text was twice reprinted in English (the last edition being known to John Adams, who quotes at length from Spelman's translation in the *Defence*), and later translated into French for publication during the Revolution.[113] I have already suggested that it was one of the few works that linked check and balance together as equivalents, and it may have played an important part in developing a convenient language for the notion that liberty is primarily established by power restraining power. It is also the first unambiguous defense

111. *Dissertation,* Letter XVII: *Works,* 2:224.

112. Storing, *Anti-Federalist,* 15.

113. There was an unauthorized reprint of Spelman's *Fragment* in 1747 under the title *Polybius's Glorious Discourse,* and an authorized reprint in an appendix to vol. 1 of Spelman's four-volume edition of Dionysius of Halicarnassus (1758). Adams reproduces lengthy passages from Spelman's translation of Polybius in the *Defence, Works,* 4:435–39; he also reproduces passages from Spelman's translation of Dionysius. Spelman's preface but not his translation was reproduced in the French Revolutionary text *Fragment de Polybe.* Selections from Spelman are reproduced in J. A. W. Gunn, ed., *Factions No More* (London: Frank Cass, 1972), 151–53, and in Peter Campbell, "An Early Defence of Party," *Political Studies* 3:166–67. On Spelman see A. Momigliano, "Polybius Between the English and the Turks" (1974) in Momigliano, *Sesto contributo alla storia degli studi classici e del mondo antico,* 2 vols. (Rome: Edizione di storia e letteratura, 1980), 125–41; Caroline Robbins, "'Discordant Parties,' A Study of the Acceptance of Party by Englishmen," *Political Science Quarterly* 73 (1958): 505–29, 527.

of party in English, the consensus until then having been that, since there was a single common interest, parties are in principle unnecessary and that where there are two parties there must be at least one faction.[114] Spelman, by contrast, argues that "In all free governments there ever were and ever will be parties," and that party conflict is not an effect but a precondition of liberty. The cities of ancient Greece were divided into supporters of aristocracy and democracy, but "It was not the existence of the two parties I have mentioned that destroyed the liberties of any of those cities, but the occasional extinction of one of them by the superiority the other had gained over it. And if ever we should be so unhappy as to have the balance between the three orders destroyed; and that any one of the three should utterly extinguish the other two, the name of a party would, from that moment, be unknown in England, and we should unanimously agree in being slaves to the conqueror."

Party thus becomes a crucial mechanism for checking the power of government:

> Whatever may be the success of the opposer, the public reaps great benefit from the opposition; since this keeps ministers upon their guard, and, often, prevents them from pursuing bold measures which an uncontrolled power might, otherwise, tempt them to engage in. They must act with caution, as well as fidelity, when they consider the whole nation is attentive to every step they take, and that the errors they may commit will not only be exposed but aggravated.

But Spelman also provides a subtle account of party, distinguishing sharply between the motives of a party's supporters who want to see certain policies adopted and its leaders who want power. The thirst for power provides the leaders with a stronger incentive than any dis-

114. See, for example, Nedham, *Excellencie*, 160: "Now that you may know what faction is, and which is the factious party in any state of kingdom, afflicted with that infirmity; the only way is first to find out the true and declared interest of state; and then if you observe any designs, counsels, actings, or persons, moving in opposition to that which is the true public interest, it may be infallibly concluded that there lies the faction, and the factious party."

interested concern for the public good, and opposition provides a training ground for future rulers. There thus exists an inherent tension between a party's leaders and its followers, for the leaders have an incentive to sacrifice their principles to attain power, while the followers, who will never be rulers, have an interest in seeing the powers of government restrained. A simple confirmation of this theory in Spelman's view is the complete failure of the political elite to repeal the Septennial Act and institute annual elections: although the whole nation would benefit from such a measure, politicians as a class have an interest in limiting the electorate's ability to control their actions.[115] A similar account appears in de Lolme's *Constitution of England,* for de Lolme argues that politicians rely on popular support to give them access to power, but as they acquire power and status, as they are promoted for example from the Commons to the Lords, the people cease to trust them and become convinced that their interests are no longer at one with those of their rank-and-file supporters.[116]

In 1787 the proposed federal Constitution for the United States necessarily multiplied both checks and balances, for it established a new constitutional tension, that between federal and state powers. Adams's new phrase immediately became the language of the hour. But well before then a new notion of balance had come into existence to supplement the Polybian and Plutarchan balance between monarchical, aristocratic, and democratic institutions. This was the notion of a natural balancing mechanism at work, first of all between parties and then between the governing elite and those they represent. This new conception of representative government made it easy to recognize that there were several balances at work as well as several checks. Neither Spelman nor de Lolme coined the phrase "checks and balances," but this is a mere accident of history, for the phrase accords well with what they wanted to say, and their notion of a balance between electors and elected is central to Adams's list of the different balances at work in the American Constitution.

115. Spelman, *Fragment,* v–viii.
116. De Lolme, *Constitution,* 206–13; see also 271–80.

3. AUTOMATIC MACHINERY

So far I have argued that there is a radical discontinuity between the Polybian or Plutarchan notion of the balance and the new mechanical language of controls, clogs, and checks, and of counterpoise, balance, and equilibrium that establishes itself after 1697. Second, I have argued that there are several types of check and more than one type of balance, and that it is important to distinguish between them. Thirdly, I have argued that where checks were plural from the beginning, the balance was singular and only became plural with a new account of the role of parties and political leaders in representative government and with the birth of federalism. At this point you might think the idea of checks and balances has been pretty thoroughly explored; this then is the time to turn to that aspect of the new mechanical thinking which seems to me to be missing from modern usages of the language of checks and balances.

Let us start with the translation of Plutarch on the balance which we find in the Dryden edition:

> For the state, which before had no firm basis to stand upon, but leaned one while towards an absolute monarchy (when the Kings had the upper hand) and another while towards a pure democracy (when the people had the better of it), found in this establishment of the Senate a counterpoise, which always kept things in a just equilibrium. For the Twenty Eight always adhered to the weaker side, and put themselves like a weight into the lighter scale, until they had reduced the other to a balance.[117]

If we take Dryden's translator to be describing not the decisions of politicians but the working of a machine, then what we have here is an automatic mechanism where a feedback loop enables the machine to regulate itself. What is involved here is not a static but a dynamic equilibrium: first the balance tips slightly one way and then the other, but each time it is brought back toward the horizontal. Where, before the establishment of the Senate, it seesawed wildly; after its establishment it oscillates gently, always close to the horizontal.

Perhaps I am reading too much into this brief passage, for the idea

117. Plutarch, *Lives* (1683), 1:141–42.

of a self-stabilizing system was not a familiar one in the late seventeenth century. In 1721 Thomas Gordon could see that the precondition for "control and counterpoise" was "a perpetual struggle: But by this struggle liberty is preserved, as water is kept sweet by motion."[118] The mixing of metaphors here, as in *The King's Answer*, shows mechanical thinking pressing at its limits. Gordon, after all, could not use the example of a self-stabilizing system with which we are most familiar, the market, where there is constant movement and change but where competition works to match supply to demand and to bring profits toward an average rate. Nor would he have been familiar with any self-stabilizing machines. He did not, for example, have the benefit of central heating. Here the temperature in the house oscillates around a norm established by a thermostat: when it falls significantly, the furnace is switched on; when it rises, the furnace is switched off.

In the second half of the eighteenth century, there was, for the first time, considerable interest in self-stabilizing systems, and it was soon claimed that under certain conditions—a separation between legislature, executive, and judiciary; a bicameral legislature; a unified executive; juries judge of law as well as fact; regular elections and a free press —representative government had a self-stabilizing character where excess in any direction would tend to correct itself automatically. Societies with representative government appear to be in a constant state of agitation, yet we believe them to be peculiarly resilient. Like a tree in a storm, the political fabric bends, but it does not break.[119] We all unthinkingly rely on this idea that certain mechanisms enable the political system to correct its own mistakes when we maintain that an independent judiciary and jury trials are guarantees of liberty or when we say that it is essential to the democratic process that there should be effective opposition or when we take it for granted that we are un-

---

118. *Cato's Letters*, No. 70, 504. Compare Nedham, in *A True State of the Case of the Commonwealth*, 36, arguing the need for frequent elections: "And how unapt men are of their own accord to part with such power, when they have got it once into their hands, how apt they are to corrupt like standing Pools, and contract an arbitrary distemper in execution of Law, and what miserable inconveniences must follow thereupon, we, and all the people of the Land can tell by too sad experience."

119. De Lolme, *Constitution*, 533–34.

likely to live through a violent revolution in England or America. This self-stabilizing system was first identified as functioning within English politics and then deliberately constructed in the American Constitution.

This revolution is of fundamental importance, for if we feel secure in the enjoyment of our liberties, it is because we believe that the political system is in some way or other self-stabilizing, that given time the consequences of bad decisions will be mitigated, not exacerbated. There are a number of reasons why this revolution has remained invisible. It was not formulated in a "classic" text of political theory. Indeed the ideas involved still remain somewhat unfamiliar and inchoate so that we have little idea of under what circumstances and to what extent they are true—could one, for example, imagine a Nazi party coming to power within a well-designed constitution, and if not, why not? Moreover, to discuss them in an eighteenth-century context it is necessary to talk about ideas of equilibrium in mechanics, a subject of little interest except to historians of science. Above all, the new theory of politics as self-stabilizing was masked by its superficial similarity to the far older theory of Polybius and Plutarch. The classical formulations of the idea of a self-stabilizing system, however, were designed to describe political systems which had the capacity to evolve into either monarchy, aristocracy, or democracy but in fact stabilized in an in-between condition. What made this equilibrium possible was not just an arrangement of political institutions but also a set of extra-institutional powers, or what one eighteenth-century commentator called "weight in the community"[120]—even if Polybius did not make this explicit, any eighteenth-century theorist familiar with Harrington's *Oceana* (1656) would have read this back into the text.[121] Thus Trenchard and Moyle wrote that "This balance [the constitution of England] can never be preserved but by a union of the natural and artificial strength of the kingdom . . . or otherwise the government is violent and against nature."[122] The new theory, by contrast, assumed

120. Storing, *Anti-Federalist*, 15.

121. In other words, they would have read Polybius as if corrected along the lines proposed by Moyle: see his *Essay Upon the Constitution of the Roman Government* in Robbins, *Two English Republican Tracts*, 231.

122. Trenchard and Moyle, *Argument*, 565.

that an overwhelming preponderance of power lay with a relatively un-differentiated "people," but that, despite there being no equilibrium in the social distribution of power, a self-stabilizing political system could exist.

Precisely because it involved a rejection of the traditional idea of a mixed government, the only system for which the claim that it was self-stabilizing had previously been made, many contemporaries found the new theory incomprehensible, implausible, or paradoxical. It re-lied, they recognized, on the idea of checks on power; it claimed that the checks involved were not simply "parchment barriers," but as far as they could see the checks were after all only "checks on paper"— Patrick Henry was blunter still, calling them "specious imaginary bal-ances, your rope-dancing, chain-rattling, ridiculous ideal checks and contrivances"—that is to say they relied purely on institutional mecha-nisms.[123] Their puzzlement and incomprehension continues to inter-fere with our ability to understand the intellectual revolution that had taken place.

Let us go back to the mechanical metaphor. The power of this de-pends partly on the quality of the clockwork mechanism one has in mind. The heart, which de Mornay likened to a clock constructed by God, does not beat steadily but sometimes races, and for John Donne, in the early seventeenth century, clockwork was a symbol of unreli-ability to be compared unfavorably with the genuinely regular move-ment of the sun through the heavens. René Descartes (1596–1650) obviously represents a key moment of transition, for in arguing that animals were mere machines, he not only deprived animals of intelli-gence, he also attributed remarkable capacities to mere machines. It took time for men to construct in their minds the idea of a perfect mechanism, of what Trenchard at the end of an essay on the mechani-cal philosophy described as "a watch which will go for a thousand years" without winding or mending.[124] First Arnold Geulincx (1624–

---

123. *The Federalist* No. 48, 309, 312; No. 73, 418; Storing, *Anti-Federalist*, 319; Frohnen, *Anti-Federalists*, 686.

124. *Cato's Letters,* No. 116, 814. There are certainly connections to be made between systems analysis, the mechanical philosophy, and materialism: a valu-able starting point is provided by Harold J. Cook, "Body and Passions: Material-ism and the Early Modern State," *Osiris* 17 (2002): 25–48, but it is worth remem-

69) and then Gottfried Leibniz (1646–1716) took the idea of mechanical perfection even further when they claimed that the mental world and the physical world correspond only because both are automata which have been perfectly synchronized, two clocks beating as one, unfailingly keeping time.[125]

This theoretical concept of the perfect mechanism takes form at roughly the same time as a quite different metaphor which contributed equally to the scientific revolution, that of the law of nature. The idea of a law as the expression of uniformity and regularity also involved the mental construction of a new species of perfection. Robert Boyle is an important pioneer in the use of both metaphors for regularity, that of the machine and that of the law, in a world where neither machines nor laws actually performed predictably. It is worth remembering that *regular* itself is a dead metaphor, derived from the term for a monastic rule; de Quincey in 1722 appears to have been the first to have used it to mean constant and uniform in opposition to irregular—to use it in the sense we now take for granted.[126]

In order to be accurate, clocks have to be designed to continue marking regular intervals of time even as the arc of the pendulum diminishes or the spring unwinds. All good clocks are in that sense self-regulating, and the history of clockwork is a history of regulatory mechanisms such as the verge-and-foliot escapement and the fusee. But a clock cannot tell when it has gone wrong and correct itself. Clocks lack feedback mechanisms, and to think of the universe as clockwork is to invite the notion that God may make occasional adjustments, as Newton believed he did to the orbits of the planets. Harrington insisted that a constitution, if constructed according to the right principles, could continue forever, a self-regenerating system, but the claim explicitly involved a comparison between the political and the divine architects.

However, a century after what we might call the mechanical revo-

---

bering that one could be a mechanist and materialist without wanting a complex state system—one need think only of Helvétius.

125. Arnold Geulincx, *Metaphysics,* trans. Martin Wilson (Wisbech, U.K.: Christoffel Press, 1999), 45, 114.

126. OED CD-ROM, s.v. *regular.*

lution, a second much less well-understood revolution took place, a revolution which saw the invention of self-regulating or self-governing or self-stabilizing machines. A simple example is the fantail windmill, where the fantail points the windmill into the wind, and constantly adjusts the direction in which the windmill points as the wind changes direction. The fantail is an eighteenth-century English invention—one apparently never adopted in France, where millers preferred to steer their windmills into the wind, not leave them to their own devices. It is on the basis of contemporary windmill technology that James Watt invented in 1788 the most famous self-regulating mechanism of the industrial revolution, the centrifugal speed governor for steam engines. Around the same time, self-regulating mechanisms that had long been known were finding new uses—the thermostat, for example, and the ball-cock valve. All such machines involve—though the term itself is a twentieth-century one—some sort of feedback mechanism.[127]

At the same time and almost ahead of the technological revolution, what we might call mind machines (remember Adam Smith describes theoretical systems as "imaginary machines") are being invented (again in the English-speaking world) which have self-regulating qualities: Hume invents the modern theory of the balance of trade in 1750 (in 1741 he had written of English politics as involving a "fluctuation" between support for government and opposition, implying perhaps a self-correcting mechanism),[128] and Smith formulates what we now call the market mechanism (he does not use the term "mechanism" himself, but he would have acknowledged that the market was an imaginary machine) in *The Wealth of Nations* (1776). The whole point of the market mechanism is not that it is a machine but that it is self-regulating or self-stabilizing, that it is a feedback system. Modern economics, as much as modern natural science, is thus dependent on a new understanding of the possibilities of mechanical systems, for even imaginary machines, if they are to be seen to work, must abide by recognizable mechanical principles. Even natural science needed the concept of self-regulation: Shaftesbury as early as 1709 describes the

127. See Mayr, *Authority, Liberty,* and also Mayr, *The Origins of Feedback Control* (Cambridge: MIT Press, 1970).

128. *Essays,* 65.

mechanical philosophy as relying on "some exquisite system of self-governed matter," and I take it self-governed here means in effect self-regulating.[129]

It is worth noting that the process described by Spelman and de Lolme, the new balance between politicians and the public, is one of constant fluctuation around an equilibrium: government provokes opposition, opposition moves into government, and government provokes opposition. The process is never at rest but is constantly self-stabilizing, just like the market or the fantail windmill. It implies, in fact, the idea of dynamic rather than static equilibrium, for what is at work is a feedback mechanism. Indeed any careful formulation of the claim that the people control their representatives through elections involves an appeal to a feedback mechanism. It is also worth stressing that Nedham and Harrington, who seem in so many respects to be the founders of the modern republican tradition, are systematically opposed to feedback mechanisms. They want a wholesale rotation or revolution in elected representatives at every election rather than seeing elections as an opportunity to assess the performance of the people's representatives.[130] And they want political discussions to take place in secret, as in Venice, not in public.[131] Their assumption is that any passage of time represents an opportunity for corruption, while for later theorists time provides scope for correcting mistakes and adjusting to developments.

We can see the new, contrasting conception best in a passage from de Lolme:

> As the representatives of the people will naturally be selected from among those citizens who are most favored by fortune, and will consequently have much to preserve, they will, even in the midst of

129. OED CD-ROM, s.v. *self-governed*.

130. Thus Nedham is careful to insist that frequent elections are not enough but must be accompanied by term limits: *Excellencie*, 42–43, 60–61, 76–77, 107–9.

131. Thus Nedham insists that all citizens should know the principles of liberty and attacks the Venetian constitution as tyrannical; nevertheless, he recommends that all debates of the senate should be held in secret: ibid., xvi, 31–32, 103–5, 138–39.

quiet times, keep a watchful eye on the motions of power. As the advantages they possess will naturally create a kind of rivalship between them and those who govern, the jealousy which they will conceive against the latter will give them an exquisite degree of sensibility on every increase of their authority. Like those delicate instruments which discover the operations of nature while they are yet imperceptible to our senses, they will warn the people of those things which of themselves they never see but when it is too late; and their greater proportional share, whether of real riches or of those which lie in the opinions of men, will make them, if I may so express myself, the barometers that will discover, in its first beginning, every tendency to a change in the constitution.[132]

The representatives thus serve as a thermostat, enflaming or damping down public opinion depending on the presence or absence of a threat to liberty and property. Again, the process involves constant movement as representatives compete simultaneously for power and public support, but as long as the circuit of election, representation, sensitivity, publicity, and new elections is unbroken, the mechanism to check power will continue to function. De Lolme, we have seen, likens the representatives to barometers, not thermostats, for like barometers they act on men's minds. But while a barometer changes one's behavior, encouraging one to set to sea or carry an umbrella, one's resulting behavior does not in itself affect the weather. In politics, by contrast, the acute sensitivity of the elected representatives actually serves to change the political situation as a result of the information being fed back to the public in the same way that a thermostat serves to change the temperature in the room by supplying information to the furnace. What de Lolme is describing is a self-regulating system, and it is because his understanding of politics reaches this level of sophistication that we find him in later editions of his book criticizing Adam Smith's view that a standing army is not a threat to liberty if the sovereign is the supreme commander and the social elite supply the officer caste: "The author we are quoting has deemed a government to be a simpler machine, and an army a simpler instrument, than they in reality are."

132. De Lolme, *Constitution*, 259.

It is only when we see that de Lolme understands England's constitutional machinery to be self-stabilizing that we can understand just how far from simple he thinks it is. We can also recognize why he was in a good position to identify and admire Smith's "great abilities."[133]

It was the need to find checks and balances with which to control representative democracy which most concerned the framers of the American Constitution. When Adams was asked by the state of Massachusetts to preside over a state constituent convention in 1820 (a convention called to revise the constitution of 1780, which Adams had drafted single-handedly), he was praised for "demonstrating to the world, in his defense of the constitutions of the several United States, the contested principle, since admitted as an axiom, that checks and balances in legislative power are essential to true liberty."[134] But the great political work which sought to clarify and formulate the new understanding of politics which came to be embodied in the phrase "checks and balances" and draw from it a new design for the machinery of politics was not Adams's *Defence* but Hamilton's and Madison's *The Federalist*, and it is only by putting that work in the sort of context I have constructed here that we can hope to measure its originality and its success. *The Federalist* needs to be read against the key texts in the development of the new theories of checks and balances — the texts of Nedham, Moyle, Trenchard, Gordon, Bolingbroke, Blackstone, Spelman, Hume, and de Lolme. At the moment *The Federalist* is read almost exclusively in the context of Hume (who had been the first to recognize that an increase in scale could itself serve as a check upon the democratic element in a constitution). Hume pioneered the idea of self-regulating systems in economics, but he scarcely employed the

133. Ibid., 448–50. The earliest direct comparison between a constitutional mechanism (in this case a form of bicameralism) and a self-regulating machine that I know is in Sieyès. "Sur l'organisation du pouvoir législatif et la sanction royale" (September 7, 1789) in *Orateurs de la Révolution française*, vol. 1, *Les Constituants*, ed. F. Furet and R. Halévi (Paris: Gallimard, 1989), 1033: "Je ne vois pas, en effet, pourquoi, si l'exercice d'un *veto* suspensif est bon et utile, on le sortirait de la place que la nature des choses lui a destinée dans la législature elle-même. Le premier qui, en mécanique, fit usage du *régulateur*, se garda bien de la placer hors de la machine dont il voulait modérer le mouvement trop précipité."

134. "Life of John Adams" (in Adams, *Works*), 625.

concept in his discussion of politics.[135] Indeed he felt sure that in the long run the British constitution would fail to correct its own faults and would dissolve into tyranny or democracy.

In *The Federalist* No. 50, Madison (for those unfamiliar with the text I should explain that we know who wrote each of the essays which appeared under the byline of Publius) rejects the idea that the working of the Constitution can be supervised by some external body. He then begins No. 51 with this question:

> To what expedient, then, shall we finally resort, for maintaining in practice the necessary partition of power among the several departments as laid down by the Constitution? The only answer that can be given is that as all these exterior provisions are found to be inadequate the defect must be supplied by so contriving the interior structure of the government as that its several constituent parts may, by their mutual relations, be the means of keeping each other in their proper places. Without presuming to undertake a full development of this important idea I will hazard a few general observations . . . the great security against a gradual concentration of the several powers in the same department consists in giving to those who administer each department the necessary constitutional means and personal motives to resist encroachments of the others. The provision for defense must in this, as in all other cases, be made commensurate to the danger of attack. Ambition must be made to counteract ambition. The interest of the man must be connected with the constitutional rights of the place. It may be a reflection on human nature that such devices should be necessary to control the abuses of government. But what is government itself but the greatest of all reflections on human nature? If men were angels, no government would be necessary. If angels were to govern men, neither external nor internal controls on government would be necessary. In framing a government which is administered by men over men, the great difficulty lies in this: you must first enable the government to con-

---

135. Bolingbroke's influence in America is stressed in Bailyn, *Ideological Origins;* for Hume and *The Federalist,* see Wills, *Explaining America* (under "Adair" in the index), and Douglass Adair, *Fame and the Founding Fathers* (Indianapolis: Liberty Fund, 1998).

trol the governed; and in the next place oblige it to control itself. A dependence on the people is, no doubt, the primary control on the government; but experience has taught mankind the necessity of auxiliary precautions.

Here the conviction so clearly formulated in *Cato's Letters* that "whilst men are men, ambition, avarice, and vanity . . . will govern their actions" has been turned from a psychological principle into the fundamental principle of the constitution.[136]

Indeed in *Cato's Letters*, a work that Madison must certainly have known, Trenchard had momentarily formulated this general constitutional principle himself. Taking as his premise that "There has always been such a constant and certain fund of corruption and malignity in human nature, that it has been rare to find that man, whose views and happiness did not center in the gratification of his appetites," Trenchard concluded that experience had shown there was only one type of free government that could survive: one where

the power and sovereignty of magistrates in free countries was so qualified, and so divided into different channels, and committed to the discretion of so many different men, with different interests and views, that the majority of them could seldom or never find their account in betraying their trust in fundamental instances. Their emulation, envy, fear, or interest, always made them spies and checks upon one another . . . The only secret therefore in forming a free government is to make the interests of the governors and the governed the same, as far as human policy can contrive. Liberty cannot be preserved any other way.

But Trenchard expected the conflict between political leaders and the institutions with which they identified to be far more ruthless and far less successfully channeled into a harmless jockeying for position than Madison did. "Disgrace, torture, and death," he tells us, should be "the punishment of treachery and corruption."[137] For hanging, draw-

136. *Cato's Letters*, No. 70, 504 (Gordon's words).

137. Ibid., No. 60, 416–17. See also Adam Ferguson, *An Essay on the History of Civil Society* (1767; rev. ed. of 1773; Farnborough, Hants., U.K.: Gregg International, 1969), 214 ("Liberty is maintained by the continued differences and

ing, and quartering, Madison substituted ambition and place-seeking. In so doing he was following the example of Hume, whom he perhaps had in mind. In "Of the Independency of Parliament" (1741), Hume had moved directly from arguing that it is "as just *political* maxim, *that every man must be supposed a knave*" to imagining a political system in which "the skilful division of power" sets one institution against another, forcing all together to pursue the public interest.[138]

Bernard Manin has correctly said that the system of internal controls which Madison is describing can properly be termed a self-enforcing equilibrium.[139] One might then say—for it is the same idea expressed in different language—that the Constitution is intended to be a self-regulating machine. We have seen that this was already de Lolme's idea and that he had elaborated this idea most clearly in his account of "the primary control," the relationship between the government and the people.

We do not know for sure that Madison had read de Lolme. It seems highly unlikely that he had not read an author whom Hamilton admired and whose book Adams (who shared de Lolme's preoccupation with the British constitution) had described as "the best defense of the political balance of three powers that ever was written."[140] Adams's enthusiasm rather blinded him to the fact that de Lolme was not interested in a balance of monarchy, aristocracy, and democracy (Adams's primary concern) but rather in a balance of executive, legislative, and judiciary and, in order to achieve this, in legislative balances and checks. In *The Federalist* No. 70, Hamilton, who wanted a strong and unified executive, stated that he and de Lolme thought as one on the question of executive power and made his own the judgement of Junius, that de Lolme was "deep, solid, and ingenious."[141] I rather suspect that Madison had read de Lolme and read him with care, for

-----

oppositions of numbers, not by their concurring zeal in behalf of equitable government") and 268 ("to prevent the practice of crimes, by balancing against each other the selfish and partial dispositions of men").

138. *Essays*, 43.

139. Manin, "Checks," 57–58.

140. Adams, *Works*, 4:358.

141. *The Federalist* No. 70, 407. Hamilton's No. 9, 119, which includes the phrase "legislative balances and checks" reads to me like a summary of de Lolme.

every step of Madison's argument in No. 51 is foreshadowed in de Lolme.

No quotation from Madison is more famous than the statement (from *The Federalist* No. 55) that "If men were angels, no government would be necessary. If angels were to govern men, neither external nor internal controls on government would be necessary." De Lolme had made a similar argument: in a world where men "had neither any ambition, nor any other private passions," then direct democracy would be practical, but "in such a society, and among such beings, there would be no occasion for any government."[142] And indeed this whole chapter (bk. 2, ch. 5) on the evils of direct democracy might be said to illustrate Madison's astonishing claim—the decisive attack on the notion that it is executives not legislatures that need to be checked— that "Had every Athenian citizen been a Socrates, every Athenian assembly would still have been a mob."[143] (Again, there is a precedent in Hume, who tells us that "Cardinal de Retz says that all numerous assemblies, however composed, are mere mob.")[144] We have seen Madison arguing that every attack must be met with an equivalent defense, that ambition must counteract ambition. De Lolme's response to the excessive concentration of power is the same: the people must employ "for their defense the same means by which their adversaries carry on their attack . . . using the same weapons as they do, the same order, the same kind of discipline . . . the arts and ambitious activity of those who govern will now be encountered by the vivacity and perseverance of opponents actuated by the love of glory."[145] Underlying the principle of ambition counteracting ambition is the conviction that there can be no disinterested exercise of power and that mere rules and regulations can never be effective checks. As de Lolme says, "Those who are in a condition to control it [power] from that very circumstance become its defenders." Thus "The people are necessarily betrayed by those in whom they trust."[146] The only remedy to an excess of power is

142. De Lolme, *Constitution*, 247.
143. *The Federalist* No. 55, 336.
144. *Essays*, 523.
145. De Lolme, *Constitution*, 256–58.
146. Ibid., 271, 276.

therefore to turn power against power, ambition against ambition. De Lolme was in fact the first theorist of legislative balances and checks, of the measures required to control an overwhelmingly powerful legislature.[147] No reading could have been more apposite for the authors of *The Federalist*, particularly as de Lolme had no interest in what one might term the antiquated elements of the British constitution such as a hereditary aristocracy, a limited franchise, or an executive veto but was interested only in those elements which could be shown to be superior to the democracy of Rousseau's *Social Contract*, which along with classical republicanism is as much de Lolme's subject as is the English political system.

Perhaps Madison had also read or reread Spelman just before writing *The Federalist* No. 51, for we catch an echo of Spelman's argument that "It was not the existence of the two parties I have mentioned, that destroyed the liberties of any of those cities, but the occasional extinction of one of them, by the superiority the other had gained over it. And if ever we should be so unhappy as to have the balance between the three orders destroyed, and that any one of the three should utterly extinguish the other two, the name of a party would, from that moment, be unknown in England, and we should unanimously agree in being slaves to the conqueror" in Madison's statement toward the end of *The Federalist* No. 50 that "an extinction of parties necessarily implies either a universal alarm for the public safety, or an absolute extinction of liberty."[148] But whether or not Madison was consciously aware of his predecessors, he shared with them a common purpose: the construction of a mental machine, a political system in which threats to liberty would be automatically counterbalanced, in which "a kind of rivalship" would pit ambition against ambition with the unintended consequence that liberty would be secured.

147. Hume, like de Lolme, thought the representative assembly needed to be weakened and the executive strengthened, but he was happy to see both objectives attained through corruption.

148. *The Federalist* No. 49, 318. The extensive discussion of party in Wills's *Explaining America* contains no hint that Madison ever wrote a sentence comparable to this one.

4. ELECTIVE DESPOTISM

In this essay I have traced the origins of the idea of checks and balances. I hope I have shown that, far from being an idea so straightforward that it has no history, it in fact has a double origin. On the one hand, as Noah Webster's "checks and balance," it is a complex amalgam of two theories which until the middle years of the eighteenth century were assumed to be incompatible: the theory of mixed government and the theory of the separation of powers. Here what made it possible to bring checks and balances together was a new understanding of the possibility of an equilibrium of independent (and also unequal) forces so that the powers within a mixed government could be thought of as always separate rather than as being obliged eventually to act in concert. The importance of this theory (born of opposition to Walpole) was that it legitimized opposition to the government and rejected the traditional quest for consensus. On the other, as Gouverneur Morris's "every legislative check and balance," it derives from the view that in a representative democracy the greatest danger is that the legislature will acquire the defects of a popular assembly, and that if it does, the executive and the judiciary may prove incapable of checking its actions. The legislature had therefore to be balanced as well as checked: by elections, by political opposition or factional division, by public opinion, by a second chamber, by a strengthened executive. The importance of this theory (born both of a recognition that power was now concentrated in the House of Commons and of a critique of Rousseau and ancient republicanism) was that it identified and addressed the possibility of a "tyranny of the majority."[149]

Thus checks and balances came to be linked by two quite different routes. In addition the checks or balances (for once the two were

149. This phrase originates with de Tocqueville's *Democracy in America,* translated into English in 1835, though the first usage given by the OED is from Mill's *On Liberty* (1859). Classical and Renaissance views that are similar but not identical to the concept of majority tyranny are collected by Nedham in his attack on the Levellers: Marchamont Nedham, *The Case of the Commonwealth of England Stated* [1650], ed. Philip A. Knachel (Charlottesville: University Press of Virginia, 1969), 99–101. Nedham's *Excellencie* with the self-perpetuating Rump Parliament in mind insists that a representative assembly can easily become tyrannical, particularly when it is not held to account through frequent elections (pp. 96–101).

coupled together the distinction between them became increasingly difficult to sustain) that were understood to be at work changed radically over time as the veto was supplemented by the idea of accountability and as the electorate, the political party, and the press came to be recognized as having a crucial part to play in preventing the abuse of power. By coining the phrase "checks and balances," Adams thus made it possible to link together three distinct traditions—mixed government (Polybius), separation of powers (Montesquieu), the need for precautions against the tyranny of the majority (de Lolme)—within a single catchphrase. This was a rhetorical not an intellectual achievement, for Adams did not grasp the full significance of the new legislative balances and checks identified by Spelman and de Lolme. Although he had some sense that the English constitution was self-regulating, he did not go much beyond Polybius and Montesquieu in his understanding of why this was so. Nevertheless he was convinced that "the English constitution is, in theory, both for the adjustment of the balance *and the prevention of its vibrations,* the most stupendous fabric of human invention."[150]

So the history of the idea of checks and balances is much more complicated than has previously been recognized, and that history can only be understood in relation to the idea of a constitution as a machine, sometimes a self-regulating machine. Without mechanical thinking, the first form of systems analysis, there could have been no "modern" (as opposed to ancient or medieval) form of liberty.[151] The idea of limited government, of checks and balances, originally depends on the metaphor of a constitution as a machine in a state of equilibrium and in its sophisticated form depends on some practical acquaintance with feedback mechanisms. For Madison, representation was "this great mechanical power . . . by the simple agency of which

150. Adams, *Works,* 4:358 (emphasis added). *Vibration* had been used as a technical term by Sir James Steuart for the process by which a market moves about an equilibrium position: e.g., *Inquiry,* 2:146.

151. Benjamin Constant, "The Liberty of the Ancients Compared with that of the Moderns" [1819], in id., *Political Writings,* ed. Biancamaria Fontana (Cambridge: Cambridge University Press, 1988), 309–28. In making this claim, I part company, I think, with Paul Rahe's indispensable *Republics Ancient and Modern,* which sees modern republicanism as largely complete with Harrington.

the will of the largest political body may be concentered and its force directed"; hence the need to check and balance it with care.[152] In this sentence the phrase "mechanical power" is to be taken seriously as a tool with which to think. I started with Nietzsche's statement that truths are really metaphors. If Nietzsche is right, the first task of the historian of ideas must be to bring back to life all the long-dead metaphors. I have tried to make a start here by showing that the metaphor of "constitutional machinery" was once vigorous and capable of doing real work; indeed it is to this metaphor that we owe all but the most elementary components of the idea of limited government.

For it should now be apparent that the whole modern tradition of constitutional theory, from Trenchard and Moyle onward, is concerned to limit the power of government. Initially the emphasis was on limiting the executive, but, over time, checks-and-balances theorists became increasingly concerned to limit government in general, and eventually they came to see the chief danger as coming from the legislature in particular. Trenchard and Moyle were supposed to have said (and Fletcher of Saltoun certainly did say in 1698), "For not only that government is tyrannical which is tyrannically exercised, but all governments are tyrannical which have not in their constitution sufficient security against the arbitrary power of their prince."[153] For Fletcher and his associates, the executive was the problem. Bolingbroke made a similar point in much more general terms: "Tyranny and slavery do not so properly consist in the stripes that are given and received, as in the power of giving them at pleasure, and the necessity of receiving them, whenever and for whatever they are inflicted."[154] And we have seen Gouverneur Morris writing in 1776 of the need to diminish political liberty, the freedom of action of our rulers, in order to increase

152. *The Federalist* No. 14, 141.

153. The passage appears in Anon., *An Argument Shewing That a Standing Army with Consent of Parliament Is Not Inconsistent with a Free Government* (London: E. Whitlock, 1698), 14, as a quotation from Trenchard and Moyle's *Argument,* but I cannot find it there. It is to be found in a contemporary work by an author linked to them, Fletcher of Saltoun's *Discourse of Government with Relation to Militias* (1698): see his *Political Works* (1732), 9.

154. Bolingbroke, *Dissertation*, Letter XIII: *Works,* 2:177.

civil liberty: it was checks on the legislature that he had particularly in mind.

These last two quotations from Fletcher and Bolingbroke are examples of what Quentin Skinner has termed the neo-Roman republican theory: the theory that for liberty to exist it is not sufficient that there is no tyranny; rather it is necessary that no one has the power to act tyrannically.[155] As we have seen, checks-and-balances theorists maintained that where someone has the power to act tyrannically, tyranny is the inevitable outcome. On Skinner's account, neo-Roman theorists were committed to a particular type of guarantee against tyranny: they held that a state was free if it was governed by its citizens, either assembled or through their representatives. Any claim to a prerogative power which could be exercised against the wishes of the representatives of the political community was (as in the quotation from Fletcher) a claim to a tyrannical power. Thus if, after the Restoration, neo-Roman theorists claimed to be able to accept the idea of monarchy, they could do so only because they intended to make the monarch a merely symbolic figurehead without any real power, a Venetian doge. Rousseau and Paine, one might comment, would have understood this argument for autonomy or self-government: a political community must be its own master if it is to be no one's slave.

But the argument for popular sovereignty is not the only way of responding to the problem of the potential for tyranny, and it is the alternative to it which I have been exploring here. This response is based in the first place on the recognition that representative government can never be the same as self-government: it acknowledges the problem of corruption and of the emergence of elites. This was a problem which preoccupied the true Whigs in their opposition to the court Whigs. Second, it faces up to the fact that the majority may wish to tyrannize the minority. "It is a mistaken notion in government," writes Gordon in 1721, "that the interest of the majority is only to be consulted, since in society every man has a right to every man's assistance in the enjoyment and defense of his private property; otherwise the greater number may sell the lesser, and divide their estates among themselves;

155. Skinner, *Liberty Before Liberalism.*

and so, instead of a society, where all peaceable men are protected, become a conspiracy of the many against the minority."[156] Here the key issue was not so much property but, as Gordon immediately went on to emphasize, religion, for the House of Commons had repeatedly shown itself hostile to the rights of religious minorities. In order to recognize this problem of majority tyranny, a conceptual shift was necessary, for it is not until Locke's *Two Treatises* that the word "majority" is used in the sense of "the greater number or part" (rather than, for example, to refer to the age of majority), the usual assumption until then being that the decisions of an assembly properly reflected a consensus.[157] And the passage from Gordon I have just quoted may be the first occasion on which "minority" is used to mean the smaller number—the earliest example given by the OED is from 1736.[158]

This shift involved rejecting the view, which Skinner says lay at the heart of neo-Roman political theory, that one could think in terms of "the body" of the political community and attribute a single will to the nation; and it thus prepared the ground for an eventual recognition that party-political divisions might be essential to the preservation of liberty. Advocates of checked-and-balanced government held that the power of the state must be limited so that it is incapable of summoning the strength to act tyrannically. "Only the checks put upon magistrates make nations free; and only the want of such checks makes them slaves," writes Trenchard in 1722 in an essay on "The encroaching nature of power, ever to be watched and checked," but as he goes on to develop this argument, it becomes clear that he is not simply concerned to check the power of the executive and make it subordinate to the legislature but rather to make the more general claim that all

156. *Cato's Letters*, No. 62, 427.

157. On the idea and language of "majority," see J. H. Burns, "Majorities: An Exploration," *History of Political Thought* 24 (2003): 66–85; OED CD-ROM, s.v. *majority* gives a later example than Locke, from 1691. Hobbes, as Burns points out, had already clearly expressed the principle: "If the Representative consist of many men, the voice of the greater number, must be considered as the voice of them all."

158. OED CD-ROM, s.v. *minority*. The classic text on consensus politics is Mark Kishlansky, "The Emergence of Adversary Politics," *Journal of Modern History* 49 (1977): 617–40.

power tends to corrupt and must be confined within limits: hence the reluctance of Parliaments to vote for annual elections. "The Romans, who knew this evil [the divergence between the interests of the rulers and the ruled], having suffered by it, provided wise remedies against it; and when one ordinary power grew too great, checked it with another. Thus the office and power of the tribunes was set up to balance that of the consuls. . . . And when the authority of the tribunes grew too formidable, a good expedient was found out to restrain it" by requiring that the tribunes always act unanimously.[159] Even the representatives of the people needed to be restrained in the cause of liberty. John Adams regarded it as a fundamental axiom that "*A single assembly is liable to all the vices, follies, and frailties of an individual.*"[160] "An *elective despotism* was not the government we fought for," wrote Jefferson in 1784, "but one which should not only be founded on free principles, but in which the powers of government should be so divided and balanced among several bodies of magistracy, as that no one could transcend their legal limits, without being effectually checked and restrained by the others."[161]

The argument that power tends to corrupt was not new: it had been clearly formulated by Nedham in *The Excellencie of a Free State.* Earlier theorists would surely have accepted that power has, as Nedham explained, its own peculiar temptations:

The reason is, because (as the Proverb saith) *honores mutant mores;* "Honours change men's manners"; accessions, and continuation of power and greatness, expose the mind to temptations: they are sails too big for any bulk [i.e. hull—cf. OED, s.v. *bulk*] of mortality to steer an even course by.

The kingdoms of the world, and the glories of them, are baits that seldom fail when the Tempter goes a-fishing, and none but He that was more than man, could have refused them.

But Nedham was able to place a whole new emphasis on the tendency of power to corrupt because he had a new theory, the separation of

159. *Cato's Letters,* No. 115, 803–5.
160. Adams, *Political Writings,* 494 (letter to John Penn, 1776).
161. *Notes on the State of Virginia* in *The Portable Thomas Jefferson,* 164.

powers, of how it was possible for a people "so to regulate their affairs, that all temptations and opportunities of ambition, may be removed out of the way."[162]

Thus the same neo-Roman definition of individual liberty as the antithesis of slavery could be used for a variety of political purposes. Skinner, in arguing for the coherence of the neo-Roman conception of liberty, appears to think that a doctrine of popular sovereignty always follows from it—and indeed Trenchard ends his essay with the claim that the Roman mechanism of "an appeal to the people" is the best of all protections for liberty. But even for Trenchard (who acknowledges that the people may sometimes, if rarely, abuse their sovereign power) and for Gordon (who fears a conspiracy of the many against the minority) and even more clearly for Nedham (who had been reprinted in 1767) and for de Lolme and for the Founding Fathers, what also followed from the neo-Roman account of liberty was an argument for the separation of powers and for checks on the power of the legislature as well as the executive, for any concentration of power (even in the hands of the majority) was now held to be dangerous. Even now this is not—in Great Britain at least—simply an academic issue, for a debate between those who insist on the need to maintain a unified Parliamentary sovereignty (which, it is claimed, is the only reliable guarantee against tyranny) and those who are willing to see sovereignty distributed through the organs of a federal Europe (which, it is claimed, is the best way of taming the nation state and of preventing the emergence of a new Hitler or Mussolini) has been central to British political debate over the last half century.

The new argument for limited government did not simply displace existing discourses.[163] Historians of political thought have tended to write as if there were a number of alternative languages—ancient con-

---

162. Nedham, *Excellencie,* 134–35; see also 18–19 on "the lust of mankind after dominion" and 147–53 on the separation of powers. For a classical text which comes near to expressing the view that power corrupts, see Plutarch, "Sallust" in *Fall of the Roman Republic,* trans. Rex Warner, rev. ed. (Harmondsworth: Penguin, 1972), 104.

163. D. Wootton, "From Commonwealth to Common Sense" in Wootton, ed., *Republicanism, Liberty, and Commercial Society* (Stanford: Stanford University Press, 1994), 1–41, 18, entirely misses the point which now seems to me crucial.

stitutional or Cokean; natural rights or Lockean; republican or neo-Harringtonian—available in the eighteenth century for discussing politics. To stress the importance of one language, it has been assumed, implies a reduction in the significance of the others so that John Pocock's work has been read (and is intended to be read) as implying that republican discourse was much more important than the argument from natural rights. But this way of thinking does not do justice to the texts we have been considering. No one had a higher opinion of Locke than Moyle (who quotes with approval the view that the *Two Treatises* are "the ABC of politics")[164] yet Moyle is one of the founders of the new mechanical language and an admirer of classical republics. So, too, in *Cato's Letters*, Trenchard and Gordon seem to oscillate from one moment to the next between a Lockean and a republican language. For these thinkers, however, these were not several alternative languages for discussing politics; they were rather several languages, each of which was appropriate for a different aspect of politics. Locke established natural rights and the principle of government by consent, thereby providing a theoretical foundation for liberty (including religious liberty). The neo-Roman republican theory defined liberty as the absence of the capacity to tyrannize. And the language of checks and balances explained how a constitution could be constructed so that liberty was maximized. Just as one would expect an architect to be familiar with issues of the aesthetics of form, structural engineering, and quantity surveying, so the language of politics had a normative discourse of rights, a theory of liberty grounded in an account of human psychology, and a value-free account of constitutional engineering. These were not seen as alternative languages: each was taken (one can see the process at work in *Cato's Letters*, No. 60 to No. 62, for example) to imply the next. They were mutually supporting. Similarly in *The Federalist*, Lockean and Humean arguments are taken to be complementary, not (as a modern reader might naturally assume) at odds with each other.[165]

I promised that my history of "checks and balances" could help us

164. Moyle, *Whole Works*, 58.

165. See Morton White, *Philosophy, "The Federalist," and the Constitution* (New York: Oxford University Press, 1987), pt. 2, "The Different Legacies of Locke and Hume."

rethink our own political commitments, and it will if it makes us take constitutional machinery seriously. This should be evident from the way in which my account of the implications of neo-Roman arguments diverges from Skinner's. But one must recognize that to seek to limit government so that it cannot act tyrannically, to check and balance, to internally divide it so that power is set against power may well be to weaken its capacity to do good as well as ill. In the United Kingdom we have a strong and powerful government: there is no effective division between legislature and executive; the powers of the second chamber are weak (it cannot, for example, oppose legislation to implement manifesto commitments made by the governing party nor can it initiate budgetary measures); the judiciary is not fully independent; the legislature has a limited and diminishing capacity to hold the executive to account; the first past the post system tends to ensure one-party government; the government can call elections whenever it chooses; the independence of the civil service (a check new in the nineteenth century) is under threat; and so on. Proper checks and balances would mean a far weaker government, a government which would find it much harder to "deliver," to use the word which is currently the most popular in government speeches. A weaker government might have to recognize that it had no option but to hand over the task of managing schools, universities, and hospitals to genuinely independent management, management released from the checks and balances that are entirely appropriate in a political context. This is an old argument, and I hardly need to rehearse it at any length here, but it is worth noting that it is different from, even if it often points in the same direction as, arguments against government monopolies and in favor of competition. The standard "Thatcherite" arguments for privatization of public services derive from Smith, while this argument derives from Madison.

But I have a new argument to make as well. Harrington believed that his constitution could remain unchanged and unchanging because the ballot and rotation would prevent corruption and so would constantly return the political system to its original starting point. He mocked Machiavelli for thinking that political reform required the irregular intervention of bold politicians who would bring the political system back to its founding principles; his system was constantly self-reforming. We can still see something of this way of thinking in the arguments of Spelman and de Lolme. Their balance may be dynamic, but its oscillations or vibrations do not alter the system. Madison, it seems to me, takes a cautious step away from this way of thinking. When he discusses the conflict between factions, he assumes that factions can simply cancel each other out. But when he talks about the parts of government keeping each other in their proper places, he envisages them as being in a constant struggle for power, an unending series of attacks and counterattacks. Out of this struggle will come political decisions and political action. In such a world there will be (as in the international struggle for power which constantly re-creates a balance of power) long-term winners and losers. As the decades pass, the system may begin to be quite different from what it was at its first foundation. In rejecting external control Madison was rejecting the possibility of restoring the American Constitution, as Machiavelli believed all constitutions needed periodically to be restored, by recalling it to its founding principles; but in his description of internal control he was also rejecting the Harringtonian conviction that the Constitution could be prevented from ever changing. He was, it seems to me, proposing to let the system run on the presumption that, as long as power was divided against power, as long as there were adequate barriers to a monopoly of power, the system could be allowed to evolve over time. In other words, what Madison had in mind was something much more like a market (he was an early reader of Smith), which is self-stabilizing but never repeats itself, than like a fantail windmill which comes back again and again to the same starting point.

Two surprising consequences follow. The first affects our idea of a written constitution, for although Madison was defending a written constitution, he was thinking in terms of a flexible and developing system, despite the fact that the two are normally thought to be, if not incompatible, then certainly in a dynamic tension. The second affects our idea of checks and balances, for if Madison had the idea not just of a dynamic equilibrium but of a dynamic evolution of what one might call a political ecology in which equilibria are constantly being established and reestablished but change radically over time, then the idea of checks and balances is not necessarily as static, as fixed, as negative as is usually assumed. Unlike Montesquieu, Madison did not imagine that the various organs of government could be required to act in concert; rather he envisaged a system where the conflict between the organs of government would have unintended consequences that were beneficial to the public. A political system in which there are numerous checks and balances could also be one which is flexible, adaptable, resilient. It is precisely because the idea of checks and balances can be used to think about dynamic interactions, not just restrictions on freedom of action or static equilibria, that it contains a largely untapped potential to help us think about political change and about a central political problem: how a political system can be engineered to be both limited in its power to do evil and at the same time quick to adapt to changing circumstances. Trenchard and Moyle were concerned that "the very excellence of our government betrays it to some inconveniences, the wheels and motions of it being so curious and delicate that it is often out of order," and this was because they conceived of the constitution as a complex mechanism incapable of self-regulation.[166] Madison, by contrast, imagined a constitution so curious and delicate that it need never go out of order, and this not because it would never go wrong but because it would have the capacity to right itself when it did go wrong. If Trenchard and Moyle were the first of the political engineers, he was the founder of a new discipline which we may term (despite the obvious anachronism) political cybernetics.

What makes adaptation possible is that checks and balances not only serve to secure our liberty, they also entrench disagreement into the political system, and thus protect our collective capacity for critical reflection; we need them not only as a bulwark against tyranny but also to preserve our capacity for innovation. Only where conflict is institutionalized within government will debate and disagreement flourish, in the process encouraging novelty without (the claim is a remarkable one) endangering stability.

166. Trenchard and Moyle, *Argument,* 566.

Moral Sense Theory and the Appeal to Natural Rights in the American Founding

In intellectual histories of the American Founding, it is common to find speculation as to the intellectual sources for the ideas that we have come to associate with the American Founders.[1] In a way, this speculation has been allowed to run rampant, both because Jefferson, Madison, Hamilton, and the others did not often quote from the texts which they were using and because in the absence therefore of compelling evidence of influence in letters, diaries, and the like, one is left to read their texts and, as it were, to find influence where one will. Given the importance we attach to the Founding and thereby to the ideas which informed and shaped it, this kind of speculation seems inevitable. Claims of influence have been made for all kinds of individuals. To be sure, some sources seem to be agreed on all sides: in the appeal to natural rights that figures in the American Declaration of Independence, the hands of Grotius, Pufendorf, and, of course, Locke are seen to be at work, and Montesquieu is thought to lurk behind numerous writings of the period. Indeed, claims of influence are made on behalf of others, such as Richard Price and Joseph Priestley,

1. E.g., Carl L. Becker, *The Declaration of Independence: A Study in the History of Political Ideas* (New York: Random House, 1958); Garry Wills, *Inventing America: Jefferson's Declaration of Independence* (New York: Vintage Books, 1979); Forrest McDonald, *Novum Ordo Seculorum: The Intellectual Origins of the Constitution* (Lawrence: University Press of Kansas, 1986). Of more recent vintage, see Hans L. Eicholz, *Harmonizing Sentiments: The Declaration of Independence and the Jeffersonian Idea of Self-Government* (New York: Peter Lang, 2001); Bernard Bailyn, *The Ideological Origins of the American Revolution* (Cambridge: Belknap Press, 1992); Jack Rakove, *Original Meanings: Politics and Ideas in the Making of the Constitution* (New York: Vintage Books, 1997); Jack Rakove, *Declaring Rights: A Brief History with Documents* (New York: St. Martin's Press, 1998); Pauline Maier, *American Scripture: Making the Declaration of Independence* (New York: Vintage Books, 1998); Gordon Wood, *The Creation of the American Republic, 1776–1787* (Chapel Hill: University of North Carolina Press, 1998). All these are now "standard" works.

who otherwise have been allowed to slip into a more quiet backwater of intellectual history. More recently and more importantly, there has been widespread speculation about the influence of the thinkers of the Scottish Enlightenment—Hume, Adam Smith, Francis Hutcheson, Lord Kames, Adam Ferguson—upon various of the Founders, especially Jefferson and Madison,[2] in a way that goes far beyond the earlier claims by Douglas Adair of the influence of Hume upon Madison's *The Federalist* No. 10[3] or the even more detailed speculations about the influence of Hume upon Madison and Hamilton in Elkins and McKitrick's *The Age of Federalism.*[4]

A moral philosopher can probably best contribute to our understanding of liberty and the American Founding not by putting forward his own candidate for influence—after all, in the absence of compelling evidence, this exercise remains highly speculative at best—but by discussing some of the intellectual currents in moral philosophy that swirl around the Founding. One of these currents—the influence of figures of the Scottish Enlightenment upon the Founders—has, as I have indicated, recently come into high fashion,[5] and it is upon an

2. There is debate, of course, about the degree of influence of the Scottish thinkers and exactly how this influence was transmitted to the American Founders. See Richard B. Sher and Jeffrey Smitten, eds., *Scotland and America in the Age of Enlightenment* (Princeton: Princeton University Press, 1990); D. Walker Howe, "Why the Scottish Enlightenment Was Useful to the Framers of the American Constitution," *Comparative Studies in Society and History* 31 (1989): 572–87; D. F. Norton, "Francis Hutcheson in America" in *Studies on Voltaire and the Eighteenth Century* 154 (1976): 1547–68. For recent discussions by philosophers of this influence in addition to Norton, see Knud Haakonssen, *Natural Law and Moral Philosophy: From Grotius to the Scottish Enlightenment* (Cambridge: Cambridge University Press, 1996), esp. ch. 12; Samuel Fleischacker, "The Impact on America: Scottish Philosophy and the American Founding," *William and Mary Quarterly*, forthcoming. I am indebted to these works by Haakonssen and Fleischacker.

3. Douglas Adair, "'That Politics May Be Reduced to a Science': David Hume, James Madison, and the Tenth *Federalist*," *Huntington Library Quarterly* 20 (1957): 343–60.

4. Stanley Elkins and Eric McKitrick, *The Age of Federalism: The Early American Republic, 1788–1800* (New York: Oxford University Press, 1993). The notes to this volume contain an extensive reading list on numerous aspects of the period of the Founders.

5. The popularity of Garry Wills's *Inventing America,* recently brought this in-

aspect of this particular claim of influence that I want to focus. Because these Scottish figures had read earlier English moral thinkers, especially Locke, Shaftesbury, and Butler, these earlier English figures —themselves forming a kind of English Enlightenment—in fact help define the moral ideas that arise in Scotland in the eighteenth century and that ultimately find their way to America. I want to suggest that there is a tension between some of these ideas, specifically between moral-sense theory and the claim that there are natural rights, a tension that has in the end to do with different kinds of reflections upon the foundation of morality.

One of the most remarkable features of the period that saw the American and French Revolutions and the dramatic appeal to the so-called "rights of man" as an integral part of political liberty was how relatively quickly these appeals faded from the scene. Of course, there were differences between the rights claimed in the American Declaration of Independence and the French Declaration of the Rights of Man, and it is perhaps not accidental that the French *philosophes*, anticlerical to a degree, could see the "rights of man" in a more secular light than the rights enunciated by the American Declaration, with which we were "endowed by our Creator," were seen. No matter; whether as a result of the excesses of the French Revolution or not, in a few short years the "rights of man" that Paine and others had appealed to had effectively disappeared as a rallying cry for revolution. One philosophical reason for their disappearance can almost certainly be traced to the attack on natural rights that would soon emerge from political thinkers as diverse as Bentham and Marx. Indeed, in one sense Bentham's claim that such rights were "nonsense on stilts" perfectly captures the problem of giving such rights a ground that can withstand philosophical scrutiny in the "Age of Reason."[6] His reported dismay

---

fluence to the attention of the public though not, of course, to philosophers or historians.

6. Jeremy Bentham, "Anarchial Fallacies" in J. Bowring, ed., *The Works of Jeremy Bentham* (London: Murray, 1843), 2:489–534. Bentham is never sympathetic to natural rights, neither in *Introduction to the Principles of Morals and Legislation*, ed. J. H. Burns and H. L. A. Hart (London: Athlone Press, 1970) nor in *A Comment on the Commentaries and a Fragment on Government*, ed. J. H. Burns and H. L. A. Hart (London: Athlone Press, 1977).

with the American Declaration is in part just the foundational worry
that such rights have a philosophically defensible ground, and nothing about their invocation by Jefferson and Madison puts such worries
to rest.

We do not have to wait until Bentham for such worries and doubts
to arise, however; for, as is well-known, Hume himself has no such
rights as part of his ethical theory. Neither does Shaftesbury or Butler,
both of whom Hume had read and both of whom were moral-sense
theorists before him. Hutcheson, on the other hand, does feature such
rights, and here is one more reason why it is vitally important not to
run Shaftesbury and Hutcheson together as moral-sense theorists and
to ignore their differences. And Smith, at least to some extent, follows
his teacher Hutcheson, at least if we read his *Lectures on Jurisprudence*
into his *Theory of Moral Sentiments* and Book V of *The Wealth of Nations*.[7]
Here, of course, if we do read the latter works in this way, is one more
reason not to run Hume and Smith together as moral theorists. Accordingly, these Enlightenment thinkers divide: Shaftesbury, Butler,
and Hume do not try to graft natural rights onto moral-sense theory;
Hutcheson and to some extent Smith do. I think the former group has
much the better of this dispute, but the important point here is to be
aware of it. For it is not Bentham who first seeks to give morality a foundation other than religion, whether natural or revealed, though, to be
sure, it is true that he and his followers, including the younger Mill,
are adamant in the matter. For the moral-sense theorists had already
grounded morality in human nature and had put in motion empirical
accounts of that nature that may be accompanied by, but do not require, any form of religious belief. It is precisely into this divide that
Jefferson and Madison step, with their joint appeals to natural rights
and to moral-sense theory. Even before Hume, these joint appeals lead
to difficulties.

I shall not be concerned here with the exact course of the transmis-

7. See Haakonssen, *Natural Law and Moral Philosophy*, chs. 4, 7; Charles Griswold, Jr., *Adam Smith and the Virtues of Enlightenment* (Cambridge: Cambridge University Press, 1999), ch. 6; Knud Haakonssen, *The Science of a Legislator: The Natural Jurisprudence of David Hume and Adam Smith* (Cambridge: Cambridge University
Press, 1981). The most detailed discussion I know is Samuel Fleischacker, *Adam
Smith's Theory of Justice*, forthcoming. I am deeply indebted to these works.

sion of English and Scottish thought to Jefferson and Madison and so, among other things, with the influence of William Small at the College of William and Mary upon the former or of John Witherspoon at the College of New Jersey upon the latter. Witherspoon is in his own right an interesting character, a firebrand in the Church of Scotland with a pen that itches to prick the theological/moral bubbles of any but the most staunch Calvinists, as evidenced by his *Ecclesiastical Characteristics*.[8] Rather remarkably, upon translation to his position in New Jersey, Witherspoon appears to have become a much more moderate character whose lectures on moral philosophy, while unsympathetic to Shaftesbury and especially to the skeptical Hume but not to Hutcheson, acquainted generations of students with moral-sense theory, at least as Hutcheson considered it to be. Much speculation exists about the influence of Witherspoon upon Madison, though the fact that comparatively little is known of Madison's college days makes such speculation of uncertain accuracy. But there is little doubt that *Ecclesiastical Characteristics* can be read as an anti-Shaftesbury treatise, with attendant praise of Hutcheson,[9] and that Witherspoon would have recoiled in horror not only at Hume's strictures upon revealed religion but also at his moral theory, from which it was thought God had been effectively banished. What Witherspoon correctly realizes, however, is that Shaftesbury and Hutcheson are on different sides of the fence so far as the relation of religion and morality is concerned, and this is true whether or not the former is the deist he is usually portrayed as being and whether or not the latter is the pious Presbyterian he is usually taken to be.

The term "enlightenment" can be used to mean many things, and

8. John Witherspoon, *Ecclesiastical Characteristics* (Edinburgh, 1763). On Witherspoon and his thought, see "John Witherspoon" in W. Thorp, ed., *The Lives of Eighteen from Princeton* (Princeton: Princeton University Press, 1946), 68–85; Vernum L. Collins, *President Witherspoon: A Biography*, 2 vols. (Princeton: Princeton University Press, 1925). For a brief, general assessment of Witherspoon's overall influence on the American Founding, see Walter Berns, *Making Patriots* (Chicago: University of Chicago Press, 2001), chs. 2–4.

9. In this regard, see Isabel Rivers, *Reason, Grace, and Sentiment*, vol. 2, *A Study of the language of religion and ethics in England, 1660–1780* (Cambridge: Cambridge University Press, 2000), ch. 3. This excellent volume presents different accounts of the works of Shaftesbury and Butler from what is given here.

it often is used of English and Scottish thought in the eighteenth century in something approaching a technical sense. Yet, it probably best captures what English and Scottish thinkers were about morally in this period if it is understood to refer to two very broad though interrelated themes, namely, the attempt to eliminate mystery and metaphysics in statements about our knowledge of the world and the people in it and, as a result, the attempt to mute direct reference to theological matters in the articulation of moral theory. The so-called "Age of Reason," in which phrases such as a "science of man" or a "science of morals" gained currency, did not mean that every thinker was to turn himself into a practicing scientist; morally, it did mean, however, that mystery and metaphysics were to be downplayed in moral theory and that empirical claims about how people are were to figure much more prominently in claims about human nature as the foundation of morals. There is no question that the tone of ethical reflection that issues from Shaftesbury's *Inquiry Concerning Virtue or Merit* (1699; reissued in *Characteristics of Men, Manners, Opinions, Times,* 1711) is one in which religious reflection upon the nature of man is largely replaced by empirical reflection upon how we find people in the world to be. Of course, it may be claimed that Hobbes had already gone down this path of secularizing ethical reflection, but the outright linkage of that secularization with an account of human nature as the ground of ethics occurs more clearly in Shaftesbury (strangely so, in some respects, for while Shaftesbury is most usually counted a deist, deism would not have implied to him atheism.)

The term "moral sense" can also be used in a wide variety of ways. Occasionally, Shaftesbury, Butler, Hutcheson, Hume, and Smith are called moral-sense theorists, even though there are marked differences among their ethical views. I shall use the term to refer to certain accounts of the ground or foundation of ethics, namely, to accounts which locate that ground in human nature and in the empirical components that make up the moral psychology of that nature. Not all such accounts make use of the metaphor of aesthetics and beauty, though all do make use of talk of balance and proportion in the parts of our nature.

The term "natural rights" can be and has been used to mean all kinds of things. I shall use it to mean justified claims to something that (1) do not issue from or depend for their existence upon a government, organized state, or group of people, (2) cannot be revoked by a government, organized state, or group of people, (3) antedate the existence of any government or organized state and help to determine what kind of government or organized state can legitimately be established, and (4) cannot be violated, infringed, or set aside by a judgment by the majority of people that the collective good warrants such violation, infringement, or setting aside.[10] Since rights in this sense are not conferred by government, state, or law, and since they have usually been seen against the backdrop of natural law and religious accounts of man and man's place in the world, God is often said to be their author. The American Declaration of Independence envisages the existence of natural rights in this sense as does, for example, Madison's *Memorial and Remonstrance Against Religious Assessments,* and both Jefferson and Madison affirm that such rights are conferred upon us by God. Moreover, there do not appear to be very many of these rights. (Whether they are essentially negative, as opposed to positive, rights is not at issue here.) Locke's trinity of life, liberty, and property, even as transposed and altered by Jefferson in the Declaration, may be thought to touch upon the central issues of (political) life, but one natural right that Madison stresses (as does Jefferson as well), namely, the right to freedom of conscience, certainly loomed large to the Founders.

The issue before us, then, is this: how are we to understand the joint appeal to natural rights and moral-sense theory? What can natural

10. Today, even though we live in a more secular age, many people would treat so-called "human" rights as natural rights in this sense, implying thereby that such rights are neither granted nor capable of being revoked by some national or international body such as the United Nations. All the U.N. Declaration of Human Rights does is to recognize the rights we all as human beings have from the outset. We have these rights because we belong to the species *Homo sapiens,* or, if this makes them appear too magical, because they are required for creatures of our nature to flourish. Why are we entitled to the conditions in which we can flourish? Different stories get told at this point, some, I suppose, more believable than others.

rights be if a moral-sense account of the ground of morality is given? Because Hume's work is so well known, or at least well canvassed, I shall use Shaftesbury and Butler to illustrate what the problem with the joint appeal is.

(It may be thought, of course, that, so long as we construe "enlightenment" to mean "movement away from overtly religious influence," it is comparatively easy to show a growing secularization of thought in England and Scotland during the course of the eighteenth century. What is under discussion here is not, for example, a growing secularization of thought about the physical world through the adoption of something akin to a mechanistic view of the physical world; rather, it is the secularization of moral thought that is part of my focus. To be sure, a movement away from religion in the explanation of the physical world may have helped inspire a movement away from religion in the discussion of the ground of morality, but I am not here concerned with any account of this influence. Rather, I want to show how the attempt to ground morality in human nature puts pressure upon the attempt to hang on to natural rights, as defined earlier in this paper.)

In a famous letter to his kinsman Peter Carr in 1787, Jefferson sets out his view of the ground of morality:

> Man was destined for society. His morality therefore was to be formed to this object. He was endowed with a sense of right & wrong merely relative to this. This sense is as much a part of his nature as the sense of hearing, seeing, feeling; it is the true foundation of morality. . . . The moral sense, or conscience, is as much a part of a man as his leg or arm. It is given to all human beings in a stronger or weaker degree. . . . It may be strengthened by exercise, as may any particular limb of the body. This sense is submitted indeed in some degree to the guidance of reason; but it is a small stock which is required for this: even a less one than we call common sense. State a moral case to a ploughman & a professor. The former will decide it as well, & often better than the latter, because he has not been led astray by artificial rules.[11]

11. J. Appleby and T. Ball, eds., *Jefferson: Political Writings* (Cambridge: Cambridge University Press, 1999), 253.

This letter draws attention to several items about man. First, Jefferson endorses the social nature of man and, by implication, rejects the purely egoistic accounts of human nature given by Hobbes and Mandeville. Second, all human beings are endowed with a moral sense, the "foundation of morality," that, unless distracted by "artificial rules" that reason has suggested to us, will correctly guide us through life. Third, this moral sense is not to be identified with reason; indeed, while reason can guide it, not even the amount of reason manifested in "common sense" is required in order for the ploughman to decide matters "well."

In reaction to Hobbes and Mandeville, the social nature of man becomes a common theme among the thinkers of the eighteenth century, and this idea becomes merged often, if even indirectly, with the idea that man is a creature of benevolence, which one's account of the nature of virtue will then reflect. This in turn leads one either to eliminate or radically to reduce the role of self-love in one's account of virtue. Jefferson goes down this path. In a letter to Thomas Law in 1814, Jefferson writes:

> Nature hath implanted in our breasts a love of others, a sense of duty to them, a moral instinct, in short, which prompts us irresistibly to feel and to succor their distresses, and protests against the language of Helvetius . . . , 'what other motive than self-interest could determine a man to generous actions? It is as impossible for him to love what is good for the sake of good, as to love evil for the sake of evil.' The Creator would indeed have been a bungling artist, had he intended man for a social animal, without planting in him social dispositions.[12]

Here morality or virtue is held to be concerned with a "love of others." Notice that one could agree that man is a social animal, with social instincts and dispositions, without also agreeing that virtue is concerned only with a "love of others." What Jefferson does is to run these two thoughts together so that he moves from the fact that man is a social animal to the view that virtue is wholly other-regarding. That this is Jefferson's tack he makes clear in his letter to Law:

12. Ibid., 287.

Self-interest, or rather self-love, or *egoism,* has been more plausibly substituted for the basis of morality. But I consider our relations with others as constituting the boundaries of morality. With ourselves we stand on the ground of identity, not of relation, which last, requiring two subjects, excludes self-love confined to a single one. To ourselves, in strict language, we can owe no duties, obligation requiring two parties. Self-love, therefore, is no part of morality. Indeed, it is exactly its counterpart. It is the sole antagonist of virtue, leading us constantly by our propensities to self-gratification in violation of our moral duties to others. Accordingly, it is against this enemy that are erected the batteries of moralists and religionists, as the only obstacle to the practice of morality. Take from man his selfish propensities, and he can have nothing to seduce him from the practice of virtue.[13]

This rather rosy picture of human beings is not shared by all moralists, of course, and there is little question that the central claim that Jefferson makes—if morality is concerned with our duties to others, self-love cannot be a part of morality—misses altogether the motivational part of the quotation he earlier makes from Helvétius. Nevertheless, it is clear Jefferson moves rather easily—and quickly—from the social nature of man to the fact that virtue is wholly a matter of the "love of others" or, more generally, benevolence. Self-love is "no part of morality." To be sure, Jefferson may well intend to reject Hobbes and Mandeville here, but the fact is that Shaftesbury, Butler, and Hume all emphasize the social nature of man but emphatically affirm that self-love is a part of morality. They are all what we might call harmony theorists; that is, they hold that virtue is a function of harmony in the parts of our nature, of which self-love is one of the most important parts.

It is sometimes alleged that it is developments in epistemology and corresponding developments in religion to do with belief in God and the rise of deism and atheism that affect claims about natural rights in the eighteenth century. In fact, whatever role these forces might have played in lessening the appeal to natural rights in accounts of morality or virtue, it is important not to underestimate the influence of Shaftes-

13. Ibid., 286–87.

bury's moral views and Butler's extension of those views (after all, in Scotland, the influence of Shaftesbury was most often felt through the moral views of Butler) in this regard. For after Shaftesbury and Butler, it is not clear exactly what role is left for natural rights to play in the account of virtue, and this is true whatever role may be assigned skepticism, deism, and atheism in producing this outcome over natural rights.

Rather remarkably, Shaftesbury begins his *Inquiry Concerning Virtue or Merit* (1699, 1711)[14] by distinguishing between religion and ethics and in a commonsense way, unlike anything to be found in Locke, his mentor. Indeed, he wonders whether an atheist can be moral and sees no reason why he cannot be: some who show great zeal in matters of religion have "wanted even the common Affections of *Humanity*" and have shown themselves "extremely degenerate and corrupt," where some of those considered to be atheists have shown themselves "to practise the Rules of *Morality*" and to act in such a way "as might seem to force an Acknowledgment of their being *virtuous*" (Shaftesbury, 192). He continues:

> If we are told, a Man is religious, we still ask, 'What are his Morals'?' But if we hear at first that he has honest moral Principles, and is a Man of natural Justice and good Temper, we seldom think of the other Question, 'Whether he be *religious* and *devout*'?' (Shaftesbury, 192)

14. Anthony Ashley Cooper, Earl of Shaftesbury, *Characteristics of Men, Manners, Opinions, Times, etc.,* ed. John M. Robertson, 2 vols. (Gloucester, Mass.: Peter Smith, 1963), vol. 1, Treatise IV (*An Inquiry Concerning Virtue or Merit*). The *Inquiry* is hereafter cited as "Shaftesbury," with page numbers in Robertson's edition given. For relevant discussions of Shaftesbury's thought, see Stephen Darwall, *The British Moralists and the Internal 'Ought,' 1640–1740* (Cambridge: Cambridge University Press, 1995); Isabel Rivers, *Reason, Grace, and Sentiment,* vol. 2; and Stanley Grean, *Shaftesbury's Philosophy of Religion and Ethics* (Athens: Ohio University Press, 1967). Rivers's book is the most careful and detailed discussion of the philosophy I know, and Darwall's is among the most philosophically challenging. Of some relevance, though, is Lawrence Klein's *Shaftesbury and the Culture of Politeness* (Cambridge: Cambridge University Press, 1994) and the biography by Robert Voitle, *The Third Earl of Shaftesbury 1671–1713* (Baton Rouge: Louisiana State University Press, 1984).

We can talk and think about virtue without talking and thinking about God and religion, and while it is true that Shaftesbury does not consistently maintain this distinction throughout the *Inquiry*, he certainly envisages the possibility that an ethical theory could be set out that was neither grounded in nor made essential reference to some one or other revealed (or natural) religion. This thought has nothing to do as such with one's belief in God; it has to do with one's view of the ground of morality. By all means continue to believe in God, whether in a form as given by revealed or natural religion: it is not necessary in order to give an account of the foundation of morality to make reference to God. However undeveloped this distinction may be in Shaftesbury, it initiates one of the main distinguishing features of moral thought during the British Enlightenment, namely, the move to free ethics from explicitly religious underpinnings. This in turn sets in motion (or continues the movement toward, depending upon the view one takes of the ethical views of Hobbes and Mandeville) the search for an alternative foundation or ground to ethics. Shaftesbury finds that ground in human nature but in a completely naturalistic account of that nature, not one as in the case of Hobbes and Mandeville that is skewered toward construing human beings to be entirely creatures of self-love, prudence, and the self-affections. And human nature, of course, is in common between the sceptic, deist, and atheist on the one hand and the religious believer on the other.

Human nature, according to Shaftesbury, is a system, the parts of which must be brought into harmony, if we are to be virtuous; virtue consists in just this harmony, balance, or right proportion of the parts. In particular, our self-affections must be in balance with our natural or other-regarding affections, which Shaftesbury treats, *contra* Hobbes and Mandeville, as an obvious, fundamental part of our nature (Shaftesbury, 285–93). We have also unnatural affections, or propensities to evil, which must be controlled and, to the extent possible, eliminated from our nature. While Shaftesbury envisages the possibility that the natural affections may be more powerful than the self-affections (and prudence), just the reverse, he thinks, is the chief imbalance in most men's natures. In turn, he is emphatic that this preponderance of the self-affections leads to misery (Shaftesbury, 317–30), something, of course, that Mandeville scathingly ridicules in *The*

Fable of the Bees (2d ed., 1723).[15] The unnatural affections lead to misery as well. To avoid misery, then, we must bring our self-affections and our natural affections into some right proportion, and fortunately we are equipped with a moral sense—almost aesthetic in its sensitivity to and perception of balance and harmony—that tells us when our affections are in or have achieved that proportion. (This aesthetic analogy to the moral sense requires qualification, not least because it really only enters Shaftesbury's thought after the initial appearance of the *Inquiry* in 1699; but my aim here is simply to make apparent that, far from seeing self-love or the self-affections as antithetical to virtue, Shaftesbury sees them as part of it.)

Thus, the virtuous man is one who has brought his self-affections and natural affections into a balance or harmony that his moral sense approves. He remains motivated by his passions, as Hobbes and Mandeville insisted, but now by his harmonized passions. This implies (e.g., Shaftesbury, 292) that his self-affections are not too strong nor his natural affections too weak and that he has perhaps tempered the strength of his self-affections by allowing himself to feel in full measure his natural affections. In this way, the specific balance in his passions that his moral sense approves always reflects his possession of other-regarding affections and, of course, of his self-affections. Man is a social animal, then, possessed of other-regarding affections, but these are but part of his nature and in no way constitute, motivationally, the whole of virtue.

There are several points to notice about this picture of virtue. First, it locates the ground or foundation of virtue in human nature and in the balance or harmony in the parts of that nature, and there is nothing in the account that requires religious belief. We may, of course, have such beliefs, and it may—or may not—be true that such beliefs come to make a good deal of our doing our duty or being moral; but these beliefs are not required in order to give an account of the ground of morality or of our acting morally. Second, virtue can only be made to be wholly other-regarding if one simply denies one whole

15. For a discussion of Mandeville's account of how social benefits flow from actions based upon self-interest, see Edward Hundert, *The Enlightenment's Fable: Bernard Mandeville and the Discovery of Society* (Cambridge: Cambridge University Press, 1994).

side of our nature. The problem that Jefferson purports to find with self-love—that it seems in conflict with our moral duties to others— is by Shaftesbury's account of the harmonized passions shown not to be a problem at all. For what motivates us morally in Shaftesbury is always our harmonized passions, and these reflect perpetually our self-affections. Equally, the problem that Hobbes and Mandeville allege (and that Jefferson ascribes to Helvétius), namely, how genuine other-regarding action is possible for a creature motivated exclusively by self-love and the self-affections, is not a problem; for we are not creatures motivated exclusively by self-love and the self-affections. Virtue is grounded in human nature, and it is an empirical matter what that nature is; what observation and introspection reveal to us is that it is neither wholly self-regarding nor wholly other-regarding and so not subject to the complaints that stem from construing it to be wholly one way or the other. God may be held by some to be the author of our nature, but that nature does not require any statement about God or God's (benevolent) attributes in order to ground an account of virtue. Like a mosaic in which the parts fit together into a harmonious whole, the beauty of which we can then detect, the parts of our nature can achieve a balance or harmony that our moral sense approves. Third, exactly what mixture of self- and natural affections our moral sense finds rightly proportioned is an empirical matter and may not, or so we cannot assume from the outset, be the same in all men. This does not mean that we cannot or will not find overlaps among different men in the matter, but each man must determine whether his own moral sense finds the mixture of the parts of his own nature to be in balance or harmony vis-à-vis the act he contemplates. There is, as it were, nothing external to his own nature that a man consults to find out the balance or harmony in his own nature, though, to be sure, he may find that the traits of character that he finds behind another's action reflect the traits that he finds his own moral sense usually approves when he contemplates acts of a similar sort in his own case. Natural rights, viewed as external constraints that bind the natures of all men, run against the grain of this picture. This is not to confuse a right with an act's being right; rather, it is simply to note that we cannot tell in advance what mixture in the parts of our nature our moral sense will approve. In this sense, natural rights do not bind our moral sense, and it is the latter, not the former, that is the ground of virtue. Therefore, whatever role might be assigned natural rights, they are not required for us to give an account of the ground of morality or for us to be virtuous. We can be virtuous if we act in accordance with human nature, and that nature is accessible to religious sceptics, deists, and atheists through introspection and observation.

Importantly, even if one were to hold that religious belief helped motivate people to be moral through fear of future divine punishment or through getting them to love virtue for its own sake, such belief is not required in order for a person to find a quite persuasive motive — namely, self-interest — to be moral. Indeed, the great peroration with which the *Inquiry* ends makes this motive manifest, even as it gushes over virtue in a tone that well explains why Mandeville itched to puncture the balloon of Shaftesbury's reputation:

> virtue, which of all excellences and beauties is the chief and most amiable; that which is the prop and ornament of human affairs; which upholds communities, maintains union, friendship, and correspondence amongst men; that by which countries, as well as private families, flourish and are happy, and for want of which everything comely, conspicuous, great, and worthy, must perish and go to ruin; that single quality, thus beneficial to all society, and to mankind in general, is found equally a happiness and good to each creature in particular, and is that by which alone man can be happy, and without which he must be miserable. (Shaftesbury, 338)

If to be virtuous can serve as our motive for harmonizing our affections, then to achieve enjoyment or happiness can serve as our motive for being virtuous. A desire for our own happiness neither precludes nor impedes our coming to desire to be virtuous for its own sake. Yet, even if we never come to desire this, we have a self-regarding motive for (1) bringing our affections into some right proportion, which actual men typically cannot do without allowing themselves fully to feel their natural affections and (2) pursuing virtue. Plainly, then, though the pursuit of virtue for virtue's sake by actual men would be a fine thing, though it would be admirable if we came actually to resemble Shaftesbury's idealized view of ourselves, nevertheless actual men can know, *whether or not* they come to resemble this view, that it is in their interest to be virtuous. Thus, the account of virtue, of virtuous action, and of the motive to be virtuous does not *require* belief in God or any appeal to natural rights.

To a rather remarkable degree, Butler, the Anglican clergyman, follows Shaftesbury in distinguishing between religion and ethics. In *Fifteen Sermons Preached at the Rolls Chapel* (1726), the *Preface* to the 1729 edition of the *Sermons,* and the *Dissertation II: Of the Nature of Virtue* (1736),[16] morality is neither grounded in nor made to rest upon revealed religion or Christianity.[17] Butler stresses that, exclusive of any belief in revelation, man's nature is of a particular order and that that nature makes of man *"in the strictest and most proper sense a law to himself"* (*Sermons,* III, 3; italics in the original). Accordingly, he says, man "hath the rule of right within." He continues (in a way not entirely dissimilar to an expression by Jefferson): "Let any plain honest man, before he engages in any course of action, ask himself, Is this I am going about right, or is it wrong? Is it good, or is it evil? I do not in the least doubt but that this question would be answered agreeably to truth and virtue, by almost any fair man in almost any circumstance" (*Sermons,* III, 4). There is nothing in the *Sermons* that bars a sceptic of Christianity, indeed, a sceptic of natural as well as revealed religion, from being just such a "plain honest man" and a "fair man" and nothing that limits the power of intuition or reflection such as Butler describes only to adherents of Christianity (*Sermons,* II, 9–11) or natural religion. All of us can be moral "if we will fall in with, and act agreeably to the constitution of our nature" (*Sermons,* II, 19). To act morally is to act in accordance with our nature, and Butler's analysis of that nature, whose author, of course, he the clergyman takes to be God, is not in Christian terms. It

16. Joseph Butler, *The Works of Joseph Butler, D.C.L.,* ed. W. E. Gladstone, 2 vols. (Oxford: Clarendon Press, 1896), vol. 2 (*Sermons*). The *Fifteen Sermons* is hereafter cited as "*Sermons,*" and I give, in addition to the sermon number, the section number in Gladstone. "Preface" refers to Butler's Preface to the second edition of *Fifteen Sermons,* added in 1729.

17. For excellent discussions of Butler's thought, see Stephen Darwall, *The British Moralists;* Isabel Rivers, *Reason, Grace, and Sentiment,* vol. 2; Terence Penelhum, *Butler* (London: Routledge, 1985). I do not agree on some central points in the interpretation of Butler's ethical views. For the flavor of some of these disagreements, see my "Butler on Self-Love and Benevolence" in C. Cunliffe, ed., *Joseph Butler's Moral and Religious Thought* (Oxford: Clarendon Press, 1992).

is accessible to introspection, observation, and reason, none of which sceptics are held as a matter of principle to lack. As with Shaftesbury, then, it would seem that sceptics, deists, and atheists can be moral.

Nor does Butler think that belief in an afterlife necessary in order to provide an account of our obligation to be moral. He affirms that, "Though a man should doubt of everything else, . . . he would still remain under the nearest and most certain obligation to the practice of virtue" (Preface, 22). Little is gained by vice, he believes, and the question arises of "whether it be so prodigious a thing to sacrifice that little to the most intimate of all obligations," a question that may be pressed "even upon supposition that the prospect of a future life were ever so uncertain" (Preface, 23). Thus, the obligation remains in force and "intimate" even if an afterlife is problematic. Man is a law to himself, in Butler's view, and one's obligation to obey this law is grounded not in belief in God and fear of future punishment but, as he stresses, in "its being the law of your nature" (*Sermons*, III, 6). Whether belief in an afterlife and fear of divine retribution stiffen one's resolve to keep this obligation is a contingent matter; the obligation itself does not depend upon acceptance of Christianity. The same is true of the motive to keep this obligation: even before presenting his detailed account of human nature, Butler, just as Shaftesbury, indicates how self-interest can provide just such a motive, how, that is, appeal "even to interest and self-love" can justify the sacrifice of what little vice can really bring "to the most intimate of all obligations" (Preface, 23). This motive is as available to sceptics as to believers, all of whom are capable of acting morally if they "fall in with" and "act agreeably to" the constitution of our nature.

This view about the ground of morality has further repercussions. First, the orthodox attempted to silence dissent by appeal to the argument from immorality: deism and freethinking generally lead to religious scepticism and ultimately atheism, and scepticism and atheism lead to immorality. This argument had force even during the Age of Reason; for if religious scepticism really does lead to immorality, then reasonable men have reason to avoid it. If, moreover, the propagation and acceptance by others of such scepticism ultimately leads to widespread immorality in the public domain, then we are not far from the then rather common view that construed an attack upon Christianity and so the moral order as tantamount to an attempt to undermine the stability of the state.

But where is the argument from immorality left if, as with Shaftesbury and Butler, the link between religious scepticism and immorality is severed and if sceptics, and in the end atheists, can be moral? These individuals will still not believe the Christian stories, but why this is supposed to impress reasonable men is unclear when these stories themselves have yet to be shown acceptable to reason. But even if this can be shown, if a sceptic or atheist can be moral, why must he bother with those stories? Why must he believe what the Christian—or any other religious person—believes? The effect of moral-sense theories in the hands of Shaftesbury and Butler is precisely, on the one hand, to make morality rest upon aspects of human nature and, on the other, to make belief in natural rights apparently irrelevant both to the account of virtue and virtuous action and to the account of the obligation to be virtuous.

The issue of tolerance is also affected. In his first *Letter Concerning Toleration* (1689), Locke excludes atheists from those to whom toleration should be extended on the basis of the argument from immorality. If atheists are necessarily either immoral or amoral, why should we tolerate those who will not, for example, respect their promises and oaths and who thereby, we may suppose, will harm other people and the state? Burke also accepts the argument. In *Reflections on the Revolution in France* (1790), he discerns among the horrors produced by that revolution a corrupting atheism, which, in its irreligion and consequent corruption of morals, feeds political instability. This, together with his lament for the past, his extolling of tradition and the political/social institutions which embody and preserve it, and his commitment to a theological foundation of the state, makes it clear that atheism has no place in a Burkean conservatism. With Shaftesbury and Butler, however, there is not the same rigidity as in Locke and Burke. Because that position is not enmeshed in the argument from immorality, there is per se no reason for not extending toleration to sceptics and atheists; social and political instability are not necessarily or inevitably the consequences of severing morality from Christianity.

When we ask, then, what role natural rights can play in the picture sketched by Shaftesbury and Butler, the answer does not turn upon an account involving appeal beyond human nature either of the ground of morality or of the ground of the obligation to be moral; it also does not turn upon some claim that social/political instability inevitably ensue if there are not such rights by which to orient human behavior. We have no reason to believe this last claim, any more than we have reason to believe that such rights form external constraints upon the moral senses of individual men. Notice, again, unlike Bentham's discussion and his insistence upon atheism, that belief in God is perfectly compatible with this picture; such belief, however, is not part of the ground of morality or required either for us to account for our obligation to be moral or to enable us to tell when the parts of our nature are in harmony or right proportion.

Briefly, Butler follows Shaftesbury in holding that human nature is a system, consisting for him of four parts, namely, the particular appetites, affections, and passions on the one hand and the principles of self-love, benevolence, and conscience on the other. According to Butler, the system of human nature is ordered in terms of natural authority, not force or strength (Preface, 14), and he usually is read as maintaining that the principles of self-love and benevolence possess greater authority than the particular passions and that conscience possesses greater authority than self-love and benevolence. (I do not myself accept this view of the relative ordering of self-love, benevolence, and conscience, but the point of my discussion here is unaffected by this disagreement.)[18] Authority is distinguished from strength (*Sermons*, II, 15–19); thus, while self-love is a "superior principle to passion" (*Sermons*, II, 16), particular passions may be so strong as to overwhelm it. Then, passions motivate us at the expense of interest, as when one seeks revenge, even though it is not in one's (long-term) interest to do so. And what is true of self-love is equally true of conscience: while it is naturally superior to revenge and hatred, these can overwhelm it and so come to motivate us.

Where Shaftesbury emphasizes balance and harmony, so too does Butler. The system of human nature is in harmony and right proportion when the passions, benevolence, self-love, and conscience exhibit their ordered authority. Acts may be proportionate or dispropor-

18. See note 17.

tionate to this ordered nature; when they are proportionate, they are natural; when disproportionate, unnatural. Disproportionateness and unnaturalness in acts, then, involve the transgression of ordered authority by strength (*Sermons,* II, 16). Butler maintains that virtue consists in acting in accordance with the constitution of man when the parts of this constitution are ordered in relation to each other; the acts in question, natural and proportionate, are right. Vice involves disproportion: one allows a lower principle (in this regard Butler usually treats the particular passions as a single principle of action) to dominate a higher one, and one acts accordingly. The disproportion that wrongness and vice involve is determined by comparing the act in question "with the nature of the agent" (*Sermons,* II, 19). Nothing external to this comparison of the act to the nature of the agent is required in order for us to determine what is right.

Just as Shaftesbury and Hume in the second *Enquiry,* Butler rejects the reductionist thesis of the selfish school, which he identifies with Hobbes (and that Hume identifies as well with Locke). We have, he maintains, all kinds of appetites, affections, and passions; these include hunger, thirst, revenge, compassion, friendship, love, and so on. He usually groups all these appetites, etc., together as particular passions, in order to compare and contrast them with self-love (*Sermons,* XI, 3–5) and conscience (*Sermons,* II, 17–19). If some of our particular passions tend to "private good," others tend to "public good" (*Sermons,* I, 6). That we have other-regarding or benevolent passions, such as love, compassion, and desire for friendship, Butler treats as obvious to inspection, and he is critical of Hobbes's view that compassion, though elicited by awareness of another's distress, is really about the possibility of future calamity to oneself (*Sermons,* I, 4n). In short, other-regarding or benevolent passions are as much a part of our nature as self-regarding ones, and we are as much made for society and tending the public good as we are for promoting and tending our own good (*Sermons,* I, 3). The reductionist thesis of Hobbes, therefore, is a mistaken account of human nature.

Obviously, too, for Butler, it is a mistake to restrict virtue to benevolence in the way we noticed earlier with Jefferson. Virtue for Butler involves self-love and self-regarding passions every bit as much as it involves benevolence and other-regarding passions. Indeed, as with Shaftesbury, his is a harmony view involving a harmony among the parts of our nature.

In *An Enquiry Concerning the Principles of Morals* (1751),[19] Hume's account of human nature in many respects resembles the accounts of Shaftesbury and Butler. They endow men with other-regarding, natural affections; so too does Hume. They reject psychological egoism; so too does Hume. They allow that the satisfaction of our benevolent passions can make us happy, and so too does Hume. Most especially, they warn of the dangers of excess in self-love and strongly urge that it and our powerful self-affections as well be brought under control. This too Hume endorses. Yet, these warnings in the end, in all three men, are just that: the excesses Hume ascribes to self-love in Appendix 2 of the second *Enquiry* do not lead him, as they do not lead Shaftesbury and Butler, to seek to eradicate self-love and the self-affections from our nature and so from figuring prominently in their accounts of virtue. For Hume, just as the others, is a harmony theorist. To be sure, especially in Book 3 of Hume's *A Treatise of Human Nature* (1739–40),[20] rights do make an appearance in Hume's account of the artificial virtues, where, basically as the result of utilitarian appeals, institutions involving rights and duties have been devised by us to allow us to ensure that justice is done and property is transferred, but these

19. David Hume, *Enquiries Concerning Human Understanding and Concerning the Principles of Morals,* ed. L. A. Selby-Bigge and Peter H. Nidditch (Oxford: Clarendon Press, 1975), 3d ed. The second *Enquiry* is hereafter cited as "Hume," with page numbers given in the above edition. For relevant discussions of Hume's thought, see D. F. Norton, *David Hume: Common-Sense Moralist, Sceptical Metaphysician* (Princeton: Princeton University Press, 1982); D. F. Norton, ed., *The Cambridge Companion to Hume* (Cambridge: Cambridge University Press, 1993), esp. the pieces by Norton and Haakonssen; Stephen Darwall, *The British Moralists;* Peter Jones, *Hume's Sentiments: Their Ciceronian and French Context* (Edinburgh, Edinburgh University Press, 1982); James Moore, "Hume and Hutcheson" in M. A. Stewart and J. P. Wright, eds., *Hume and Hume's Connexions* (Edinburgh: Edinburgh University Press, 1994). See also Haakonssen's *The Science of a Legislator.* I am deeply indebted to the work of Norton and Moore.

20. David Hume, *A Treatise of Human Nature,* D. F. Norton and M. J. Norton, eds. (Oxford: Oxford University Press, 2000).

institutional or conventional rights can in no way be construed to be natural rights that have a noninstitutional, nonconventional grounding and setting.

Interestingly, in Part 2 of the Conclusion to *An Enquiry Concerning the Principles of Morals,* Hume also follows Shaftesbury and Butler in maintaining that we have an "interested *obligation*" to virtue (Hume, 278; italics in the original). When Hume asks "whether every man, who has any regard to his own happiness and welfare, will not best find his account in the practice of every moral duty" (Hume, 278), he answers affirmatively and believes it a particular feature of his moral position that it facilitates such an answer. When the "dismal dress" in which "many divines" and "some philosophers" have clothed virtue falls away, she will reveal her "sole purpose" to be making "her votaries and all mankind, during every instant of their existence, if possible, cheerful and happy" (Hume, 279). Now this passage might be interpreted to mean that the overall purpose of virtue is to make us happy without it being implied that any particular duty that virtue recommends must be to our interest. But Hume quickly goes on:

> What theory of morals can ever serve any useful purpose, unless it can show, by a particular detail, that all the duties which it recommends are also the true interest of each individual. The peculiar advantage of the foregoing system [Hume's] seems to be, that it furnishes proper mediums for that purpose. (Hume, 280)

This passage commits Hume to the view not that the sole purpose of virtue is to make us happy but that virtue can only serve a useful purpose *at all* if *all* the duties it recommends are the *true interest* of *each* individual. This is, in Hume's terms, a restatement of Butler's view that "duty and interest are perfectly coincident" (*Sermons,* III, 13), and one sees Hume the harmony theorist, just as Shaftesbury and Butler, trying to control and moderate self-love and the self-affections. His path follows that of Shaftesbury and Butler. Here, I shall give only a general indication of this path.

In the second *Enquiry,* Hume makes a familiar point: while we are endowed with self-affections and self-love as well as other-regarding affections and benevolence, and while it is always possible that the latter may be stronger in us than the former, the reverse is typically the case.

Of course, benevolence and the other-regarding passions are every bit as much a part of our nature as self-love and our self-regarding passions, and Hume, as the others, stresses this (Hume, 218–32). But when Hume writes of benevolence and the other-regarding passions, he does not typically do so in terms of their extraordinary force or strength or energy within us; whereas when he writes of self-love he always does so in terms of its "extensive energy" (Hume, 218), either directly or indirectly, in terms of how this forceful part of our nature, augmented at times by the self-affections, can seize control of our lives.

To resist this control, Hume might follow Butler and appeal to a generalized compassion for others; yet, much beyond family and friends, what we might find in most people may be compassion (or a form of benevolence) in a much-weakened state, and it may be unclear how it is to cope with the power of self-love and the self-affections within us. Obviously, were Hume to assert the existence in us of a passion such as the love of mankind generally and to ascribe it a force equal to the power of self-love and the self-affections, we might use that passion to restrain self-love and the self-affections. But Hume never asserts any such things as these.

Sympathy, if taken as augmenting and reinforcing our other-regarding passions, may be appealed to by Hume's readers to counteract self-love and the self-affections. In the second *Enquiry*, however, sympathy is considerably less in evidence than in the *Treatise*, and when it is in evidence, it is circumscribed by avowed limitations on its strength and scope. Thus, Hume writes that sympathy "is much fainter than our concern for ourselves, and sympathy with persons remote from us much fainter than that with persons near and contiguous" (Hume, 229). If then by "sympathy" is meant merely being affected in some degree by what befalls others, that degree may be insufficient by itself to motivate the agent. Accordingly, if it is true that sympathy (or, as Hume says, generosity of man) is typically confined in any considerable degree to family and friends, then the question arises of how, making all due allowance for our benevolent passions and for sympathy, something this limited and comparatively weak is to battle successfully the strength of self-love and the self-affections within us. Hume's move is to talk about usefulness and the happiness of mankind, but it is really only in Part 2 of the Conclusion that he faces up to this central, motivational issue. And he meets it in exactly the way that Shaftesbury and Butler meet it: he claims that duty and virtue coincide and thereby, just as they did, hitches the forcefulness of self-love to the wagon of virtue.

In an interesting passage, Hume affirms that "We must renounce the theory, which accounts for every moral sentiment by the principle of self-love" (Hume, 219). We must, he thinks, "adopt a more public affection, and allow, that the interests of society are not, even on their own account, entirely indifferent to us" (Hume, 219). Suppose that we do this: what do we do if the pull of our own interests is simply stronger than the pull of the interests of society? Hume envisages that this might well occur, that private interest might be "separate" from public interest and even "contrary" to it (Hume, 219); but he does not tell us how to resolve the ensuing motivational problem. What he does is to go on to make a point about the usefulness of what contributes to the happiness of society and, importantly, to link this to a partial account of the very origin of morality. He writes:

Usefulness is only a tendency to a certain end; and it is a contradiction in terms, that anything pleases as means to an end, where the end itself no wise affects us. If usefulness, therefore, be a source of moral sentiment, and if this usefulness be not always considered with a reference to self; it follows, that everything, which contributes to the happiness of society recommends itself directly to our approbation and good-will. Here is a principle, which accounts, in great part, for the origin of morality. (Hume, 219)

There are two points to notice here. First, even if it is true that "everything which contributes to the happiness of society recommends itself directly to our approbation and good-will," we are given no instruction about what to do if the degree of recommendation or approbation simply cannot cope with the power of self-love and concern for self. We may still feel positively toward that which contributes to society's happiness, but that feeling cannot simply be assumed in and of itself in all cases to dwarf the strength of self-love. Hume says that, when private and public interest clashed, we "observed the moral sentiment to continue, notwithstanding this disjunction of interests" (Hume, 219). There is no reason to dispute this: the point is not that, when private interest and public interest pull in different directions, public interest (and so the moral sentiment) is extinguished; it is rather that, even allowing the moral sentiment to persist, we need some reason for thinking its motive force at least equivalent to that of private interest and self-love. Second, by speaking of "the origin of morality" in the context of our approbation and goodwill toward that which contributes to the happiness of society, Hume enables us to see that the motivational problem that Shaftesbury and Butler confronted and tried to solve through linking duty and interest confronts Hume. Put baldly, if private and public interest conflict, what reason have we to think that we shall be motivated sufficiently by the latter to harm the former? Since there can in Hume the epistemologist be no a priori guarantee that we shall be so motivated, we seem to be left hoping that there will not be, as a matter of fact, very many such clashes with which to contend. Pursuit of virtue, then, turns upon whether we shall be motivated to pursue it, and in this regard we are left to hope that (1) benevolence, sympathy, and our approbation of that which contributes to the happiness of society are jointly stronger than the power of self-love and the self-affections (including prudence) and (2) the number of occasions on which self-love clashes with these others are few.

The difficulty here, obviously, as Hume well realizes, is that much is left to chance: pursuit of virtue seems not quite assured on this picture. This fits well with Hutcheson's complaint of Hume's ethics lacking warmth in the cause of virtue. But warmth in this respect is not what is needed; what is needed is some more certain basis upon which to claim a sufficiently powerful degree of motivation to pursue virtue. Hume could come out with the wondrous claim that we will all just come to love virtue for its own sake, however implausible this may be to assume; but he does not. Instead, he simply follows the lead of Shaftesbury and Butler, both of whom seek to put the motivational issue beyond doubt by the claim that individual happiness and virtue are linked and accordingly that it is in our interests to be moral. As we have seen, this is what Hume proceeds to do in Part 2 of the Conclusion, with his claim that a theory of morals only serves a useful purpose if it can show "that all the duties which it recommends are also the true interest of each individual" (Hume, 280). Thus, Hume seeks to show that we have an "interested *obligation*" (Hume, 278; italics in the original) to virtue by showing that virtue facilitates our interest or happiness, not in general or in the vast run of cases, but, if he is to be believed, in all cases. We need not agree with Hume about all cases, in order to see that he seeks to replicate the strategy of Shaftesbury and Butler of arguing for the coincidence of virtue and interest. Far from accepting Jefferson's banishment of self-love from the realm of the moral, the three men all seek to tie it and its powerful force within us to the cause of virtue. Put differently, we have good reason to pursue virtue, which these moral-sense theorists see as harmony in the parts of our nature; it facilitates our own happiness. This reason holds *whether or not* we come to love virtue for its own sake, *whether or not* we come to believe in God, *whether or not* we assume that there are any natural rights by which to guide our moral thinking.

Hume finishes off this line of argument by remarking that, contrary to vulgar supposition, there really is no contradiction "between the *selfish* and *social* sentiments or dispositions" (Hume, 281). The passage here is straight Butler and echoes a footnote in the 1748 edition of *An Enquiry Concerning Human Understanding* to Butler's *Sermons* (which note was removed in subsequent editions). In essence, this footnote appears in Part 2 of the Conclusion to the second *Enquiry,* only now stated in terms of a denial of a contradiction or incompatibility between selfish and social sentiments instead of selfish and benevolent ones. Giving vent to our social sentiments can make us happy. Hume continues:

> Besides this advantage, common to all, the immediate feeling of benevolence and friendship, humanity and kindness, is sweet, smooth, tender, and agreeable, independent of all fortunes and accidents. These virtues are besides attended with a pleasing consciousness or remembrance, and keep us in humour with ourselves as well as others; while we retain the agreeable reflection of having done our part towards mankind and society. (Hume, 282)

If satisfaction of the social sentiments is as much productive of our happiness as the satisfaction of the self-regarding sentiments, then the search for our happiness, which is a part of all of us, plays its role as a motive for us to seek harmony in the parts of our nature and to behave virtuously. At the level of foundations, there simply is no room for natural rights in this kind of picture, not because Hume is an epistemological sceptic but because the account of virtue, of virtuous conduct, and of the motive to be virtuous neither require them in their exposition nor see human nature as involving their assumption.

Harmony theorists set out a picture of the ground of morality that turns fundamentally upon human nature and upon balance or proportion among the parts of that nature, of which self-love and the self-affections remain important parts.[21] Natural rights draw upon a different picture of the ground of morality, one, as Butler might put it, that moves away from the view that man is a law unto himself, with the rule of right within, toward the view that man is a being subject to laws— natural laws—which he has neither the capacity nor the entitlement to change. They bind him and render morally appropriate that which they specify. For those who identify natural laws with moral laws, there is a temptation to identify natural rights with moral rights, but, as we saw in our definition of natural rights, we must not confuse natural rights with moral rights that can be altered (and permissibly violated or infringed) by men. Any moral rights of this latter kind would not qualify traditionally as natural rights, and there would be a clear implication that, if we could alter and amend them, they do not bind in the requisite fashion of natural rights. It is precisely this picture of binding our nature that the moral-sense theorists seem intent on rejecting. Of course, natural law (and natural rights) also requires perhaps a different metaphysical picture of the world and man's place in it. Butler, who is far from being a Humean sceptic, tries to indicate this in the *Sermons:*

> There are two ways in which the subject of morals may be treated. One begins from inquiring into the abstract nature of things: the other from a matter of fact, namely, what the particular nature of man is, its several parts, their economy or constitution; from whence it proceeds to determine what course of life it is, which is correspondent to this whole nature. (Preface, 7)

Unlike Samuel Clarke and the Cambridge Platonists, such as Henry More (*Enchiridion Ethicum,* 1688, translated as *An Account of Virtue,*

---

21. In this regard, see D. D. Raphael, *The Moral Sense* (Oxford: Clarendon Press, 1949).

1690) and Ralph Cudworth (*Treatise Concerning Eternal and Immutable Morality*, 1731), Butler, together with Shaftesbury and Hume, embraces the second of these two approaches. The aim of the *Sermons,* he says, is to explain "what is meant by the nature of man, when it is said that virtue consists in following, and vice in deviating from it" and to show that this claim about virtue or morality "is true" (Preface, 8). Appeal to natural rights runs against the grain of this approach to ethics.

There seem to be two obvious ways of trying to deal with this tension between moral-sense theory, as an account of the ground of morality, and appeal to natural rights, viewed as constraints on the nature of man that render morally appropriate what they specify. Both involve a deviation from the traditional view of natural rights, and neither, I think, is satisfactory. The first way is to make natural rights subject to the moral sense; the second is to turn them into facets of the moral sense. (What I mean by this latter will become apparent below.) The first way, as best I can tell, is adopted by Jefferson, the second by Hutcheson.

Surprisingly, Jefferson, who is not, as it were, a practicing philosopher, seems to see the philosophical clash between these two different pictures of the ground of morality and the pressure this in turn puts upon his appeal to natural rights; his solution is to change the nature of natural rights. In 1793, in his *Opinion on the French Treaties,* in a discussion of the right of self-liberation, he writes:

> Questions of natural right are triable by their conformity with the moral sense & reason of man. Those who write treatises of natural law, can only declare what their own moral sense & reason dictate in the several cases they state. Such of them as happen to have feelings & a reason coincident with those of the wise & honest part of mankind, are respected & quoted as witnesses of what is morally right or wrong in particular cases. Grotius, Puffendorf [*sic*] Wolf, & Vattel are of this number. Where they agree their authority is strong. But where they differ, & they often differ, we must appeal to our own feelings and reason to decide between them.[22]

22. Appleby and Ball, *Jefferson: Political Writings,* 559–60.

This passage submits claims of natural right to the moral sense and reason of man. If taken strictly, it enunciates the view that those who claim or point to natural rights ("those who write treatises of natural law") are simply declaring what their moral sense tells them is right or wrong in particular cases. Such rights pose no external constraint on virtue since they are only, in particular cases, claims founded upon some individual's moral sense and upon the fact that the moral senses of other individuals agrees with what this individual says in the particular case at hand. This radically changes the nature of natural rights as traditionally understood; it also effectively mutes the religious overtones that such rights (through natural law) were taken to have and to represent.

Moreover, the agreement of others with "the wise & honest part of mankind" presumes us to know who these individuals are, and it should be apparent from my earlier discussion that Shaftesbury, Butler, and Hume see no reason why, since sceptics and atheists can be moral, these individuals may not be counted among the wise and honest part of mankind. So, in their cases, if there are any natural rights, such rights would represent simply another way of talking about what such individuals would see in particular cases as the right courses of action. Certainly, there would be no suggestion of anything particularly religious or theological about natural rights, and no suggestion, if people's moral sense so indicated, that what had previously been taken to be a natural right was no such thing. After all, the ultimate guide in each individual's case is his moral sense, not some claim to a natural right, which claim is nothing more than another way of speaking of the agreement of the moral senses of some of the wisest and most honest among us.

Part of what one can do, then, to relieve the tension between moral-sense theory and natural rights is to make the rights subject to each individual's moral sense, which radically changes them from what they have traditionally been understood to be. They only matter morally to the extent that our moral sense can endorse the course of action that they recommend. In short, natural rights do not pose external constraints on our moral sense but are submitted to it, and they in fact are nothing more than claims to which the moral senses of "the wise and honest part of mankind" are in the main in agreement. This is what the natural rights that figure in the American Declaration of Independence amount to: they are claims to which the moral senses of "the wise and honest part of mankind," which can include sceptics and atheists, are in the main in agreement. They have no binding force apart from this consideration, and should the moral senses of such men change, they would have no binding force whatever. This not only deviates from what was traditionally understood by those who "write treatises of natural law" and of natural rights; it deviates even from what Locke, in his *Second Treatise of Government* (1689), took his rights to life, liberty, and property to represent.[23] Locke, of course, was no moral-sense theorist, so he had no need to address himself to problems involving clashing pictures of the foundation of morality. Jefferson does not enjoy this luxury.

The second way of dealing with the tension between moral-sense theory, as an account of the ground of morality, and appeal to natural rights, viewed as constraints on the nature of man that render morally appropriate what they specify, is, as it were, to turn natural rights into facets of the moral sense. This, in essence, is Hutcheson's proposed solution. It has three main pillars: the identification of virtue with benevolence, the claim that what the moral sense actually detects in action or character and approves of is its benevolent motivation or aspect, and the claim, in effect, that natural rights reflect both benevolent qualities in our nature and mark off possibilities of benevolent action on our parts.

Hutcheson's moral thought is often difficult to render a coherent whole between his writings in the 1720s, especially *An Inquiry into the Original of Our Ideas of Beauty and Virtue in Two Treatises* (1725)[24] and the *Essay on the Nature and Conduct of the Passions and Affections, with Illus-*

23. Relevant here is A. John Simmons, *The Lockean Theory of Rights* (Princeton: Princeton University Press, 1992); S. Buckle, *Natural Law and the Theory of Property: Grotius to Hume* (Oxford: Clarendon Press, 1991); J. Tully, *A Discourse on Property: John Locke and His Adversaries* (Cambridge: Cambridge University Press, 1980).

24. Francis Hutcheson, *An Inquiry into the Original of Our Ideas of Beauty and Virtue in Two Treatises* (1725; 4th ed., London: Midwinter, 1738). Hereafter cited as *Inquiry* with page numbers given.

trations on the Moral Sense (1728)[25] and the work that appeared posthumously, *A System of Moral Philosophy* in 1755.[26] Any problems of interpretation arising from this difficulty need not concern us here since my focus is not only upon the earlier material but upon the central role of benevolence in Hutcheson's thought which does not change. Indeed, the emphasis he places upon benevolence is apparent even in his earliest work in the 1720s, such as his *Reflections on the Common Systems of Morality* (1724).[27] He virtually begins this work by announcing the identity of virtue and benevolence, an identity, of course, that Shaftesbury, Butler, and Hume do not endorse: "All virtue is allowed to consist in affections of love towards the Deity, and our fellow creatures, and in actions suitable to these affections" (*Reflections*, 97). From this, he thinks one of the things we may conclude is that "Whatever scheme of principles shall be most effectual to excite these affections [of love], the same must be the truest foundation of all virtue" (*Reflections*, 97). He then comes out strongly in favor of the "kind affections." He castigates Hobbes and others for not speaking of the "bright side

25. Francis Hutcheson, *Essay on the Nature and Conduct of the Passions and Affections, with Illustrations on the Moral Sense* (1728; 3d ed., London: A. Ware, 1742). Hereafter cited as *Essay* with page numbers given.

26. Francis Hutcheson, *A System of Moral Philosophy*, 2 vols. (London, 1755). Hereafter cited as *System* with page numbers given.

27. Francis Hutcheson, *Reflections on the Common Systems of Morality* in T. Mautner, ed., *On Human Nature* (Cambridge: Cambridge University Press, 1993). Hereafter cited as *Reflections* with page numbers given. Relevant works on Hutcheson—and ones that have strongly influenced me—include James Moore, "Hume and Hutcheson"; James Moore, "Natural Rights in the Scottish Enlightenment" in M. Goldie and R. Wokler, eds., *The Cambridge History of Eighteenth-Century Political Thought* (Cambridge: Cambridge University Press, forthcoming); D. F. Norton, "Hutcheson's Moral Realism," *Journal of the History of Philosophy* 23 (1985): 392–418; D. F. Norton, "Hutcheson's Moral Sense Theory Reconsidered" in *Dialogue* 13 (1974): 3–23; James Moore, "The Two Systems of Francis Hutcheson: On the Origins of the Scottish Enlightenment" in M. A. Stewart, ed., *Studies in the Philosophy of the Scottish Enlightenment* (Oxford: Clarendon Press, 1990), 37–59; Samuel Fleischacker, "The Impact on America: Scottish Philosophy and the American Founding." It is Hutcheson, of course, who is the star of Garry Wills's *Inventing America*. These works by Moore and Fleischacker have influenced me in my accounts of Hutcheson and natural rights.

of human nature" (*Reflections,* 100), and he goes on to give a glowing account of it. He continues:

> Every action is amiable and virtuous, so far as it evidences a study of the good of others, and a real delight in their happiness: . . . innocent self-love, and the actions flowing from it, are indifferent; . . . nothing is detestably wicked, but either a direct study and intention of the misery of others, without any further view; or else such an entire extinction of the kind affections, as makes us wholly indifferent and careless how pernicious our selfish pursuits may be to others. (*Reflections,* 101)

The problem here is with the kindly affections: what do we do if they are much weaker in us than the self-affections and self-love? Hutcheson stresses the role of education in *Reflections,* as well as in the *Inquiry* and the *Essay,* and he clearly hopes that we can educate men into feeling their kindly affections in full measure. Yet, he, too, it may seem, thinks to invoke interest on their behalf, as his claim in the Preface to the *Essay* may be thought to indicate:

> It may seem strange, that when in this *Treatise* Virtue is supposed *disinterested;* yet so much Pains is taken, by a *Comparison* of our several *Pleasures* to prove the *Pleasures* of *Virtue* to be the greatest we are capable of, and that consequently it is our truest *Interest* to be *virtuous.* (*Essay,* viii: italics in the original)

Now this may look like a move in a familiar direction, but it fails to be such; for there is no sense at all for Hutcheson in which interest can be a part of virtue. All he is trying to do here is to use interest to further the case of benevolence, which is all and the only content of virtue. As he makes clear, self-love, even when it is innocent, is morally indifferent; if it is pernicious, and so amounts to selfishness, it is evil. It *never* forms part of virtue. This, of course, is in line with Jefferson's earlier claim.

Equally, moreover, Hutcheson is clear that self-love or the self-affections cannot form part of virtuous motivation (*Reflections,* 97); only the kindly affections can serve this role. Indeed, in, for example, the *Essay,* he even describes virtue as kind affection (*Essay,* xv). So there is a kind of purity demanded of us, if we are to be morally motivated: we must be motivated only by the kindly affections. Self-love and the self-affections cannot form any part of such motivation. Thus, unlike the case with Shaftesbury, Butler, and Hume, Hutcheson's apparent move to hitch interest to the cause of enhancing the kindly affections is productive of harm, if it produces the outcome that we are even in part motivated by interest. To tell someone, then, that he can further his interest by acting morally is really in a sense to lead him astray if he actually does seek his interest; what he has to do is to know that his interest will be furthered but come to be motivated, if he is to be morally motivated, only by love of others. And he must be so motivated even when his own interest or happiness is sacrificed if he is to act morally. This is a major difference with Shaftesbury, Butler, and Hume, none of whom identify virtue with benevolence or virtuous motivation with motivation only by the love of others. Indeed, in all three thinkers, part of what they are concerned to do is to provide people with a motive to virtue, even if they never come to love virtue for its own sake, even if they never come to be motivated exclusively or only by the love of others. In this sense, they take themselves to be realists about human nature, as exhibited empirically by the people we meet in daily life, in whom self-love and the self-affections are powerful features of their (moral) psychology and for whom virtue is balance and proportion between this and other aspects of their nature.

Hutcheson provides an extraordinarily positive, optimistic view of people, their character, and especially their propensities to be motivated for the good of others, and this view is evident throughout his writings, including *Reflections*. We find in ourselves, he says, that love of others is "one of the great springs" of action. He goes on:

> We shall find strong natural affections, friendships, national love, gratitude; scarce any footsteps of disinterested malice, or study of mischief, where there is no opposition of interests; a strong delight in being honoured by others for kind actions; a tender compassion towards any grievous distress; a determination to love and admire every thing which is good-natured and kind in others, and to be highly delighted in reflecting on such actions of their own. And on the other hand, a like determination to abhor everything cruel or

unkind in others, and to sink into shame upon having done such actions themselves. (*Reflections*, 101–2)

We take delight in our kindly affections and strongly approve actions motivated by them; we admire the kindly affections we find in others and strongly approve their actions that are motivated by them; and we admire and strongly approve the characters of people when we call up to our minds in reflection the benevolent motivation (the love of others) that their acts exhibit. What Hutcheson has done is to identify virtue with benevolence and virtuous motivation with benevolent motivation. Shaftesbury, Butler, and Hume are harmony theorists and seek to bring self-love and benevolence and our self-affections and natural affections into balance and some right proportion; Hutcheson takes benevolence to be the whole of virtue and plays up the role of benevolence and the kindly affections in us. As he says, he has sketched human nature "on the bright side." Of human beings in the round, he claims that "their intention, even when their actions are justly blameable, is scarce ever malicious, unless upon some sudden transitory passion, which is frequently innocent, but most commonly honourable or kind, however imperfectly they judge the means to execute it" (*Reflections*, 102). It is not only Hobbes and Mandeville who would find such a picture of us to be unrealistic.

To be sure, all kinds of passages in, for example, the *Inquiry* try to show us pleased by benevolent motivation, but the emphasis so far as virtue is concerned is never upon the pleasure to us as such but always upon the benevolence we "perceive" the action or character to betray. God has made us to be creatures who respond to benevolence with approval or approbation, and what we prize in ourselves and our character, we prize in others and in their characters. Here lies, I think, the key to understanding Hutcheson's view of natural rights whatever his view in *A System of Moral Philosophy* of their relation to natural law, to utility, to the common good, and to the distinction between perfect and imperfect rights and their relation to the issue of coercion. His view here, which I have characterized as making natural rights into facets of moral sense, has three planks to it.

First, God has made us creatures who respond with approbation to benevolence. We are "naturally" this way. Hutcheson puts the matter:

Human Nature was not left quite indifferent in the affair of Virtue, to form to itself Observations concerning the *Advantage* or *Disadvantage* of Action. . . . The Author of Nature has much better furnished us for a virtuous Conduct, than our Moralists seem to imagine. (*Inquiry*, xiii–xiv)

The "Author of Nature" has done this by making us naturally certain sorts of creatures. We do not choose to be creatures who approve of and take pleasure in benevolence:

> *Approbation* is not what we can *voluntarily* bring upon ourselves when we are contemplating Action, we do not *chuse* to approve because *Approbation* is pleasant. . . . *Approbation* is plainly a *Perception* arriving without previous *Volition.* . . . The Occasion of it is the *Perception of benevolent Affection* in ourselves or the discovering the like in others. (*Essay,* 248; italics in the original)

Thus, nature has made us to be creatures who respond to benevolence with delight and pleasure whether that benevolence be found in our own character or in the characters of others. Approbation arises spontaneously when we apprehend the benevolent motivation of acts; we do not choose to find benevolence pleasurable and approve of benevolent motivation because it gives us pleasure. Second, something which is not chosen is natural. Hutcheson labels natural, for example, "that *State,* those *Dispositions* and *Actions, natural,* to which we are inclined by some part of our Constitution, antecedently to any *Volition of our own;* or which flow from some *Principles* in our Nature, not brought upon us by our own *Art,* or that of others" (*Essays,* 201; italics in the original). Third, our moral sense, therefore, naturally responds or reacts to benevolence with approbation and approval, and our moral sense, so regarded, gives rise to a certain view of obligations and of rights.[28] For such things amount in essence to little more than possibilities for benevolent action on our parts, given appropriate circumstances. Put differently, one is obliged to act benevolently means on this view that

---

28. In this regard, see James Moore, "Natural Rights in the Scottish Enlightenment," and Samuel Fleischacker, "The Impact on America: Scottish Philosophy and the American Founding."

one's moral sense would condemn one for not doing so, for omitting to act benevolently or leaving such action undone, and it seems likely that one's moral sense would approve the use of coercion to see that the obligation to act benevolently is carried out. Given that virtue and benevolence are identical and given that we naturally respond or react to benevolence with approbation, it would be surprising if we did not feel obliged to act benevolently or to do those acts that exhibit a love of others. One has a right to act benevolently means that one's moral sense always approves action based on the motive of benevolence and that, other things equal, it would be wrong to interfere with one's action on this motive. This is a natural right in the sense indicated for Hutcheson; for the fact that our moral sense approves action based on the motive of benevolence is not something chosen by us but part of our nature. Obligations and rights, therefore, are connected centrally to Hutcheson's account of virtue and to the emphasis in that account upon benevolence and upon our natural disposition to respond positively to it. In a sense they are reflections of the benevolent aspect of our nature in that they mark off possibilities for benevolent action on our parts: to see oneself as obliged to act benevolently and to see oneself with a right to act benevolently is to see oneself acting virtuously. And one is doing this, moreover, for the love of virtue, out of the love we have for others; one is not motivated either wholly or partially by interest, though it is a happy truth about us that we take delight in benevolence and benevolent action.

The discussion of rights in *A System of Moral Philosophy* takes place in a different climate, one in which natural law figures, in which jurisprudential concerns are manifest, and in which political society, the common good, and aspects of utility are discussed.[29] It is there that he famously claims that a man "hath a *right* to do, possess, or demand any thing" when "his acting, possessing, or obtaining from another in these circumstances tends to the good of society, or to the interest

29. See Haakonssen, *Natural Law and Moral Philosophy*, ch. 2; Isabel Rivers, *Reason, Grace, and Sentiment*, vol. 2; James Moore, "Utility and Harmony: The Quest for the *Honestum* in Cicero, Hutcheson, and Hume," Utilitas 14 (2002): 365–86; James Moore, "Natural Rights in the Scottish Enlightenment." My discussion here has been influenced by these works.

of the individual consistently with the rights of others and the general good of society, and obstructing him would have the contrary tendency" (*System*, 2:iii, 1). This relation of rights to the general good, and through this ultimately to broader utilitarian concerns, is not really part of the moral-sense position set out by Hutcheson in the 1720s where the attempt to link duties and rights to his account of virtue predominates. Whatever the relation of this subsequent account of natural rights to natural law, the appeal to the "general good of society" and so to broader utilitarian concerns in the account of rights would have been certain to set off alarms in the Founders and others of the period for whom "the rights of man" do not appear to be or appear even to be linked to what today we would call more generally utilitarianism. For to build concerns of the general good into one's account of rights and so to construe even perfect rights (rights that foster community and social living) as subject to the constraints of the general good is implicitly to allow them to be infringed if so doing serves the general good. This in turn raises the whole issue of what exactly the cash value of a scheme of *individual* rights is if it can be evaded or overcome by appeals to more general considerations of the overall collective good. This kind of issue is less apparent in the writings of the 1720s. (Involved in all this, of course, is a standard complaint against Benthamite utilitarianism or, indeed, any form of classical or act-utilitarianism, namely, that collective concerns of the general good erode individual protections.)

Hutcheson might try to resist this clash between the general good and individual protections by arguing in *A System of Moral Philosophy* that God will ensure that there is no clash of this sort; in this sense, God has ordered the world in such a way that things work out for the best not only for individuals through honoring their rights but also for the collective as well through everyone's having their perfect rights honored. This assumption—that God has ordered the world in such a way that if only everyone acts on their perfect rights the general good will be served—assumes a harmony of interest between individuals and the collective that, per se, we have no reason to believe. Certainly, there appear to be obvious examples of its falsity, as when acting on my right to have a promise kept produces a catastrophe for others.

In the writings of the 1720s, the tension we noted earlier between moral-sense theory, as an account of morality, and the appeal to natural rights, as constraints on the nature of man that render morally appropriate what they specify, is allegedly dissolved by Hutcheson by making natural rights into facets of moral-sense theory. They are linked to, if not a product of, it. They are not (external) constraints on the nature of man but reflections of that nature, at least so far as they exhibit love of others. They are not subject to the moral sense, they are products of it; they do not stand outside moral-sense theory as constraints but inside moral-sense theory as creations of it. If this kind of position dissolves the tension in question, it does so by making natural rights facets or products of human nature into reflections of our benevolence (and of the identity between benevolence and virtue).

The problem with this line of argument is not simply that it deviates from the traditional understanding of natural rights, though, of course, it does so. Rather, the problem is that the very identification of virtue with benevolence upon which the dissolution of the tension relies is problematic and for two reasons. First, we have seen that Shaftesbury, Butler, and Hume reject the identification. It does not correspond to the empirical description of human nature as we find it in real people in whom self-love and the self-affections are fundamental parts of their nature. So why should we agree to limit virtue to benevolence or so exclusively to see human nature "on the bright side"? And why should we believe that motivation by self-love can never be moral? As it were, we face a choice over competing views of virtue, as between Shaftesbury, Butler, and Hume on the one hand and Hutcheson on the other: we need a reason for taking virtue to be all and only benevolence in a way that taints self-love and the self-affections from ever being part of the moral.

Second, Hutcheson's account makes natural rights into products or creations of his account of virtue (and the happy fact that we are so made as to be creatures that greet benevolence and benevolent motivation with approbation). In a sense, then, such rights are utterly contingent, contingent upon our nature and so how we were made. Had we been made differently, they need not have been as they are. Moreover, had God not made us to be creatures that love virtue for its own sake, then the account of virtue would need to be different; as we have seen, Shaftesbury, Butler, and Hume all give the search for our happiness, or self-interest, as a reason why we should be virtuous, which implicitly allows for the possibility that we are not creatures who love virtue for its sake. The very status of the claim that we are creatures who greet benevolence with approbation is in doubt in the sense that, while it is perfectly true that we do this on occasion, it is not obvious that we do it always, inevitably, without exception. Nor, realistically, could Hutcheson insist otherwise. So, he, too, seems likely to have to have recourse to our happiness, or self-interest, in order to address those occasions when the love of others is, as it were, at a low point within us. While important, however, this likelihood misses the crucial point: the claim that we are made so as to greet benevolence with approbation must not be run together with the claim that virtue is all and only benevolence. In principle, we could accept the former without accepting the latter: we could agree that we are made so as to respond positively to benevolence without agreeing that virtue is, and is only, benevolence. Again, we could agree that it is part of our nature to exhibit love of others, without agreeing that virtue consists in all and only love of others. Put differently, even if we were to agree that benevolence or love of others is an important part of our nature, nothing but the identification of virtue with benevolence makes it the case that virtuous motivation is exhausted by benevolent motivation. Nothing about how God made us makes *this* the case. One cannot deduce from the claim that we are fortunately made to love benevolence that virtue is exhausted by benevolence; we cannot use God, therefore, to defend this claim, which is what produces or creates natural rights, according to Hutcheson's moral-sense theory. Definitional stances do not amount to an argued defense.

To relieve the tension between moral-sense theory, as an account of the ground of morality, and appeal to natural rights, as constraints upon the nature of man that render morally appropriate what they specify, then, one may make the rights subject to each individual's moral sense or one may make them the products or creations of moral sense. Both options lead to difficulties, and tension between moral-sense theory and such rights remains.

Adam Smith follows his teacher Hutcheson and appeals to natural rights, at least if we read his *Lectures on Jurisprudence* (1976)[30] into *The Theory of Moral Sentiments* (1759)[31] and *An Inquiry into the Nature and Causes of the Wealth of Nations* (1776).[32] Notes of Smith's lectures on jurisprudence are all that we have, and these effectively surfaced for scholars in the 1950s. Since neither *Moral Sentiments* nor *The Wealth of Nations* makes use of natural rights, they do not contain any discussion of how such rights might be made compatible with moral-sense theory. This does not mean that there is not room for natural rights in those works. For example, in Book 5 of *The Wealth of Nations*, Smith presents one of the first discussions of limited government, wherein he ascribes the state three tasks, one of which is the administration of justice. It now is evident that, based upon the discussion of justice in the *Lectures on Jurisprudence*, natural rights would figure prominently in his treatment of this subject.[33] (They do not so figure in Hume's discussion of this topic, of course, and this is another area in which the two men have significant philosophical differences.)

As best one can judge, Smith exerted little influence upon the Founders, so far as moral theory is concerned, and I know of nothing in that period which tries to integrate his discussion of justice and natural jurisprudence into his discussion of the moral sentiments. *The Wealth of Nations* seems to have fared better and was certainly known by Jefferson and Madison; and Hamilton, as might be expected in an economist, is said to have taken extensive notes on the work. But none

30. Adam Smith, *Lectures on Jurisprudence,* ed. R. L. Meek and D. D. Raphael (Indianapolis: Liberty Fund, 1982). There are two sets of lectures, denominated A and B.

31. Adam Smith, *The Theory of Moral Sentiments,* ed. A. L. Macfie and D. D. Raphael (Indianapolis: Liberty Fund, 1982).

32. Adam Smith, *An Inquiry into the Nature and Causes of the Wealth of Nations,* ed. R. H. Campbell and A. S. Skinner, 2 vols. (Indianapolis: Liberty Fund, 1976).

33. See Haakonssen, *Natural Law and Moral Philosophy,* esp. ch. 4; Griswold, *Adam Smith and the Virtue of Enlightenment,* esp. chs. 6 and 7. This last work contains an extensive bibliography of recent writings on this issue. See also Samuel Fleischacker's detailed account in *Adam Smith's Theory of Justice,* forthcoming; James Moore, "Natural Rights in the Scottish Enlightenment." These works provide excellent discussions of the relevant Hutcheson/Smith issues.

of this engages the moral side of Smith's thought and so how he might have been thought to render compatible or at least to integrate natural rights with moral-sense theory. So there is little prospect that the Founders relied upon Smith in this regard.

In the end, then, moral-sense theory and appeals to natural rights remain in tension. I have tried to show how moral-sense theory split, with Shaftesbury, Butler, and Hume going in one direction and Hutcheson going in another. The former group has no role for natural rights to play and moral-sense theory seems to draw upon a picture of the foundation of morality that runs against the grain of one that features appeals to natural rights. As we saw, one can then, like Jefferson, try to make natural rights subject to each individual's moral sense or, like Hutcheson, try to make them products or creations of an account of virtue as benevolence. Each option has difficulties.

Why, ultimately, does all this matter? What is the upshot? The answer would seem to be that Bentham is right, that the rights featured in the American Declaration of Independence are not well-grounded, if moral-sense theory is thought to supply that ground. Appeals to God or the Creator leave only believers as thinking those rights well-grounded, and in the "Age of Reason," wherein the "rights of man" are part of the explanation of in what liberty consists, that is not a place where reasonable men wish to be left.

But there is also a deeper matter at issue, I think, one that Madison certainly realizes. In the *Memorial and Remonstrance Against Religious Assessments* (1785),[34] he assembles a whole series of reasons why it would be a bad idea for the Virginia General Assembly to enact a bill establishing "a provision for teachers of the Christian Religion," in effect, giving the state's support for Christianity.[35] After claiming a right of conscience to be a natural right that is conferred upon us by our "Cre-

---

34. James Madison, *Writings* (New York: The Library of America, 1999), 29–36.

35. Of relevance here is Lance Banning, *The Sacred Fire of Liberty: James Madison and the Founding of the American Republic* (Ithaca: Cornell University Press, 1995), esp. chs. 3 and 9; Jack Rakove and Oscar Handlin, eds., *James Madison and the Creation of the American Republic* (New York: Longman, 2001). For a series of essays on Madison's religious beliefs and on his writings pertinent to religion, see R. S. Alley, ed., *James Madison on Religious Liberty* (Buffalo: Prometheus Books, 1985).

ator" or "Governour of the Universe" or "Universal Sovereign," which right we have prior to the establishment of civil society (this is the standard view of Locke), he comes to the point:

> We maintain therefore that in matters of Religion, no mans right is abridged by the institution of Civil Society and that Religion is wholly exempt from its cognizance. True it is, that no other rule exists, by which any question which may divide a Society, can be ultimately determined, but the will of the majority; but it is also true that the majority may trespass on the rights of the minority.[36]

If fear of faction is a recurring theme throughout Madison's writings, so too is fear of the majority. In this passage he not only expresses this latter fear but also maintains that all other issues that divide society are to be settled by the will of the majority. What both he and Jefferson do, since they both, as it were, inherit the natural law tradition of Grotius and Pufendorf and the natural rights of Locke, is to use talk of "natural rights" in order to separate out concerns of vital moral/social/political importance to individuals from concerns of lesser such importance. Calling something a "natural right" as Madison does the right of conscience is simply to indicate that it is one of those vital moral concerns. He seems to say in the above passage that it is the only such concern that lies beyond the will of the majority. Yet, at the end of *Memorial and Remonstrance* he seems to go further and in a way that allows us to see the true significance of calling something a "natural right." He writes of the right to conscience as held by us with "the same tenure with all our other rights." He then goes on:

> If we weigh its importance, it cannot be less dear to us; if we consult the "Declaration of those rights which pertain to the good people of Virginia, as the basis and foundation of Government," it is enumerated with equal solemnity, or rather studied emphasis. Either then, we must say, that the Will of the Legislature is the only measure of their authority; and that in the plenitude of this authority, they may sweep away all our fundamental rights; or, that they are found to leave this particular right untouched and sacred. Either

36. James Madison, *Writings*, 30.

we must say, that they may controul the freedom of the press, may abolish Trial by Jury, may swallow up the Executive and Judiciary Powers of the State; nay that they may despoil us of our very right of suffrage, and erect themselves into an independent and hereditary Assembly or, we must say, that they have no authority to enact into law the Bill under consideration.[37]

There are in Madison's mind some rights thought of as fundamental, among which no doubt are those he earlier ascribed to the Creator, and these mark off concerns of fundamental moral/social/political importance to individuals. He calls these "natural." He clearly sees that, unless he can mark off some rights as fundamental, then they will all fall into the class of rights granted by legislatures and other bodies, and what is granted us can be taken away. This latter notion, sometimes captured by the expression "conventional rights," stands he thinks to us in a completely different degree of importance than, say, the right of conscience (or Jefferson's rights to life and liberty). The problem is that he does not have the philosophical paraphernalia to capture this notion of fundamental moral importance except by ascribing the rights in question to the Creator and thereby trying to place them beyond the powers of legislatures (or other bodies) to amend, alter, or abolish. He sees clearly that conventional rights can be tinkered with, and he thinks this likely to be productive of harm.

Fear of the majority, then, gets translated into fear of what can happen unless we place certain fundamental moral/social/political concerns beyond the powers of legislatures (and other bodies) to tinker with. Yet, he also sees clearly that this leaves him in an odd situation: there are any number of things that can strike the citizens of Virginia as of fundamental moral/social/political importance, and doubtless it will strike many that there are numerous things which must be kept from being tinkered with by the majority (in the legislature). The more such things held to be of fundamental importance and so removed from action by the majority, the less scope the majority of the state's citizens will have to express their democratic wishes.

Bentham is alive to all this: the general good has to contend with

37. Ibid., 35–36.

claims by some that certain things are of such fundamental importance that they have to be placed beyond all scope of amendment, alteration, and abolition. One searches for terminology in which to express this and, given the earlier natural law traditions, finds this terminology in natural rights talk. But who gets to determine which things are of fundamental importance and so placed beyond all scope of change? Which of their concerns carry the most weight? Why do they have this weight? These questions, when addressed by moral-sense theorists, admit of no answers that can withstand criticism since the whole burden of such theories in the first place is that each of us determine in our own case what our moral sense approves and finds important.

The problem, then, is that moral-sense theory gives us no real way of privileging certain of our concerns, of marking them off as fundamental in a way that bars another person's moral sense in principle from objecting. Bentham, I think, realizes all this in his understanding of Hume on justice, in which utility creates a case for the institution or rules of justice and property and in which rights and duties figure, but where the rules, rights, and duties in question all must rise to and meet the bar of utility. In the appropriate sense, *nothing* gets marked off as fundamental to the extent that it *lies beyond* this bar. To be sure, one can reject Bentham's claims on behalf of utility, but one will have done nothing thereby to have resuscitated the case for natural rights in a moral-sense theory.

"Riches Valuable at All Times and to All Men": Hume and the Eighteenth-Century Debate on Commerce and Liberty

To declaim against present times, and magnify the virtue of
remote ancestors, is a propensity almost inherent in human nature.
—David Hume, *Essays*

In almost precisely the middle of the eighteenth century (one could use as a marker the publication of Rousseau's *Discourse on the Sciences and Arts* in 1750), a variety of thinkers on both sides of the Atlantic engaged in a vigorous, complex, and extensive debate about commerce. Reduced to its essentials, the argument was about whether a free society is possible if commercial activities flourish, that is, if citizens are allowed to devote themselves to the enterprises associated with gain and prosperity. Free societies were generally believed to depend on patriotic citizens, and it was alleged that patriotism cannot survive in a commercial society. "A nation in no other period of its progress is so flourishing, as when patriotism is the ruling passion of every member: during that period, it is invincible," averred Lord Kames (Henry Home, Scotsman, friend and "cousin" to David Hume). But, he also observed, "successful commerce is not more advantageous by the wealth and power it immediately bestows, *than it is hurtful ultimately by introducing luxury and voluptuousness, which eradicate patriotism.*"[1]

This controversy about commerce and liberty echoes in the writings and debates of the American Founding generation. James Madison's

1. Henry Home, Lord Kames, *Sketches of the History of Man* (1774; Edinburgh, 1813), vol. 1 (bk. 2, sketch 7), 467, 474 (emphasis added). For the relationship between Kames and Hume, see Ernest Campbell Mossner, *The Life of David Hume* (Oxford: Clarendon Press, 1980).

1790's essays in the *National Gazette,* in particular, show one Founder wrestling with some of the central issues in the debate about commerce. My focus here, however, will be on the political economy essays of David Hume, arguably the first great political economist. No one any longer disputes the claim that Hume had an important influence on some members of the American Founding generation, and on Madison in particular.[2] But Hume's influence seems to have been confined to his earlier and more purely political essays (and his *History of England*); the political economy essays appear to have had negligible influence. Yet it is difficult to believe these essays were not familiar to the Americans—according to Hume himself the *Political Discourses* (as the 1752 set of essays was first known) was "the only work of mine that was successful on the first publication."[3] What can explain this failure of the American Founders to appreciate Hume's political economy, or, to put it the other way around, why did Hume's views make not even a dent in the Founders' preconceptions about the characteristics of a free society? I will argue here that the widespread admiration for the classical republics of Sparta and Rome[4] and the mistaken belief that they were free societies (of a sort that would be desirable in the new world) presented especially powerful obstacles to the success of the "modern project"—the project of Hume's intellectual forebears

2. The starting point on this matter is Douglas Adair, "'That Politics May Be Reduced to a Science': David Hume, James Madison, and the Tenth Federalist," in *Fame and the Founding Fathers,* ed. Trevor Colbourn (Indianapolis: Liberty Fund, 1998), 132–51. See also Gordon S. Wood, *The Creation of the American Republic, 1776–1787* (Chapel Hill: University of North Carolina Press, 1969 and 1998), 504–6. See also Samuel Fleischacker, "Adam Smith's Reception Among the American Founders, 1776–1790," *William and Mary Quarterly* 59, no. 4 (October 2002).

3. David Hume, "My Own Life" in *Essays: Moral Political and Literary,* ed. Eugene Miller (Indianapolis: Liberty Fund, 1985), xxxvi.

4. One might begin from the Founders' predilection to assume the names of Roman patriots—Publius, Brutus, Agricola, etc.—as pen names for their pamphlets and newspaper columns. For a thorough and excellent discussion of the deployment of classical heroes as symbols and as models, see Carl J. Richard, *The Founders and the Classics: Greece, Rome, and the American Enlightenment* (Cambridge: Harvard University Press, 1994), especially chs. 2 and 3.

Hobbes and Locke (from whom he is more commonly separated because of his criticisms of early modern rationalism). At the core of that project was a new understanding of politics and its place in human life, and Hume was one of the clearest proponents of the new view whose success he helped to assure.[5] Perhaps it would be too much to expect political men—statesmen—to welcome with open arms the denigration of politics.[6]

1. SCHOLARSHIP AND THE
POLITICAL ECONOMY ESSAYS

Hume's political economy essays, when not simply ignored, have been read for the most part in two ways. The first is quite narrow. Hume himself noted in an early essay that "trade was never esteemed an affair of state till the last century; and there scarcely is any ancient writer on politics, who has made mention of it,"[7] and thus his interest in political economy has led to his being considered one of the founders of modern economic science. Though occasionally dismissed as little more than an unsystematic precursor to Adam Smith, Hume's solid contribution to the emerging science of economics is not really in dispute. Read in this way, the significance of Hume's political economy has been thought to lie in his attack on mercantilism, a school of thought as prominent in 1750 as it is today. The most thorough presentation and analysis of Hume's political economy essays from this per-

---

5. A similar view can be found in Roy Porter, *The Creation of the Modern World: The Untold Story of the British Enlightenment* (New York: W. W. Norton, 2000). See esp. 247–51, where Porter writes: "Hume thus blew the trumpet for the modern: Scotland should not copy Sparta, nostalgia was wasted on that imagined community" (251).

6. For a somewhat different take on the result—at least—of the American Founders' work, see the superb study by Gordon Wood, *The Radicalism of the American Revolution* (New York: Alfred A. Knopf, 1992). Wood presents a compelling case that the aristocratic and hierarchical world (marked, for example, by "patriarchal dependence") of pre-Revolutionary America was completely overturned or eliminated as a result of the American Revolution. But Wood does not trace this to any revolutionary political theory, offering instead a primarily sociological account.

7. Hume, *Essays*, 88.

spective is still without doubt Eugene Rotwein's excellent monograph, now five decades old.[8]

More recently scholars have turned to the political economy essays with an eye toward assessing their broader significance in the history of political thought. The primary focus has been on Hume's relevance to what is called the civic humanist or classical republican paradigm in eighteenth-century British politics. This approach has illuminated the eighteenth-century controversy about republics and has convincingly demonstrated the importance of that controversy to an understanding of Hume. But there is less agreement than one might wish on the question of Hume's relation to civic humanism. John Robertson, for example, who attributes his understanding of the civic humanist tradition to the "magisterial investigations" of J. G. A. Pocock, sees in Hume's "The Idea of a Perfect Commonwealth" a design for a political order which shows that "Hume's thinking remained to the end within the framework of the civic tradition."[9] On Robertson's view, Hume accepted the classical republican view that political participation—necessary for a fully human life—can only occur where citizens have achieved the material basis for political activity (wealth and leisure). But Hume grafted onto this understanding a progressive view of economic development, which he believed "will . . . tend to bring an ever larger proportion of society within reach of material independence and moral fulfillment—and thus will tend to universalize the capacity for citizenship." Robertson sums up the claim as follows:

> The liberty to be provided by regular, free government must take not one but two forms. Priority must initially be given to the "jurisprudential" form of liberty: liberty under the law, liberty *from* neighbours and government. But as economic and moral betterment diffuses the capacity for citizenship ever wider, so in the perfect

8. Eugene Rotwein, ed., *David Hume: Writings on Economics* (1955; Madison: University of Wisconsin Press, 1970).

9. John Robertson, "The Scottish Enlightenment at the Limits of the Civic Tradition" in *Wealth and Virtue: The Shaping of Political Economy in the Scottish Enlightenment,* ed. Istvan Hont and Michael Ignatieff (Cambridge: Cambridge University Press, 1983), 139, 174.

commonwealth the civic liberty *to* participate will in the end become equally important and extensive.[10]

As Robertson reads him, then, Hume understood economic life as a means to participation in political life, which is of higher dignity. This is indeed the classical or Aristotelian view. But is it Hume's?

Pocock himself, writing in the same volume, presents a different view. He describes several paradigms which have been used to explain eighteenth-century Scottish thought (the "alternative paradigms" are "civic humanism, Addisonian morality, and natural jurisprudence"),[11] and although he gives no definitive statement of his own view, Pocock more than Robertson sees a tension between virtue and commerce.[12] He seems to lean toward a combination of the second and third paradigms, viewing Scottish thought as "a response to the civic humanist paradigm." This, he writes, "presents the Scottish Enlightenment as directed less against the Christians than against the ancients. It replaced the *polis* by politeness, the *oikos*, by the economy."[13] According to Pocock, this approach challenges conventional wisdom: "Since it presents the ideal of republican virtue as an ideological assault on the Whig regime, it presents Scottish social theory as the latter's ideological defense; from which it follows that the delineation of commercial society was not a criticism of aristocracy, but a vindication of it in its Whig form."[14] Although Pocock does not appear to endorse this view wholeheartedly, he observes that it "encourages us to look questioningly on the convention that the ideology of commerce sprang from the political and epistemological individualism of Hobbes and Locke."[15]

10. Hont and Ignatieff, *Wealth and Virtue*, 175.

11. J. G. A. Pocock, "Cambridge Paradigms and Scotch Philosophers: A Study of the Relations Between the Civic Humanist and the Civil Jurisprudential Interpretation of Eighteenth-Century Social Thought," in Hont and Ignatieff, *Wealth and Virtue*, 251.

12. Ibid., 252.

13. Ibid., 242.

14. Ibid., 243.

15. Ibid.

There is something to be said for each of these views, but it seems to me that reading Hume in this way leads us, in the end, to miss the forest for the trees. My purpose here is to give at least a sketch of the forest. I believe that Hume's political economy essays, indeed his writings altogether, present a subtle and complex argument against what could be called "the primacy of the political," a primacy which was at the core of not only classical republicanism but also, with qualifications, of ancient or classical political philosophy (which in other respects was often opposed to classical political practice).[16] In this denigration of the political life, Hume seems to me to be thoroughly modern and to agree in important respects with Hobbes and Locke with whom in some other ways Hume had important disagreements (above all epistemologically). If my assessment is correct, it is not too much to say that Hume's political economy essays[17] presented a set of arguments which were indispensable in tipping the scale toward Hobbes and Locke in the quarrel between the ancients and the moderns.

One final word on the historiographical issues surrounding Pocock's interpretation. One learns with some surprise that, according to Pocock, "historians are trained to think in linear, progressive and quasidialectical patterns, in which the movement is 'from' one state of affairs 'to' another." As a consequence "they are disposed to think in terms of one reigning paradigm at a time. . . . But the civic humanist paradigm, whose rise as a tool of historical explanation we have been exploring here, encourages us to think of the civic and commercial ideologies as struggling with one another at least down to the lifetimes of Adam Smith and John Millar."[18] Without presuming to comment on how historians are educated, we may observe that perhaps in one respect there is an advantage in studying political philosophy the old-fashioned way: students of political philosophy would be surprised to find any age (at least one where philosophical questioning

16. For an excellent and thorough discussion of this see Paul Rahe, *Republics Ancient and Modern: Classical Republicanism and the American Revolution* (Chapel Hill: University of North Carolina Press, 1992), 364–98 and passim.

17. This means primarily the first ten essays published under the title "Political Discourses" in 1752 together with the essay "Of the Jealousy of Trade" which was written in 1758 and later added to the original (1752) collection.

18. Pocock, "Cambridge Paradigms," 244.

goes on) where a paradigm rules without challenge. It should be no surprise that the civic and commercial "ideologies" could coexist in tension with each other; it would be surprising if they did *not* and not only during the lifetimes of Smith and Millar. There were proponents of both ways of life in Plato's time as there were in the eighteenth century and indeed are today. It seems to me that the very historiography we are concerned with discloses this quite clearly. There are many who dislike and oppose liberal commercial social order today, and not coincidentally they call for more public spiritedness, more sacrifice (higher taxes), more virtue, and less selfishness. Their catalogue of evils (materialism, luxury, self-indulgence, etc.) cannot help but remind us of what the opponents of commercial society in Hume's day warned against. The controversy we are considering—whether we see it as a clash of paradigms or simply as different conceptions of the good for man and society—played a large role in the eighteenth century, partly because it lies near the heart of the challenge posed by early modern thinkers to the understanding of human nature and political life which had been regnant for nearly two thousand years. In the next section I turn to a sketch of the classical formulation of the issue of politics versus commerce, or virtue versus acquisitiveness.

2. CLASSICAL REPUBLICS AND COMMERCE

Civic humanism is generally equated with the ideals of classical republicanism, which means above all the ideals of the most celebrated republics of antiquity, Sparta and Rome. The ancient political philosophers were in some respects critical of ancient political practice, but it is not difficult to show that, in respect to the denigration of commerce, the philosophers not only agreed with political practice but offered thoughtful justifications of what might otherwise seem to have been only the prejudices of the aristocracy. Thus we can learn more from the philosophers about this aspect of the classical republic than from the record of their institutions and practices alone. We are considering—when we consider commerce or trade or economics— the "low things," and although philosophers and statesmen or gentlemen might have disagreed about what is highest, there was general agreement about the lower part of the ranking of the human goods.

That the concern with politics, ruling, and honor—characteristic of the aristocratic class or gentlemen of the classical republics—is higher and more humanly fulfilling than a concern with trade or commerce seems to have been universally accepted by the ancients.[19] Plato's Socrates does not hesitate to tell his companions in *Republic* that wealth "produces luxury, idleness, and innovation"; even with regard to craftsmen, wealth (along with poverty) is said to "corrupt them so as to make them bad" (*Republic*, 422a1–2, 421d2).[20] Socrates and his codesigners of the city in speech sneer at the idea of even attending to the details of "that market business—the contracts individuals make with one another in the market, and . . . any market, town, or harbor regulations, or anything else of the kind. Shall we bring ourselves to set down laws for any of these things?" Socrates asks, only to be answered that "it isn't worthwhile . . . to dictate to gentlemen" (ibid.).

The ancient thinkers were nonetheless aware, of course, that most people do not share the elevated views characteristic of the gentleman. Indeed the overwhelming power or attraction of the objects of the lower desires were readily acknowledged, and precisely this fact seems to have been a major part of the justification for an aristocratic regime: the classical thinkers favored aristocracy *because* it would help to draw the attention of most or some men to higher things than commerce and the pursuit of wealth. On the other hand Aristotle, who surely had his feet on the ground even as a philosopher, recognized that wealth was not thought to be "the good and happiness" even by the vulgar: "the common run of people and the most vulgar" identify the good and happiness with "pleasure, and for that reason are satisfied with a life of enjoyment. For the most notable kinds of life are

19. The cardinal principle of classical republicanism is well stated by Pocock: "the ancient belief that the fulfillment of man's life was to be found in political association" (J. G. A. Pocock, "Between Machiavelli and Hume: Gibbon as Civic Humanist and Philosophical Historian" in *Edward Gibbon and the Decline and Fall of the Roman Empire*, ed. G. W. Bowersock and John Clive [Cambridge, Mass.: 1977], 104). As Aristotle expressed it, "man is by nature a *polis* animal" (*Politics*, bk. 1, ch. 2: 1253a3; my translation). Since the nature of a thing can be seen only in its completion or perfection (its *telos* or end), this amounts to the belief than anyone who is not fortunate enough to be active in a *polis* or political association cannot be said to live as a full human being.

20. Quotations are from Plato, *The Republic*, trans. Allan Bloom (New York: Basic Books, 1968).

three: the life just mentioned, the political life, and the contemplative life" (*Nicomachean Ethics,* 1095b16–20). Whatever the merits of the latter two alternatives, Aristotle makes very clear his judgment of the first. "The common run of people, as we saw, betray their utter slavishness in their preference for a life suitable to cattle" (1095b19–20), although even for them "wealth is not the good . . . for it is only useful as a means to something else" (1096a7–9). The love of gain, then, is really a form of love of pleasure—and this will be important when we consider Hume's economic psychology below.

The ancient thinkers were also alive to the connection between commerce and character. This is perhaps most succinctly expressed in Socrates' conversation with Cephalus in *Republic I,* when Socrates asks the old gentleman how he came by his wealth. Upon learning that it was mostly inherited, the philosopher responds, "the reason I asked, you see, . . . is that to me you didn't seem overly fond of money. For the most part, those who do not make money themselves are that way. Those who do make it are twice as attached to it as the others" (330b8–c3). In fact, he adds, those who make money are "hard even to be with because they are willing to praise nothing but wealth" (330c6–7). Ancient philosophers believed that the souls of merchants or traders were not suitable for political life; one could not expect in them the largeness of vision, the understanding of nonpecuniary motives, necessary for ordering the life of the city. A city or *polis* is not merely "an association for residence on a common site, or for the sake of preventing mutual injustice and easing exchange. These are indeed conditions which must be present before a *polis* can exist; but the presence of all these conditions is not enough, in itself, to constitute a *polis*" (Aristotle, *Politics,* 1280b30–34).

For the classical thinkers, then, (1) there is a ranking of the goods human beings seek, and the pursuit of wealth through commerce ranks low; (2) the appreciation of this principle is unfortunately confined to a few, generally wellborn or perhaps of philosophic disposition. This is a fact with political implications. And (3) there is an unavoidable connection between commercial pursuits and the souls or characters of those who are preoccupied with them. From these three principles or tenets it follows that a well-ordered city will enact restrictions to prevent commercial men from engaging in political activity or ruling.[21] It is also important, in the better sort of political order, to make sure economic activity is not considered honorable. (Hume, as we shall see, recognized this attitude as characteristic of monarchies and thought it harmful to economic progress.)

One of the most careful analyses of the place of economics in human life and perhaps the one with the most enduring legacy is Aristotle's account of the two kinds of acquisition in the first book of his *Politics*. That treatment is important here because the distinction Aristotle drew between natural and unnatural acquisition became the basis for condemning a certain kind of economic activity that I will call arbitrage. The belief that there is something objectionable about such activity has persisted for more than two thousand years; Hume's political economy sought to overcome the opprobrium attached to what Aristotle called unnatural acquisition.

The first book of Aristotle's *Politics* is devoted to subpolitical matters, including household management generally (and the unattractive issue of slavery). One subpolitical matter is the "business of acquiring goods" (*chrematismos*). "One kind of acquisitive expertise (*chrematistikê*), then, is by nature a part of expertise in household management (*oikonómia*)," Aristotle concludes approvingly. This is the art of acquiring what Aristotle calls "genuine wealth," which means "those goods a store of which is both necessary for life and useful for partnership in a city or a household" (1256b26–29). The key words here are "necessary" and "useful," since Aristotle teaches that such acquisition must aim only at "self-sufficiency." There is a natural limit or "boundary" to such acquisition, "just as in the other arts; for there is no art that has an instrument that is without limit either in number or in size, and wealth is the multitude of instruments belonging to expert household managers and political [rulers]" (1256b33–37). One with a proper understanding of economic affairs, then—even a gentleman—knows that the acquisition of wealth is necessary, that it may involve trade (even exchange using money or currency), but that when pursued naturally it is a bounded or limited activity.

21. For example, "In Thebes there used to be a law that one who had not abstained from the market for ten years could not share in office," says Aristotle, and "the best city will not make a vulgar person a citizen" (*Politics,* 1278a20–25, 1278a7–8).

In the next chapter Aristotle continues: "But there is another type of acquisitive expertise that they particularly call—and justifiably so—expertise in business, on account of which there is held to be no limit to wealth and possessions" (1256b40–1257a2). And this kind of acquisition or business is by most people confused with the first kind, notwithstanding the fact that "the one is by nature, while the other is not by nature but arises through a certain experience and art." The difference can be seen most clearly, according to Aristotle, if we "take the following as our beginning. Every possession has a double use. Both of these uses belong to it as such, but not in the same way, the one being proper and the other not proper to the thing" (1257a6–8). What follows is a lucid account of the distinction between use-value and exchange-value, as drawn later by Adam Smith and Karl Marx. Aristotle seems to say that exchange is perfectly natural if you exchange for some necessary object, that is, if you barter. But the invention of money—at first only a convenience because "the things necessary by nature are not in each case easily portable"—led to the second, unnatural kind of acquisition. "Once a supply of money came into being as a result of such necessary exchange, then, the other kind of expertise in business arose—that is, commerce" (1257a42–b2). At first this was probably quite simple, but "later through experience it became more a matter of art—[the art of discerning] what and how to exchange in order to make the greatest profit" (1257b3–5). Commerce and maximizing profit on this view should be regarded as not merely low, but unnatural (some things are low even though natural, that is, necessary or appropriate, for human beings).

Now if Aristotle means only that we should remember that wealth and material things are not the only important things in life, his counsel is obviously quite sensible. But something else lurks here. The enduring legacy of these passages (and they are not untypical of classical philosophy, indeed of classical poetry and history) was, in the West at least, the view that economic activity as such—commerce or the acquisition of wealth—is not merely low; it is unnatural, a perversion of nature, and unworthy of a decent human being. (It is worth noting that the formulation is in terms of wealth *acquisition*, not wealth *generation*—as if the wealth already exists somewhere, and needs only to be acquired in what thus must amount to a zero-sum game. More on this below.) Nobel laureate Harry Markowitz told a story which captures nicely the attitude:

> A few years ago a friend asked me to have dinner with him and a Russian emigré mathematician. I was disturbed to hear the mathematician predict that the Gorbachev reforms would not succeed. "The basic problem is the Russian people's attitude toward profit," he explained. "If there are goods in one place that are needed someplace else and someone makes a profit moving these goods from the one place to the other, he is considered greedy and evil."[22]

If arbitrage is making a profit by buying and selling in view of price discrepancies (which is what "moving goods from where they are to where they are needed" means), Aristotle's condemnation of unnatural acquisition seems to be echoed very precisely in the Russian condemnation of arbitrage.[23] The attitude toward commerce here is connected to a variety of other conceptions (or misconceptions): the doctrine of just price and the "natural" value of things, the idea that wealth is acquired rather than generated, the notion that money is wealth, and so forth. In his political economy essays, Hume attempted to rethink some of these matters and to put us right about them.

3. THE LIMITS OF THE POLITICAL

It is a commonplace that political economy developed only in modern times (after 1650, if Hume's remark quoted above is accurate). The elevation of trade to "an affair of state," however, can be viewed from a different angle. Perhaps it would be better to describe the change as the devaluation of politics and the political rather than the elevation of trade. At least in a general sense this seems obvious

22. Harry M. Markowitz, "Markets and Morality, Or Arbitragers Get No Respect," *Wall Street Journal*, May 14, 1991, A16.

23. Markowitz makes explicit the commonsense observation that maximizing well-being is not the same as maximizing wealth. "I believe that most people find that once some moderate needs for food and shelter are satisfied, it depends more on how you spend your time than on how much money you make." If this is all Aristotle meant, who could disagree? But unlike Aristotle, Markowitz seems to believe that a commercial life, which accumulates (generates?) wealth, can be very satisfying so long as one finds "time for other interests" (ibid).

and undeniable. Hobbes was perhaps the first to articulate the new understanding of the place of politics, captured some eighty years later in Pope's famous lines from the *Essay on Man:* "For forms of government let fools contest; Whate'er is best administered is best."[24] This amounts to an emphatic rejection of the core of ancient political science which was the study of regimes, the various constitutions or forms of government, and the types of character or soul they engender or depend on. Curiously enough the ground of that wholesale rejection of Aristotelian political science was a deeper agreement with Aristotle about human nature: Hobbes agreed with the ancients that most people, left to themselves, will pursue prosperity, wealth, well-being, or "commodious living." The difference was that Hobbes was prepared to let them do so rather than try to direct political life to higher aims. On Hobbes's view, the political order will be more stable (peaceful) if it is grounded solidly on the common, indeed nearly universal, human desire for security and prosperity. If the political order can be understood as merely a means to security and prosperity rather than virtue (or salvation or empire), no shaping of souls or characters need occur, because the shape most are already in (as even Aristotle agreed) is perfectly acceptable. Of course this amounts to an enormous demotion of politics, now to be seen as merely instrumental, as something we engage in only to satisfy what Aristotle would have said are our lowest, most animal needs.

I rehearse these matters of common knowledge only to prepare the ground for an argument about the significance of Hume's political economy. In the century after Hobbes's masterpiece was published, the scene of British political thought was of course enormously complicated, as Pocock and others have ably and abundantly demonstrated. Nevertheless it is possible to say that the central and defining issue was the great contest known as the quarrel between the ancients and the moderns, that is, between the principles of classical political science and political practice on the one hand and the radically new

---

24. Hume cites this dictum in order to take issue with it at the beginning of one of his early essays ("That Politics May Be Reduced to a Science"), *Essays*, 14. Obviously Hume is not of one mind with Hobbes on the issue of regimes (see below, pp. 331–33).

vision of human nature and politics which issued from thinkers as diverse as Bacon, Descartes, Hobbes, Spinoza, Locke, and Defoe on the other. At the center of that controversy, I believe, was the question of the place and purpose of politics itself. It is to this issue that Hume speaks in the essays on political economy. Although he addresses the large issue only indirectly in the course of examining topics such as taxes, interest, money, luxury, and the relation of commerce to national power, Hume supplies a set of arguments critical in overcoming the lingering traces of the classical view of politics.

A good point of departure is an issue on which we find Hume in profound agreement with the ancient writers: the importance of regimes. Hume rejects Pope's dictum that forms of government don't matter because "whate'er is best administered is best" (this presumably rests on the Hobbesian premise that all legitimate governments are trying to do precisely the same things: to provide security and tranquillity so that individuals can pursue their own private ends). One of the recurring themes in his essays, even in the early essays which preceded the *Political Discourses* by a decade, is the fundamental difference between monarchies and republics (Hume saw the British government as falling somewhere in between). In "Of Civil Liberty" Hume reveals his agreement with the ancients most clearly. He speaks there of his reason for thinking that "there is something hurtful to commerce inherent in the very nature of absolute government, and inseparable from it."[25] Hume's contemporaries who detected in monarchies an antipathy to commerce took the reason to be the insecurity of property in absolute governments, but he disagrees. "Private property seems to me almost as secure in a civilized EUROPEAN monarchy, as in a republic."[26] And human avarice, "the spur of industry," is so nearly universal a passion that "it is not likely to be scared by an imaginary danger," so its absence cannot explain the fact that commerce is less likely to flourish in a monarchy. "Commerce, therefore, in my opinion, is apt to decay in absolute governments, not because it is less *secure,* but because it is less *honourable.*" The principle of the regime (in this case honor, as Montesquieu had observed), then, does have a powerful effect on the way of

25. Hume, *Essays,* 92.
26. Ibid., 92–93.

life of subjects or citizens. In a monarchy "birth, titles, and place must be honoured above industry and riches," and "while these notions prevail, all the considerable traders will be tempted to throw up their commerce, in order to purchase some of these employments, to which privileges and honours are annexed."[27] Here Hume seems in complete agreement with Aristotle on the close connection between the regime (what is honored or thought important) and the way of life of a people.

But when we come to the issue of which sort of regime is preferable, Hume is entirely on the side of the moderns. There is nothing in Hume's writings to suggest that he believed human beings are not fully human unless they engage in politics or are interested in political considerations. Although man is a social creature, the social needs can be fulfilled in a variety of ways including even economic activity. If we take the core of Hobbes's and Locke's thought to have been not "the rigorous individualism of self-interest" (Pocock) but the view that political life is merely a means to satisfy prepolitical needs (and therefore not necessary to human fulfillment), Hume is in the same camp with his seventeenth-century predecessors. But Hobbes's and Locke's great political masterpieces had not carried the day against the classical view, and Hume undertook the task of completing what they had begun. We can begin to appreciate the significance of his political economy only when we get this issue in proper perspective. Perhaps this is only another way of saying that the historians are surely correct who have demonstrated how widely accepted was the paradigm of classical republicanism (in 1750). They are mistaken only in seeing Hume as endorsing the ancient political understanding, or indeed as ambivalent about it.

4. CIVIC GREATNESS, LUXURY, AND MANNERS

Hume published his first volume of essays in 1741, and a second volume appeared in 1742. Ten years later he issued a new collection called *Political Discourses*. It is these which constitute the heart of Hume's political economy, though the full story would need to include important passages from his masterwork, the *History of England*. I have suggested that Hume's approval of the kind of society he saw emerg-

27. Ibid., 93.

ing in England—a commercial republic—places him on the side of his early modern predecessors in the debate with the ancients over the priority of politics. But in Hume's century, a lingering nostalgia for the grandeur of classical republics was quite strong, and he undertook to consider the basis of the various antipathies to commercial society. We find him in the political economy essays addressing (and refuting) claims which one might call relics of the classical outlook, such as the belief that commerce draws wealth away from the public treasury and thus weakens the state, or that luxury is itself vicious and should be suppressed in any decent political order. Hume lays out a subtle but compelling account of human psychology in relation to what he calls the "manners and customs" of peoples to explain his qualified endorsement of the large modern commercial republic in which politics is merely instrumental and the center of life need not be located in the public realm.

Let us begin by sketching Hume's arguments in the first few political economy essays. We will find they address directly the kinds of anxieties voiced about commerce by a wide spectrum of statesmen and political pamphleteers in the middle of the eighteenth century, both in Britain and in her American colonies. First, according to Hume, the ancient republics were not genuinely free nor did their institutions and practices accord with human nature. Thus the classical republics are not attractive models for a free political order. Second, such republics did indeed depend on the suppression of trade, commerce, and manufactures, but the usual consequence of such suppression is not a robust *polis* with a virtuous citizenry but rather indolence and poverty.[28] Third, although where trade and commerce flourish one generally finds luxury, luxury is not itself the source of political corruption, as is often thought, but a spur to industry (thus luxury enhances the power of the state or sovereign). The explanation of this phenomenon, which involves the psychological disposition to be active, points in turn to

28. There is a close parallel between this claim and Locke's account of how in the state of nature, before the invention of money, there is no way for men to escape the grinding poverty and insecurity of hand-to-mouth existence. See ch. 5 of Locke's *Second Treatise* and John Danford, *Roots of Freedom* (Wilmington, Del.: ISI Books, 2000), 92–99.

the benefits of a commercial as opposed to an aristocratic order of landed wealth. Fourth and finally, political men—those who exalt political action as rewarding in itself—overstate the effectiveness of political agency. Economic matters in particular are too complicated to be managed or directed by human wisdom, no matter how clear the purpose or how firm the resolve of the manager. And notwithstanding its pretensions, political activity is not directive anyway since it consists for the most part in factious struggle, for example among "zealots" who "kindle up the passions of their partizans, and under pretence of public good, pursue the interests and ends of their particular faction."[29] Hume notes that "the ages of greatest public spirit are not always most eminent for private virtue," and in the end finds private virtue more natural and thus more to be relied on in human institutions.[30]

The first of the political economy essays, "Of Commerce," contains Hume's most direct consideration of classical republicanism, along with "Of the Populousness of Ancient Nations" which concludes the set. He approaches the theme by way of an inquiry concerning the foundation of "the greatness of the state" by examining the apparent tension or "opposition between the greatness of the state and the happiness of the subject," an opposition not "merely chimerical" but "founded on history and experience." The relevant history is the history of the two greatest of the ancient republics, Sparta and Rome. Hume does not doubt the greatness of these two republics, and in fact he appears to admit that those who see a danger in commerce are correct. "The republic of SPARTA was certainly more powerful than any state now in the world, consisting of an equal number of people; and this was owing entirely to the want of commerce and luxury."[31] But Hume is at pains to show that it would not be possible for modern sovereigns to "return to the maxims of ancient policy," not least

---

29. The formulation comes from one of Hume's earliest essays, "That Politics May Be Reduced to a Science," in *Essays*, 27.

30. Ibid., 25. This receives its most extensive treatment in Hume's treatise on morals, the *Enquiry Concerning the Principles of Morals* (Oxford: Oxford University Press, 1975). See Danford, *David Hume and the Problem of Reason* (New Haven: Yale University Press, 1990), ch. 8.

31. Hume, *Essays*, 257.

because of the system of slavery Hume shows ancient policy to have rested upon. Considered in light of a broad historical survey, "ancient policy was violent, and contrary to the more natural and usual course of things." The freedom of the ancient republics was not freedom for the citizens themselves as individuals; it was only freedom from foreign domination. "A continuall succession of wars makes every citizen a soldier: He takes the field in his turn: And during his service he is chiefly maintained by himself. This service is indeed equivalent to a heavy tax; yet is it less felt by a people addicted to arms, who fight for honour and revenge more than pay, and are unacquainted with gain and industry as well as pleasure" (259).

Hume believed that only very special circumstances made it possible for Sparta and Rome to flourish by the suppression of trade and commerce. The more general effect of "the want of trade and manufactures" is simply poverty and indolence, which are "the consequences of sloth and barbarity" (260). The ancient republics did not, as many writers claimed, decline because of the spread of commerce and luxury. "It would be easy to prove, that these writers mistook the cause of the disorders in the ROMAN state, and ascribed to luxury and the arts, what really proceeded from an ill modelled government, and the unlimited extent of conquests. Refinement on the pleasures and conveniencies of life has no natural tendency to beget venality and corruption" (276). The explanation for this claim is one of the key insights of Hume's political economy:

> The value, which all men put upon any particular pleasure, depends on comparison and experience; nor is a porter less greedy of money, which he spends on bacon and brandy, than a courtier, who purchases champagne and ortolans. Riches are valuable at all times, and to all men; because they always purchase pleasures, such as men are accustomed to, and desire: Nor can any thing restrain or regulate the love of money, but a sense of honour and virtue; which, if it be not nearly equal at all times, will naturally abound most in ages of knowledge and refinement. (276)

The second argument, then, is based on Hume's insight that at the most general level our genuine alternatives are societies which suppress commerce (and thereby condemn themselves to rustic poverty

and aristocratic extravagance), and those in which commerce flour-
ishes and produces luxury, which in turn stimulates most people to
productive labor.[32] Hume calls the latter, with his customary delicacy,
"ages of refinement," and insists they are "both the happiest and most
virtuous."[33]

Many others believed, however, that commerce is inimical to liberty
because they accepted what one might call the life-cycle theory of republican government, according to which only in the middle period
of a republic's life can citizens be free and the polity healthy and vigorous. As Richard Price observed in the year of the Declaration of Independence,

> Our American Colonies . . . have been for some time in the happi-
> est state of society, or in that middle state of civilization, between
> its first rude and its last refined and corrupt state. . . . The colonies
> consist only of a body of yeomanry supported by agriculture, and
> all independent and nearly on a level; . . . they must live at their
> ease and be free from those cares, oppressions, and diseases which
> depopulate and ravage luxurious states.[34]

Most desirable, in this view, is the middle stage of economic self-
sufficiency and virtuous liberty; this is, however, eventually and in-

---

32. Compare the pithy formulation of Edward Gibbon: speaking of the various refinements "of conveniency, of elegance, and of splendour" which "under
the odious name of luxury, have been severely arraigned by the moralists of every
age," Gibbon observes that "it might perhaps be more conducive to the virtue,
as well as happiness, of mankind, if all possessed the necessaries, and none the
superfluities, of life. But in the present imperfect condition of society, luxury,
though it may proceed from vice or folly, seems to be the only means that can
correct the unequal distribution of property. The diligent mechanic, and the
skilful artist, who have obtained no share in the division of the earth, receive a
voluntary tax from the possessors of land . . ." (Edward Gibbon, *The History of
the Decline and Fall of the Roman Empire,* ed. David Womersley [London: Penguin
Books, 1994], vol. 1, ch. 2, 80).

33. Hume, *Essays,* 269.

34. Richard Price, *Observations on the Nature of Civil Liberty* (London, 1776), 70.
An excellent discussion of this theme can be found in Drew McCoy, *The Elusive
Republic: Political Economy in Jeffersonian America* (Chapel Hill: University of North
Carolina Press, 1980; republished as a Norton paperback, 1982), 48–67.

evitably replaced by a corrupt phase of luxury and vice. The corrupt stage is associated with urbanization, manufacturing, and in general too much wealth.[35] James Madison expressed a similar view sixteen years later in one of his *National Gazette* essays, "Republican Distribution of Citizens." According to Madison, "the life of the husbandman is pre-eminently suited to the comfort and happiness of the individual. . . . *Competency* is more universally the lot of those who dwell in the country, when liberty is at the same time their lot. The extremes both of want and of waste have other abodes. 'Tis not the country that peoples either the Bridewells or the Bedlams. These mansions of wretchedness are tenanted from the distresses and vices of overgrown cities."[36] McCoy cites dozens of such passages (one example from Samuel Deane: "Continued prosperity is apt to bring political evils in its train; such as luxury and idleness, dissipation and extravagant expenses; which tend to, and end in, wretchedness and ruin").[37] Although in one case Hume uses language which seems to accept this,[38] he is without doubt arguing against the life-cycle view. In the passage just alluded to, for example, he suggests that the only time fancy has not confounded her wants with those of nature is "in the first and more uncultivated ages of any state," when "men, content with the produce of their own fields, or with those rude improvements which they themselves can work upon them, have little occasion for exchange, at least for money, . . . the common measure of exchange" (291). This is part of his larger argument that in "rude, uncultivated

35. See McCoy, *The Elusive Republic,* chs. 1 and 2.

36. From James Madison, *Writings,* edited by Jack N. Rackove for Library of America (New York: Literary Classics of the United States, 1999), 511–12.

37. Samuel Deane, *A Sermon Preached February 19th, 1795* (Portland, Mass.: 1795), quoted in McCoy, *The Elusive Republic,* 172.

38. Hume writes, "Ere fancy has confounded her wants with those of nature . . ." (*Essays,* 291), a passage which might be taken as a lament (in the vein of Rousseau) about the unnatural accretions to human needs caused by civilized or urbane life. But in the very sentence in which this phrase appears, Hume identifies the period of very simple wants as an age "the first and more uncultivated . . . of any state" and goes on to contrast "rude, uncultivated" ages with "times of industry and refinement" (291). There is no doubt about which Hume prefers or recommends.

ages," or when "men live in the ancient, simple manner" (293), they must necessarily be divided into two classes, a prodigal and extravagant landed gentry who consume their wealth in rustic hospitality, and a peasantry condemned, with no outlets for their energy or industry, to hardship at least, and probably to "sloth and an indifference to others."[39]

The chief problem centers on the misleading term "luxury." Hume understands that the notion of luxury is relative to time and place.

> Luxury is a word of an uncertain signification, and may be taken in a good as well as in a bad sense. In general, it means great refinement in the gratification of the senses; and any degree of it may be innocent or blameable, according to the age, or country, or condition of the person. The bounds between the virtue and the vice cannot here be exactly fixed, more than in other moral subjects. To imagine, that the gratifying of any sense, or the indulging of any delicacy in meat, drink, or apparel, is of itself a vice, can never enter into a head, that is not disordered by the frenzies of enthusiasm. . . . Indulgences are only vices, when they are pursued at the expense of some virtue, as liberality or charity; in like manner as they are follies, when for them a man ruins his fortune, and reduces himself to want and beggary.[40]

Without tracing the reasoning here, Hume's conclusion is that "Refinement on the pleasures and conveniencies of life has no natural tendency to beget venality and corruption. The value, which all men put upon any particular pleasure, depends on comparison and experience; nor is a porter less greedy of money, which he spends on bacon and brandy, than a courtier, who purchases champagne and

39. Ibid., 300–302, 280.

40. Ibid., 268–69. John Dickinson, author of *Letters from a Federal Farmer,* wrestles with the same issue. Speaking of what today we call demand elasticity, he admits that the terms "luxury" and "necessity" change with time: "This must be decided by the nature of the commodities and the purchasers demand for them. If they are mere luxuries, he is at liberty to do as he pleases, and if he buys, he does it voluntarily: But if they are absolute necessaries, *or conveniences which use and custom have made requisite for the comfort of life,* and which he is not permitted, by the power imposing the duty, to get elsewhere, there the seller has a plain advantage, and the buyer must pay the duty" (73–74; emphasis added).

ortolans. Riches are valuable at all times, and to all men" (276). Hume's understanding of this issue—if correct—means that Madison, Jefferson, Franklin, and others who decried the spread of luxury are thoroughly wrong.

The principle that "riches are valuable at all times, and to all men; because they always purchase pleasures, such as men are accustomed to, and desire" is at the core of another argument taken up by Hume in the third and fourth essays of the set ("Of Money" and "Of Interest"), which are normally read quite narrowly since they appear to be no more than careful examinations of widely held mercantilist prejudices (in the former case, that "any particular state is weak, though fertile, populous, and well cultivated, merely because it wants money" and in the latter that plenty of money leads to low interest rates).[41] In both cases Hume's approach is the same. He finds that the common misunderstanding results from regarding as a cause what is really only a "collateral effect: . . . a consequence is ascribed to plenty of money; though it be really owing to a change in the manners and customs of the people."[42] The deeper argument, then, rests on Hume's understanding of human nature and specifically his understanding of the effects of certain "manners and customs of the people." The basic principle is found in many of Hume's writings (here is his formulation from the fourth essay, "Of Interest"): "There is no craving or demand of the human mind more constant and insatiable than that for exercise and employment; and this desire seems the foundation of most of our passions and pursuits" (300).

This principle—the constant craving of the mind for exercise and employment—has enormous social and political implications which Hume simplifies here to make his point about the superiority of commercial societies. In the second essay, Hume suggests that "in rude unpolished nations, where the arts are neglected, all labour is bestowed on the cultivation of the ground; and the whole society is divided into two classes, proprietors of land, and their vassals or tenants" (277).

41. For excellent discussions of them in this light see Rotwein, *David Hume*, lx–lxxvi.

42. Hume, *Essays*, 294.

He characterizes these classes more specifically. "The latter are necessarily dependent, and fitted for slavery and subjection; especially where they possess no riches, and are not valued for their knowledge in agriculture; as must always be the case where the arts are neglected." The landed proprietors, on the other hand, will "erect themselves into petty tyrants," and Hume thinks it most likely something like a feudal order will emerge, where the aristocracy submits to a master "for the sake of peace and order." Now the consistent lesson (in history) of societies based on landed wealth is that those with wealth dissipate it on frivolities.

> As the spending of a settled revenue is a way of life entirely without occupation; men have so much need of somewhat to fix and engage them, that pleasures, such as they are, will be the pursuit of the greater part of the landholders, and the prodigals among them will always be more numerous than the misers. In a state, therefore, where there is nothing but a landed interest, as there is little frugality, the borrowers must be very numerous, and the rate of interest must hold proportion to it. The difference depends not on the quantity of money, but on the habits and manners which prevail. (298)

Something quite different happens when commerce and trade disrupt the stability of a landed aristocracy, as they inevitably do. In a stable order of landed property, most men are "content with the produce of their own fields, or with those rude improvements which they themselves can work upon them" (291). Thus they have "little occasion for exchange, at least for money." The result is largely a sort of barter economy. "The wool of the farmer's own flock, spun in his own family, and wrought by a neighboring weaver, who receives his payment in corn or wool, suffices for furniture and cloathing." Even the landlord himself, "dwelling in the neighbourhood, is content to receive his rent in the commodities raised by the farmer." But "after men begin to refine on all these enjoyments, and live not always at home, nor are content with what can be raised in their neighbourhood, there is more exchange and commerce of all kinds" (291). Obviously there is nothing mysterious in this, but the economic effects are dramatic. In the stable landed order, as we have seen, the tendency on the part of those with wealth is toward prodigality ("deprive a man of all business and serious occupation, he runs restless from one amusement to another; and the weight and oppression which he feels from idleness is so great, that he forgets the ruin which must follow from his immoderate expenses" [300–301]).

But when commerce enters the picture, the life of the idle landlord is transformed.

> Give him a more harmless way of employing his mind or body, he is satisfied, and feels no longer that insatiable thirst after pleasure. But if the employment be lucrative, especially if the profit be attached to every particular exertion of industry, he has gain so often in his eye, that he acquires, by degrees, a passion for it, and knows no such pleasure as that of seeing the daily encrease of his fortune. And this is the reason why trade encreases frugality, and why, among merchants, there is the same overplus of misers above prodigals, as, among the possessors of land, there is the contrary. (301)

The lesson is that trade and commerce, where they are permitted to flourish, produce not luxury (or not only luxury) but industry and frugality. One could say that what begins as a desire for pleasure of activity is converted into a narrower kind of activity: "It is an infallible consequence of all industrious professions, to beget frugality, and make the love of gain prevail over the love of pleasure."[43] As Hume sums up his argument, "thus an encrease of commerce, by a necessary consequence, raises a greater number of lenders, and by that means produces lowness of interest" (302).

5. STABILITY, INNOVATION, AND THE LIMITS OF POLITICS

In one of the best known of his *National Gazette* essays, "Fashion," James Madison laments that mere changes in the taste of consumers can result in thousands of workers being thrown out of work.

43. Ibid., 301. It is instructive to compare Hume's reasoning with the words of the Platonic Socrates in *Republic I* (at 330b8–c3), quoted above (see p. 327). As noted earlier, Hume agrees with the ancients about the psychology associated with commerce but draws contrary political conclusions.

He has learned, he writes, that "the BUCKLE MANUFACTURERS of Birmingham, Wassal, Wolverhampton, and their environs," who employ "more than TWENTY THOUSAND persons," are fallen on hard times, and of that number many, "in consequence of the prevailing fashion of SHOESTRINGS & SLIPPERS, are at present without employ, almost destitute of bread, and exposed to the horrors of want at the most inclement season."[44] This leads Madison to conclude that "the most precarious of all occupations which give bread to the industrious, are those depending on mere fashion, which generally changes so suddenly, and often so considerably, as to throw whole bodies of people out of employment."

> *Twenty Thousand* persons are to get or go without their bread, as a wanton youth, may fancy to wear his shoes with or without straps, or to fasten his straps with strings or with buckles. Can any despotism be more cruel than a situation, in which the existence of thousands depends on one will, and that will on the most slight and fickle of all motives, a mere whim of the imagination.

One might quibble about the use of the word despotism, but Madison's sentiment is familiar in all ages. Changes in economic arrangements often result in hardship and are almost always disturbing. It is always easier to see the costs of change (which are relatively immediate) than the benefits, which take time to emerge. Hence we are tempted to regard change itself as the problem.

Hume would have us ask, first, what are the genuine alternatives here? Would not the elimination of innovation—by the name of fashion or any other—require us to extinguish liberty? The only real alternative to the situation Madison deplores would be somehow to freeze all economic development or change (perhaps by rigorous sumptuary laws, which however are always unavailing) and then to live in a state of rude simplicity, a state which has its own drawbacks. As Hume says in a different context, "that provisions and labour should become dear by the encrease of trade and money, is, in many respects, an inconvenience; but an inconvenience that is unavoidable, and the effect of that public wealth and prosperity which are the end of all our

44. James Madison, *Writings*, 513.

wishes."[45] Moreover, as Hume points out, all economic activity is subject to changes and shocks and dislocations, and that economy is best able to cope with them which is wealthy and diversified. As Hume puts it, once a nation has developed commercially, it "may lose most of its foreign trade, and yet continue a great and powerful people. If strangers will not take any particular commodity of ours, we must cease to labour in it. The same hands will turn themselves towards some refinement in other commodities, which may be wanted at home. *And there must always be materials for them to work upon; till every person in the state, who possesses riches, enjoys as great plenty of home commodities, and those in as great perfection, as he desires;* WHICH CAN NEVER POSSIBLY HAPPEN" (264; emphasis added). In a later passage, Hume addresses the issue even more directly, acknowledging that "any people is happier who possess a variety of manufactures, than if they enjoyed one single great manufacture, in which they are all employed. Their situation is less precarious; and they will feel less sensibly those revolutions and uncertainties, to which every particular branch of commerce will always be exposed" (330).

The last of Hume's insights demanding our attention here is one scattered widely throughout Hume's later writings, including especially the *The History of England.* One of the clearest formulations is in the eighth and briefest of the political economy essays, "Of Taxes." "I shall conclude this subject with observing, that we have, with regard to taxes, an instance of what frequently happens in political institutions, that the consequences of things are diametrically opposite to what we should expect on the first appearance" (347). This happens in political matters, as we learn from the first essay, because they are of awesome complexity, so that *general* reasonings about them are rarely accurate. Most people judge tolerably well about *particulars,* but

> they cannot enlarge their view to those universal propositions, which comprehend under them an infinite number of individuals. . . . Their eye is confounded with such an extensive prospect; and the conclusions, derived from it, even though clearly expressed, seem intricate and obscure. But however intricate they may seem,

45. Hume, *Essays,* 284.

it is certain, that general principles, if just and sound, must always prevail in the general course of things, though they may fail in particular cases; and it is the chief business of philosophers to regard the general course of things.[46]

Hume is attempting in his political economy to "regard the general course of things," and he hopes to explain, for example, why Sparta and Rome are poor models because they are rare exceptions to the "general course of things," according to which "industry and arts and trade encrease the power of the sovereign as well as the happiness of the subjects" (260).

As we learn from *The History of England,* the general principles of commerce or political economy are even more complex and less easy to grasp than those of "the police of the kingdom." In the reign of Henry VII, Hume observes, regulations regarding police were "contrived with much better judgment" than were those affecting commerce. "The more simple ideas of order and equity are sufficient to guide a legislator in everything that regards the internal administration of justice: But the principles of commerce are much more complicated, and require long experience and deep reflection to be well understood in any state. The real consequence of a law or practice is there often contrary to first appearances."[47] When we consider political economy, then, our task is more difficult than one might expect, and the tendency to magnify the importance of politics is especially dangerous. This renders the political science of the ancients not only useless (in part) but dangerous for us. The exaltation of politics and ruling is fraught with problems, and Hume is happy to remind us of the inadequacy of that view. Even if political agency is effective in small, simple societies, in a complex commercial republic the sovereign power ought to be diffident about what sovereign power can accomplish.

Most political activity, as Hume saw it around him, is the pursuit of factious interests under the guise of promoting the public good, as we

46. From the introductory section to the whole set of (1752) political economy essays, in Hume, *Essays,* 254.

47. David Hume, *The History of England, from the Invasion of Julius Caesar to the Revolution in 1688* (Indianapolis: Liberty Fund, 1983), 3:74.

noted above. He concluded an early essay about the politics of court and country in the time of Walpole with an admonition to both sides of factional disputes to moderate their zeal. If politics is mostly about low matters (not virtue, but interests), surely the rhetoric of patriotic defense of the constitution is out of place:

> I would employ the same topics to moderate the zeal of those who defend the minister. *Is our constitution so excellent?* Then a change of ministry can be no such dreadful event; since it is essential to such a constitution, in every ministry, both to preserve itself from violation, and to prevent all enormities in the administration. *Is our constitution very bad?* Then so extraordinary a jealousy and apprehension, on account of changes, is ill placed; and a man should no more be anxious in this case, than a husband, who had married a woman from the stews, should be watchful to prevent her infidelity. Public affairs, in such a government, must necessarily go to confusion, by whatever hands they are conducted; and the zeal of *patriots* is in that case much less requisite than the patience and submission of *philosophers.*[48]

Hume's own temper was of course philosophic, and the imagery of this paragraph is suggestive of his view of politics, which sets Hume apart from his classical predecessors.[49] For Hume, private life and private virtues are not an unsatisfactory alternative to life on the public stage. To be fully human one does not need to live in a *polis;* indeed a commercial republic is preferable. Hume does caution that he "would not be understood to mean, that public affairs deserve no care and attention at all. Would men be moderate and consistent, their claims might be admitted; at least might be examined."[50] But moderation is more likely to be found in the kind of society to which Hobbes and

---

48. Hume, *Essays,* 30.

49. For additional evidence that Hume did not endorse "republican self-government," see Robert A. Manzer, "A Science of Politics: Hume, *The Federalist,* and the Politics of Constitutional Attachment," *American Journal of Political Science* 45, no. 3 (July 2001): esp. 513: "Despite all his work to cultivate public opinion, however, Hume did not embrace republican self-government."

50. Ibid.

Locke pointed the way than in Sparta or Rome or indeed Athens. Hume's rich, complex, and profound reflections on political economy were intended to persuade those with lingering nostalgia for the classical republics, or the ancient understanding called civic humanism, that modern commercial republican societies are superior.[51]

51. See also Arthur Herman, *How the Scots Invented the Modern World* (New York: Crown Publishing, 2001).

Scottish Thought and the American Revolution: Adam Ferguson's Response to Richard Price

When Richard Price's *Observations* were originally published at the beginning of February 1776, the colonies had not yet determined to declare independence from Great Britain although time appears to have been on the side of those supporting some declaration of colonial sovereignty. On November 29, 1775, the Continental Congress appointed a Committee of Secret Correspondence[1] charged with establishing diplomatic relations and seeking military aid from any of the European nations that might be friendly to the colonies, and on December 11, 1775, King George issued a royal proclamation declaring the American colonies beyond his protection and closing them to all trade and commerce. Of even greater impact was the publication in January 1776 of Thomas Paine's *Common Sense,* possibly the most effective political polemic ever written, which presented a vigorous argument for colonial independence and was to have a decisive effect on American sentiments. In inspired and electrifying language Paine showed that the cause of the colonists was the cause of all mankind and that nothing was gained from a continued connection to Great Britain.[2]

1. The Committee can justifiably be regarded as the earliest intelligence-gathering arm of the newly formed United States.

2. "O ye that love mankind! Ye that dare oppose, not only the tyranny, but the tyrant, stand forth! Every spot in the old world is overrun with oppression. Freedom hath been hunted around the globe. Asia and Africa have long expelled her. Europe regards her like a stranger, and England hath given her warning to depart. O! receive the fugitive and prepare in time an asylum for mankind. . . . We have in our power to begin the world over again. The birthday of a new world is at hand, and a race of men, perhaps as numerous as all Europe contain, are to receive their portion of freedom from the events of a few months. The Reflexion is awful—and in this point of view, How trifling, how ridiculous, do the little, paltry cavellings, of a few weak or interested men appear, when weighed against the business of the world." *Common Sense,* in Thomas Paine, *Collected Writings,* ed.

Paine's essay not only sold extensively in the colonies but was also for sale, as were a whole array of American publications, in the London bookshops.[3] In addition, there appear to be at least two editions published in Great Britain that year, one in London published by J. Almon and a second in Edinburgh and Stirling sold by Charles Elliot and by William Anderson.[4] But even had Paine remained unread in Britain, the wider importance of the events in America would not have been lost on the English radicals, such as Richard Price, who were keenly aware of the broader implications of the colonial struggle. In addition, Paine's emphasis on man's rational nature, on the notion of rights, and on political contract, all appealed to the radical Whigs, who saw echoed there their own notions regarding the basis of legitimate government. Price particularly was energized by what he regarded as a holy struggle against oppression and corruption then being staged in America.

Of the various supporters of the American cause in England, Richard Price proved to be one of the most articulate. Indeed, so highly was he regarded by his American contemporaries that in October 1778 the Continental Congress approved a motion that the honorable Benjamin Franklin, Arthur Lee, and John Adams, Esquires, or any one of them, be directed forthwith to apply to Dr. Price, and inform him, that it is the desire of Congress to consider him as a citizen of the United States; and to receive his assistance in regulating their finances. That if he shall think it expedient to remove, with his family, to America, and afford such assistance, a generous provision shall be made for requiting his services.[5]

Eric Foner (Library of America; New York: Literary Classics of the United States, 1995); 36, 52–53.

3. Colin Bonwick, *English Radicals and the American Revolution* (Chapel Hill: University of North Carolina Press, 1977), 38–40.

4. Both publications appear in the catalogues of the British Library and the Bodleian. The Edinburgh imprint carries the following statement on its title page: "To shew the real spirit and views of the colonies, or rather of their leaders in rebellion; which cannot fail to rouse the indignation of every Briton, without leaving them from henceforth a single advocate, who is not utterly lost to loyalty, to patriotism, and to common sense."

5. *Journals of the Continental Congress, 1774–1789,* ed. Worthington C. Ford

It is indicative of the regard in which he was held by the new nation that he was extended the privileges of citizenship and invited to settle there. Price's essay in support of the American colonies became for a time the focus on which debate over the colonial cause centered. Its sales in Britain were spectacular, in some ways mirroring the effect created by Paine's *Common Sense* in America.

At the time Price published his *Observations* in 1776, he had already gained a reputation as one of the most ardent defenders of civil and religious liberty and republican values in Great Britain. The son of a Congregationalist minister, Price was born in the parish of Llangeinor in Glamorgan, Wales, in 1723. At the age of seventeen, Price entered Coward's Academy in Tenter Ailey, Moorfields, where he studied under John Eames, a friend and disciple of Isaac Newton. It was doubtless while a student at the Academy that Price gained his lifelong interest in mathematics and his philosophical rationalism. While Price rejected his father's harsh Puritanism, he appears quite early in his education to have determined to prepare for the ministry and was ordained a Nonconformist minister in 1744. His church at Newington Green, a center of dissent for a number of years, soon became a magnet for reformers and radicals, among them Mary Wollstonecraft, John Howard, Benjamin Franklin, John Adams, and Adam Smith. Price's principal philosophical work, *A Review of the Principal Questions and Difficulties in Morals,* was published in 1758, and it was this work that resulted in his being awarded a Doctorate of Divinity by Marischal College, Aberdeen, in 1769. Price's "discourse on the love of our country," a ringing defense of the revolutionary events in France preached in November 1789, provided the immediate stimulus not only for Burke's *Reflections* but for a huge number of responses. In 1791, the year in which he died, Price became a founding member of the Unitarian Society.

The *Observations on the Nature of Civil Liberty, the Principles of Government, and the Justice and Policy of War with America,* prepared in the winter of 1775–76, made its appearance on February 8 and became an immediate success. Several thousand copies were sold within a few days of its publication, 60,000 copies by the close of 1776. The work ran

---

et al. (Washington, D.C.: Library of Congress, 1904–37), 12:984–85 (Tuesday, October 6, 1778).

into five editions within five weeks and into twelve editions within the year.[6] No one interested in the affairs of the Empire was ignorant of its contents. The essay prompted the Council of the City of London to award Price its highest honor, the Freedom of the City, for laying bare "those pure principles of which alone the supreme legislative authority of Great Britain over her colonies can be justly or beneficially maintained."[7] The essay was quickly republished across the Atlantic, with editions appearing in Boston, New York, Charleston, and Philadelphia.[8] And while its effect on the pro-independence forces was not nearly as great as was that of Paine's pamphlet, the *Observations* did contribute to the arsenal at the disposal of those seeking a separation from Great Britain.

Price's pamphlet was regarded as so significant a challenge both to the government's position on America and to the arguments put forward by those who accepted the authority of Parliament to tax the colonies that it gave birth to a profusion of responses. The government's policy was ardently defended by, among others, Josiah Tucker, John Fletcher, and the Methodist John Wesley.[9] Dr. John Shebbeare, who was regularly paid by the government to defend its positions and who had previously been pilloried for libel, penned one of the most scurrilous of the replies, while Burke's response was one of the mildest, calling for conciliation with the rebellious colonies while not repudiating the abhorrent Declaratory Act,[10] which had been enacted

6. Roland Thomas, *Richard Price: Philosopher and Apostle of Liberty* (Oxford: Oxford University Press, 1924), 74.

7. London's Roll of Fame, at the Guildhall Library, quoted in Thomas, *Richard Price*, 76.

8. "Preface," in Bernard Peach, ed., *Richard Price and the Ethical Foundations of the American Revolution* (Durham, N.C.: Duke University Press, 1979), 9.

9. Josiah Tucker, *A Series of Answers to Certain Popular Objections, Against Separating from the Rebellious Colonies, and Discarding Them Entirely* (Gloucester: R. Raikes, 1776); John Fletcher, *American Patriotism Farther Confronted with Reason, Scripture, and the Constitution* (Shrewsbury: J. Eddowes, 1776); John Wesley, *Some Observations on Liberty, Occasioned by a Late Tract* (London: R. Hawes, 1776).

10. The Act, passed in March 1766, declared that the colonies in America "have been, are, and of right ought to be, subordinate unto, and dependent upon the imperial crown and parliament of Great Britain; and that the King's majesty, by and with the advice and consent of the lords spiritual and tempo-

during the administration of the Marquis of Rockingham with whom Burke was associated.[11]

One of the most measured of the published rebuttals was that written by Adam Ferguson, the Scottish philosopher and professor of pneumatics and moral philosophy at the University of Edinburgh. Ferguson's sympathies, like those of many other Scottish men of letters, were with the British government, whose understanding of the constitutional relationship of the American colonies to the authority of Westminster was regarded as consistent with both British tradition and British law.[12] Ferguson had earlier shown some sensitivity to the colonial cause and had condemned the Stamp Act as politically inept and foolish. In a letter to John Macpherson, probably written in 1772, he noted that "I think Greenevilles Stamp Act a very unlucky affair for this Countrey. It has brought on a disspute in which this Mother Countrey as it is very properly called has made a very shabby figure, And I am affraid cannot mend the matter."[13] Even as late as the beginning

---

ral, and commons of Great Britain, in parliament assembled, had, hath, and of right ought to have, full power and authority to make laws and statutes of sufficient force and validity to bind the colonies and people of America, subjects of the crown of Great Britain, in all cases whatsoever." 6 George III, c. 12; *The Statutes at Large*, ed. Danby Pickering (Cambridge: J. Bentham, 1767), 27:19–20. So heinous did Price find this Act that he wrote of it, "I defy any one to express slavery in stronger language." "Observations on the Nature of Civil Liberty, the Principles of Government, and the Justice and Policy of the War with America" in Peach, *Ethical Foundations*, 82–83 (hereafter cited as "Observations").

11. John Shebbeare, *An Essay on the Origin, Progress and Establishment of Natural Society; in Which the Principles of Government, the Definitions of Physical, Moral, Civil, and Religious Liberty, Contained in Dr. Price's Observations, etc. Are Fairly Examined and Fully Refuted* (London: J. Pew, 1776); Edmund Burke, *A Letter from Edmund Burke, Esq., One of the Representatives in Parliament for the City of Bristol, to John Farr and John Harris, Esqrs., Sheriffs in that City, on the Affairs of America* (Bristol: William Pine, 1777).

12. Neither Hume nor Smith was in complete agreement with this view. Hume was contemptuous of government policy and urged that the colonies should be allowed their independence, while Smith proposed that the colonies be extended representation in Parliament in proportion to the taxes levied on them. See Dalphy I. Fagerstrom, "Scottish Opinion and the American Revolution," *William and Mary Quarterly*, 3d series, 11 (April 1954): 259–60.

13. Ferguson to Sir John Macpherson, Edinburgh, 1772 (no. 59), in Vincenzo

of 1776, Ferguson, while convinced of the legality of the government's position, expressed concern that Britain would not be able to extricate itself from the impasse it had arrived at with the colonies. These speculations were occasioned by his having received a copy of James Macpherson's pamphlet "on the Rights of this Countrey against the Claims of America."[14] "I have never had any doubt on any of the rights Established in this Pamphlet," Ferguson maintained. "The only Question with me was what this Countrey in Wisdom ought to do in the Situation at which the Colonys were Arrived. This Question becomes every Day more complicated & more difficult."[15]

It appears that as early as 1772 Ferguson had been approached by the administration to publish his views on the American crisis, doubtless in the expectation that the high reputation in which he was held by educated colonists might work to blunt their increasing hostility toward Britain. As one of the leading figures of the Scottish Enlightenment, Ferguson was well known and his work highly respected. Indeed, the Scottish Enlightenment, as one historian has noted,

> was probably the most potent single tradition in the American Enlightenment. From Hutcheson to Ferguson, including Hume and Adam Smith, came a body of philosophical literature that aroused men from their dogmatic slumbers on both sides of the Atlantic.[16]

Merolle, ed., *The Correspondence of Adam Ferguson*, 2 vols. (London: William Pickering, 1995), 1:95.

14. James Macpherson, *The Rights of Great Britain Asserted Against the Claims of America; Being an Answer to the Declaration of the General Congress* (London: T. Caddell, 1775). Following publication of Price's *Observations on the Nature of Civil Liberty* in 1776 and beginning with the sixth edition of Macpherson's pamphlet, the essay was expanded and the following added to its title: *To Which Is Now Added a Refutation of Dr. Price's State of the National Debt*.

15. Ferguson to John Home, Edinburgh, January 27, 1776 (no. 83), in *Ferguson Correspondence*, 1:134.

16. Herbert W. Schneider, *A History of American Philosophy*, 2d ed. (New York: Columbia University Press, 1963), 216. See also the detailed discussion of the favorable reception given eighteenth-century Scottish moral philosophy and epistemology by American intellectuals in Elizabeth Flowers and Murray G. Murphey, *A History of Philosophy in America*, 2 vols. (New York: Capricorn Books, 1977), 1:203–361. William R. Brock deals with the extensive influence of Scottish thought in the colonies in *Scotus Americanus: A Survey of Sources for Links Between*

Scottish moral philosophy was decisively established in America through the mediation of John Witherspoon, who arrived in the colonies from Scotland to take up the position of president of Princeton (then known as the College of New Jersey) in 1768. Witherspoon, one of the more outspoken Evangelical ministers in the Church of Scotland, brought with him an intimate knowledge of the work of the leading Scottish writers, which he kept current and attempted to impart to his students. Thus, Ferguson's principal work, *Essay on the History of Civil Society*, appears among the works comprising Witherspoon's recommended reading list for his course in political theory.[17] A student of Witherspoon's, James Madison was especially receptive to Ferguson's writings,[18] but Madison was certainly not alone among Americans in having studied Ferguson. Data presented by Lundberg and May indicate that between 1777 and 1813 the *Essay* appeared in no less than 22 percent of the American library catalogues and booksellers' lists examined.[19] Jefferson had been introduced to the works of the major Scottish thinkers when a student at the College of William and Mary,[20] and

Scotland and America in the Eighteenth Century (Edinburgh: Edinburgh University Press, 1982), 87–113.

17. Dennis F. Thompson, "The Education of a Founding Father: The Reading List for John Witherspoon's Course in Political Theory, Taken by James Madison," *Political Theory* 4 (1976): 528. See also John Witherspoon, *Lectures on Moral Philosophy,* ed. Varnum Lansing Collins (Princeton: Princeton University Press, 1912), 144.

18. Madison's debt to Scottish-Enlightenment thinking is discussed at some length in Roy Branson, "James Madison and the Scottish Enlightenment," *Journal of the History of Ideas* 11 (1979): 235–50.

19. David Lundberg and Henry F. May, "The Enlightened Reader in America," *American Quarterly* 28 (1976): 262–93.

20. The basic library list that Jefferson prepared for a friend in 1771 contained works by Adam Smith, Thomas Reid, David Hume, and Henry Home, Lord Kames. Jefferson to Robert Skipwith, August 3, 1771, in Julian Boyd, ed., *The Papers of Thomas Jefferson* (Princeton: Princeton University Press, 1950), 1:78–80. Having studied for two years under William Small at the College of William and Mary, it is inconceivable that Jefferson had not also read and digested Ferguson's works. One commentator has gone so far as to maintain that Jefferson was so thoroughly immersed in the thought of the Scottish Enlightenment that the Declaration of Independence cannot be properly understood except in terms of Scottish political and moral philosophy. See Garry Wills, *Inventing America: Jeffer-*

among the items listed in the catalogue of books sold to the Library of Congress in 1815 was a copy of the *Essay*.[21]

In New England the effects of Scottish philosophy in shaping the American Enlightenment were even more profound than in the South. Scottish thought was to prove crucial in temporalizing Calvinist doctrine and replacing it with secular conceptions of history and progress. As one intellectual historian has observed, one can only imagine the effect of sentiments such as these on minds steeped in a Puritan theology that viewed man as entirely dependent on God, whose earthly magistrates we are obligated to obey.[22] It was Adam Ferguson who gave this sweeping secularization its best expression: "We speak of art as distinguished from nature," he wrote,

> but art itself is natural to man. He is in some measure the artificer of his own frame, as well as his fortune, and is destined, from the first age of his being, to invent and contrive. . . . If we are asked therefore, Where the state of nature is to be found? we may answer, It is here, and it matters not where we are understood to speak in the island of Great Britain, at the Cape of Good Hope, or the Straits of Magellan. . . . If the palace be unnatural, the cottage is so no less; and the highest refinements of political and moral apprehension, are not more artificial in their kind, than the first operations of sentiment and reason.[23]

When the first shots were fired at Lexington in April 1775, Ferguson was almost fifty-two years old and had held the chair of philosophy at the University of Edinburgh for eleven years. He was born at Logierait, Perthshire, on the border of the Scottish Highlands, on

---

son's Declaration of Independence (Garden City, N.Y.: Doubleday, 1978). While there is no historical warrant whatever for this eccentric conclusion, there is much evidence that Jefferson was familiar with the major Scottish writers.

21. Ferguson, *Essay*, 2d ed., corr.; London: A. Millar and T. Caddell, 1768. E. Millicent Sowerby, comp., *Catalogue of the Library of Thomas Jefferson*, 5 vols. (Washington, D.C.: Library of Congress, 1952–59), 3:20–21, item 2348.

22. Schneider, *American Philosophy*, 38.

23. Adam Ferguson, *An Essay on the History of Civil Society*, ed. Fania Oz-Salzberger (Cambridge: Cambridge University Press, 1995), 12, 14 (hereafter cited as *Essay*).

June 20, 1723, the youngest child of the parish minister. Having received his early education at the parish school and the local grammar school, he was sent to the University of St. Andrews in 1738, where he gained a reputation for classical scholarship. Ferguson took his M.A. degree in 1742 and in the same year entered the Divinity Hall at St. Andrews. Soon thereafter he transferred to Edinburgh University and in 1745, after having completed only three years of the required six-year course of study in theology, he was offered the deputy chaplaincy of the Black Watch Regiment, largely it appears because of his knowledge of Gaelic. In July 1745 he was ordained in the Scottish Kirk and raised to the rank of principal chaplain. He remained with his regiment until 1754, at which time he resigned his commission and quit the clerical profession.

With the help of his friend David Hume, Ferguson was appointed to the post of Keeper of the Advocates Library, Edinburgh, in 1757, having succeeded Hume to that office (and thus providing Ferguson with access to one of the best libraries in Europe). Following the death of the professor of natural philosophy at the University of Edinburgh, and again through the intercession of, among others, David Hume, Ferguson was named to that chair in 1759; five years later, in 1764, he transferred to the chair of pneumatics and moral philosophy, which he held until his retirement in 1785. It was during his tenure as professor of moral philosophy that three of his four most important works were published: the *Essay on the History of Civil Society* in 1767; the *Institutes of Moral Philosophy,* a synopsis of his lectures on moral philosophy, in 1769; and the *History of the Progress and Termination of the Roman Republic* in five volumes in 1783.[24]

24. Citing the condition of his health, Ferguson resigned his professorship in 1785 at the age of sixty-two, to be succeeded in that position by his one-time student and friend, Dugald Stewart. In lieu of a pension, Ferguson had made arrangements with the university to continue to draw a salary as senior professor of mathematics. The position was, of course, a sinecure, and all lectures in the field were, in fact, to be delivered by a junior professor. During his retirement Ferguson completed his major work in moral philosophy, a revision and expansion of his *Institutes* entitled *Principles of Moral and Political Science* which appeared in two volumes in 1792. Ferguson died on February 22, 1816, in his ninety-third year at St. Andrews, Scotland, and is buried in the grounds of the cathedral there. By

The *Essay on the History of Civil Society* was early recognized as Ferguson's most important work. Not only did it go through at least seven editions in the author's lifetime, but it also appeared in French, German, Swedish, Italian, and Russian translations. The first edition of the *Essay* was published simultaneously in London, Edinburgh, and Dublin, and at least two pirated English-language editions were issued before the end of the century.[25] So popular did the *Essay* prove that despite the ready availability of British editions of the work in America, at least two American editions appeared by 1819.[26] Indeed, the *Essay*

---

far the best biographical essay is by Jane B. Fagg, "Biographical Introduction" in Vincenzo Morelle, ed., *The Correspondence of Adam Ferguson,* 1:xx–cxvii. See also the biographical chapter on Ferguson in David Kettler, *The Social and Political Thought of Adam Ferguson* (Columbus: Ohio State University Press, 1965), 41–82.

25. A French edition was published in Paris in 1783 with a second edition appearing in 1796 under the title *Essai sur l'histoire de la société civile,* translated by Claude Bergier and Alexandre Meunier. A German translation by C. F. Jünger, entitled *Versuch über die Geschichte der bürgerlichen Gesellschaft,* appeared in Leipzig in 1768. In 1790 a Swedish translation by Johan A. Carlbohm was published titled *Försök till Historien om borgerligt Samhälle.* The work was published in an Italian translation done by P. Antonutti in Venice in 1807 under the title *Saggio circa la storia di civile societá.* Finally, a Russian translation by Ivan Timkovskii appeared between 1817 and 1819 bearing the title *Opyt istorii grazhdanskogo obshchestva,* published in Saint Petersburg in three volumes. The two pirated editions carry the imprint "Basil: J. J. Toureisen, 1789" and "Basel, Thurneysen, 1791."

26. There was a printing of the seventh edition, published in Boston by Hastings, Etheridge and Bliss in 1809, and an eighth edition, published in Philadelphia by A. Finlay in 1819. Charles R. Hildeburn's bibliography of Pennsylvania imprints lists an edition of the *Essay* printed in Philadelphia by Robert Bell in 1773 — *A Century of Printing: The Issues of the Press in Philadelphia, 1685–1784,* 2 vols. (New York: Burt Franklin, 1968), 2:164, item 2878, originally published in 2 vols. (Philadelphia: Press of Matlack & Harvey, 1885–86). Hildeburn's evidence for the existence of this edition is based on an advertising circular issued by Bell in that year, announcing that the *Essay* "by a living Author of much Estimation whose elegant Performance will greatly delight" would be published by subscription in the fall of 1773 (ibid., 160, item 1857). There appear to be no copies of this edition extant. The editors of the Madison papers, however, maintain that the copy of the *Essay* obtained for James Madison by William Bradford in 1773 is the 1773 Bell edition (William Bradford to James Madison, January 4, 1775, in William T. Hutchinson and William M. E. Rachel, eds., *The Papers of James Madison* [Chicago: University of Chicago Press, 1962], 1:133n).

proved a remarkable success and gained for Ferguson an international reputation as a man of letters.[27]

The *Essay*'s primary purpose is to set forth the social history of mankind. It was this approach to understanding man's nature, rooted as it was in an empirical study of how man behaves, that has led intellectual historians to credit him with being one of the founders of modern sociology.[28] All societies, Ferguson maintained, progressed from "rude" to "polished" nations, most evolving through three clearly distinct stages defined by their primary mode of subsistence—hunting, pastoral and/or agricultural, and commercial, each of which reflected differing notions of property and distinct legal and political institutions. Of the varieties of precommercial society, the most primitive are those based on hunting and fishing, and in these the notion of private property except in its most rudimentary sense is absent. Lacking a concept of property, these communities possess no formal system of subordination and, consequently, no government.[29] Such societies Ferguson denominated *savage*. Most agrarian and pastoral societies, however, are likely to be those in which property has ceased to remain communal and in which private wealth takes the form of agricultural products or of a herd of animals. Although private property will not have yet become institutionalized into a formal system of laws

27. Among the many marks of favor the publication of the *Essay* conferred upon its author was the award of an honorary LL.D. by the University of Edinburgh.

28. See Theodor Buddeberg, "Ferguson als Soziologe," *Jahrbücher für National-ökonomie und Statistik* 123 (1925): 609–12; Werner Sombart, "Die Angänge der Soziologie" in Melchoir Palyi, ed., *Hauptprobleme der Soziologie: Erinnerungsgabe für Max Weber*, 2 vols. (Munich and Leipzig: Duncker & Humblot, 1923), 1:9; and Harry E. Bames, "Sociology before Comte," *American Journal of Sociology* 23 (1917): 234.

29. As Ferguson explains it, "Where no profit attends dominion, one party is as much averse to the trouble of perpetual command, as the other is to the mortification of perpetual submission" (*Essay*, 83). That the institution of a formal political structure rests upon the prior establishment of a system of private property was a concept common to the Scottish historical school. See, for example, Adam Smith, *Lectures on Jurisprudence*, R. L. Meek, D. D. Raphael, and P. G. Stein, eds. (Oxford: Clarendon Press, 1978), 404, and, in a more extensive treatment, in his *An Inquiry into the Nature and Causes of the Wealth of Nations*, R. H. Campbell and A. S. Skinner, eds., 2 vols. (Oxford: Clarendon Press, 1976), 2:709–10 (V.i.b 21).

in these communities, it is a principal object of individual and social concern. Societies thus marked by the emergence of personal property Ferguson called *barbarian*. The transmutation of barbarian societies into modern commercial communities comes about when some members begin applying their skill and labor apart and seek the exclusive possession of goods. At that point "The individual no longer finds among his associates the same inclination to commit every subject to public use, [and] he is seized with concern for his personal fortune; and is alarmed by the cares which every person entertains for himself."[30] With the advent of modern notions of property, the members of the community can now be distinguished one from the other by unequal possessions, which in turn lays the foundation for a permanent subordination of rank and for the emergence of government restrained by law.

Ferguson's analysis of the stages of social development and their relation to changes in the extent of private property had been adumbrated in slightly altered form by several of his fellow Scotsmen.[31] Of all these conjectural accounts, however, Ferguson's is the most fully elaborated and most convincingly argued. In addition, in his discussions of the various civilized societies, both ancient and modern, the forces at work in shaping their social and political institutions, and the origins and character of despotic regimes,[32] Ferguson brought to bear a wealth of observations from a wide range of sources and occasionally showed great insight.

While Ferguson's political sympathies were decidedly Whiggish, he regarded the American position on taxation as without merit. The

30. *Essay,* 95.

31. See Sir John Dalrymple, *Essay Towards a General History of Feudal Property in Great Britain* (London: A. Millar, 1757); Henry Home, Lord Kames, *Historical Law-Tracts,* 2 vols. (Edinburgh: A. Millar, London, and A. Kincaid & J. Bell, Edinburgh, 1758) and the second edition of his *Essays on the Principles of Morality and Natural Religion* (Edinburgh: R. Fleming & A. Donaldson, 1758); and, in particular, Adam Smith, in his 1762–63 *Lectures on Jurisprudence,* 1–394.

32. Ferguson's discussion of the causes and nature of despotism was regarded as particularly astute. Indeed, Price, among many others, quoted him authoritatively on the subject. Richard Price, "Additional Observations on the Nature and Value of Civil Liberty, and the War with America" (1777) in *Ethical Foundations,* 161 (hereafter cited as "Additional Observations").

notion that England should underwrite the costs of garrisoning an army in North America to protect the colonists while being blocked from taxing the beneficiaries of this policy struck Ferguson as nonsensical. Having received the benefits of subjects, it followed that the colonists were subject to the duties of subjects. It is true that England had profited from its trade with America, but this held equally true of America in its trade with the mother country. Indeed, the laws of nature clearly provided that one body politic could legally submit itself to the authority of and to contribute to the supplies of another as was the case, Ferguson maintained, with the American colonies in its relation with the Parliament of Great Britain.

These conclusions, well known to the authorities, prompted the North administration in 1772 to approach Ferguson with a view to publishing a pamphlet in support of the government's policies in North America. To this suggestion, Ferguson, in writing to Sir John Macpherson,[33] declined, noting that "I could come under no Obligations which I am affraid the Step of your Friendship Suggests would seem to Promise."[34] Ferguson adds that, while he will not write a pamphlet, "I will continue to write you what occurs to me" and noted that he would have no objection to his comments being brought to the attention of Lord Grafton.[35]

In 1776 Ferguson was again approached, this time by Sir John Dalrymple, who had at first suggested that Ferguson participate in a plan to contribute regularly to a weekly journal defending the government's policies, but this scheme appears never to have been implemented. However, Dalrymple was successful in gaining for Ferguson a handsome government stipend at the beginning of 1776. Dalrymple argued

33. While Macpherson was, at the time, a lower-ranking administrator of the East India Company, he was very well connected and eventually became Governor-General of India.

34. Ferguson to Sir John Macpherson, Edinburgh, 1772 (no. 59), in *Ferguson Correspondence*, 1:96.

35. "If I had written the best that the occasion requires I should [not] be averse to be mentioned to Grafton as a writer." Letter to Sir John Macpherson, Edinburgh, 1772 (no. 59), ibid. The Duke of Grafton served as Prime Minister from late 1767 to 1770 and was appointed Privy Seal in the North government.

that Ferguson had been a faithful adherent of administration policy on numerous occasions, especially with regard to the colonies. However, his support, unlike that of so many of his colleagues, had never been acknowledged with some favor or another, and as a consequence, according to Dalrymple, Ferguson had begun to grow somewhat bitter. As a consequence, he was awarded a grant of £200 per annum, conferred on him on January 23, 1776, by the King's Warrant under the Privy Seal of Scotland.[36]

The effect of this subsidy appears to have been immediate. Price's *Observations* appeared on February 7, and Ferguson quickly began work on a rejoinder to the essay, which he sent to the government to be used as they wished. On behalf of the government, Sir Grey Cooper, who held the post of secretary of the treasury, instructed the publisher William Strahan in Edinburgh to print Ferguson's essay,[37] and it was soon republished by a group of printers in Dublin.[38] The pamphlet, which appeared under the title *Remarks on a Pamphlet Lately Published by Dr. Price, Intitled Observations on the Nature of Civil Liberty, the Principles of Government, and the Justice and Policy of the War With America, etc., In a Letter from a Gentlemen in the Country to a Member of Parliament,* sold for one shilling[39] and was very well received, being quoted at length in the *Critical Review* and the *Monthly Review,* two of the leading magazines of the day. Even Price referred to its author as "one even of the most candid as well as the ablest of my opponents."[40]

36. Fagg, "Biographical Introduction" in *Ferguson Correspondence,* 1:xlix–l.

37. See Letter from Grey Cooper, London, March 23, 1776 (no. 85), ibid., 1:137.

38. Fagg, "Biographical Introduction," ibid., 1:l. The practice of rewarding authors sympathetic to the government and hiring publishers to place the administration's point of view before the public was extremely common. See Solomon Lutnick, *The American Revolution and the British Press, 1775–1783* (Columbia: University of Missouri Press, 1967), 12–34.

39. It should be pointed out that a professional such as a surgeon or high-level government clerk earned on average no more than £2 per week, and consequently, once bought, pamphlets of this nature were widely circulated from one reader to another and often read aloud in coffeehouses. See Lutnick, *British Press,* 2.

40. "Additional Observations," 140.

Ferguson's attitude toward the colonies appeared to have hardened following publication of his *Remarks*. Again writing to John Macpherson, on October 27, 1777, Ferguson expressed the hope that British forces "for our own Credit, [would inflict on] that people . . . a sound drubbing." Once having done so, however, Ferguson supported the removal of British troops from the rebellious colonies inasmuch as their upkeep would be beyond the financial capacities of the colonies to sustain. He writes:

> I protest that if we had news to morrow that Howe had beat Washington and Burgoyne Arnold the use I would make of it would be to leave America with contempt. For it looks as if no Calamity would force them to Submission & if it did their Submission is not worth haveing. Their whole resource for any Visi[ble] time to Come will not pay the Army that ke[eps] them in Submission. So I am partial enough to Great Britain to wish them to the bottom of the Sea.[41]

What occasioned this mean-spiritedness and led Ferguson to such a foolish miscalculation regarding the colonies' economic capacities is impossible to say. He continued in the same vein three months later when, after outlining a military campaign that he felt would prove sufficient to subdue the rebellion, he noted: "In our Way to this Object the Rebels may be induced to prefer accommodation to the Continuance of Such A War. But Lord have mercy on those who expect any Good in this business without Sufficient Instruments of Terror in one hand & of Moderation and justice in the Other."[42] Having been selected to join the Commission appointed to seek some accommodation with the colonies, Ferguson felt it expedient to moderate his views somewhat prior to setting sail to America in early 1778. He noted in yet another letter to John Macpherson that he hoped the administration would signal to the colonies that they had no intention of invading American liberties and that they supported the establishment of a general parliament for America.[43]

---

41. Ferguson to John Macpherson, October 27, 1777 (no. 100) in *Ferguson Correspondence*, 156.

42. Ferguson to John Macpherson, January 15, 1778 (no. 105), ibid., 162.

43. Ferguson to John Macpherson, February 12, 1778 (no. 108), ibid., 1:

In the fall of 1777, General John Burgoyne, who had led an invasion force from Canada with the intention of linking up with the British army in New York City, suffered a decisive defeat at Saratoga, and on October 17 Burgoyne and his whole army surrendered to General Horatio Gates. The news of Burgoyne's defeat caused a sensation across the Atlantic. The French government set in train formal diplomatic efforts to recognize America's independence, and the British government in an effort to be as conciliatory as possible abruptly reversed its policies. In February the North administration introduced bills in Parliament repealing all acts passed since 1763 of which the colonies complained. At the same time, a commission was struck whose purpose was to enter into negotiations with the Americans to grant to the colonies anything they wished,[44] provided they remain loyal to the Crown.

The commissioners were appointed by George III, who personally had little hope that they would prove successful. As its head, the Crown appointed Frederick Howard, fifth Earl of Carlisle, and its membership comprised William Eden (later Lord Auckland), a close friend of Lord North, and George Johnstone, who had been appointed the first governor of West Florida in 1763.[45] It was Johnstone, an old friend of Ferguson, who was responsible for inviting Ferguson to accompany the Commission to America.[46] Upon arriving at Philadelphia in June,

---

166. "My Idea of a General Parliament for America may appear odd," Ferguson wrote. "What Unite them; should they not rather be keept Separate that we may govern by dividing. I have much to say on that Subject being much impressed with a notion that one great state is much more easily Governed than many Small ones."

44. The principal exceptions revolved around responsibility for the redemption of colonial paper money and assuming the financial burden undertaken by the colonies in the war.

45. It appears that Lord Shelburne had given serious thought to offering the post to Ferguson after Johnstone had returned to England in 1766. Fagg, "Biographical Introduction" in *Ferguson Correspondence*, 1:xl.

46. Johnstone had entered Parliament following his tenure as governor of West Florida and over the course of the next decade had been an outspoken defender of the American cause. Ferguson's biographer recounts that Johnstone was encouraged by others to choose Ferguson as a companion in part because of Johnstone's hotheadedness which, it was felt, would be moderated by Fergu-

the Commission appointed Ferguson its secretary and immediately attempted to enter into negotiations with several members of Congress.[47] These proved a complete failure, nor was the Commission any more successful in prevailing upon Washington to grant Ferguson a passport through the American lines to treat directly with Congress.[48] Having been defeated at reaching agreement with the colonies short of recognizing their independence and withdrawing all British troops, the Commission returned home in late 1778. Ferguson continued to occupy himself with Commission business until the spring of the following year, at which point he resumed his chair at the university.[49]

Despite having spent six months in the colonies, Ferguson's sentiments regarding the colonial cause had not softened since having written in reply to Price two years earlier. Indeed, if the Manifesto and Proclamation issued by the Conciliation Commission in October 1778,

---

son's more temperate disposition. Fagg, "Biographical Introduction" in *Ferguson Correspondence,* 1:li.

47. The Commission's official letter to Congress was accompanied by personal notes from both Eden and Johnstone warmly commending Ferguson. Eden referred to the favorable reception to which Ferguson was entitled by virtue of his eminence in the literary world (Eden to Washington, June 9, 1778, in Benjamin Franklin Stevens, ed., *Stevens's Facsimiles of Manuscripts in European Archives Relating to America, 1773–1783,* 24 vols. [London: Malby & Sons, 1889–95], 5:401, facsimile 498), while Johnstone's letter was even more generous. "I beg to recommend to your private civilities my friend Dr. Ferguson," he wrote. "He has been engaged from his early life, in inculcating to mankind the virtuous principles you practise." (Johnstone to Washington, June 10, 1778, in Jared Sparks, ed., *Correspondence of the American Revolution,* 4 vols. [Boston: Little, Brown, 1853], 2:136).

48. There are good reasons to explain the colonists' refusal to treat with the Commission. The United States had just entered a treaty of alliance with France, and it was clear that there were deepening divisions in Parliament regarding America. Washington was particularly adamant that the Commission's terms be rejected out of hand. Finally, with respect to the Commission's secretary, one is tempted to speculate that Washington was familiar with Ferguson's rejoinder to Price's essay and, as a result, was especially ill-disposed toward the writer.

49. Extensive discussions of the Carlisle Commission appear in Weldon A. Brown, *Empire or Independence: A Study in the Failure of Reconciliation, 1774–1783* (Baton Rouge: Louisiana State University Press, 1941), 244–92, and Carl Van Doren, *Secret History of the American Revolution* (Garden City, N.Y.: Garden City Publishing Co., 1941), 63:116.

of which Ferguson was one of the authors,[50] is any indication, Ferguson's animus toward the colonists had deepened in the wake of America's alliance with France, a nation, it was argued, that traditionally opposed freedom of conscience and that held religious toleration, which Englishmen took for granted, in contempt.[51] A treaty with France, the Manifesto observed, would convert the existing hostilities between those sharing a common heritage into a world struggle. In light of this, it went on, self-preservation would justify England's destruction of the colonies.[52] Thomas Paine was especially offended by the Manifesto's claim that France was the "natural enemy" of both England and America and devoted a good part of "The Crisis" no. 6 to criticizing Ferguson for his use of the notion "natural enemies," which Paine characterized as a meaningless barbarism.[53]

Richard Price, it need hardly be added, was not moved to alter his views in light of America's alliance with France although he appears to have shared Ferguson's aversion to a treaty between a people dedicated to establishing a free society and a nation as closely tied to its feudal past as was France. In early 1778, he had published a new edition of his *Observations* to which he appended a second essay replying to his numerous critics. This second pamphlet, which first appeared in February 1777 under the title *Additional Observations on the Nature and Value of Liberty*, was issued with the *Observations* in January 1778 as *Two Tracts on Civil Liberty*, to which he added a general introduction and supplement.[54] Price's introductory observations pointed to the need to hasten a resolution of the conflict with the colonies by acceding to their demands, a comment prompted by his belief that an American-French alliance was imminent.[55] Indeed, once the alliance was con-

---

50. Fagg, "Biographical Introduction" in *Ferguson Correspondence*, 1:liii.

51. The Commission sought to remind the clergy that "the foreign power with which the Congress is endeavouring to connect them has ever been averse to toleration." Van Doren, *Secret History*, 112–13.

52. Brown, *Empire or Independence*, 284–85.

53. Thomas Paine, "The Crisis," no. 6, October 20, 1778, in Thomas Paine, *Collected Writings* (New York: Library of America, 1995), 186–90.

54. *Two Tracts on Civil Liberty, the War with America, and the Debts and Finances of the Kingdom* (London: T. Caddell, 1778).

55. "The consequences [of not acceding to America's demands] must be that

cluded, Price saw even less reason to deny the United States its independence. "France," he wrote,

> has acknowledged the independence of America. Every power in Europe is ready to do it. All *real* authority is gone; and it cannot be expected that by any *nominal* authority we can bind them to anything that interferes with their interest. In these circumstances, all hesitation about yielding independence to them seems unreasonable.[56]

A reading of Price's *Observations* and Ferguson's response naturally raises the question: In which ways did these two writers, who shared so much of the Whig tradition and who were both highly regarded for their political insights by so many colonists, differ from each other in their assessment of the events in America? In this regard it will prove useful to contrast Price and Ferguson with respect to the philosophical differences that bore most decisively on their views of the American crisis.

EPISTEMOLOGY AND ITS RELATION TO ETHICS

While Locke was clearly a major influence in shaping Price's views, the underlying epistemology that shaped Price's political philosophy differs markedly. In his *A Review of the Principal Questions in Morals,* first published in 1758, Price maintains that certain ideas, for example those having to do with identity and causation, are simply not derivable from our sensory experiences but rather are known through rational intuition. Equally, our intellectual perceptions of right and wrong, our notions of moral rightness, follow immediately from our understanding and, once having been intuited, are appealable to noth-

---

the colonies will become the allies of France, that a general war will be kindled and, perhaps, this once happy country be made, in just retribution, the seat of that desolation and misery which it has produced in other countries." Richard Price, "The General Introduction and Supplement to the Two Tracts on Civil Liberty, the War with America, and the Finances of the Kingdom" in Peach, *Ethical Foundations,* 60.

56. D. O. Thomas, *The Honest Mind: The Thought and Work of Richard Price* (Oxford: Clarendon Press, 1977), 261–62.

ing more fundamental. Among these immutable and objective truths of which the mind is aware are our duty to God and our sense of justice. And justice, in turn, is the duty to respect property, which includes an individual's life, limbs, faculties, and goods.[57] Alongside this view, Price also asserted that utility and benevolence constituted legitimate criteria for judging the rightness of an act. At the point at which these several principles of morals might conflict, Price asserts, reason will dictate which principle has priority.

It is this epistemological foundation that underlies Price's discussion of civil liberty in the *Observations*.[58] When Price notes that civil liberty entails that every man act as his own legislator (that is, that each of us participates in some capacity or another in determining the rules that govern us)[59] and that no community can rightfully assume authority over a person or his property without adequate representation, he regarded these claims as deductively true. It is, Price would contend, in the nature of free societies that those who live in them have the right to legislate for themselves since as truly free agents their disposition is such that they would legislate correctly.

Ferguson's approach to ethics varies considerably from that of Price. His *Essay*, while apparently a work in conjectural sociology, was regarded by Ferguson as primarily an extension of his researches into moral philosophy, the starting point for which he believed was the study of the way man functions, both as an individual and in conjunction with others. He regarded all aprioristic notions of man's nature as unsatisfactory and maintained that the only adequate method of gaining information about the principles of ethics was by studying man within the context of his history. "Before we can ascertain the rules of morality for mankind," he wrote, "the history of man's nature, his dispositions, his specific enjoyments and sufferings, his condition and

57. Martha K. Zebrowski, "Richard Price: British Platonist of the Eighteenth Century," *Journal of the History of Ideas* 55 (1994): 29. See also Bernard Peach, "The Indefinability and Simplicity of Rightness in Richard Price's Review of Politics," *Philosophy and Phenomenological Research* 14 (1954): 370–85.

58. The ethical foundations of Price's political views are discussed at some length in Peach, "Introduction" in *Ethical Foundations*, 18.

59. "Observations," 70.

future prospects, should be known."[60] Indeed, Ferguson insisted, we are as capable of gaining real knowledge about the nature of human beings and the laws governing how they are to be treated as we are about the physical universe.

This, coupled with Ferguson's belief in the inevitable moral progress of the human species, led him to conclude that it was possible to define the ends toward which man ought to move and, indeed was moving as he approaches a more perfect condition. An empirical investigation of man's nature would provide the facts from which we are able to determine what his ends are. "Our knowledge of what any nature ought to be," he observed, "must be derived from our knowledge of its faculties and powers and the attainment to be aimed at must be of the kind which these faculties and powers to fitted to produce."[61]

The sharply divergent epistemological presuppositions that shaped the arguments that Price and Ferguson put forward account in part for Ferguson's criticisms of Price's notions of liberty, one of whose divisions Price characterizes as our "power of following our own sense of right and wrong." Ferguson notes that were we to accept this definition, then it follows that any constraint whatever on our behavior constitutes a species of slavery. However, Price is here claiming that we are morally unfree to the extent that we are prevented from complying with our sense of what is right; this formulation, when applied to civil liberty, leads inexorably to the conclusion that to be truly free entails our being able to legislate for ourselves. As one commentator has observed, Ferguson's response that this interpretation would empower thieves and pickpockets to make their own laws misses the point since what Price is claiming is that it is in the nature of things that in a truly free society all its citizens as morally free agents would act rationally in keeping with rectitude and virtue.[62] Further, Ferguson argues that, inasmuch as the great end of government is to secure to each of us our persons and our property by restraining others from invasive acts,

60. *Institutes of Moral Philosophy* (Edinburgh: A. Kincaid and W. Creech, 1769), 2.

61. *Principles of Moral and Political Science,* 2 vols. (Edinburgh: A. Strahan and T. Cadell, 1972), 1:5 (hereafter cited as *Principles*).

62. Peach, "Introduction" in *Ethical Foundations,* 19.

it follows that liberty as Price understands the term, that is, the absence of any restraint, is inconsistent with peace and civil society. But, again, Price's argument has reference to external restraints on truly free agents whose choices would already be restrained by their moral sense.

It is true that Price later concedes that freedom is consistent with "limitations on our licentious actions and insults to our persons, property, and good name," but, Ferguson argues, Price has recourse to this amendment only after having been shown that his earlier formulation is far too broad. Interestingly, Price's addendum serves to bring his notion of liberty into line with that offered by Locke and reflects Ferguson's own conception of personal liberty as not so much a power but the security of our rights.[63] Doing what we please, Ferguson argues, is not what liberty is about. Rather, being free to act as we choose, circumscribed by the rights of others and secure in our right to so act, is the defining characteristic of a truly free society. In point of fact this seems to be very close to what Price is suggesting.

Thus it appears that both Price and Ferguson, by completely divergent routes and despite differing epistemological underpinnings, arrive at similar conclusions respecting the nature of liberty. Independent of exactly how rights are defined, both Price and Ferguson agree that a free society is one, in Ferguson's words, "which secures to us the possession of our rights, while it restrains us from invading the rights of others."[64]

RIGHTS

Price had defended America in its controversies with the Crown since their inception. Indeed, he regarded the cause of the colonies as the cause of all free Englishmen and saw in colonial resistance to the depredations of the North administration the best hope that freedom would be preserved in Britain. The colonists, Price main-

---

63. [Adam Ferguson], *Remarks on a Pamphlet Lately Published by Dr. Price* (London: T. Caddell, 1776), 7 (hereafter cited as *Remarks*). "The liberty of every class and order is not proportional to the power they enjoy," Ferguson writes, "but to the security they have for the preservation of their rights" (ibid., 11).

64. Ibid., 5.

tained, in fighting the English battle for liberty, were preserving a future asylum for those seeking freedom.[65]

The concept of liberty Price puts forward in the *Observations,* bor-
rows heavily from Locke and differs only in minor particulars.[66] While
he was prepared to put forward utilitarian arguments in support of
certain political ends, Price does not rest his case for freedom on any
doctrine of utility but bases it firmly on a foundation of natural rights
whose principles are eternally valid. Price divides liberty into four aspects, physical, moral, religious, and civil, all of which reflect some
notion of self-direction. Physical liberty entails the power to act as an
agent free from physical restraint; moral liberty consists in the power
to conduct oneself in accord with one's sense of right or wrong; religious liberty lies in being able to choose those beliefs and modes of
worship that conform to the dictates of one's conscience; and civil liberty refers to the community's power to govern itself by laws of its own
making.

Price's understanding of rights is purely Lockean. Rights, he maintains, derive from our nature as human beings and are inalienable.
They are to be understood in their negative designation only, prohibit-
ing certain actions on the part of others directed at the rights-holder,
that is, one's right to something entails that others may not intervene
should the rights-holder attempt to exercise it. It does not entail that
others are positively obligated to help the rights-holder to exercise it.
My right to my life denotes that I may do all within my power consistent with the rights of others to keep myself alive (that is, that I am
under no obligation not to prevent myself from dying) and that others
are prohibited from intervening should I attempt to preserve my life.
Thus, when Price writes of religious liberty, that it is the power of acting as we choose with respect to our religious beliefs,[67] he notes that,

65. Carl B. Cone, *Torchbearer of Freedom: The Influence of Richard Price on Eighteenth Century Thought* (Lexington: University of Kentucky Press, 1952), 73.

66. Price admits as much. In the Preface to the fifth edition of the "Observations," Price acknowledges that "the principles on which I have argued form the
foundation of every state as far as it is free; and are the same with those taught
by Mr. Locke, and all the writers on civil liberty who have been hitherto most
admired in this country" (65).

67. "Religious liberty signifies the power of exercising, without molestation,

inasmuch as we each possess the same inalienable right to this liberty, no one may use this right in such a way that he encroaches on the equal liberty of others. Price argues that this is self-evidently true since were it not then "there would be a contradiction in the nature of things, and it would be true that every one had a right to enjoy what every one had a right to destroy."[68] However, my right does not imply any positive duty on the part of others that they help save me. The right to one's life does not connote that one will be free from disease nor that it is incumbent on others to do all they can to prevent one from dying but only that they not actively intervene to kill you. Even under circumstances where two people are confronted with conditions such that one man's life is contingent on the other's death, neither may raise his hand against the other under pain of violating this right, despite the fact that both will die. Or, put more simply, my right to something, say my liberty or my life, entails only prohibitions on others and not positive commands.

All civil government, Price maintains, both originates with the people and exists to advance their happiness by securing these rights.[69] Those governments that operate on principles at variance with this debase the natural ends of government and enslave their citizens. Free governments, furthermore, are the only kind that are favorable to human improvement. Since the essential function of government is to ensure that we may peaceably enjoy our rights and since this conduces most to our happiness, nations that are administered in conformity with other ends pervert the natural and inherent equality with which God has endowed each of us.

Ferguson's conception of rights is at sharp variance with that offered by Price. Just as notions of private property evolve as societies develop from the rudest to the most polished, so it is with rights, whose primary function is to secure property and thus ensure our liberty. These rights evolve over time and owe their origin to the inequalities of station and the attempts to curb the abuse of power that arise as societies

---

that mode of religion which we think best or of making the decisions of our consciences respecting religious truth the rule of our conduct, and not any of the decisions of our fellow-men" (ibid., 68).

68. "Additional Observations," 81.

69. "Observations," 69.

advance from savagery to civilization. This subordination of rank that marks all societies except the most primitive is, Ferguson writes, natural and salutary. "It is a common observation," he notes,

> that mankind were originally equal. They have indeed by nature equal rights to their preservation, and to the use of their talents; but they are fitted for different stations; and when they are classed by a rule taken from this circumstance, they suffer no injustice on the side of their natural rights. It is obvious, that some mode of subordination is as necessary to men as society itself; and this, not only to attain the ends of government, but to comply with an order established by nature.[70]

Unlike Price, Ferguson rejects the idea that our rights and the personal liberty that they allow are natural and attach to us by virtue of our humanity, independent of our history. In fact, he argues, they take their specific shape from the totality of events that shape our past and differ in particulars as society evolves. He observes:

> Liberty, in one sense, appears to be the portion of polished nations alone. The savage is personally free, because he lives unrestrained, and acts with the members of his tribe on terms of equality. The barbarian is frequently independent from a continuance of the same circumstance, or because he has courage and a sword. But good policy alone can provide for the regular administration of justice, reconstitute a force in the state, which is ready on every occasion to defend the rights of its members.[71]

The distinction between Price and Ferguson on the issue of rights emerges most clearly in Ferguson's *Remarks* where he juxtaposes Price's appeal to the concept of natural universal rights to the historical obligations and privileges that in law determine the relation of the colonists to Great Britain. "The Doctor is pleased to say," Ferguson writes, "that the question of right, with all liberal inquirers, ought to be, not what jurisdiction over them, precedents, statutes, and charters give,

70. *Essay,* 63–64.
71. Ibid., 247.

but what reason and equity, and the rights of humanity give."[72] Ferguson expressed amazement at this approach to politics which he felt could only lead to expressions of private interest and opinion, depriving one of the fixed landmarks provided by precedents, statutes, and charters.

In any case, Ferguson did not regard liberty as dependent on the presence of abstract rights. Rather, the crucial determinant of a free society was the stability of those institutions that guaranteed our ability to enjoy what rights we in fact had. Throughout his writings Ferguson emphasizes the singular importance of the security of property, without which justice and liberty would be impossible. It is the preservation of our property and station that makes society possible and secures to each of us the rights that we have acquired. Indeed, the paramount function of government is to ensure to its citizens this security. "Liberty consists in the security of the citizen against every enemy," Ferguson maintained in his *Principles,*

> whether foreign or domestic, public or private, from whom, without any provision being made for his defence, he might be exposed to wrong or oppression of any sort: And the first requisite, it should seem, towards obtaining this security, is the existence of an effective government to wield the strength of the community against foreign enemies, and to repress the commission of wrongs at home.[73]

THE NATURE OF EMPIRE

No distinction between the presuppositions of Price and Ferguson is clearer than on the question of the nature of empire. It seems clear that Ferguson conceives of the Empire covering the home islands and the American colonies as a unitary political structure comprising one people bound together by the same laws, customs, and traditions. He observes that the colonies by virtue of having been part of the British Empire are subject to the sovereignty of the mother country and to its legislature.[74] Price, on the other hand, offers a conception

72. *Remarks,* 16.
73. *Principles,* 2:461.
74. *Remarks,* 41.

of empire that is clearly federative, with each constituent unit independent of the others with regard to its internal affairs and all paying loyalty to the same sovereign. "An empire," Price maintains,

> is a collection of states or communities united by some common bond or tie. If these states have each of them free constitutions of government and, with respect to taxation and internal legislation, are independent of the other states but united by compacts or alliances or subjection to a great council representing the whole, or to one monarch entrusted with the supreme executive power, in these circumstances the empire will be an empire of freemen. If, on the contrary, like the different provinces subject to the Grand Seignior, none of the states possess any independent legislative authority but are all subject to an absolute monarch whose will is law, then is the empire an empire of slaves.[75]

Ferguson's notion of the British Empire of the eighteenth century is far more traditional. Having expanded its territory and having originally populated these new areas with its own people who carried with them British law, the Empire constituted nothing more than a geographical extension of the original state whose ultimate political authority remained where it was previously lodged. In fact, the colonies, economic satellites of the mother country, had as their primary function the generation of wealth for Britain. The mere expansion of territory, Ferguson would have maintained, was not sufficient justification for the creation of separate, constituent sovereignties, each independent of the others and reliant on the central authority only on issues touching the whole. The history of mankind, Ferguson contended, reflects this motive to empire, a desire to extend the limits of the existing state and uniting the whole under one central power while severely limiting the degree of self-government in the provinces.

In America's case especially, justice demanded that the colonies contribute to the upkeep of this centralized empire inasmuch as they were the recipients of the most essential benefits the mother country could extend to them by securing their property from domestic and

75. "Observations," 80.

foreign assault and by providing them with an outlet for their goods.[76]
Britain's relation to her colonies was indeed particularly generous[77]
and it was incumbent on the American colonies to indemnify her for
the expenses that the central authority had determined had been in-
curred on their behalf.

It is interesting that in his *Essay* Ferguson called attention to the
dangers that adhere in too extensive an empire, the effect of which is
to deprive us of a stage on which men of political integrity and sagacity
can play a role. "When we reason in behalf of our species," Ferguson
writes,

> although we may lament the abuses which sometimes arise from in-
> dependence, and opposition of interest; yet, whilst any degrees of
> virtue remain with mankind, we cannot wish to croud, under one
> establishment, numbers of men who may serve to constitute sev-
> eral; or to commit affairs to the conduct of one senate, one legisla-
> tive or executive power, which, upon a distinct and separate foot-
> ing, might furnish an exercise of ability, and a theater of glory, to
> many.[78]

Despite this caution, however, he remained committed to supporting
the conflict with the colonies until Britain was successful in reestab-
lishing its North American empire. At some point following the return
of the Carlisle Commission to Plymouth in December 1778, Ferguson
penned a memorial regarding American independence in which he
maintained that "the danger and the consequences of this separation
are so great as to justify every tryal that can be made to prevent it."[79]

In any event, the success of the American cause put an end to the
empire as Ferguson conceived and transformed its essential nature
from one of political dominion to one of economic penetration. It has
recently been noted:

76. *Remarks,* 18–19.

77. Ferguson goes so far as to make the following claim: "It is certainly true,
that no nation ever planted Colonies with so liberal or so noble a hand as England has done" (ibid., 26).

78. *Essay,* 61.

79. "Appendix H," in *Ferguson Correspondence,* 2:556.

British statesmen in the late eighteenth century were sometimes given to musing that a world-wide network of commerce was preferable to an Empire of rule over land and people. Some historians have argued that a "revulsion against colonization," accentuated by the quarrel that led to the loss of most of Britain's dominions in North America and coinciding with the rise of industrialization, brought about a shift away from an empire of rule to the pursuit of trade and influence throughout the world. Trade, it has been argued, came to be preferred to dominion.[80]

STATE OF NATURE AND GOVERNMENT BY CONTRACT

Price, like Locke, holds that political authority derives, and indeed can only derive, from the people. Men have no more a natural obligation to obey their government than they do their neighbor. The obligation to conform to the dictates of the civil magistrate stems solely from the freely extended consent of the person governed, without which one cannot become the subject of another or be constrained by law not of one's making. As Price argues:

> All civil government, as far as it can be denominated *free*, is the creature of the people. It originates with them. It is conducted under their direction; and has in view nothing but their happiness. All its different forms are no more than so many different modes in which they chuse to direct their affairs, and to secure the quiet enjoyment of their rights. In every free state every man is his own Legislator. All *taxes* are free gifts for public services. All *laws* are particular provisions or regulations established by COMMON CONSENT for gaining protection and safety. And all *Magistrates* are Trustees or Deputies for carrying these regulations into execution.[81]

80. P. J. Marshall, "Introduction," P. J. Marshall, ed., *The Oxford History of the British Empire*, vol. 2: *The Eighteenth Century* (Oxford: Oxford University Press, 1998), 25–26.

81. "Observations," 69. Every man is his own legislator in a free state, according to Price, in the sense that every man in a truly free state participates in making the political decisions or in choosing those who make the political decisions that govern him. See "Additional Observations," 140.

Indeed, in one significant area Price goes significantly further than does Locke in leaving greater power in the hands of the people. Locke's social contract, like those of most other political theorists who invoke the notion, is such that it empowers its signers to determine the form of political authority that will prevail together with its duration and its limits. Once having established the terms of the original social contract, however, those bound by its terms are forever constrained to observe its provisions unless the magistrate violates his obligations. They hold no residual power to change the form of government, having ceded such a right when removing themselves from the state of nature. Price, on the other hand, maintained that ultimate sovereignty over the form and style of government was never surrendered and remained in the keeping of those who were governed throughout. The political sovereignty of the people is continuous and may be exercised as and when they see fit.[82]

Price's arguments supporting the colonists' demands for a change in the civil magistracy are thus even stronger than those that would have been put forward by Locke. Not only had the civil magistrate, in the form of the Royal Court and the various administrations responsible for American policy since the end of the French and Indian War, violated the terms of the original contract whereby the English colonists who settled in the New World were guaranteed their rights, but it was also the case that the American people wished to reorder their political institutions to better reflect their needs and wishes, which they had every right to do. Despite the fact that the history of the relationship between Great Britain and her American colonies was an oppressive and despotic one, the colonists were under no obligation to prove that the British magistracy had breached the contract it had entered into with its subjects to protect their rights. It was sufficient that they wished to replace the political authority of the mother country with one more in keeping with their welfare.

Unlike Price, Ferguson rejected the notion that civil society and

---

82. "Without all doubt, it is the choice of the people that makes civil governors. The people are the spring of all civil power, and they have a right to modify it as they please." "Additional Observations," 148.

government are artifacts, creations of some original contract whereby free and equal beings living independently in some natural state devoid of political authority came together to confer their natural rights and powers on a newly designated sovereign. Committed to approaching the study of man and society scientifically, that is, to describing man as he is actually observed, Ferguson rejected the notion of "man in the state of nature" in the sense of man before the advent of society. "Mankind are to be taken in groupes," he wrote, "as they have always subsisted." That society is coeval with man is confirmed by the fact that the individual is the bearer of social dispositions and that regardless of where we find man, we find him gathered together with others.[83]

Ferguson rejected the social contract theory as a valid account of the origins of government with many of the same arguments earlier offered by Hume.[84] The establishment of formal rules enforceable by a permanent political institution emerge, claimed Ferguson, not from the desire to create a stronger social union but rather in response to the abuses that arise from an imperfect distribution of justice. Ferguson held that a system of formal political arrangements did not rest on consent but was gradually shaped to meet the interests of justice with respect to securing private property.[85] It is a useless analytical tool, he claimed, to posit the idea of universal consent to what was, in fact, the gradual emergence of formalized rules of action which took their origin in earlier modes of behavior. "What was in one generation a propensity to herd with the species," Ferguson observed, "becomes, in the ages which follow, a principle of national union. What was originally

83. *Essay*, 10.

84. See David Hume, *A Treatise of Human Nature*, ed. L. A. Selby-Bigge, 2d ed. (Oxford: Clarendon Press, 1978), 534–39.

85. *Essay*, 1:22–26. The notion that government itself, far from being the product of conscious design, took its form gradually and without deliberate intent has led one commentator to refer to Ferguson's rejection of the social contract as the boldest attack on the contractarian theory of political obligation that had been made up to that time (Hermann Huth, "Soziale und Individualistische Auffassung im 18. Jahrhundert, vornehmlich bei Adam Smith und Adam Ferguson," *Staats- und Sozialwissenschaftliche Forschungen* [Leipzig: Duncker & Humblot, 1907], 46).

an alliance for common defence, becomes a concerted plan of political force."[86]

Ferguson does, however, make use of the term "state of nature," but he confines its use to his ethics rather than to his political theory. He regarded a progression toward excellence or perfection as the governing principle of all moral life. Thus, at one and the same time, Ferguson enunciated a law of perfection that offered an explanation both for individual morality and for social progress. For Ferguson, the natural development of the individual and the species toward perfection describes the "state of nature." Any point that lies along this continuum of development is as much man's "state of nature" as is any other point.[87] In his major work on moral philosophy, Ferguson noted:

> The state of nature or the distinctive character of any progressive being is to be taken, not from its description at the outset, or at any subsequent stage of its progress; but from an accumulative view of its movement throughout. The oak is distinguishable from the pine, not merely by its seed leaf; but by every successive aspect of its form; by its foliage in every successive season; by its acorn; by its spreading top; by its lofty growth; and the length of its period. And the state of nature, relative to every tree in the wood, includes all the varieties of form or dimension through which it is known to pass in the course of its nature.[88]

COMMERCE

Despite the fact that both Price and Ferguson were aware of the advantages to be derived from commerce, in the case of neither writer was their support unreserved. While the nature of their fears regarding an unrestrained commercial society were similar, Price was particularly fearful that a substantial increase in luxury might pose a fatal threat to liberty. This is not to suggest that Price advocated an

86. *Essay,* 118.

87. "If the palace be unnatural," wrote Ferguson in an often-quoted passage, "the cottage is so no less; and the highest refinements of political and moral apprehension, are not more artificial in their kind, than the first operation of sentiment and reason" (ibid., 14).

88. *Principles,* 1:192.

austere and frugal lifestyle as alone compatible with a free and independent nation. He appears to have been aware of the benefits that accrued to Great Britain from its flourishing trade with the American colonies. "This trade," he maintained,

> was not only thus an increasing trade, but it was a trade in which we had no rivals, a trade certain, constant, and uninterrupted, and which, by the shipping employed in it, and the naval stores supplied by it, contributed greatly to the support of that navy which is our chief national strength. Viewed in these lights it was an object unspeakably important. But it will appear still more so if we view it in its connexions and dependencies. It is well known that our trade with Africa and the West-Indies cannot easily subsist without it. And, upon the whole, it is undeniable that it has been one of the main springs of our opulence and splendour and that we have, in a great measure, been indebted to it for our ability to bear a debt so much heavier than that which, fifty years ago, the wisest men thought would necessarily sink us.[89]

Despite these sentiments, however, Price's preferences were clear. He saw in a society that devoted itself primarily to commerce and the acquisition of wealth a source of servility and venality that would inevitably lead to corruption and the loss of liberty. With respect to the decline in trade with Britain on the American colonies, Price noted, "Having all the necessaries and chief conveniencies of life within themselves they have no dependence upon [their pre-Revolutionary trade], and the loss of it will do them unspeakable good, by preserving them from the evils of luxury and the temptations of wealth and keeping them in that state of virtuous simplicity which is the greatest happiness."[90] These views are particularly surprising inasmuch as Price was fully aware of the benefits of international trade in encouraging tolerance among diverse communities and in fostering peaceful relations between states, a sentiment raised to a principle of liberal ideology in the following century. "Foreign trade," he wrote,

89. "Observations," 102–03.
90. Ibid., 115.

has, in some respects, the most useful tendency. By creating an intercourse between distant kingdoms it extends benevolence, removes local prejudices, leads every man to consider himself more as a citizen of the world than of any particular state, and, consequently, checks the excesses of that love of our country which has been applauded as one of the noblest, but which, really, is one of the most destructive principles in human nature. Trade also, by enabling every country to draw from other countries conveniencies and advantages which it cannot find within itself, produces among nations a sense of mutual dependence, and promotes the general improvement.[91]

Yet, despite Price's economic sophistication,[92] he repeatedly viewed America as exempt from these benefits. Indeed, immediately following the passage just quoted, Price wrote that "There is no part of mankind to which these uses of trade are of less consequence than the American states."[93] And, in a letter to Ezra Stiles written after the war's conclusion, he observed that "It may be best for the united states that their rage for foreign trade should be checked, and that they should be oblig'd to find all they want within themselves, and to be satisfy'd with the simplicity, health, plenty, vigour, virtue and happiness which they may derive from agriculture and internal colonization."[94] Price appears to have believed that men in an agrarian society, who were under

91. "Observations on the Importance of the American Revolution, and the Means of Making It a Benefit to the World, To Which Is Added, a Letter from Mr. Turgot, Late Comptroller of the Finances of France" in Peach, *Ethical Foundations,* 210 (hereafter cited as "Importance of the Revolution").

92. Price was a seminal contributor to the study of finance and insurance and was universally so regarded. His *Appeal to the Public on the Subject of the National Debt* (London, 1771) argued decisively against the increasing British public debt and called for its elimination. In the same year he published an essay, *Observations on Reversionary Payments,* that was of crucial importance in making possible a workable system of life insurance and pensions.

93. "Importance of the Revolution," 210.

94. Price to Ezra Stiles, Newington Green, August 2, 1785, in Bernard Peach and D. O. Thomas, eds., *The Correspondence of Richard Price,* 3 vols. (Durham, N.C.: Duke University Press, 1991), 2:297.

no compulsion to act in their narrow self-interest and whose connections with one's fellowmen and with the community were deeper, were more likely to defend their rights against domestic and foreign invasion. Price expanded on these views in 1785 when he returned to the subject of American independence.

> Better infinitely will it be for them to consist of bodies of plain and honest farmers, than of opulent and splendid merchants. Where in these states do the purest manners prevail? Where do the inhabitants live most on an equality and most at their ease? Is it not in those inland parts where agriculture gives health and plenty, and trade is scarcely known? Where, on the contrary, are the inhabitants most selfish, luxurious, loose, and vicious, and at the same time most unhappy? Is it not along the sea coasts and in the great towns where trade flourishes and merchants abound? So striking is the effect of these different situations on the vigour and happiness of human life, that in the one, population would languish did it receive no aid from emigration, while in the other, it increases to a degree scarcely ever before known.[95]

Ferguson was far more positive in his assessment of the benefits of commerce than was Price, despite what he regarded as its potential dangers. He was prepared to concede that commercial societies, which he equated with societies based on the principle of private property, would inevitably display an uneven distribution of wealth. But this inequality, he argued, served the function of acting as a spur to industry and an incentive to the labor of the great mass of the population,[96] the ultimate effect of which would serve to encourage the production of ever-greater quantities of wealth, thus benefitting all members of the community. "The object of commerce is wealth," wrote Ferguson, and "in the progress, as well as in the result of commercial arts, mankind are enabled to subsist in growing numbers; learn to ply their resources, and to wield their strength, with superior ease and success."[97]

He further argued that active participation in commercial life en-

95. "Importance of the Revolution," 211.
96. *Principles,* 2:371.
97. Ibid., 1:254, 253.

couraged men in the exercise of a host of virtues, including industry, sobriety, frugality, justice, even beneficence and friendships.[98] Although Ferguson contended that civilization was not invariably accompanied by a high degree of commercial activity, he did insist that the prime motive force for individual and social progress was ambition, "the specific principle of advancement uniformly directed to this end, and not satiated with any given measure of gratification." And ambition, in turn, he noted, operated no less "in the concerns of mere animal life; in the provision of subsistence, of accommodation, and ornament," as "in the progress of society, and in the choice of its institutions."[99] Further, and more important, Ferguson saw no conflict between those social arrangements that acted as guarantees of individual liberty and those that encouraged an increase in wealth.[100] He contended that the forces that lead to an expansion in population, which Ferguson equated with social wealth, required the successful pursuit of commerce coupled with a vigorous defense of individual rights. "The growth of industry," he wrote, "the endeavours of men to improve their arts, to extend their commerce, to secure their possessions, and to establish their rights, are the most effectual means to promote population."[101] Indeed, one intellectual historian has observed that one of the chief reasons for the popularity of Ferguson's *Essay* among Americans was its unambiguous defense of commercial society over more primitive cultures, despite other social costs that might possibly accompany civilization.[102]

98. Ibid., 254.

99. Ibid., 235.

100. Ferguson writes in his *Essay* that "The laws made to secure the rights and liberties of the people, may serve as encouragements to population and commerce" (131).

101. Ibid., 135.

102. "What generally emerges from Ferguson's *Essay* and from others like it, is a simple and clear demonstration from conjectural history of a proposition which Americans, in their feelings of pity and censure over the fate of the Indians, needed desperately to believe; that men in becoming civilized had gained much more than they had lost; and that civilization, the act of civilizing, for all of its destruction of primitive virtues, put something higher and greater in their place" (Roy Harvey Pearce, *The Savages of America: A Study of the Indian and the Idea of Civilization,* rev. ed. [Baltimore: Johns Hopkins Press, 1965], 85).

All this is not to deny that Ferguson dealt extensively with the harmful effects of the increasing division of labor that marked advanced commercial societies. These effects he regarded as possessing the potential of producing a permanent subordination of rank, thus allowing for the rise of despotism.[103] "Many mechanical arts," he wrote,

> require no capacity; they succeed best under a total suppression of sentiment and reason; and ignorance is the mother of industry as well as of superstition. Reflection and fancy are subject to err; but a habit of moving the hand, or the foot, is independent of either. Manufactures, accordingly, prosper most, where the mind is least consulted, and where the workshop may, without any great effort of imagination, be considered as an engine, the parts of which are men.[104]

In elaborating the consequences of the division of labor, however, Ferguson did not conclude that it would inevitably prove to be a Trojan horse whose ultimate social effect would invariably be the destruction of a free and virtuous society. Although the division of labor might well place strains upon the social fabric and make possible a permanent subordination of the many by the few, it also facilitates the fullest expression of each individual's natural abilities and personal excellences and hence serves a particularly valuable moral and social purpose. "With the benefit of commerce . . . [and the division of labor which naturally accompanies it]," Ferguson noted, "every individual is enabled to avail himself, to the utmost, of the peculiar advantage of his place; to work on the peculiar materials with which nature has furnished him; to humour his genius or disposition, and betake himself to the task in which he is peculiarly qualified to proceed."[105]

Ferguson's response to the question of whether the dangers inherent in commercial societies could be averted was unambiguous. So long as the members of the community take an active role in civic affairs, so long as they prevent the division of labor from embracing the

103. Ferguson's views respecting the dangers arising out of the division of labor are discussed at some length in Ronald Hamowy, "Adam Smith, Adam Ferguson, and the Division of Labour," *Economica* 35 (1968): 249–59.

104. *Essay*, 174.

105. *Principles*, 2:424.

more crucial aspects of political and military life,[106] it is possible to secure the nation against despotism. In sum, while it is true that commercial societies bring with them the risks of despotism in the form of an overspecialization of function and a permanent system of subordination, a decline into tyranny need not follow. The stifling of public involvement in the affairs of state—either through the throttling of individual capacity consequent on an extensive division of labor or out of an all-consuming concern solely for one's private wealth—is, in the end, what makes despotism possible. Encourage the populace to actively participate in the civic and military affairs of the nation and tyranny can be averted. Man's ability to uncover the laws that determine his condition provides him the opportunity to avoid what might otherwise be regarded as that corruption to which all commercial societies might descend.

These differences in their approach to political philosophy persisted in regard to the events in France two decades later. While Price was a fervent champion of the Revolutionary cause, Ferguson was to express grave reservations respecting French attempts to "transform their Monarchy into a Democracy."[107] He could not tolerate the pretensions of French revolutionary ideology[108] and was dubious that any of the political tinkering undertaken by the various revolutionary bodies would prove of value in either establishing or maintaining a freer polity. At one point he even refers to the revolutionary forces as "the Antichrist himself in the form of Democracy & Atheism."[109] Ferguson maintained that by abetting the revolutionaries in America the

106. Ferguson was a strong supporter of a civilian army and had written tracts pointing out the serious dangers that followed the creation of a professional military force and calling for the establishment of a civilian militia. See his *Reflections Previous to the Establishment of a Militia* (London: R. & J. Dodsley, 1756), published anonymously.

107. Ferguson to Sir John Macpherson, Edinburgh, July 31, 1790 (no. 269) in *Ferguson Correspondence,* 2:340.

108. With reference to the French Convention, for example, Ferguson wrote ironically, "[they] are Surely very impudent in pretending to prescribe to the great Infallible Sovereign People of France whom they shall elect." Ferguson to Sir John Macpherson, Nydpath Castle, September 17, 1795 (no. 297), ibid., 370.

109. Ferguson to Alexander Carlyle, Edinburgh, November 23, 1796 (no. 322), ibid., 408.

French court had set a dangerous example to its own people.[110] The cataclysm in France, he argued, posed a significant threat to the security of Great Britain and to the peace of the continent. Indeed, Ferguson's particular concern was that Britain would be dragged into what had started as an internal French conflict but would likely become international.[111]

Price's views on the Revolution are, of course, well known, primarily because of Edmund Burke's *Reflections on the Revolution in France,* written in response to Price's comments. The sermon Price gave at the Old Jewry on November 4, 1789, before the Society for Commemorating the Revolution in Great Britain reflected his enormous enthusiasm for what was taking place in France. The nominal purpose of the address, which Price entitled *A Discourse on the Love of Our Country,* was to celebrate the hundredth anniversary of the Glorious Revolution. In doing so Price linked the events of 1688–89 with the American Revolution and the reforms in France in one of the most impassioned speeches delivered during the course of this tempestuous period. "I have lived to see the rights of men better understood than ever," he said,

> and nations panting for liberty, which seemed to have lost the idea of it. I have lived to see thirty millions of people, indignant and resolute, spurning at slavery, and demanding liberty with an irresistible voice, their king led in triumph, and an arbitrary monarch

110. Ferguson to Sir John Macpherson, Edinburgh, January 19, 1790 (no. 265), ibid., 336–37.

111. Ferguson seems to have blamed the French military, drunk with notions of democracy, for the revolution. "The French Revolution," he wrote in 1797, "it seems is still a Curiosity; many things certainly led to it and the French heads a stir after new things made bolder and wider steps than ever were made before by Mankind in any case whatever; but all this would have come to nothing if the French Army had Adhered to their noblesse officers & to the Crown: but they did not; & they made the Revolution. They made & will continue to make every change that is to happen in France to the end of time. They were struck with democracy as with a Spark of Electricity or a Stroke of Lightening & have continued changed ever Since. They will follow no General that swerves from Democracy & will cut the throats of all Representatives of the People of France if the Cry of Royalism is raised against them." Ferguson to Alexander Carlyle, Hallyards, October 2, 1797 (no. 332), ibid., 423.

surrendering himself to his subjects. After sharing in the benefits of one Revolution, I have been spared to be a witness to two other Revolutions, both glorious. And now, methinks, I see the ardor for liberty catching and spreading, a general amendment beginning in human affairs, the dominion of kings changed for the dominion of laws, and the dominion of priests giving way to the dominion of reason and conscience.

Be encouraged, all ye friends of freedom and writers in its defence! The times are auspicious. Your labours have not been in vain. Behold kingdoms, admonished by you, starting from sleep, breaking their fetters, and claiming justice from their oppressors! Behold, the light you have struck out, after setting America free, reflected to France and there kindled into a blaze that lays despotism in ashes and warms and illuminates Europe!"[112]

It is a reflection on the scope of the eighteenth-century Whig tradition that it could encompass two writers whose views were as dissimilar in certain particulars as were those of Price and Ferguson. Yet both were legatees of the Revolutionary Settlement of 1688 and both accepted its ideological premises. Both agreed that a free society was one that recognized the primacy of private property and the critical importance of the rule of law and both identified individual liberty with the rights of citizens to act as they chose, limited only by a modestly intrusive government. Finally, both had original insights into the nature of freedom and despotism that enlightened and informed. In light of this, it is not difficult to see why, despite their differences, the American colonists were receptive to both these thinkers.

---

112. "A Discourse on the Love of Our Country" in D. O. Thomas, ed., *Political Writings*, Cambridge Texts in the History of Political Thought (Cambridge: Cambridge University Press, 1991), 195–96.

Federalism, Constitutionalism, and Republican Liberty: The First Constructions of the Constitution

Within three years of the inauguration of the Constitution, its greatest champions, accompanied or followed by a host of other leaders, found themselves irreparably divided over how the first great democratic revolution might be most effectually secured. The reasons for their conflict were enormously complex and utterly profound, stretching from the first—and ever more apparently as both sides tried to mobilize the public—over nearly every aspect of the nation's public life. Clashing views about the foreign, economic, and financial policies appropriate for the American republic welled from deeply different regional perspectives and from radically opposing lessons drawn from the experience and the inheritance of thought from eighteenth-century Britain. Contrasting attitudes toward popular participation hinted at fundamentally contending visions of the nature of a sound republic. So, however, did the rapidly emerging parties' differing conceptions of the nature of the federal union and a sound interpretation of the document on which it rested. The Constitution may have been the longest step toward defining how liberty could be secured in an extended, federal republic, but it did not by any means resolve this question. The workability and wisdom of the novel federal system conceived by the Constitutional Convention was the central issue in the national debate over whether the Constitution should be ratified or not. The ambiguities inherent in the constitutional division of authority continued to divide the Founders through the rest of their careers.

There is nothing truly new, of course, in any of these points. They bear reemphasis primarily because, for much of the twentieth century, as "states' rights" were discredited and national power grew, the finest scholarship about the Founding tended to be more concerned with different topics, as did the nation and the courts. Nevertheless, in the years surrounding the adoption of the Constitution, federalism seemed as crucial as republicanism to the aspirations of the Revolutionary generation—as crucial and as problematic. These master concepts were, indeed, inseparably connected by a general agreement that the great experiment in liberty—that is, in the creation of a governmental system grounded exclusively on popular consent and popular control but at the same time offering firm securities for individual rights—could not succeed without a continental union, yet would just as surely fail in a consolidated or unitary national republic. Continental union seemed the only guarantee that North America would not become another Europe, where a multitude of rival states or small confederations would arm themselves with standing military forces, powerful executives, large debts, high taxes, and other unrepublican equipage. A single national government, however, seemed hardly less consistent with protection for the rights of all or with the sorts of bonds between the rulers and the ruled that characterized a genuine republic.

The eighteenth-century British Empire was a working federal system, in practice though not in theory. Judged by the prosperity and power of the Empire, the system was successful, though many British politicians were convinced that it was failing. Setting out to fix what may not have needed fixing, they tightened supervision of the colonies and after 1763 attempted Parliamentary taxation. The Empire shattered on its inability to solve or even to define the federal problem: how might political authority be safely, effectively, and lastingly divided between the central and subordinate governments? In the end the colonies would fight rather than concede that there were no definable limits to Parliamentary sovereignty. The English would fight rather than concede that Parliament's authority was "constitutionally" constrained by the subordinate authority of the colonial assemblies. As Americans declared their independence, they concluded from the conflict with a distant, unresponsive central government that liberty must be secured by written constitutions grounded wholly on elections and a union carefully restricted to a narrow range of general concerns. Ten years later, nevertheless, the new American union was itself in danger of collapse over the difficulties posed by its own initial effort to resolve the federal problem.

Early on, to put it quickly, the federal riddle seemed to have a fairly obvious solution. As Thomas Jefferson expressed it, "To make us one nation as to foreign concerns and keep us distinct in domestic ones gives the outline of the proper division of powers between the general and particular governments."[1] The union would be a firm and perpetual league of friendship between the several new republics, whose Continental Congress would concern itself almost exclusively with war and international relations. Surprisingly little systematic thought was given to the matter. The Articles of Confederation, not even ratified until 1781, did little more than formalize the institutions and authority that had evolved in practice in the years since 1774.[2]

By 1781, however, it was clear to the majority of national leaders that the Articles were seriously flawed; and by the middle 1780s, even relatively localistic leaders thought the union was in crisis. Constitutional reform would not have taken the distinctive shape it took if many of those leaders had not been disgusted with the policies adopted in the several states during a sharp postwar depression. The Constitution was deliberately designed to correct the democratic errors that many of its Framers thought had been committed in the states.[3] But constitutional reform would not have come about at all if the Confederation had been able to confront the economic downturn, pay its debts, and handle other problems—if many, for that matter, had not believed that the union was in imminent danger of dissolution and even that the failure of the republican Revolution could follow the collapse of union.

Even at this point, the reach of national consensus seems as striking as any of the arguments that would ensue. The Constitutional Convention easily achieved a firm agreement that the current federal arrangement was inherently and irredeemably defective: a sovereignty over sovereigns, a general government requiring independent action by the states to execute its measures, would have to be replaced by one

1. Jefferson to James Madison, December 16, 1786, in *The Republic of Letters: The Correspondence Between Thomas Jefferson and James Madison, 1776–1826*, ed. James Morton Smith, 3 vols. (New York: Norton, 1995), 458. Punctuation, spelling, and capitalization have been modernized here and throughout the essay.

2. The best recent discussion is Jack N. Rakove, *The Beginnings of National Politics: An Interpretive History of the Continental Congress* (New York: Johns Hopkins University Press, 1982).

3. The classic study is Gordon S. Wood, *The Creation of the American Republic, 1776–1787* (Chapel Hill: University of North Carolina Press, 1969).

deriving more directly from the people and possessing independent means of compelling obedience to its commands.[4] Still, the Constitutional Convention worked within a general agreement, also, on the powers or responsibilities that ought to be in federal hands, and these were generally conceded to be relatively few: an independent power of taxation, regulation of the country's trade, the powers vested in the general Congress by the old Confederation, and a handful of additional responsibilities requiring general supervision. Accordingly, a reconstructed central government responsible for a limited range of general concerns was placed atop a confederation of republics. Indeed, I would suggest, the Framers' consciousness that they were framing a general government of specific and limited powers is the best explanation even for their greatest mistake: their unanimous decision not to frame a bill of rights.

Original understandings are, in most respects, a troublesome, contentious issue. Remarkably, however, few participants on either side of the impressive national debate about adoption of the Constitution broke from the agreement that a firm, effective union was essential to the liberty, prosperity, and happiness of the United States while a consolidated national government would prove destructive to them all. *The Federalist* was vitally concerned to demonstrate that every power granted to the central government was at once essential and guarded as carefully as reason could require against the possibility of abuse, that the Constitution was not so much an addition of new powers to the general government as a means of rendering its current powers more effective, and that the mass of powers granted to the central government would not endanger the residual rights of the people and the states. The finest writers on the other side, "Brutus" and "The Federal Farmer," acknowledged that the document did not create a unitary system and admitted that the union needed to be strengthened. Their argument with "Publius" was over whether any system structured as the new one was and armed not only with the powers actually enumerated

4. This paraphrases the language of *The Federalist* No. 15, which had echoed throughout the Constitutional Convention. For the ease with which the Convention agreed that repairs of the existing Articles of Confederation would not do, consider that the members needed less than three full days of direct comparison to reject the New Jersey alternative in favor of the amended Virginia Plan.

in the Constitution but also with the power to enact such other laws as might be "necessary and proper" to carry the enumerated powers into action would continue to be limited for any great length of time. There can be little doubt that people ratified the Constitution understanding, as Virginia put it, "that every power not granted thereby remains with [the people]" and, as New York added, "that those clauses in the said Constitution which declare that Congress shall not have or exercise certain powers do not imply that Congress is entitled to any powers not given by the said Constitution, but such clauses are to be construed either as exceptions to certain specified powers or as inserted merely for greater caution."[5]

But even a Constitution many times as long as this one was could not have answered every question. Thus, as soon as the first new Congress turned to the creation of a presidential cabinet, a puzzle was immediately apparent. The document was clear about who had the power of appointing major officers of state: the president, acting with the consent of the Senate. The Constitution said nothing, however, about who had the power to dismiss these great executive officials. Implications and interpretations were impossible to do without. And two years later in 1791 when Alexander Hamilton proposed the creation of a national bank, James Madison, the other "Publius," initiated an enduring argument between proponents of strict and broad constructions of the "sweeping clauses."[6] Indeed, with a single, partial exception—the Alien and Sedition Acts of 1798—every constitutional debate within

5. Virginia's ratification and proposed amendments, including a clause similar to New York's, can be found in *Creating the Bill of Rights: The Documentary Record from the First Federal Congress,* ed. Helen E. Veit, Kenneth R. Bowling, and Charlene Bangs Bickford (Baltimore: Johns Hopkins University Press, 1991), 17–21; New York's ratification is from Jonathan Elliot, ed., *The Debates in the Several State Conventions on the Adoption of the Federal Constitution* (New York: J. B. Lippincott, 1888), 1:327–31.

6. "Sweeping clauses" is a term of convenience (seldom used initially) for the opening and concluding clauses of Article I, Section 8: "The Congress shall have power to lay and collect taxes, duties, imposts and excises, to pay the debts and provide for the common defense and general welfare of the United States" and "To make all laws which shall be necessary and proper for carrying into execution the foregoing powers, and all other powers vested by this Constitution in the government of the United States, or in any department or officer thereof."

the Founders' lifetimes centered not on different understandings of the Bill of Rights as most contemporary controversies do but on a sound construction of these "general clauses" and the constitutional limits of federal power. Hamilton, followed by the Marshall Court, effectively rebutted Thomas Jefferson's insistence that measures were not "necessary" unless an enumerated power could not be carried into effect without them.[7] Still, neither Hamilton nor Marshall ever really answered Madison's original objection: if the means need not be *directly* conducive to the end, if a "necessary" measure need not be *clearly incidental* to it, what is to prevent chains of implication capable of reaching "every object of legislation" and completely overturning the effects of an enumeration? Nor was everybody willing to agree that all such questions should be settled by the courts. Thus, Andrew Jackson stood on good Jeffersonian ground when he insisted that he would perform his executive duties according to his own reading of the Constitution, not John Marshall's.

Suppose, moreover, that all three branches of the federal government should unite in "a deliberate, palpable, and dangerous exercise of . . . powers not granted" by the Constitution, which was the problem that Madison and Jefferson perceived in the legislation of 1798. In that event, Virginia and Kentucky (Madison and Jefferson) said, the states which were the parties to the constitutional compact should interpose to take "the necessary and proper measures . . . for maintaining unimpaired the authorities, rights, and liberties reserved to the states respectively, or to the people."[8] But then, again, interposition led, in no great time, to nullification and secession. Even Madison, perhaps the greatest constitutional theorist the country has ever produced, was never able to sit securely between the horns that seem to stick us either with disunionism (and the tyranny of local majorities) or with what we've come to call an imperial judiciary (and the tyranny of unelected, unresponsive judges). In 1788 and 1789, Madison worried that the process of judicial review "makes the judiciary depart-

7. *M'Culloch v. Maryland*, 4 Wheaton 316 (1819).

8. The quotations are from the Virginia Resolutions of 1798, in *The Papers of James Madison* (hereafter cited as Madison, *Papers*), ed. William T. Hutchinson et al. (Chicago and Charlottesville: University Press of Virginia, 1962–), 17:189–90.

ment paramount . . . to the legislature, which was never intended and can never be proper," anticipating Andrew Jackson.[9] In 1800 in defense of the Virginia Resolutions, he suggested that the courts *might* be the "last resort . . . in relation to the authorities of the other departments of the [general] government," but "not in relation to the rights of the parties to the constitutional compact," tempting John Calhoun.[10] Yet in the 1830s he insisted that the nullifiers had gotten it all wrong, that the Supreme Court *was* the penultimate arbiter of disputes between the nation and the states and that the nullifiers were dramatically at odds with the republican principle of majority control, a stand not wholly incompatible with that of Abraham Lincoln who would settle the dispute by force.[11]

The understandings of the Founders—and sometimes even of a single Founder—often prove impossible to capture, not least when different Founders plainly disagreed. Whether those understandings, so far as they can be discovered, should control our own is yet another question. It pays us, nevertheless, to probe the Founders' views. For on the reasons why our system should be only partly national in nature, on the intimate relationship between federalism and republicanism, and on the ways in which a federal division of authority can be maintained, we've yet to find Americans who thought so deeply or so well.

In 1789 the triumph of the Constitution was conditional and incomplete. Two states, North Carolina and Rhode Island, had rejected the reform. Several others had approved it only on the understanding that amendments would be framed, and the division over its adoption had intensified a feeling in its friends and foes alike that liberty itself might stand or fall on the decisions of the next few years. Supporters of the Constitution thought that it had saved the Union from the danger of a speedy dissolution and had armed that Union after

9. "Observations on Jefferson's Draft of a Constitution for Virginia" (1788) in Madison, *Papers*, 11:293. See also his 1789 speech on executive removal, discussed more fully below.

10. Madison, *Papers*, 17:424.

11. A full and superb discussion of Madison's late-life battle with the nullifiers is in Drew R. McCoy, *The Last of the Fathers: James Madison and the Republican Legacy* (Cambridge: Cambridge University Press, 1989), ch. 4.

years of ineffectuality with powers equal to its duties. But even its most ardent champions were painfully aware that every measure of the first new Congress would establish precedents for everything to come and that the Federal Convention had reserved for them a number of decisions needed to complete the system: creation of judicial and executive departments, not to mention resolution of the problems that had wrecked the old Confederation.[12] Even its most ardent champions, moreover, differed more than they were currently aware about the policies that would be necessary to restore the nation's health, the character of the regime created by the Constitution, and the strategies most likely to secure it.[13]

At the Constitutional Convention, Alexander Hamilton had candidly confessed that, if the nation's sentiments did not forbid it, he would favor abolition of the states or turning them into administrative districts of a national republic.[14] James Madison, by contrast, had been searching since the opening of the deliberations for a "middle ground" between excessive "independence" for the states and a complete consolidation.[15] Hamilton and Madison were able to collaborate effectively in their magnificent defense of the Convention's work because they both believed that the completed Constitution was a safe and necessary remedy for pressing national ills. Beneath their large agreements, nonetheless—beyond the topics that they needed to pursue in order to defend the Constitution—the authors of *The Federalist* had vastly different visions of the sort of nation the United States should be, contrasting attitudes about the document itself, and different ideas about the policies most likely to attach the people to it.

Hamilton, as ought to be notorious from recent scholarship, in-

12. As Madison told his father, July 5, 1789, the members were in "a wilderness without a single footstep to guide us," Madison, *Papers*, 12:278.

13. Full documentation of many of the following statements about the Founders would burden these notes unduly. This, with fuller argumentation, can be found in Lance Banning, *The Sacred Fire of Liberty: James Madison and the Founding of the Federal Republic* (Ithaca, N.Y.: Cornell University Press, 1995).

14. See his great speech of June 18, 1787, in *The Records of the Federal Convention of 1787*, ed. Max Farrand, 4 vols., rev. ed. (New Haven, Conn.: Yale University Press, 1937), 1:287.

15. See his preconvention letters to Edmund Randolph and George Washington, April 8 and 16, 1787, in Madison, *Papers*, 9:369, 383.

tended over time to arm the infant government with the financial, economic, and administrative tools that would permit it to compete with European empires on the Europeans' terms. "The premiere state-builder in a generation of state-builders," as Isaac Kramnick has called him,[16] he hoped to overcome endemic localism which he always saw as the outstanding danger to the Union by detaching vital portions of the nation's natural leadership from their connections with the states and binding them by solid ties of interest to the central government's success. No one's preferences, he told the great Convention, differed more than his from the completed Constitution. He supported it because he calculated, privately, that it would make it possible for an efficient administration to promote prosperity, secure the people's loyalty, and move the country gradually toward greater centralization.[17]

Madison, by contrast, understood the Constitution as an instrument by which America could long avoid the European institutions Hamilton associated with a modern state.[18] His politics had always been affected more than some contemporaries saw (and more than modern scholarship has generally detected) by early revolutionary condemnations of the British system of administration and finance, which Hamilton as secretary of the treasury would replicate as far as he was able. As the Federal Convention closed, Madison, as well as Hamilton, was doubtful that the reconstructed government could actually correct the failings of the old Confederation.[19] But as they wrote *The Federalist*,

16. *The Federalist Papers*, ed. Isaac Kramnick (Harmondsworth, U.K.: Viking Penguin, 1987), 67.

17. The crucial document here is an undated, private memorandum written shortly after the convention adjourned: "Conjectures About the New Constitution" in *The Papers of Alexander Hamilton* (hereafter cited as Hamilton, *Papers*), ed. Harold C. Syrett and Jacob E. Cooke, 26 vols. (New York: Columbia University Press, 1961–79), 4:275–77.

18. The quickest reference here may be his speech of June 29, 1787, in Farrand, *Records of the Convention*, 1:464–65.

19. See his letters to Jefferson of September 6 and October 24, 1787, Madison, *Papers*, 10:163–64, 207–16, suggesting that state equality in the Senate and the omission of a federal veto on state laws made it probable that the Constitution would "neither effectually answer its national object nor prevent the local mischiefs which everywhere excite disgusts against the state governments."

Madison was more successful than his colleague in concluding that the Constitution was a better document than he had thought when it was signed—indeed, that in the Constitution's complex, partly federal features, the Convention had contrived the best expedient that human ingenuity had yet discovered for securing liberty completely. Madison did not believe that it was possible (much less desirable) to integrate America in imitation of Great Britain; its citizens were too diverse, too nearly equal, and too little deferential. Unlike Hamilton, who would dismiss complaints about the regional inequities of his designs as simply selfish and divisive, Madison, who was distinctively Virginian in his thinking, was convinced that the United States could hold together only if its leaders consciously displayed a spirit of accommodation. Certainly he would accommodate demands for the addition of a bill of rights, not least because there was a good deal in the hopes and fears of sensible opponents of the Constitution to which he was, in fact, quite sympathetic.

"Brutus," Madison confessed, not long before agreeing to enlist in Hamilton's defense of the reform, struck plausibly at the foundations of the Constitution.[20] "Although the government reported by the convention does not go to a perfect and entire consolidation," Brutus wrote, "yet it approaches so near to it that it must, if executed, certainly and infallibly terminate in it." The central government was granted "absolute and uncontrollable power" over "every object to which it extends," including power to enact such laws as might be "necessary and proper" to carry its enumerated powers into execution; and "the powers of the general legislature extend to every case that is of the least importance." Federal laws and treaties would be the supreme laws of the land, binding every judge throughout the country, and there would be no need for any action by the states to carry them into effect. Certainly the federal taxing powers would extend to every object whatever, since Congress would itself determine what was "for the general welfare." In consequence, the states would find it so impossible to raise the money they required that they would soon be "annihilated,

20. Madison to Edmund Randolph, October 21, 1787, Madison, *Papers,* 10:199 and note 4.

except so far as they are barely necessary to the organization of the general government." But "a free republic," Brutus argued, could not "succeed over a country of such immense extent."

> If the people are to give their assent to the laws, by persons chosen and appointed by them, the manner of the choice and number chosen must be such as to possess, be disposed, and consequently qualified to declare the sentiments of the people; for if they do not know or are not disposed to speak the sentiments of the people, the people do not govern, but the sovereignty is in a few. . . . In a large extended country, it is impossible to have a representation possessing the sentiments and of integrity to declare the minds of the people without having it so numerous and unwieldy as to be subject in great measure to the inconveniency of a [direct] democratic government.

In a genuine republic, laws were executed "by the people turning out to aid the magistrate," not by military force. The people would do this, however, only if the government was "so constructed as to have the confidence, respect, and affection of the people," which would not be likely in a country as extensive as the United States. The people could not know their rulers, follow their proceedings, change them with facility, or unite with citizens in distant sections of the country to force a change nor could their representatives be familiar with local conditions and needs. Without the confidence of the people, there would be no way to make the laws effective "but by establishing an armed force to execute the laws at the point of the bayonet."[21]

"A fair and equal representation," another anti-Federalist observed, "is that in which the interests, feelings, opinions, and views of the people are collected in such manner as they would be were the people all assembled." It was dishonest to assure the people that they could choose their rulers "if they cannot, in the nature of things, choose men from among themselves and genuinely like themselves." But this could never be the case in an American legislature smaller than a mob.

21. "Brutus," No. 1, in *The Documentary History of the Ratification of the Constitution,* ed. Merrill Jensen et al. (Madison: State Historical Society of Wisconsin, 1976–), 1:412–21.

Legislators would inevitably be chosen from the four or five thousand natural aristocrats in the country: state governors or judges, members of the general Congress, state senators, army and militia officers, large property owners, and eminent professionals. The huge variety among the people would not be mirrored among legislators whose sympathies and associations would be entirely with people like themselves. The members of the legislature would inevitably be "too far removed from the people in general to sympathize with them, and too few to communicate with them." The people would be governed by an unresponsive few.[22]

Madison, though often understood too narrowly as the ratification contest's most determined champion of large republics, was not insensitive to these concerns. Even in the famous essay arguing that large republics are superior to small ones in their capacity "to secure the public good and private rights against the danger of" majority factions, he admitted that "there is a mean on both sides of which inconveniences will be found to lie."

> By enlarging too much the number of electors, you render the representative too little acquainted with all their local circumstances and lesser interests; as by reducing it too much, you render him unduly attached to these, and too little fit to comprehend and pursue great and national objects. The federal Constitution forms a happy combination in this respect; the great and aggregate interests being referred to the national, the local and particular to the state legislatures.[23]

Madison was not, in truth, an advocate of large republics simply defined. He argued, rather, that "the larger the society, provided it lie within a practicable sphere, the more duly capable it will be of self-government. And happily for the *republican cause,* the practicable sphere may be carried to a very great extent by a judicious modifi-

22. "Letters from the Federal Farmer," No. 7, in *The Anti-Federalist: An Abridgment of the Complete Anti-Federalist,* ed. Herbert J. Storing (Chicago: University of Chicago Press, 1985), 73–79.

23. *The Federalist,* ed. Jacob E. Cooke (Cleveland: Wesleyan University Press, 1961), No. 10, 63.

cation and mixture of the *federal principle*."[24] In *The Federalist* No. 39, he offered the most impressive contemporary analysis of the unprecedented blend of "federal" and "national" features in the Constitution; and he was centrally concerned throughout his numbers to persuade opponents that this novel compound would endure. "In the compound republic of America," he wrote, "the power surrendered by the people is first divided between two distinct governments and then the portion allotted to each subdivided among distinct and separate departments." Within each set of governments, the different branches would be chosen sometimes more and sometimes less directly by the people, which would guarantee a due concern for both their short- and long-term needs. The state and general governments would each be charged exclusively with the responsibilities that each was best equipped to handle, guarding the society against the threat of unresponsive rulers. The state and general governments would each control the other "at the same time that each will be controlled by itself" —and by the sovereign people. As long as that common master continued to be fit for freedom, Madison believed, future generations would continue to enjoy as much self-government as human nature would allow.[25]

But once (and if) the people have approved a Constitution properly dividing state and general responsibilities, how can this division be maintained? Amendments, anti-Federalists insisted, were essential; and despite initial reservations, Madison, the leader of the House of Representatives in 1789, decided that amendments could be framed that would accommodate their fears without affecting the federal division of authority.[26] Drafting them himself, he offered mostly what he understood as "additional securities"—redundant guarantees—against the possibility of federal intrusions into matters over which the federal government had not been granted any power to begin with (although

24. Ibid., No. 51, 353.

25. This interlines and expands *The Federalist* No. 51, 351.

26. For Madison's initial reservations and the reasons for his change of mind, see "Parchment Barriers and Fundamental Rights" in Lance Banning, *Jefferson and Madison: Three Conversations from the Founding* (Madison, Wis.: Madison House, 1995), 1–26.

he also sponsored an amendment barring *state* infringements of the most essential rights and one assuring that the federal House of Representatives would be enlarged). State preserves as well as individual rights received additional protection. Madison was careful to insert provisions that became the Ninth Amendment, without which, he believed, an effort to enumerate essential rights might prove more dangerous than safe: "The enumeration in the Constitution of certain rights shall not be construed to deny or disparage others retained by the people." The Tenth Amendment, in his view, encapsulated the agreement reached in the course of the recent national debate: "The powers not delegated to the United States by the Constitution, nor prohibited by it to the states, are reserved to the states respectively, or to the people."

Already, nonetheless, events had shown that even an amended Constitution could not answer every question. The episode, indeed, was surely one of many reasons why Madison and other Congressmen refused to write a Tenth Amendment that would have declared that powers not "expressly" granted were reserved, which was the language of the Articles of Confederation.

On May 19, 1789, three months before the House felt free to turn to constitutional amendments, Madison had moved for the creation of executive departments whose heads could be dismissed by the president acting alone. William Loughton Smith, a South Carolina congressman, objected that impeachment was the only method of removing officers mentioned in the Constitution, while Theodorick Bland, Madison's Virginia colleague, believed that the requirement of concurrence by the Senate in appointments might imply that its concurrence should be necessary also for removals. Madison, who was determined to defend the separation of powers, responded, first, that he believed the Constitution's silence on the matter left it to Congressional discretion.[27] On second thought, however, he retracted this idea as ill-digested. A sound interpretation of the Constitution, he remarked, was certainly among the most important tasks that early Congresses would face. Their decisions would inevitably "become the permanent exposition of the Constitution; and on a permanent exposition

27. Madison, *Papers*, 12:172–73.

of the Constitution will depend the genius and character of the whole government."[28] Nor could Congress simply leave such matters to the courts, as some of his colleagues suggested. In the ordinary course of governmental operations, it was true, "the exposition of the laws and Constitution" would of course devolve upon this branch.

> But I beg to know upon what principle it can be contended that any one department draws from the Constitution greater powers than another in marking out the limits of the powers of the several departments. . . . If the constitutional boundary of either be brought into question, I do not see that any of these independent departments has more right than another to declare their sentiments on that point. . . . In all [governmental] systems there are points which must be adjusted by the departments themselves, to which no one of them is competent. If it cannot be determined in this way, there is no resource left but the will of the community, to be collected in some mode to be provided by the Constitution or one dictated by the necessity of the case.

It was "incontrovertibly of as much importance" to the House as to any other branch of government, Madison maintained, "that the Constitution shall be preserved entire"; and this, he now believed, would demand that Congress consider all "the great departments" in their constitutional relationship to one another, taking guidance from the fundamental principles that underpinned the charter. On this view, he argued now, the legislature could not constitutionally extend the limited exception to the executive power represented by the Senate's role in appointments, for this was dangerously at odds with the critical principle of executive independence.[29]

To Madison, a sound interpretation of the Constitution might be hard to reach,[30] but the construction of the fundamental law was never

28. Speech of June 17, ibid., 232–39.

29. Ibid. The long quotation is at p. 232.

30. "I feel great anxiety," he said, when "called upon to give a decision . . . that may affect the fundamental principles of the government and liberty itself. But all that I can do is to weigh well everything advanced on both sides, with the purest desire to find out the true meaning of the Constitution and to be guided by that and an attachment to the true spirit of liberty" (ibid.).

to be merely instrumental to the ends that Congress wanted to pursue. The Constitution was the people's law, to be revered and not continually remolded by their servants.[31] Accordingly, it was by no means out of character for him, as the First Congress moved toward its conclusion, to object ferociously to Hamilton's proposal to create a national bank. This proposition, to be sure, went far toward showing him to what a very great degree the secretary of the treasury was seeking to reinstitute a British system of finance, an enterprise to which he had a multitude of deep objections. Thus, he opened his remarks of February 2, 1791, with substantive objections to the plan. But he was even more alarmed, he indicated, by the implications of the scheme for the interpretation of the Constitution, and we are well advised to take him at his word. It was a lifelong principle for Madison that "precedents of usurpation" have to be resisted on their first appearance as they had been early in the Revolution, and the precedents that might be instituted by approval of the bank might well initiate the very process of degeneration that "Brutus" or the "Federal Farmer" had predicted. Three years before, the leader of the House of Representatives had seen slight danger from this quarter. Nevertheless, he quite agreed with former anti-Federalist opponents that a unitary national system would inevitably prove incompatible with freedom. A single national legislature could never regulate the countless matters currently overseen by the states. Thus, a further concentration of authority in central hands would necessarily entail so great an increase of executive offices, responsibilities, and prerogatives as might transform the president into a monarch. The legislature, too, would steadily become more independent of the people, since it would prove impossible to gather and enforce the genuine opinion of the people if they were deprived of the "local organs" through which their sentiments were currently conveyed.[32] However difficult the task, the maintenance of the federal division of responsibilities must never be abandoned, for there were

31. Written constitutions, he would soon be writing, might justly "be pronounced the most triumphant epoch of [world] history," and it was critical that public opinion "should guarantee, with a holy zeal, these political scriptures from every attempt to add to or diminish from them." "Charters," *National Gazette,* January 18, 1792, reprinted in Madison, *Papers,* 14:192.

32. "Consolidation," *National Gazette,* December 3, 1791, ibid., 139.

no alternatives but "schism or consolidation; both of them bad, but the latter the worst, since it is the high road to monarchy, than which nothing worse, in the eye of republicans, could result from the anarchy implied in the former."[33]

The Constitution, Madison reminded the House, was "not a general grant, out of which particular powers are excepted—it is a grant of particular powers only, leaving the general mass in other hands. So it had been understood by its friends and its foes, and so it was to be interpreted." Nothing in the Constitution, he insisted, specifically empowered Congress to incorporate a national bank. A bank was not a borrowing of money, not an act for laying taxes, not an exercise of any power listed in the constitutional enumeration. And whether a bank was "necessary and proper" to carry the enumerated powers into action had to be determined by considering "its incidentality to an express authority," its intrinsic importance, and "the probability or improbability of its being left to construction." "Necessary and proper" meant "direct and incidental means" for carrying an enumerated power into execution. The clause was not to be interpreted in such a way as would give "an unlimited discretion to Congress"; it was "in fact merely declaratory of what would have resulted by unavoidable implication," authorizing only such measures as were "*necessary* to the *end* and *incidental* to the *nature* of the specified power." To construe it as permitting *any* means that might "conduce" to execution of a delegated power, as suggested in the preamble to the bill, would destroy "the essential characteristic of a government . . . composed of limited and enumerated powers. . . . Mark the reasoning on which the validity of the bill depends," Madison objected:

> To borrow money is made the *end* and the accumulation of capitals *implied* as the *means*. The accumulation of capitals is then the *end* and a bank *implied* as the *means*. The bank is then the *end* and a charter of incorporation, a monopoly, capital punishment [for forging notes], etc. *implied* as the *means*.

If implications thus remote and multiplied can be linked to-

33. "Government of the United States," *National Gazette*, February 4, 1792, ibid., 218.

gether, a chain may be formed that will reach every object of legislation, every object within the whole compass of political economy.

The power of incorporation, Madison insisted, could not be considered merely "an accessory or subaltern power to be deduced by implication . . . ; it was in its nature a distinct, an independent and substantive prerogative," a power which he well remembered had been specifically rejected by the Constitutional Convention. The bank bill was a "usurpation," he maintained. It would establish precedents for an interpretation "levelling all the barriers which limit the powers of the general government" and destroying "the very character of the government" the Constitution created. It was "condemned by the exposition of the friends of the Constitution, whilst depending before the public; was condemned by the apparent intention of the parties which ratified the Constitution"; was condemned by the Ninth and Tenth Amendments; "and he hoped it would receive its final condemnation by the vote of the House."[34]

As the Constitution went into effect, George Washington depended more on Madison than on any other individual for advice about the Constitution.[35] Small wonder, then, that he immediately asked his cabinet for their opinions on the bank and Madison himself to draft a veto message. Attorney General Edmund Randolph and Secretary of State Thomas Jefferson agreed with their Virginia friend, the latter in a paper destined to become a great foundation for the doctrine of "strict construction" of the federal charter.

"To take a single step beyond" the Tenth Amendment, Jefferson wrote, "is to take possession of a boundless field of power, no longer susceptible of any definition." Incorporation of a bank was not an exercise of any delegated power and not an act consistent with a sound construction of "the general phrases." One of these permitted Congress "to lay taxes to provide for the general welfare"—not to lay taxes for any purpose it pleased, and certainly not to do whatever it judged in the general welfare, for the last interpretation would render the enu-

34. Speech of February 2, 1791, ibid., 372–82.

35. Stuart Leibiger, *Founding Friendship: George Washington, James Madison, and the Creation of the American Republic* (Charlottesville: University Press of Virginia, 1999) is a very recent study.

meration absolutely useless. Clearly, too, the powers plainly granted Congress might all be carried into execution without a national bank, and the "necessary and proper" clause authorized "only the means which are 'necessary,' not those which are merely 'convenient.'" The contrary interpretation, again, would permit such "a latitude of construction . . . as to swallow up all the delegated powers" and transform the government from a limited into an unlimited one. Properly constructed, the clause authorized only "those means without which the grant of [an enumerated] power would be nugatory." Mere "convenience," Jefferson insisted—even superior convenience—could not suffice to authorize Congress to impinge on state laws to the degree that the bank bill would do. "Nothing but a necessity invincible by any other means" could authorize such an act.[36]

Alexander Hamilton, who studied his colleagues' papers before preparing his own, made fairly easy work of Jefferson's opinion which pushed a strict interpretation of federal authority a good deal farther than Madison had done. Jefferson, his colleague noted, read the "necessary and proper" clause as though it said "absolutely" or "indispensably" necessary. But

> such a construction would beget endless uncertainty & embarrassment. The cases must be palpable & extreme in which it could be pronounced with certainty that a measure was absolutely necessary, or one without which the exercise of a given power would be nugatory. There are few measures of any government which would stand so severe a test. To insist upon it would be to make the criterion of the exercise of any implied power a case of extreme necessity; which is rather a rule to justify the overleaping of the bounds of constitutional authority than to govern the ordinary exercise of it. . . . The *degree* in which a measure is necessary can never be a test of the *legal* right to adopt it. That must ever be a matter of opinion; and can only be a test of expediency. The *relation* between the *measure* and the *end*, between the *nature of the mean* employed towards the execution of a power and the object of that power, must be the criterion

36. *The Papers of Thomas Jefferson*, ed. Julian P. Boyd et al. (Princeton: Princeton University Press, 1950–), 19:275–80.

of constitutionality, not the more or less of *necessity* or *utility*. . . .
The means by which national exigencies are to be provided for, national inconveniencies obviated, national prosperity promoted, are of such infinite variety, extent and complexity, that there must, of necessity, be great latitude of discretion in the selection & application of those means.

By all of his opponents, Hamilton remarked, a corporation seemed to have been seen "as some great, independent, substantive thing — as a political end of peculiar magnitude & moment; whereas it is truly to be considered as a quality, capacity, or mean to an end," a means employed with regularity by every government whatever (and without objection by the new United States itself to create governments for the western territories). As Hamilton conceived it,

Every power vested in a government is in its nature sovereign and includes by force of the term a right to employ all the means requisite and fairly applicable to the attainment of the ends of such power; and which are not precluded by restrictions and exceptions specified in the Constitution, or not immoral. Or not contrary to the essential ends of political society.

It was, he thought, "unquestionably incident to sovereign power to erect corporations, and consequently to that of the United States" — not, of course, for every purpose whatever, but certainly "in relation to the objects entrusted to the management of the government." And in a paper several times as long as that of his colleagues, he went on to demonstrate "a natural and obvious relation between the institution of a bank and the objects of several of the enumerated powers."[37]

Washington may well have judged his secretary of the treasury the victor in this battle.[38] In comparison to Madison, Jefferson had made himself a fairly easy target, pushing his strict interpretation of federal

37. Hamilton, *Papers*, 8:62–134.

38. Although, as fierce as he had been in his denunciation of the bank, Jefferson had ended his opinion by advising the president (consistently with his republican principles) that he should defer to the legislature's judgment if he remained uncertain of the constitutionality of a measure.

authority so far as nearly to suggest that the Tenth Amendment did declare that powers not "expressly" delegated were reserved, a declaration that Madison himself had warned had bound the old Confederation so impossibly that Congress had been forced into repeated violations.[39] But Madison, as well as Jefferson, had characterized the power of incorporation as too great to have been left to implication, an opinion with which Washington was quite unlikely to agree. Hamilton, like Madison, admitted that the proper test for claims of an implicit power lay in the relationship between the measure (or the means) proposed and an enumerated power. Hamilton, as well as Madison, acknowledged that "the moment the literal meaning is departed from, there is a chance of error and abuse," and both of them expected many controverted cases. But Madison's elucidation of the test he had in mind was brief and fuzzy: the degree to which the means seemed clearly incidental and directly related to the end, the intrinsic importance of the measure, and "the probability or improbability" that authority for such a measure would have been left to construction. These were not the sorts of tests that courts could reasonably employ—an observation that might not have troubled Madison, who did not believe (at that point anyway) that the judiciary would or should resolve such questions but one that did concern both Hamilton and John Marshall. It is not surprising then that Marshall's court, disclaiming an authority to reconsider the legislature's judgment of the degree of necessity involved, would closely follow Hamilton's language, which, of course, would also prove more congenial to later, more positivistic courts: "If the end be clearly comprehended within any of the specified powers, and if the measure have an obvious relation to that end, and is not forbidden by any particular provision of the Constitution," Hamilton suggested, "it may safely be deemed to come within the compass of the national

39. *The Federalist* No. 44, 303–4, including "It would be easy to show if it were necessary that no important power delegated by the Articles of Confederation has been or can be executed by Congress without recurring more or less to the doctrine of *construction* or *implication*. As the powers delegated under the new system are more extensive, the government . . . would find itself still more distressed with the alternative of betraying the public interest by doing nothing or of violating the Constitution by exercising powers indispensably necessary and proper, but at the same time not *expressly* granted."

authority," especially if the measure proposed did not abridge "a pre-existing right of any state or of any individual."[40]

In truth, however, none of these positions was without real dangers. Neither Hamilton nor Marshall ever adequately answered Madison's essential questions, which indeed remain unanswered to this day. If "necessary" means no more than "needful, requisite, incidental, useful, or conducive to" as Hamilton maintained, what can possibly prevent a string of implications reaching any object whatever and gradually transforming a government of enumerated powers into a government with no practical limits at all (or limits defined only by exceptions such as those imposed by the Bill of Rights)?[41] And is it really possible in any large and populous nation for a single government to be republican in character and spirit—"republican," that is, in something like the sense in which the great Virginians and many others of the Founding generation defined that term? The great (and long) de-

---

40. Compare the language of *M'Culloch v. Maryland:* "Let the end be legitimate, let it be within the scope of the constitution, and all means which are appropriate, which are plainly adapted to that end, which are not prohibited, but consist with the letter and spirit of the constitution, are constitutional."

41. Which was just what Madison complained of in the aftermath of the decision, sounding almost like a critic of twentieth-century uses of the commerce clause: The problem with *M'Culloch* was "the high sanction given to [excessive] latitude in expounding the Constitution. . . . In the great system of political economy, having for its general object the national welfare, everything is related immediately or remotely to every other thing; and consequently a power over any one thing, if not limited by some obvious and precise affinity, may amount to a power over every other." A rule of construction "as broad and as pliant" as Marshall's would have defeated the ratification of the Constitution, Madison insisted. "It has been the misfortune, if not the reproach, of other nations that their governments have not been freely and deliberately established by themselves. It is the boast of ours that such has been its source and that it can be altered by the same authority only which established it. . . . It is anxiously to be wished, therefore, that no innovations may take place in other modes, one of which would be a constructive assumption of powers never meant to be granted. If the powers be deficient, the legitimate source of additional ones is always open, and ought to be resorted to." James Madison to Spencer Roane, September 2, 1819, in *The Mind of the Founder: Sources of the Political Thought of James Madison,* ed. Marvin Meyers, rev. ed. (Hanover, N.H.: University Press of New England, 1981), 359–62.

bate about the bank, accordingly, was only one more stage in the developing dispute about interpretation of the Constitution and the nature of the system it created.

A single essay cannot follow every step in this dispute, but major issues and important landmarks can at least be mentioned. Thus, Madison's and Jefferson's alarm about the progress of "consolidation," their horror at the great degree to which the prophecies of anti-Federalists appeared to be progressively unfolding, was ratcheted another notch by Hamilton's Report on Manufactures. Here, again—and more decisively this time—the economic vision underlying the report was fundamentally at odds with the Virginians' different vision of the future. They would doubtless have opposed it on those grounds alone. But they were deeply troubled also by employment of the "general welfare" clause to justify the payment of bounties to encourage native manufactures. "The national legislature," Hamilton claimed,

> has express authority "to lay and collect taxes, duties, imposts and excises, to pay the debts and provide for the *common defense* and *general welfare.*" . . . The power to *raise money* is *plenary* and *indefinite;* and the objects to which it may be *appropriated* are no less comprehensive than the payment of the public debts and the providing for the common defense and *"general welfare."* . . . The only qualification of the generality of the phrase in question which seems to be admissible is this—that the object to which an appropriation of money is to be made be *general* and not *local,* its operation extending in fact, or by possibility, throughout the union, and not being confined to a particular spot.[42]

In previous debates about implicit powers, Madison explained to Henry Lee, even the greatest champions of broad construction had tied their arguments to the enumerated powers by way of the "necessary and proper" clause. "If not only the *means* but the *objects*" of the general government were rendered "unlimited" by appeal to the "general welfare" instead, "the parchment had better be thrown into the fire at once."

42. Hamilton, *Papers,* 10:302–3.

It will no longer be a government possessing special powers taken from the general mass, but one possessing the general mass with special powers reserved out of it. And this change will take place in defiance of the true and universal construction and of the sense in which the instrument is known to have been proposed, advocated, and ratified.

"Everything, from the highest object of state legislation down to the most minute object of police would be thrown under the power of Congress," he told another correspondent, for almost any purpose "would admit the application of money and might be called, if Congress pleased, provisions for the general welfare."[43]

By this time Madison was publicly (although anonymously) developing his fear of transmutation of the Constitution in several of his nineteen essays for the *National Gazette*, which he and Jefferson had helped to found,[44] and Jefferson was saying much the same in conversations with the president, warning Washington that he had heard Hamilton say that the Constitution "was a shilly shally thing of mere milk and water, which could not last and was only good as a step to something better." Hamilton had sought in the Convention to "make an English constitution of it," and "all his measures" since were "tending to bring it to the same thing."[45]

Among the many reasons why these two Virginians feared a further concentration of authority in central hands, the necessary increase in executive responsibilities, a loosening of bonds of sympathy and intimate familiarity between the legislators and the people, and, in consequence, a loss of popular control of government were key. "Monarchy," or the gradual replacement of the current system with a British

43. James Madison to Lee and to Edmund Pendleton, January 1, 8, and 21, 1792, in Madison, *Papers,* 14:180, 193–96, 220–24.

44. The *National Gazette* essay on "Charters" appeared concurrently with the letters to Pendleton and Lee.

45. See his remarks on the "general welfare" clause in his report of a conversation of February 29, 1792, in *Thomas Jefferson, Writings,* ed. Merrill D. Peterson, Library of America (New York: Viking Press, 1984), 677, and the report of a conversation of October 1, 1792, on p. 682.

form of government, was shorthand for this bundle of concerns: a fear at once quite literal—that is, the distant outcome they envisioned if the current trends continued—and, for now, a way of saying briefly and dramatically how quickly in their view a replication of a British system of corrupting links between the secretary of the treasury and special-interest factions in the Congress, a Hamiltonian political economy, and Federalist interpretations of the Constitution were moving the new government toward "independence" from the people. This is why they took such great alarm, again, at Hamilton's defense of Washington's authority to proclaim that the United States would pursue a "friendly and impartial" conduct during the war between Great Britain and the infant French Republic. The fundamental "heresy" that Jefferson urged Madison to cut apart before the public was not neutrality itself (though Madison did see the proclamation as entrenching on the legislature's clear authority to decide on war or peace) but Hamilton's construction of the scope of the executive prerogative in international relations. This, wrote Madison, was modelled on the practices and theory of monarchical Britain and "pregnant with inferences and consequences against which no ramparts in the Constitution could defend the public liberty, or scarcely the forms of republican government." If these doctrines were accepted, Madison warned the public,

> Every power that can be deduced from them will be deduced and exercised sooner or later by those who may have an interest in so doing. . . . The history of government, in all its forms and in every period of time, ratified the danger. A people, therefore, who are so happy as to possess the inestimable blessing of a free and defined constitution cannot be too watchful against the introduction, nor too critical in tracing the consequences, of new principles and new constructions that may remove the landmarks of power.[46]

The argument about executive prerogative culminated three years later when Madison decided on a last-ditch stand against Jay's Treaty with Great Britain. Disastrous as Madison regarded this agreement, the Senate had conditionally approved it on June 24, 1795, Britain

46. "Letters of Helvidius," Nos. 2 and 4, replying to Hamilton's "Letters of Pacificus" in Madison, *Papers*, 14:80, 106–7.

had accepted the conditions, and Washington proclaimed it in effect on February 29, 1796. Madison attempted to defeat it in the House of Representatives by refusing the appropriations necessary to fund the joint commissions it created. He acknowledged that the Constitution vested power over treaties in the president and Senate, but "taken literally and without limit," he observed, this clearly clashed with the delegation to the whole Congress of powers to regulate commerce, declare war, raise armies, and such. In cases of this sort, he argued, the people's servants were obliged to construct the document in ways that "would best reconcile the several parts of the instrument with each other, and be most consistent with its general spirit and object." The Constitution surely did not mean to free the president and Senate, acting through the treaty power, to proceed without restraint on matters plainly entrusted only to Congress as a whole. On these grounds, he reasoned, treaties "required at the same time the legislative sanction and cooperation in those cases where the Constitution had given express and specific powers to the legislature." In such cases, certainly, the legislature would have to "exercise its authority with discretion," but it must still possess a will of its own.[47]

During these proceedings, Washington humiliated (and defeated) Madison by refusing a House request to deliver papers relating to negotiation of the treaty and to Jay's instructions, partly on the grounds that a proposal at the Constitutional Convention to require that treaties be confirmed by laws had been specifically rejected by that body. Madison was forced into a further explanation of his basic principles of constitutional construction, for in his famous speech against the national bank, as some of his opponents gleefully remarked, he had himself recalled that the Convention had specifically refused to enumerate a power to create corporations. But Madison was more embarrassed by the public clash with Washington than foes believed he ought to be by this apparent contradiction.[48] As he now explained, his

47. Speech of March 10, 1796, in Madison, *Papers*, 17:255–63. Obviously, this was hardly "strict construction," but it has been my point throughout that "strict construction" is a crude characterization of Madison's way of interpreting the charter.

48. Perhaps he should have been embarrassed, too, that he had really misremembered or offered a challengeable interpretation of the episode he had in

reference to the Convention in the speech of 1791 had been a passing comment, and the intent of the Constitutional Convention had never since been urged by anyone as a proper guide to the meaning of the Constitution.

Reexamination shows that Madison was right about his argument of 1791. Like the national bank, Jay's Treaty raised a question that had not until that time come clearly into view; and even Madison, as he repeatedly observed, could discover the implications of the Constitution only as new issues raised new questions. Constitutional interpretations had to be constructed over time, and no one's personal interpretation was unquestionably correct. But even in his argument against the bank, Madison had not depended mainly on the intentions of the Constitutional Convention. He had stood primarily on other ground —ground he had recurred to frequently in later writings and would take consistently from this point on. The Constitution, he had then suggested, was best understood as its friends and foes had understood it during the debates over its adoption. "In controverted cases, the meaning of the parties to the instrument"—the people who had ratified it through their several state conventions—was the most authoritative guide. When the defenders of the Constitution were confronted with demands for amendments clarifying the reach of federal powers, they had replied that powers not confided to the federal government were retained by the states or the people "and that those given were not to be extended by remote implications." They had insisted that "The terms necessary and proper gave no additional powers." The explanatory declarations and proposed amendments offered by the state conventions were based on the same assumptions, and this general understanding had been confirmed by the Ninth and Tenth Amendments. "With all this evidence of the sense in which the Constitution was understood and adopted," it was both disgracefully dishonest and an outright usurpation to revert to an opposite construction to justify

---

mind. Benjamin Franklin had suggested the addition to the enumerated powers of one to cut canals, and Madison himself had proposed extending this to a power to create corporations. These propositions were indeed rejected, but, as Hamilton noted in his opinion on the bank, this happened after a debate in which some members had objected that the power would permit a bank, but others seemed to think that a power to create corporations was already implicit.

the bank.[49] "Whatever veneration might be entertained for the body of men who formed our Constitution," Madison added now,

> The sense of that body could never be regarded as the oracular guide in expounding the Constitution. As the instrument came from them it was nothing more than the draft of a plan, nothing but a dead letter, until life and validity were breathed into it by the voice of the people, speaking through the several state conventions. If we were to look, therefore, for the meaning of the instrument, beyond the face of the instrument, we must look for it not in the general convention, which proposed, but in the state conventions, which accepted and ratified the Constitution.

Looking to this source—and beyond that, he might have added (as he had on earlier occasions) to the public writings on both sides of the ratification debate and to the amendments recommended by the several states—it was clear to him that the treaty power was a limited one. None of the state conventions had supposed that powers over commerce, war and peace, and even the disbursement of public funds could be assumed, in practice, by the Senate and executive alone.[50]

Madison's decision to retire from Congress may have been completed by his inability to hold his fellow Jeffersonian Republicans to a consistent strategy against Jay's Treaty. As all of them had feared, however, the agreement with Great Britain soon embroiled the nation in an argument with France. As John Adams replaced George Washington (and Jefferson assumed vice-presidential duties), the trouble deepened into a limited naval war. And in the summer of 1798, the Federalists in Congress, over heated opposition, set about to repress their Republican opponents. French and Irish immigrants were mostly in that camp. Congress extended to fourteen years the residency required for naturalization and authorized the deportation of any alien whose presence seemed to the president a danger to the United States.

49. Madison, *Papers,* 13:374, 380–81. And, certainly, both Madison and Hamilton had insisted that opponents need not fear the "sweeping clauses." See Alexander Hamilton's *Federalist* No. 33, 204–7 and James Madison's *Federalist* No. 41 and No. 44, 277–78, 302–6.

50. Speech of April 6, 1796, Madison, *Papers,* 17:290–301, quotations at pp. 294–96.

Aliens and citizens alike were also subjected to a new Sedition Law, which threatened with fines and imprisonment anyone who wrote, printed, uttered, or published "any false, scandalous and malicious writings against the government of the United States, or either house of the Congress of the United States, or the President of the United States, with intent to defame" them or to bring them "into contempt or disrepute." With these measures, the Republicans believed, the Federalist conspiracy against the Constitution—and against democracy itself —had burst into the open.

Enforced by a partisan judiciary, the crisis laws of 1798 imposed a bloodless reign of terror on the country. Under the Sedition Act or under color of a common law of seditious libel, all of the most important Republican newspapers in the country felt the sting of prosecutions, as did several pamphleteers. The *Argus* and the *Time Piece,* the only Republican newspapers in New York City, were driven out of business. Benjamin Franklin Bache, whose Philadelphia *Aurora* had replaced the *National Gazette* as the opposition's leading outlet, died while under indictment. What could the defenders of the Constitution do when all three branches of the federal government united in a program that opponents saw not merely as a usurpation under cover of a forced interpretation of the fundamental law but as a patent violation of express provisions of the Constitution—one that struck, moreover, at the very right that underpinned self-government itself? (In Congress, Albert Gallatin and Edward Livingston had both objected that the legislation was a patent violation of the First Amendment and a potent threat to the people's underlying right to change their rulers through free elections, which depended on their freedom to express and circulate opinions.)

Jefferson's and Madison's response was to initiate, or press, the sort of protest that had greeted British measures early in the Revolution— much the sort of protest, ironically, that Hamilton, as well as Madison, appears to have envisioned back in 1788.[51] Each prepared a set of

51. Every federal usurpation, said James Madison's *Federalist* No. 44 (on the "necessary and proper" clause), would be an invasion of the rights of the states; "these will be ever ready to mark the innovation, to sound the alarm to the peo-

resolutions, which they funnelled to the legislatures of Kentucky and Virginia. Jefferson, as was his habit, was again the more extreme, but it was Madison's conception of the Constitution, introduced in *The Federalist* No. 39, on which they both would build.

"The several states," Jefferson premised, had not united "on the principle of unlimited submission to their general government." Rather by a "compact" to which each was party "they constituted a general government for special purposes, delegated to that government certain definite powers" and reserved "each state to itself, the residuary mass of right to their own self-government." Neither did they make this general government "the exclusive or final judge of the extent of the powers delegated to itself," for that would have made the general government's discretion, not the Constitution, "the measure of its powers." Instead, each state retained "an equal right to judge for itself, as well of infractions as of the mode and measure of redress." Act by act, his draft of the Kentucky Resolutions listed legislation in which Congress had assumed authority not delegated by the Constitution, sometimes by construction but often in the face of the explicit language of the Bill of Rights. Calling each of these examples "not law" but "altogether void and of no force," he argued that, in all such cases

---

ple, and to exert their local influence in effecting a change of federal representatives" (305). Every state government, he added in *The Federalist* No. 46 (320) "would espouse the common cause. A correspondence would be opened. Plans of resistance would be concerted. . . . The same combination in short would result from an apprehension of the federal as was produced by the dread of a foreign yoke; and unless the projected innovation should be voluntarily renounced, the same appeal to a trial of force would be made in the one case as was made in the other." "The state governments," Hamilton concurred (*The Federalist* No. 28, 179–80), "will in all possible contingencies afford complete security against invasions of the public liberty by the national authority. . . . Possessing all the organs of civil power and the confidence of the people, they can at once adopt a regular plan of opposition, in which they can combine all the resources of the community. They can readily communicate with each other in the different states and unite their common force for the protection of their common liberty." The state legislatures, he had already said, would "constantly have their attention awake to the conduct of the national rulers and will be ready enough, if anything improper appears, to sound the alarm to the people and not only to be the voice but if necessary the arm of their discontent" (*The Federalist* No. 26, 169).

"every state has a natural right . . . to nullify of their own authority all assumptions of power by others within their limits." Urging the other states to concur in similar declarations, he recommended also "measures of their own for providing that neither these acts nor any others of the general government not plainly and intentionally authorized by the Constitution shall be exercised within their respective territories."[52]

Kentucky's legislators deleted Jefferson's suggestion that the rightful remedy for federal usurpations was a nullification of such acts by each state acting on its own to prevent their operation within its respective bounds, calling only for the other states to unite in declarations that the federal acts were "void and of no force" and in "requesting their repeal." Madison was similarly cautious in his draft of resolutions for Virginia and would be on solid ground years later in insisting that he never said that any single state could constitutionally impede the operation of a federal law. Nevertheless, Virginia's legislature did "peremptorily declare," with Madison,

> That it views the powers of the federal government as resulting from the compact to which the states are parties; as limited by the plain sense and intention of the instrument constituting that compact; as no farther valid than they are authorised by the grants enumerated in that compact, and that in case of a deliberate, palpable, and dangerous exercise of powers not granted by the said compact, the states who are the parties thereto have the right, and are in duty bound, to interpose for arresting the progress of the evil, and for maintaining within their respective limits, the authorities, rights, and liberties appertaining to them.[53]

Like Jefferson, Madison attacked specific violations of amendments to the Constitution, together with the federal government's attempts

52. Jefferson's rough draft and fair copy of the resolutions are printed side by side together with the resolutions as actually adopted in *The Works of Thomas Jefferson*, ed. Paul Leicester Ford, 12 vols. (New York: G. P. Putnam's Sons, 1904), 8:458–79.

53. Madison, *Papers*, 17:189.

to enlarge its powers by forced constructions of the constitutional charter . . . so as to destroy the meaning and effect of the particular enumeration which necessarily explains and limits the general phrases; and so as to consolidate the states by degrees into one sovereignty, the obvious tendency and inevitable consequence of which would be to transform the present republican system of the United States into an absolute, or at best a mixed monarchy.

Like Jefferson, Madison called on the states not only to concur in declaring these usurpations unconstitutional but also in declaring "that the necessary and proper measures will be taken by each for cooperating with this state in maintaining unimpaired the authorities, rights, and liberties reserved to the states respectively, or to the people."[54]

Madison would soon—and many times—regret his insufficient care in drafting the Virginia Resolutions. Though he had cautioned Jefferson against confusing the power of a state with that of its legislature,[55] he had not himself avoided language that confused the several senses in which "state" was commonly employed or language that could easily be taken, even if it was not meant, to recommend state actions to impede illegal measures "within their respective limits," which is pretty certainly what Jefferson appears to have envisioned and what South Carolina would attempt within the Framer's lifetime. Seven other states responded to Virginia's and Kentucky's resolutions, all of them objecting as New Hampshire did "that the state legislatures are not the proper tribunals to determine the constitutionality of the laws of the general government" and several agreeing with Rhode Island that the Constitution "vests in the federal courts, exclusively, and in

54. Ibid., 189–90.

55. James Madison to Thomas Jefferson, December 29, 1798, Madison, *Papers,* 17:191–92: "On the supposition that the [state] is clearly the ultimate judge of infractions, it does not follow that the [legislature] is the legitimate organ, especially as a convention was the organ by which the compact was made. This was a reason of great weight for using general expressions that would leave to other states a choice of the modes possible of concurring" with Virginia's views. (But, of course, as South Carolina followed later by its southern sisters was to prove, it would be easy enough to constitute a convention, rather than the legislature, as an organ.)

the Supreme Court . . . ultimately, the authority" to make this judgment.[56] In 1799, Madison reentered the Virginia legislature to respond
to these replies and clarify his stance (although without admitting that
the language of the resolutions was his own).

But Madison did not retract the fundamental logic of Virginia's (or
Kentucky's) interposition against the measures they protested. In *The
Federalist* No. 39, he had insisted that adoption of the Constitution was
undoubtedly "a federal and not a national act . . . the act of the people
as forming so many independent states, not as forming one aggregate
nation." This, he had maintained, was obvious from the consideration
that the Constitution was adopted neither by "the decision of a majority of the people of the union, nor from that of a majority of the
states" but by the voluntary act of each of the states that approved
it (each altering its own constitution in the process). Had the people
been regarded "as forming one nation, the will of the majority of the
whole people of the United States" would have bound the minority.[57]
Now, in his Report of 1800, he reaffirmed that the Constitution was
a federal compact, whose parties were "the people composing" the
several states "in their highest sovereign capacity." On these grounds,
he still maintained "that where resort can be had to no tribunal superior to the authority of the parties, the parties themselves must be
the rightful judges in the last resort, whether the bargain made has
been pursued or violated." The federal courts were not such a superior
tribunal, since on the opposite hypothesis "the delegation of judicial
power would annul the authority delegating it." In cases where there
was "a deliberate, palpable and dangerous breach of the Constitution,"
cases "dangerous to the great purposes for which the Constitution was
established," the parties to the compact could legitimately interpose
"at least so far as to arrest the evil, to maintain their rights, and to preserve the Constitution." Otherwise, "there would be an end to all relief
from usurped power . . . as well as a plain denial of the fundamental
principle on which our independence itself was declared."[58]

Clause by clause, Madison elaborated and defended each of the

56. *Documents of American History,* ed. Henry Steele Commager (New York:
Appleton-Century-Crofts, 1963), 184–85.

57. *The Federalist* No. 39, 254.

58. Madison, *Papers,* 17:307–51, quotations at pp. 308–11.

resolutions of 1798. Federal usurpations by construction, he insisted, had begun as early as the law establishing the national bank. The sweeping clauses had been used repeatedly to justify assumptions of authority not clearly granted by the Constitution or intended by the parties to the compact. The Sedition Act and prosecutions under color of a federal common law of crimes were even worse. The former exercised a power "expressly and positively forbidden" by the First Amendment—a power "levelled against that right of freely examining public characters and measures, and of free communication thereon," which was essential to elective government itself. The latter claimed authority so broad as to completely overturn the concept of enumerated powers.[59]

In condemning the Sedition Act and other measures as transgressions of the Constitution, Virginia's General Assembly, Madison insisted, was within its lawful bounds. If other states had joined it in such declarations, these and other protests by the people would have been sufficient to arrest the evils they condemned. Other means might also have been used: petitions to the Congress, instructions to their senators to move amendments to the Constitution, or an exercise of the authority of three-fourths of the states to call a constitutional convention. If the Federalists of 1788 had thought it proper to support the Constitution by referring "to the intermediate existence of the state governments between the people and [the federal] government, to the vigilance with which they would descry the first symptoms of usurpation, and to the promptitude with which they would sound the alarm to the public," it was proper now for states to interpose against a train of measures that could wreck that Constitution or extend the concentration of authority so far as to replace elections by hereditary rule.[60]

Historically, it would seem hard to doubt that Madison was right about the making of the Constitution; and, historically, although the other states refused to go along with the Virginia and Kentucky resolutions, those resolutions did assist in furthering the protests that would help to win the election of 1800 for men who were determined to retract the federal government into the limits they believed had been

59. Ibid., 312–45.
60. Ibid., 347–50.

established by the peoples of the several states at its creation. The federal government *would* operate within enumerated limits long after the Civil War. But as the foremost Framer of the Constitution lived to see, the compact theory held some dreadful dangers of its own. Its logic in less subtle hands marched readily to nullification and secession. For if indeed the peoples of the several states had been the parties to the federal compact, why are not these peoples (acting, it may be, through state conventions) the most authoritative judges of the things they had agreed to? Did they constitute a federal government which is itself, through its judiciary, final judge in its own cause?

But Madison himself was nothing if not subtle, offering perhaps as good an answer to these questions as anyone has ever done. The Constitution was, indeed, he would insist until the end, a compact entered into by the peoples of the several states, each covenanting with the others. Those peoples, ultimately sovereign, might have constituted a confederation. They might have framed a unitary national government. They chose however to do neither. Instead, they each compacted with the others to create a system partly national and partly federal in nature and "not to be explained so as to make it either."[61] They made themselves a single people *for the purposes enumerated in that charter.* These facts, however, did not mean that any of these peoples in their individual capacities could constitutionally suspend the operation of a federal law, which was fully as authoritative if the compact was created in this way as if it had been entered into by "the people in their aggregate capacity, acting by a numerical majority of the whole."[62] No single party to the compact had a right to tell the others what the compact meant (or, presumably, to break the compact by a unilateral decision). Had the states retained an individual authority to judge the constitutionality of federal laws, the Constitution would be a different document in different portions of the union. This trust was necessarily

61. Notes on Nullification (1835–36) in Meyers, *The Mind of the Founder*, 437. Both simpler forms had proven incompatible with "individual rights, public order, [or] external safety," Madison added, and those who would insist on making the Constitution one or the other "aim[ed] a deadly blow at the last hope of true liberty on the face of the earth" (ibid., 441).

62. Ibid., 440.

vested in the general government, acting through its own tribunals.[63] In case of usurpations by the general government, the states might make their declarations, might instruct their senators, might change their federal representatives through free elections, might call a constitutional convention, appealing to "the power that made the Constitution and can explain, amend, or remake it." Should all this fail, however, "and the power usurped be sustained in its oppressive exercise on a minority by a majority, the final course to be pursued by the minority must be a subject of calculation in which the degree of oppression, the means of resistance, the consequences of its failure, and consequences of its success must be the elements."[64] There is always, that is to say, the right of revolution, exercise of which is likely to be greeted as revolutions usually are.[65]

This was not, of course, an unimpeachable solution to the riddle that had ruined the British Empire: how to keep the general government within the bounds defined by natural rights, by constitutional prescription, and by the powers vested in the other governments of a complex regime. It did not prevent secession. It begged the question, still, about exactly which dimensions of their lives the parties to the compact had intended to reserve from federal intrusions and what to do if the intentions of the other parties change. In the long run Madison's opponents at the Founding may have been correct. Even if the people (or the peoples of the several states) are ultimately sovereign, governmental sovereignty may not in practice be divisible along a line that will not shift and can be recognized distinctly by an honest

63. Madison to Spencer Roane, June 29, 1821, ibid., 368.

64. Notes on Nullification, ibid., 434.

65. The issues raised by the Sedition Act and by the long succession of federal "abuses" in the years since 1791 were very like the ones James Otis and other Revolutionary pamphleteers had struggled with from 1764 until the Declaration of Independence. Like Otis, Jefferson, and even John Locke, Madison insisted in the Resolutions of 1798 and in the Report of 1800 that only a long succession of tyrannical abuses could justify resistance. But such a long succession of abuses was exactly what the Revolutionaries, the Jeffersonian Republicans, and the secessionists of 1861 believed that they were faced with—and exactly what Parliament, the Federalists, and the general government of 1861 denied were unconstitutional at all.

and dispassionate examination of the circumstances under which the compact has been made. No agency—not legislatures, federal courts, or even state conventions—can be universally acknowledged as a final judge of this division without encountering one problem or another. Europeans might take heed. Difficult as it may be to forge an effective union, such a union once established may be even harder to confine. Certainly, America has never solved the federal puzzle.

Is There a "James Madison Problem"?

Scholars used to talk about the "Adam Smith Problem" or, as the German scholars liked to call it, "Das Adam Smith Problem." This problem arose out of the presumed discrepancy between the Adam Smith of the *Theory of Moral Sentiments* and the Adam Smith of the *Wealth of Nations*. Smith seemed to be two different persons with very different views of human nature. While Smith's *Moral Sentiments* seemed to ascribe human actions to sympathy, his *Wealth of Nations* seemed to ascribe them to self-interest. Much scholarly time and energy were spent trying to account for the apparent difference between the two books. Eventually, however, more recent scholarship has shown that the problem was a figment of our scholarly imaginations and that the two books can in fact be reconciled.

But can we do the same for James Madison? Nearly everyone sees two different Madisons, two Madisons who appear to be as wildly different from one another as the two different Adam Smiths used to be.

There is the Madison of the 1780s—the fervent nationalist who feared the states and their vicious tyrannical majorities and wanted to subject them to the control of the central government. Although he did not want to eliminate the states, he seems to have wanted to reduce them to what at times appear to be little more than administrative units that, as he said, might be "subordinately useful."[1] This is the Madison who has become the "Father of the Constitution."

By contrast there is the Madison of the 1790s—the strict constructionist, states' rights cofounder of the Democratic-Republican party who feared the national government and its monarchical tendencies and trusted the popular majorities in the states. By 1798 he was even willing to invoke the right of the states to judge the constitutionality of federal acts and to interpose themselves between the citizens and

1. Gordon S. Wood, *The Creation of the American Republic, 1776–1787* (Chapel Hill: University of North Carolina Press, 1969), 473.

the unconstitutional actions of the central government. For the early Madison, popular majorities within states were the source of the problem; for the later Madison, these popular majorities in the states became a remedy for the problem. It is hard to see how these two seemingly different Madisons can be reconciled.

This first Madison is the author of the Virginia Plan, which became the working model for the Philadelphia Convention. We often forget what an extraordinarily powerful and sweeping national government the Virginia Plan proposed. According to Madison's plan both branches of the bicameral national legislature would be proportionally representative, thus eliminating all semblance of state sovereignty from the national government. Moreover, this national legislature would have the power to legislate in all cases in which the separate states were incompetent and the power to negative all state laws that in its opinion contravened the Union. Madison thought this curious veto power to be "absolutely necessary and to be the least possible encroachment on the State jurisdictions."[2]

During 1789 when the new Washington administration was getting on its feet, Madison still seemed to be the quintessential Federalist—"a great friend to strong government," concluded South Carolina Federalist William Loughton Smith in August 1789.[3] Although a member of the House of Representatives, Madison was President Washington's closest confidant. He helped shape the legislation that created the departments of government and was very important in establishing the executive's independence from Congress. Even his support for a bill of rights that dealt only with individual rights and liberties was seen as a means of subverting or diverting the anti-Federalist demand for many more substantial limits on the national government.

Only slowly did Madison seem to change. Although he reluctantly recognized the need for funding the national debt, he was not happy with Hamilton's proposal in January 1790 to pay only the current holders of the government's bonds. But Hamilton's plan for the national

2. James Madison to George Washington, April 16, 1787, Jack N. Rakove, ed., *James Madison: Writings* (New York: The Library of America, 1999), 81.

3. Stuart Leibiger, *Founding Friendship: George Washington, James Madison, and the Creation of the American Republic* (Charlottesville: University Press of Virginia, 1999), 123.

government to assume all the state debts angered him even more. These issues were not beyond compromise, however, and at a dinner arranged by Jefferson, Hamilton and Madison clinched a deal in which southerners would accept the national assumption of state debts in return for having the permanent capital on the Potomac. With Hamilton's proposal for a national bank, however, compromise appeared impossible and Madison's criticism of the secretary of the treasury's plans became even more severe.

Hamilton was not surprised by opposition to his financial plans. He knew that state and local interests would resist all efforts to strengthen national authority. But he was surprised that his harshest critic in the House of Representatives was his long-time ally James Madison. He thought that Madison had desired a strong national government as much as he had. He could not understand how he and Madison, "whose politics had formerly so much the *same point of departure*," could have diverged so dramatically.[4]

In the House, Madison argued not only that the bank bill was a misguided imitation of England's monarchical practice of concentrating wealth and influence in the metropolitan capital but, more important, that it was an unconstitutional assertion of federal power. He urged a strict interpretation of the Constitution, claiming that it did not expressly grant the federal government the authority to charter a bank.

By the end of 1790 Madison and other Virginians were openly voicing their alarm at the direction the national government was taking. By 1791 Madison was privately describing the supporters of Hamilton's program not only as "speculators" but also as "Tories," a loaded term that suggested the promoters of royal absolutism.[5] By 1792 Madison and Jefferson were emerging as the leaders of what Madison called the "Republican party" in opposition to what seemed to them to be Federalist efforts to establish a consolidated British-style monarchy.

4. Hamilton to Edward Carrington, May 26, 1792, Harold C. Syrett et al., eds., *The Papers of Alexander Hamilton* (New York: Columbia University Press, 1966), 11:432.

5. Stanley Elkins and Eric McKitrick, *The Age of Federalism* (New York: Oxford University Press, 1993), 234; James Madison to Thomas Jefferson, May 1, 1791, in James Morton Smith, ed., *The Republic of Letters: The Correspondence Between Thomas Jefferson and James Madison, 1776–1826* (New York: Norton, 1995), 2:685.

But so much was the Republican Party the result of Madison's efforts alone that it was often referred to as "Madison's Party."[6] By May 1792 Hamilton had become convinced "that Mr. Madison cooperating with Mr. Jefferson is at the head of a faction decidedly hostile to me and my administration, and actuated by views in my judgment subversive of the principles of good government and dangerous to the union, peace and happiness of the Country."[7]

With the coming of the French Revolution and the outbreak of war between republican France and monarchical Britain in 1793, the division between the Federalists and the Republicans deepened and became more passionate. The future of the United States appeared to be tied up in the outcome of the European struggle. "None of the Republicans," writes historian James Morton Smith, "was more committed to the concept of the revolution in France as an extension of the one in America than was Madison."[8]

By this point Madison was convinced that Hamilton and the Federalists were bent on making a "connection" with Great Britain and "under her auspices" were determined to move "in a gradual approximation towards her Form of Government." Until his retirement from Congress in December 1796, Madison remained the undisputed leader of the Republican Party in the Congress and its most effective spokesman in the press. When the crisis of 1798–99 came to a head, it was not surprising that Madison and Jefferson should have emerged as states' rights' advocates against the consolidationist tendencies of the Federalists.

What happened? What could account for this apparently remarkable change of sentiment? From being the leader of the nationalist and Federalist movement in the 1780s, Madison became the leader of the states' rights and anti-Federalist movement in the 1790s. Explaining this change does seem to be a major problem, one that has bedeviled Madison's biographers and historians of the Founding era.

Most biographers and historians have concluded that Madison did

6. Smith, *Republic of Letters*, 2:881.
7. Hamilton to Edward Carrington, May 26, 1792, Syrett et al., *Papers of Hamilton*, 11:429.
8. Smith, *Republic of Letters*, 2:747.

indeed change his mind about national power. "In drawing back from Hamilton's program," writes Ralph Ketcham, "Madison took another step backward from the nationalism he had first expressed so firmly in May 1787. . . . Hamilton and others," Ketcham goes on to say, "judged correctly Madison's changing attitude toward national power, and perhaps had some grounds for feeling betrayed by him." [9] During the early 1790s, writes Jack Rakove, Madison "revised many of the beliefs he had held as the radical nationalist in the late 1780s." [10] During the early part of 1790, writes Joseph Ellis, "Madison went through a conversion process . . . from the religion of nationalism to the old revolutionary faith of Virginia." [11] His was a "divided mind," write Stanly Elkins and Eric McKitrick, pulled in opposing directions by the forces of "nationalism" and "ideology." [12] Even his most sympathetic biographer, Irving Brant, suggests that the disagreement between Hamilton and Madison on social and economic matters though it had existed for a long time "grew until it produced a change in Madison's political and constitutional views, but," Brant added, "there was no deviation from the straight line he followed in economic and social issues." [13]

Scholars' explanations for Madison's apparent change of views have varied. Some have described his "sudden turn" in 1790 to be a matter of "political expediency," designed as "the opening move in a resumption of state-oriented politics." [14] Others have stressed his awakened loyalty to the sentiments of his Virginia constituents. Taking off from this new consciousness of Madison's Virginianness, still others have pointed to his inability to comprehend bond markets and mercantile affairs and have emphasized that his objection to Hamilton's

9. Ralph Ketcham, *James Madison: A Biography* (New York: Macmillan, 1971), 314.

10. Jack N. Rakove, *James Madison and the Creation of the American Republic* (New York: HarperCollins, 1990), 93.

11. Joseph J. Ellis, *Founding Brothers: The Revolutionary Generation* (New York: Alfred A. Knopf, 2000), 55.

12. Elkins and McKitrick, *Age of Federalism*, 146.

13. Irving Brant, *James Madison: The Nationalist, 1780–1787* (Indianapolis: Bobbs-Merrill, 1948), 217.

14. E. James Ferguson, *The Power of the Purse: A History of American Public Finance, 1776–1790* (Chapel Hill: University of North Carolina Press, 1961), 298.

program seemed to rest on his disgust with northern speculators and moneyed men.[15] Others have talked about his friendship with Jefferson and his willingness to defer to his older colleague, ready "always," as he told Jefferson in 1794, to "receive your commands with pleasure."[16] And still others have stressed that he "thought as a working statesman," shifting his opinion in accord with his perception of where the threats to liberty and republican government lay.[17]

As far as I know, Lance Banning, in his very formidable book, *The Sacred Fire of Liberty,* is the only present-day scholar to maintain that Madison did not change his views in the 1790s.[18] But in order to stress Madison's consistency in the 1790s, Banning has to play down Madison's nationalism in the 1780s and turn him into something less than a full-blown nationalist. "He was," says Banning, "a nationalist . . . at certain times, on certain issues, and within the limits of his revolutionary hopes." In other words, says Banning, modern scholarship has mistaken Madison's position in the 1780s. It "has generally misjudged the hopes and fears that he brought into the Constitutional Convention." It has "misinterpreted a major change of mind which started while the meeting was in process"; and therefore it has come to "hold a poorly balanced view of what he said and what he was attempting in *The Federalist.*" The opposition Jeffersonian Madison of the 1790s, concludes Banning, "was not as inconsistent with the 'father of the Constitution' as is usually believed."[19]

I have a lot of sympathy with Banning's position. I too believe that Madison was more consistent in his outlook than we historians have admitted. But I have a different explanation for that consistency. It is

15. Elkins and McKitrick, *Age of Federalism,* 136–45.

16. Madison to Jefferson, October 5, 1794, in Smith, *Republic of Letters,* 2:857.

17. Marvin Myers, ed., *The Mind of the Founder: Sources of the Political Thought of James Madison* (Indianapolis: Bobbs-Merrill, 1973), xlv.

18. In a short article written nearly a half century ago, Neal Reimer did emphasize Madison's consistency over time. Reimer, however, merely stressed Madison's lifelong commitment to republicanism, which is scarcely in doubt, and admitted that in the 1790s "Madison retreated somewhat from his earlier nationalism." Reimer, "The Republicanism of James Madison," *Political Science Quarterly* 69 (1954): 45–64, quotation at 56.

19. Lance Banning, *The Sacred Fire of Liberty: James Madison and the Founding of the Federal Republic* (Ithaca: Cornell University Press, 1995), 42, 9.

not, as Banning says, that Madison was less a nationalist in the 1780s than we used to think. Madison was, I believe, very much a fervent nationalist, eager to create a national government that would control certain kinds of behavior in the states. But he was not the kind of nationalist that other Federalists such as Hamilton were. And when he came to realize what kind of national government that Hamilton was trying to create, he naturally went into opposition. His conception of what the national government ought to be was not being fulfilled. In other words, ultimately there is not a Madison problem after all.

Trying to discover consistency in a politician who lived a long life in a rapidly changing society may be a foolish and unnecessary project. Does it really matter if he changed his views? He certainly thought so; to the end of his life he always maintained that he was consistent in his beliefs and that it was Hamilton who abandoned him.[20] Certainly we can never escape from the fact that the later Madison is different in many ways from the early Madison. No doubt he was a nationalist in the 1780s and a states' rights advocate in the 1790s. Yet at some basic level Madison remained in harmony with himself throughout his career. There were not two James Madisons.

How to explain that consistency in Madison's thinking? First of all we have to get back to the eighteenth century in order to understand exactly what Madison was trying to do in 1787. It may be that we scholars have been attributing far more farsightedness to Madison than he was in fact capable of. In our eagerness to make Madison the most profound political theorist not only in the Revolutionary and Constitution-making period but in all of American history as well, we may have burdened this eighteenth-century political leader with more theoretical sophistication than he or any such politician can bear. We want him to be one of the important political philosophers in the Western tradition. If the English have Hobbes and Locke, and the French have Montesquieu and Rousseau, then we Americans at least have Madison.

20. See Madison to C. E. Haynes, February 25, 1831, in Gaillard Hunt, ed., *The Writings of James Madison* (New York: G. P. Putnam's Sons, 1910), 9:442; and N. P. Trist, "Memoranda," September 27, 1834, in Max Farrand, ed., *The Records of the Federal Convention of 1787* (New Haven: Yale University Press, 1911, 1937), 3:534.

Convinced of the originality and sophistication of Madison's ideas, many scholars have been stumbling over themselves in their desire to explore the implications of his political thought, less, it seems, for understanding the eighteenth century and more for understanding our own time. Since Madison was central to the creation of the United States Constitution—the "Founding" as we have come to call it— Madison and his ideas have come to bear an extraordinary responsibility for the character of American politics and society.

Political scientists have been especially eager to treat Madison as America's foremost political philosopher and have compiled a small library of works analyzing his (and Hamilton's) contributions to *The Federalist*. According to many political theorists, to understand Madison is to understand American politics. So, in Robert A. Dahl's formulation, Madison is the pluralist who unfortunately concocted our fragmented structure of government in order to protect minority rights at the expense of majority rule. Or, according to Richard K. Matthews, he is the symbol of a cold-hearted American liberalism that promotes a selfish individualism that has no sense of benevolence and cares only for material wealth and property. Or in Gary Rosen's hands, he is the innovative theorist of the social compact that is the foundation of natural rights and our limited constitutional government.[21]

As these studies by political scientists and political theorists become more and more refined and precious, they seem to drift farther and farther away from Madison's eighteenth-century reality. Whatever his creativity and originality may be, we have to keep in mind that Madison was not speaking to us or to the ages. His world was not our world; indeed, our world would have appalled him. Thus in our efforts to relate his very time-bound thinking to our present predicaments, we run the risk of seriously distorting his world and what he was trying to do.

---

21. Robert Dahl, *A Preface to Democratic Theory* (Chicago: University of Chicago Press, 1956); Richard K. Matthews, *If Men Were Angels: James Madison and the Heartless Empire of Reason* (Lawrence: University Press of Kansas, 1995); Gary Rosen, *American Compact and the Problem of Founding* (Lawrence: University Press of Kansas, 1999). For more recent uses of Madison by political theorists, see John Samples, ed., *James Madison and the Future of Limited Government* (Washington, D.C.: Cato Institute, 2002).

And despite all of his achievements, we run the risk of exaggerating his creativity.

If we are to recover the historical Madison, I believe we have to soften if not discard the traditional idea that Madison was the "Father of the Constitution." He himself, of course, always held that it was "the work of many heads and many hands."[22] With good reason, for the Constitution that emerged from the Philadelphia Convention was not what he had wanted. When during the Convention Madison lost the battle over proportional representation in both houses of the legislature with the so-called Connecticut Compromise, he was deeply depressed. He even caucused the next day with his fellow Virginia delegates over whether or not to withdraw from the Convention. When he lost his congressional power to negative the states' laws, he was even more disheartened. He thought the Constitution was doomed to fail. Just before the Convention adjourned, he told Jefferson that the new federal government would accomplish none of its goals. The Constitution, he said, "will neither effectually answer its national object nor prevent the local mischiefs which every where excite disgusts against the state governments."[23] This is really a quite extraordinary statement: it gives us some idea of how little the final Constitution resembled his original intentions, more or less embodied in his Virginia Plan.

His Virginia Plan was certainly nationalistic and original, but it was a quirky, even visionary, kind of originality that it expressed—one that proved unacceptable to most Federalists. The Virginia Plan grew out of Madison's view of what was wrong with America in the 1780s. For him the weaknesses of the Confederation, which nearly everyone seemed to acknowledge, seemed secondary to the vices within the several states. Not only did the self-interested behavior of the states weaken the Union, but, more important, popular politics within the states threatened the Revolutionary experiment in self-government. Ever since independence, said Madison, the states had passed a host

22. Madison to William Cogswell, March 10, 1834, in Farrand, *Records of the Federal Convention*, 3:533.

23. Madison to Jefferson, September 6, 1787, in Smith, *Republic of Letters*, 1:491.

of laws whose "multiplicity," "mutability," and "injustice" called "into question the fundamental principle of republican Government, that the majority who rule in such Governments, are the safest Guardians both of public Good and private rights."[24] By 1787 Madison was convinced that these problems within the states contributed more to the calling of the Philadelphia Convention than did the obvious weaknesses of the Confederation. It was this conviction that led Madison to the peculiarities of his Virginia Plan—especially the power to veto state laws and the sweeping legislative authority granted to the Congress.

Of course, there were many other Federalists who shared his disgust with what was happening in the states, and agreed with his remedy of establishing an elevated national government. But many of them did not agree with the strange judicial-like way he hoped to deal with the factional politics he found in the states. Madison had a very unusual conception of American politics.

In his analysis of the sources of interest and faction in his most famous *Federalist* paper, No. 10, he seems at first to be very much the cold-eyed realist. Interest-group politics, he wrote, was an ineradicable part of American social reality. People inevitably had interests, and because they wanted to protect those interests, they divided into political factions. The causes of faction, he said, were quite simply "sown in the nature of man." It was naive to expect most people to put aside these interests for the sake of some nebulous public good. And it would be a denial of liberty to try to eliminate them. He thus realized that the regulation of these private factional interests was becoming the principal task of modern legislation, which meant that the spirit of party and faction was in the future likely to be involved in the ordinary operations of government.

At this point, even though many other Americans in 1787 were saying the same thing, we scholars have generally applauded Madison for his hardheaded realism, for his unsentimental willingness to question the utopianism of some of his fellow republicans who had hoped in 1776 that the American people would have sufficient virtue to tran-

24. Madison, "Vices of the Political System of the United States" (April 1787) in Rakove, *Madison: Writings,* 69–75.

scend their interests and act in a disinterested manner. Yet when he continues with his analysis in *Federalist* No. 10, we begin to realize that he is not quite as cold-eyed and practical as we had thought.

No government, he wrote, could be just if parties, that is, people with private interests to promote, became judges in their own causes; indeed, interested majorities were no better in this respect than interested minorities.

> No man is allowed to be a judge in his own cause, because his interest would certainly bias his judgment, and, not improbably, corrupt his integrity. With equal, nay with greater reason, a body of men are unfit to be both judges and parties at the same time; yet what are many of the most important acts of legislation but so many judicial determinations, not indeed concerning the rights of single persons, but concerning the rights of large bodies of citizens? And what are the different classes of legislators but advocates and parties to the causes which they determine? Is a law proposed concerning private debts? It is a question to which the creditors are parties on one side and the debtors on the other. Justice ought to hold the balance between them. Yet the parties are, and must be, themselves the judges; and the most numerous party, or in other words, the most powerful faction must be expected to prevail.[25]

Since the popular colonial assemblies had often begun as courts (the "General Court of Massachusetts") and much of their legislation had resembled adjudication, Madison's use of judicial imagery to describe the factional and interest-group politics in the state legislatures may seem quite understandable.[26] But it was not entirely practical and does not seem forward-looking; it tends to point back toward the colonial world, not toward our world at all.[27] For all the brilliance of Madi-

25. Madison, *The Federalist* No. 10, ibid., 160–67.

26. On the colonial legislatures acting as courts see Wood, *Creation of the American Republic,* 154–55.

27. Note, for example, Samuel Adams's traditional use of judicial imagery in 1772 in describing what happens when a man leaves the state of nature and becomes a member of society. In the state of nature, wrote Adams, man by himself was sole judge of his own rights and the injuries done him. By entering into society, however, "he agrees to an Arbiter or indifferent Judge between him and his

son's diagnosis of interest-ridden popular politics in the states, his remedy of dealing with that politics was very traditional and perhaps ultimately just as utopian, just as visionary, as the views he was contesting. Madison's conception of the new national government was not modern at all. It was idealistic and in many respects harked back to older conceptions of government. Madison hoped that the new federal government might transcend parties and become a kind of superjudge. It would become, as he put it, a "disinterested & dispassionate umpire in disputes between different passions & interests" in the various states.[28] In fact, he hoped that the new government might play the same super-political neutral role that the British King ideally had been supposed to play in the Empire.[29]

It was this kind of adjudicatory thinking that led him to conceive of a new national government with a remarkable power to veto all state laws. Such "a negative *in all cases whatsoever* on the legislative acts of the States, as heretofore exercised by the Kingly prerogative," he told Washington a month before the meeting in Philadelphia, was "absolutely necessary" and "the least possible encroachment on the State jurisdictions."[30] As Jack Rakove has pointed out, this was an extraordinarily reactionary proposal.[31] But not only was it reactionary, it was also bizarre. It evoked not only the infamous phrase of the British Declaratory Act of 1766 but as well the royal veto that Jefferson had so bitterly denounced in the Declaration of Independence. His proposal for

neighbors." Samuel Adams, "The Rights of the Colonists," 1772, in Harry Alonzo Cushing, ed., *The Writings of Samuel Adams* (New York: G. P. Putnam's Sons, 1904–08), 2:353.

28. Madison to George Washington, April 16, 1787, in Rakove, *Madison: Writings,* 81.

29. It was traditional to think that government, which for most states in the world meant a monarch, was supposed to be an impartial judge among the members of the state. A king was presumed to be more capable of this impartiality than anyone else in the society precisely because his self-interest supposedly coincided with the general interest; this, in fact, had been the best justification of monarchy through the ages.

30. Madison to George Washington, April 16, 1787, in Rakove, *Madison: Writings,* 81.

31. Jack N. Rakove, *Original Meanings: Politics and Ideas in the Making of the Constitution* (New York: Alfred A. Knopf, 1996), 51.

this national congressional power to negative all state legislation was a measure of just how peculiarly odd Madison's thinking actually was.

Madison envisioned a very strange kind of national government. He wanted a national government that was principally designed to evade popular majoritarian politics in the states in order to protect individual liberties and minority rights. He certainly had little or no interest in creating a modern state with a powerful executive. In fact, he seems to have never much valued executive authority in the states as a means of countering legislative abuses, and his conception of the executive in the new national government remained hazy at best. As late as April 1787, he told Washington that he had "scarcely ventured as yet to form my own opinion either of the manner in which [the executive] ought to be constituted or of the authorities with which it ought to be cloathed."[32] Through much of the Convention he assumed that the powers over appointment to offices and the conduct of foreign affairs would be assigned not to the president but to the Senate. Only in mid-August when Madison and other nationalists became alarmed by the states' gaining equal representation in the Senate were these powers taken away from the state-dominated Senate and granted to the president.

Madison very much desired to transcend the states and build a nation in 1787, but he had no intention of creating for this nation a modern war-making state with an energetic and powerful executive. Instead, he wanted a government that would act as a disinterested judge, a dispassionate umpire, adjudicating among the various interests in the society. Which is why he, unlike his friend Jefferson, eventually came to value the position of the Supreme Court in American political life: it was the only institution that came close to playing the role that in 1787 he had wanted the federal Congress to play.[33]

32. Madison to George Washington, April 16, 1787, in Rakove, *Madison: Writings,* 81. For Madison's downplaying of the executive in the state governments, see Madison to Caleb Wallace, August 23, 1785, ibid., 41–42.

33. Drew R. McCoy, *The Last of the Fathers: James Madison and the Republican Legacy* (Cambridge: Cambridge University Press, 1989), 70–71, 102. Of course, as Oscar and Mary Handlin pointed out in *Commonwealth: A Study in the Role of Government in American Economy: Massachusetts, 1774–1861,* rev. ed. (Cambridge: Harvard University Press, 1969), Massachusetts and presumably other state gov-

With this conception of the new national government as a neutral disinterested umpire, Madison becomes something other than the practical pluralist that many scholars have believed him to be. He was not offering some early version of modern interest-group politics. He was not a forerunner of twentieth-century political scientists like Arthur Bentley or David Truman. He did not envision public policy or the common good emerging naturally from the give-and-take of hosts of competing interests. Instead, he turns out to be much more old-fashioned and classical in his expectations. He expected that the clashing interests and passions in the enlarged national republic would neutralize themselves in the society and allow liberally educated, rational men—men, he said, "whose enlightened views and virtuous sentiments render them superior to local prejudices, and to schemes of injustice"—to decide questions of the public good in a disinterested adjudicatory manner.[34]

Madison, in other words, was not all as realistic and as modern as we often make him out to be. In his view not everyone in government had to be a party to a cause. He believed that there were a few disinterested gentlemen in the society—men like Jefferson and himself—and he hoped that his system would allow these few to transcend the interest-mongering of the many in the society and be able to act as neutral judges or referees in the new national Congress. As "an auxiliary desideratum" to his scheme, Madison predicted that the elevated and expanded sphere of national politics would act as a filter, refining the kind of men who would become these national umpires.[35] In a larger arena of national politics with an expanded elec-

---

ernments in the first half of the nineteenth century, by doling out much of their sovereign power especially in the creation of corporate charters that became private vested rights, did end up exercising just their police powers and acting to a large extent as merely impartial arbiters and umpires among the various competing interests in the society. Although these nineteenth-century liberal state governments did not very actively promote a positive public good in the way Madison and most other Revolutionaries had desired, they at least seem to have come to resemble the judicial-like government Madison had wanted for the United States.

34. Madison, *The Federalist* No. 10, in Rakove, *Madison: Writings*, 160–67.
35. Madison, "Vices of the Political System," ibid., 79.

torate and a smaller number of representatives, the people were more apt to ignore the illiberal narrow-minded men with "factious tempers" and "local prejudices" who had dominated the state legislatures in the 1780s and instead elect to the new federal government only those educated gentlemen with "the most attractive merit and the most . . . established characters." [36]

Madison's theory did not seem to have much practical effect on the character of the new national government; in fact, by March 1789 Madison was already predicting that the elevated Congress would behave pretty much as the vice-ridden state legislatures had behaved. [37] In the Congress we do not hear any more talk about his notions of an extended republic and the filtration of talent. These notions turned out to be as unrelated to reality as his idea of a congressional power to veto all state laws had been. He had other ideas now that turned out to be equally impractical. The truth is Madison was never the hard-headed realist that we have often thought him to be. Despite the often curious and probing quality of his mind, Madison was at heart a very idealistic, if not a utopian, republican, not all that different from his visionary friend and colleague Jefferson.

Madison began to reveal his peculiar conception of what the national government ought to be when he gradually became aware in the early 1790s of the kind of government that Washington, Hamilton, and other Federalists were actually creating. It was not a judicial-like umpire they were after but a real modern European-type government with a bureaucracy, a standing army, and a powerful independent executive. Like Madison, other Federalists may have been concerned about too much majoritarian democracy in the states, but these Federalists had much grander ambitions for the United States than simply controlling popular politics in the states and protecting minority rights. Hamilton and his fellow Federalists wanted to emulate the state-building process that had been going on for generations in Europe and Great Britain.

If any of the Founders was a modern man, it was not Madison but

36. Madison, *The Federalist* No. 10, ibid., 166.
37. Madison to Jefferson, March 29, 1789, in Smith, *Republic of Letters*, 1:606.

Hamilton. It was Hamilton who sought to turn the United States into a powerful modern fiscal-military state like those of Great Britain and France. Madison may have wanted a strong national government to act as an umpire over contending expressions of democracy in the states, as his Virginia Plan suggests. But he had no intention of creating the kind of modern war-making state that Hamilton had in mind. Which is why he had no sense of inconsistency in turning against the state that Hamilton was building in the 1790s.

The great development of the early modern period in the Western world was the emergence of modern nation-states with powerful executives—states that had developed the fiscal and military capacity to wage war on unprecedented scales. Over the past several decades scholars have accumulated a rich historical and sociological literature on state formation in early modern Europe.[38] From the sixteenth century through the eighteenth century, the European monarchies had been busy consolidating their power and marking out their authority within clearly designated boundaries while at the same time protecting themselves from rival claimants to their power and territories. They erected ever-larger bureaucracies and military forces in order to wage war, which is what they did through most decades of three centuries. This meant the building of ever more centralized governments and the creation of ever more elaborate means for extracting money and men from their subjects. These efforts in turn led to the growth of armies,

---

38. There is a huge literature on early modern European state-building. See especially Charles Tilly, ed., *The Formation of National States in Western Europe* (Princeton: Princeton University Press, 1975); John Brewer, *The Sinews of Power: War, Money, and the English State, 1688–1783* (New York: Alfred A. Knopf, 1989); Brian M. Downing, *The Military Revolution and Political Change: Origins of Democracy and Autocracy in Early Modern Europe* (Princeton: Princeton University Press, 1992); Lawrence S. Stone, ed., *An Imperial State at War: Britain from 1689 to 1815* (London: Routledge, 1994); Thomas Ertman, *Birth of the Leviathan: Building States and Regimes in Medieval and Early Modern Europe* (Cambridge: Cambridge University Press, 1997). It was Brewer who originated the term "fiscal-military state," and I have been much influenced by his book, *Sinews of Power*. But the work that provoked my thinking about Madison anew was Max M. Edling, *A Revolution in Favor of Government: Origins of the U.S. Constitution and the Making of the American State* (New York: Oxford University Press, 2003), and I am much indebted to it.

the increase in public debts, the raising of taxes, and the strengthening of executive power.[39]

Such monarchical state-building was bound to provoke opposition, especially among Englishmen who had a long tradition of valuing their liberties and resisting Crown power. The country Whig–opposition ideology that arose in England in the late seventeenth and early eighteenth centuries was essentially proto-republican. It was resisting just these kinds of monarchical state-building efforts taking place rather belatedly in England. When later eighteenth-century British radicals like James Burgh and Thomas Paine warned that the lamps of liberty were going out all over Europe and were being dimmed in Britain itself, it was these efforts at modern state formation that they were talking about.[40] Madison, Jefferson, and many other Americans had fought the Revolution to prevent the extension of these kinds of modern state-building efforts to America. They were not about to allow Hamilton and the Federalists to turn the United States into a modern fiscal-military state burdened by debt and taxes and saddled with an expensive standing army. Such states smacked of monarchy and were designed for the waging of war. "Of all the enemies to public liberty," wrote Madison in 1795, "war is, perhaps, the most to be dreaded, because it comprises and develops the germ of every other [enemy]." As "the parent of armies," war, he said, not only promoted "debts and taxes," but it also meant that "the discretionary power of the Executive is extended; its influence in dealing out offices, honors, and emoluments is multiplied; and all the means of seducing the minds, are added to those of subduing the force, of the people."[41] These senti-

39. For an important account of the different capacities of early modern states to extract money from their subjects or citizens without bankrupting them, see James Macdonald, *A Free Nation Deep in Debt: The Financial Roots of Democracy* (New York: Farrar, Straus and Giroux, 2002).

40. It is this opposition to modern state-building that infuses Bernard Bailyn's *The Ideological Origins of the American Revolution* (Cambridge: Harvard University Press, 1967).

41. Madison, "Political Observations," April 20, 1795, in Thomas A. Mason et al., eds., *The Papers of James Madison* (Charlottesville: University Press of Virginia, 1985), 15:518.

ments, which Madison never ceased repeating, were the source of the Republicans' sometimes hysterical opposition to the Hamiltonian Federalist state-building schemes of the 1790s.

Many American Revolutionaries, including Jefferson and Madison, wanted to end this kind of modern state-building and the kinds of international conflicts that this state-building promoted. Just as enlightened Americans in 1776 sought a new kind of domestic politics that would end tyranny within nations, so too did they seek a new kind of international politics that would promote peace among nations and, indeed, that might even see an end to war itself.

Throughout the eighteenth century, liberal intellectuals had dreamed of a new enlightened world in which corrupt monarchical diplomacy, secret alliances, dynastic rivalries, standing armies, and balances of power would disappear. Monarchy, unresponsive to the will of the people, was the problem. Its bloated bureaucracies, standing armies, perpetual debts, and heavy taxes lay behind its need to wage war. Eliminate monarchy and all its accouterments, and war itself would be eliminated. A world of republican states would encourage a different kind of diplomacy, a peace-loving diplomacy—one based not on the brutal struggle for power of conventional diplomacy but on the natural concert of the commercial interests of the people of the various nations. If the people of the various nations were left alone to exchange goods freely among themselves—without the corrupting interference of selfish monarchical courts, irrational dynastic rivalries, and the secret double-dealing diplomacy of the past—then, it was hoped, international politics would become republicanized, pacified, and ruled by commerce alone. Old-fashioned diplomats might not even be necessary in this new commercially linked world.[42]

Suddenly in 1776 with the United States isolated and outside European mercantile empires, the Americans had both an opportunity and a need to put into practice these liberal ideas about international re-

---

42. This is a much neglected topic. The only major account concerning America is Felix Gilbert's little book, *To the Farewell Address: Ideas of Early American Foreign Policy* (Princeton: Princeton University Press, 1961), which historians have much too casually dismissed. We have no major study of the Americans' Model Treaty of 1776, which attempted to embody these liberal ideas about war and commerce.

lations and the free exchange of goods. Thus commercial interest and revolutionary idealism blended to form the basis for American thinking about foreign affairs that lasted well into the twentieth century. To some extent this blending is still present in our thinking about the world.

"Our plan is commerce," Thomas Paine told Americans in 1776, "and that, well attended to, will secure us the peace and friendship of all Europe; because it is the interest of all Europe to have America a *free port.*" There was no need for America to form any partial political connections with any part of Europe. Such traditional military alliances were the legacies of monarchical governments, and they only led to war. "It is the true interest of America," said Paine, "to steer clear of European contentions." Trade between peoples alone would be enough.[43] Indeed, for Paine, Jefferson, Madison, and other idealistic liberals, peaceful trade among the people of the various nations became the counterpart in the international sphere to the sociability of people in the domestic sphere. Just as enlightened thinkers foresaw republican society held together solely by the natural affection of people, so too did they envision a world held together by the natural interests of nations in commerce. In both the national and international spheres, monarchy and its intrusive institutions and monopolistic ways were what prevented a natural harmony of people's feelings and interests.

These enlightened assumptions are what lie behind the various measures of commercial coercion attempted by Madison, Jefferson, and other Republicans throughout the 1790s and the early decades of the nineteenth century. They knew only too well that if republics like the United States were to avoid the consolidating processes of the swollen monarchical powers—heavy taxes, large permanent debts, and standing armies—they would have to develop peaceful alternatives to the waging of war. Madison was not a completely naive utopian. He feared, as he wrote in 1792, that "a universal and perpetual peace . . . will never exist but in the imaginations of visionary philosophers, or in the breasts of benevolent enthusiasts." Nevertheless, because war was so

43. Thomas Paine, *Common Sense* (1776), in *Common Sense and Other Writings,* ed. Gordon S. Wood (New York: Random House, 2003), 22–23.

foolish as well as wicked, he still hoped that the progress of reason might eventually end war, "and if anything is to be hoped," he said, "every thing ought to be tried."[44]

The ideal, of course, was to have the world become republican, that is, composed of states whose governments were identical with the will of the people. Jefferson and Madison believed that, unlike monarchies whose wills were independent of the wills of their subjects, self-governing republics were likely to be peace-loving—a view that Hamilton had only contempt for. Madison did concede that even republics might occasionally have to go to war. But if wars were declared solely by the authority of the people and, more important, if the costs of these wars were borne directly and solely by the generation that declared them, then, wrote Madison, "ample reward would accrue to the state." All "wars of folly" would be avoided and only brief "wars of necessity and defence" would remain, and even these might disappear. "If all nations were to follow [this] example," said Madison, "the reward would be doubled to each, and the temple of Janus might be shut, never to be opened again."[45] In other words, Madison believed that a republican world might be able to close the door on war forever.

In a world of monarchies, however, Madison concluded that the best hope for the United States to avoid war was to create some sort of peaceful republican alternative to war. This alternative was the use of commercial discrimination against foreign enemies backed ultimately by the withholding of American commerce; these measures were, he said, "the most likely means of obtaining our objects without war."[46] In other words, Madison proposed the use of what we now call economic sanctions—something that even today we often desperately cling to as an alternative to the direct use of military force. Given the importance

44. Madison, "Universal Peace," February 2, 1792, in Rakove, *Madison: Writings,* 505.

45. Ibid., 507. Janus, the ancient Roman god, was noted not only for two-facedness. To commemorate Janus, the Romans always left the temple of Janus open in time of war so that the god could come to their aid. The door was only closed when Rome was at peace.

46. Madison, "Political Observations" in Mason et al., *Papers of Madison,* 15: 518–19.

Republicans attached to commerce in tying nations together, it made sense to use it as a weapon in international politics.

I suggest that this republican idealism—this fear of the modern fiscal-military state and this desire to find peaceful alternatives to war —is the best context for understanding the thinking of Madison and other Republicans. It helps to explain not only their attitude toward modern state power but also their resort to trade discrimination against Great Britain in the early 1790s. Madison and the other Republicans were so outraged at Jay's Treaty in 1795 because the treaty took this essential weapon away from the United States. In the same way this context helps to explain Jefferson's and Madison's policies in the years following the lapse of Jay's Treaty in 1806—the several non-importation and nonintercourse acts against the two European belligerents, Britain and France. These efforts came to a climax with what Jefferson called his "candid and liberal" experiment in peaceful coercion—the Republicans' disastrous embargo of all American trade between 1807 and 1808, surely the most extraordinary example in American history of ideological principles brought directly to bear on a matter of public policy.[47] Actually Madison believed in the coercive purpose of the embargo more than did Jefferson. To the end of his life Madison remained convinced that the embargo would have eventually worked if it had not been prematurely repealed.[48]

But probably the most convincing evidence of Madison's being an idealistic republican seeking to avoid a strong federal government and the state-building processes characteristic of the modern European monarchies was the way he and the other Republicans prepared for and fought the War of 1812. "Prepared for" is hardly the term to use. The Republicans in the Congress talked about war, but at the same

47. Jefferson to Madison, March 24, 1793; to Tench Coxe, May 1, 1794; to Thomas Pinckney, May 29, 1797; to Robert R. Livingston, September 9, 1801; and Jefferson, Eighth Annual Message, November 8, 1808, in Merrill Peterson, ed., *Thomas Jefferson: Writings* (New York: Library of America, 1984), 1006, 1014, 1045–46, 1093, 544.

48. J. C. A. Stagg, *Mr. Madison's War: Politics, Diplomacy, and Warfare in the Early American Republic 1783–1830* (Princeton: Princeton University Press, 1983), 22, 36.

time proposed abolishing the army. They cut back the War Department and defeated efforts to build up the Navy. They abolished the Bank of the United States on the eve of hostilities, and in March 1812 they very reluctantly agreed to raise taxes, which were to go into effect, however, only if an actual war broke out.

Historians often harshly criticize Madison and the Republicans for the inept way they prepared for and conducted the war. But this criticism misses the point of what Madison and the Republicans were most frightened. As Jefferson said in 1806, "Our constitution is a peace establishment—it is not calculated for war."[49] War, the Republicans realized, would lead to a Hamiltonian monarchical-type government —with increased taxes, an overblown bureaucracy, heavy debts, standing armies, and enhanced executive power. Since war was a threat to republican principles, the Republican Party and administration would have to wage the war that began in 1812 in a manner different from the way monarchies waged war. As Secretary of the Treasury Albert Gallatin pointed out at the outset, the Republicans' dilemma was to wage a war without promoting "the evils inseparable from it . . . debt, perpetual taxation, military establishments, and other corrupting or anti-republican habits or institutions."[50]

Madison remained remarkably sanguine during the disastrous events of the war. Better to allow the country to be invaded and the capital to be burned than to build up state power in a European monarchical manner. Even during the war he continued to call for embargoes as the best means for fighting the war. He knew that a republican leader could not become a Napoleon or even a Hamilton. He knowingly accepted the administrative confusion and inefficiencies and the military failures, calm in the conviction that, in a republic, strong executive leadership could only endanger the principles for which the war was fought.[51]

So even though the war settled nothing, it actually settled every-

49. Dumas Malone, *Jefferson the President: Second Term, 1805–1809* (Boston: Little, Brown: 1974), 76.

50. Albert Gallatin to Jefferson, March 10, 1812, in Henry Adams, *The Life of Henry Gallatin* (New York: J. B. Lippincott, 1879), 455–56.

51. Ketcham, *James Madison: A Biography*, 586, 604.

thing. It vindicated the grand revolutionary experiment in limited republican government. As the City of Washington declared in a formal tribute to the president, the sword of war had usually been wielded at the expense of "civil or political liberty." But this was not the case with President Madison in the war against Britain. Not only had the president restrained the sword "within its proper limits" but he also had directed "an armed force of fifty thousand men aided by an annual disbursement of many millions, without infringing a political, civil, or religious right." As one admirer noted, Madison had withstood both a powerful foreign enemy and widespread domestic opposition "without one trial for treason, or even one prosecution for libel."[52]

Historians living in a world dominated by theories of preemptive war, a vast federal bureaucracy, a sprawling Pentagon, an enormous CIA, huge public debts, taxes beyond any the Founders could have imagined, and well over a million men and women under arms may not appreciate Madison's achievement, but contemporaries did. "Notwithstand[ing] a thousand Faults and blunders," John Adams told Jefferson in 1817, Madison's administration had "acquired more glory, and established more Union than all his three Predecessors, Washington, Adams, Jefferson, put together."[53]

We historians have gotten so used to praising Madison the author of the Tenth *Federalist* and denigrating Madison the president that we assume they must be two different Madisons. But there is no "Madison Problem" except the one that we have concocted. Maybe we ought to spend less time investigating Madison the author of the Tenth *Federalist* and more time investigating Madison the president. His conception of war and the world, whether we agree with it or not, might give us a better perspective on the confusing times in which we live.

52. Irving Brant, *James Madison: Commander in Chief, 1812–1836* (Indianapolis: Bobbs-Merrill, 1961), 419, 407.

53. John Adams to Jefferson, February 2, 1817, in Lester J. Cappon, ed., *The Adams-Jefferson Letters: The Complete Correspondence Between Thomas Jefferson and Abigail and John Adams* (Chapel Hill: University of North Carolina Press, 1959), 2:508.

Index

Ferguson-Price debate on, 373–77; government of, 332; liberty and hegemony of, 21, 23–24, 104–5; limits of, 332–33; as negotiated empire, 102; state-building in response to, 441–42

British Privy Council, 93–95, 99–100; colonial laws and power of, 33; Committee on Colonial Affairs, 89; Committee on Plantation Affairs, 78; Delap affair and, 68–69; Jamaican laws reviewed by, 41, 48, 54, 87–91; Kingston petition and, 61, 87–88; Knowles' resignation and, 71–72, 77–78

Brock, William R., 353–54n

Brooks, John, 229

Browne, Stephen H., 131

Burgh, James, 441

Burgoyne, John, 363

Burke, Edmund: on American Revolution, 6, 9–10, 20, 101; conservatism of, 292; on French Revolution, 1–5, 9–10, 350, 386; on natural rights, 182–83; political philosophy of, 1–3, 5; Price's influence on, 350–52; on religion and liberty, 107–8, 119; on taxation, 8–9; on tolerance, 292–93

Burr, Aaron, 115, 174n

Bush, Benjamin, 174n

Bush, George W., 150n

Bute, Earl of, 2

Butler, Joseph: moral-sense theory of, 277–78, 280, 282–85, 290–302, 308, 312–17; natural rights and, 292–93, 301–3; on virtue, 294–95

Butler, Samuel, 219

Butzer, Martin, 189

Calhoun, John, 394

Calvinism, 14, 189, 195, 199–200,

202, 279, 355. *See also* Scottish Enlightenment

Cambridge Platonists, 301–2

Cambridge School, 212–13

Canada: American invasion of, 114–15, 363; emigrants to, 17

Canavan, Francis, 165n

Cappon, Lester J., 115n

Carlisle Commission, 363–64, 375

Carr, Peter, 282–83

Carrington, Edward, 427n, 428n

Catholicism: Augustinian, 158; in Canada, 114–15; individualism and, 200–1; natural law in, 180–81, 186; Thomist, 200; voting rights and, 156

Cato's Letters, 219, 240–41, 251n, 253–54, 260, 268n, 271

Centinel, 247

Characteristics of Men, Manners, Opinions, Times, 280

Character of a Trimmer (Halifax), 232

Charles I (King of England): execution of, 121; Parliament and, 213–14

Charles II (King of England), 46–47, 55–56, 95

Charlton, Lionel, 228n

Chauncy, Charles, 191n

checks and balances: automated systems for, 250–63; constitutional provisions for, 230, 244, 246–47; elective despotism and, 264–66, 271–74; history of, 210–16; evolution of concepts in, 228–49; mechanics of constitution and, 218–28; in political theory, 212, 235, 256; Plutarch's concept of, 250–51; Shaftesbury's discussion of, 293–94; Trenchard and Moyle's theories on, 216–19. *See also* separation of powers

Christianity: communalism in, 175; of Founders, 155–66; humanism in,

egoism, 284; psychological, 295
elections: balance of power and,
247–49, 251; of 1800, 421–22
elective despotism, 264–74
Eliot, Andrew, 189
Elkins, Stanley, 276, 427n, 429, 430n
Ellis, Joseph, 209n, 224n, 429
embargo, Founders' belief in, 445–46
Emerson, William, 183–84
England. *See* British Empire; Great
Britain
English law: colonial reliance on,
133–37; post-Revolution rejection
of, 177–86
Enlightenment: English, 277, 286;
federalism and, 142; influence on
Founders of, 14–15, 186, 195–98,
200–1, 270–72; law and influence
of, 105–6; moral-sense theory and,
278–82; religion and, 154–61;
Scottish, 195, 276–77, 323, 353–54
*Enquiry Concerning Human
Understanding, An* (Hume), 300–1
*Enquiry Concerning the Principles of
Morals, An* (Hume), 295–97, 335n
enumerated powers, 391–92, 397,
404, 414n
epistemology: ethics and, 366–69;
natural rights and, 284–85
equality, emerging ideal of, 128,
235–36
equilibrium, checks and balances and
principle of, 211n, 234–35, 252–56
Essay on Man (Pope), 331
Essay on the History of Civil Society
(Ferguson), 354, 356–60, 367–68
*Essay on the Lacedaemonian Government,
An* (Moyle), 217, 225
*Essay on the Nature and Conduct of the
Passions and Affections, with
Illustrations on the Moral Sense*
(Hutcheson), 304–5
Essex Result, The (Parsons), 140–43

ethics: epistemology and, 366–69;
religion and, 280, 285, 290
evangelicalism, 159, 174
Evans, Charles, 113n
Evelyn, John, 215
Everson v. Board of Education, 110n
excess, 215
exchange-value, distinction between
use-value and, 329
executive powers, 236, 238, 261;
creation of, 395, 401, 411–13
extra-institutional powers, 252

Fagg, Jane, 357n
false imprisonment, protection from,
148
fantail windmill metaphor of
government, 255–56
farmers, reliance on Anglo-American
law, 134–35
fashion, a cause of unemployment,
343
federal government: constitutional
limits of, 393, 397–98; Founders'
concepts of, 389; Madison's vision
of, 436–47; religious freedom and,
161–72
federalism: birth of, 250;
constitutionalism and, 388–94,
399–400, 412–15; of Madison,
426–31, 439; original sin and,
194–95; Republican party
repudiation of, 427–29, 441–42
Federalist Papers, The, 395–97, 430;
central government's powers
discussed in, 391; checks and
balances discussed in, 210n, 229,
237, 246; constitutionalism
discussed in, 210, 391, 395–98,
400, 408, 416, 420–24; Hamilton's
contributions to, 151, 432; *Essex
Revolt* and, 142; legal principles in,
131–32, 142–45; liberty discussed

The typeface used for this book is ITC New Baskerville, which was created for the International Typeface Corporation and is based on the types of the English type founder and printer John Baskerville (1706–75). Baskerville is the quintessential transitional face: it retains the bracketed and oblique serifs of old-style faces such as Caslon and Garamond, but in its increased lowercase height, lighter color, and enhanced contrast between thick and thin strokes, it presages modern faces.

The display type is set in Didot.

This book is printed on paper that is acid-free and meets the requirements of the American National Standard for Permanence of Paper for Printed Library Materials, z39.48-1992. ⊚

Book design by Rich Hendel, Chapel Hill, North Carolina
Typography by Tseng Information Systems, Inc., Durham, North Carolina
Printed by Worzalla Publishing Company, Stevens Point, Wisconsin, and bound by Dekker Bookbinding, Grand Rapids, Michigan